Olive Smith

A MUSICAL VISIONARY

Olive Smith

A MUSICAL VISIONARY

GILLIAN SMITH

SOMERVILLE PRESS

Somerville Press Ltd,
Dromore,
Bantry,
Co. Cork, Ireland

First published 2019

Designed by Jane Stark
Typeset in Adobe Garamond Pro
seamistgraphics@gmail.com

ISBN: 978-1-9999970-4-5

Printed and bound in Spain
by GraphyCems, Villa Tuerta, Navarra

For My Family

CONTENTS

FOREWORD

I am delighted that this biography of Olive Smith has at last come to fruition after what I can only call an elephantine gestation. The lengthy embryonic period was due partly to my own procrastination and allowing other projects to get in its way, despite the fact that I held Olive Smith in high esteem and continue to regard her as one of the remarkable women of twentieth-century Ireland.

The end result has been a labour of love for Olive's daughter Gillian. Her research, particularly on her mother's involvement with the Music Association of Ireland (MAI) and the Irish Youth Orchestra (IYO), has meant long hours of delving into the records of both organisations, with many of their respective files now lodged in the inner sanctum of the National Library. Gillian's thorough exploration also demanded detailed interviews with those who worked with Olive in the wide variety of her pursuits, and those who knew her on a more personal and intimate level.

The outcome sheds not only a defining light on Olive's contribution to the musical life of our country but also provides accurate histories of both the MAI, more or less from its cradle to its grave, and the birth and early years of the IYO, happily still functioning as the National Youth Orchestra of Ireland. It continues to be a living testimonial to Olive Smith's memory.

As might be expected, the early chapters of this book deal with the family background. It shows Olive Smith, *née* Richardson, reared in a relatively prosperous environment framed within the Presbyterian tradition. The tenets of this faith moulded Olive's thinking and led to her obeying high ideals of honesty and integrity. They instilled in her a strict sense of duty that lasted her in good stead throughout her life. They were also an abiding source of inspiration to the many facets of her diverse and fascinating career, which

9

often found different strands operating on varying levels simultaneously, yet never seeming to conflict with one another.

Olive Smith's involvement with the Girl Guide movement, which she joined in 1920, helped in the development of her talents in leadership. This sterling quality would remain constantly with her and be manifested in both her music and business activities, and assist in her understanding and encouragement of young, and indeed not so young, people. As Gillian discovered from some of her mother's 'guider' peers, 'she was an inspiration and a role model.... And while she was a natural leader, she never looked on herself as being "above" those in her care'.

It was through the Guides that Olive's participation in music began to take on an extra dimension and lead eventually to her role as conductor of a number of choirs, not least the long-established Culwick Choral Society and, later on, the formation of her own Olivian Singers.

This biography also gives valuable insights into Olive Smith's academic life in Trinity College Dublin, from where she graduated in 1928 and where she worked for twelve years in the Lady Registrar's Office. In was in TCD that she gained 'not only her ability to deal with all kinds of people, but also her considerable administrative skills'. In recognition of her services to music Olive was conferred with an honorary doctorate (LL.D.) from her *alma mater* in 1978.

The concluding chapters deal with Olive's later years, when her business acumen was again called into play following the death of her husband Lyall in 1969, when she undertook the day-to-day running and long-term management of the family photographic firm of Lyall Smith Laboratories. They also cover her eventual retirement to her beloved Derrylahan in Co. Galway and her final illness.

However, the perceptive 'in-between' chapters recount in considerable detail the establishment and work of the MAI from its foundation in 1948, and Olive Smith's extraordinary contribution to its operation and expansion over the years of its lifetime. In line with the rest of the MAI's honorary officers and committee members, all of Olive Smith's time, so generously and lovingly given to the Association, was on a completely voluntary basis.

It should be remembered that through the determination of the MAI's committees, with Olive Smith one of their leading lights, there came into being a number of on-going programmes not least its Country Tours and Schools Recitals Schemes; 'Coming-Out' recitals for young artists; the youth group Ógra Ceoil; the setting up of Concert & Assembly Hall Ltd promoting the idea of a national concert hall; the members' magazine *Counterpoint*; the Dublin Festival of 20th Century Music and, maybe most importantly, the founding of the Irish Youth Orchestra in 1970.

The latter was the project dearest to Olive Smith's heart. Affectionately known to so many young musicians over the years as 'Granny' Smith, the orchestra continues to be a lasting legacy of this extraordinary woman.

My own admiration for Olive Smith came through my joining the MAI and becoming editor of its magazine *Counterpoint*. Initially I considered her formidable, even a little forbidding, but I soon found there was a very humane side to her. She liked conscientious people around her who would be responsible for whatever task they had taken on. For my part, she never interfered with whatever I wrote or what I decided to publish nor do I remember her ever criticising anything that appeared in the magazine. If she had faith in you she let you work away without ever 'looking over your shoulder'.

While this book tells the story of Olive Smith, it is also a significant historical document which I feel many will find enjoyable, informative and inspiring.

Pat O'Kelly

ACKNOWLEDGEMENTS

My original aspiration was to publish this biography in the year 2006, to coincide with the 100th anniversary of my mother's birth. With this in mind, in January 2001 I approached the music journalist Pat O'Kelly, author of books about the RTÉ Symphony Orchestra and the National Concert Hall, and asked for his assistance. Pat had known my mother well during the years of his service on the Council of the Music Association of Ireland, and was its Chairman at the time of her retirement. I am greatly indebted to him for his ready agreement to become involved with this project, and for the many hours of his valuable time which he devoted to the initial research.

It was clear from the outset that the chief source of information would be the files of the Music Association of Ireland (MAI), at that time housed in their offices over Walton's Music Shop on George's Street, Dublin 2. Pat and I began a painstaking inventory, making lists and writing up our findings. It quickly emerged that there were a number of key people who should be contacted, and I would like to record my gratitude to the following friends and colleagues of my mother whom Pat and I interviewed during 2001 and 2002: Kenneth Armstrong, Mary Boydell, Doreen Bradbury, Enid Chaloner, Ivy Kevelighan, David Laing, Máire Larchet, Sheila Larchet-Cuthbert, Eilís MacGabhann, Mairtín McCullough, Isolde McCullagh, Pat McKnight, John O'Sullivan, Vincent Trotman and Jim Wilson. Most of these are from the world of music, but I am particularly grateful to Vincent Trotman for the information he supplied about my father's business interests, and to Pat McKnight who gave me her albums of Girl Guide photographs.

For insights into my mother's family I turned to my first cousins, Brian Lusk and Helen Young (née Lusk). Pat O'Kelly and I travelled to meet them at Brian's house near Guildford, Surrey, in January 2002, for a day-long immersion in Richardson and Smith family history! Now that the book has finally taken shape, I would like to express my warmest appreciation of their assistance, support and encouragement.

Unfortunately, having made a positive start, several circumstances intervened between 2003 and 2006 to prevent consistent progress. The MAI decided towards the end of 2003 to create an archive of material and to place this in the care of the National Library of Ireland. There was a brief ceremony on 19 February 2004 to mark the occasion. Although this action should not have impeded research, the fact that the MAI records were less accessible seemed to create a stumbling-block. Pat and I were both very busy with other preoccupations, my mother's 100th anniversary came and went, and the project faltered.

Almost ten years later, in June 2015, Pat and I agreed to meet in the National Library to view the MAI material that is accessible to the general public, namely back copies of its two publications *Counterpoint* and *SoundPost* and some issues of the earlier *MAI Bulletin*. I began to feel renewed interest and obtained permission to start research on the main body of the MAI archive. Access to this is restricted as it has never been catalogued and is kept in an off-site storage facility in fifty-three boxes. At this point Pat and I decided that it would be more practical if I were to embark on a solo journey of exploration, whilst he would remain as back-up support, should I encounter major problems. In fact, the task of working through the boxes (two more appeared in due course) continued for at least two years, and I would like to thank the staff of the Manuscripts Reading Room, particularly James Harte, Avice-Claire McGovern and Frances Clarke, for their unfailing assistance.

My motivation for writing this biography is two-fold. On one level, I feel that my mother's life-story is well worth telling and that it is important to document the past achievements of pioneering and visionary Irish women. From a broader perspective, I am determined that the extraordinary work done in the cause of classical music in Ireland during the period from 1948 to 1978 – the first thirty years of the Music Association of Ireland

– should not remain in obscurity, particularly as these years cover the campaign for a National Concert Hall and the foundation of the National Youth Orchestra of Ireland.

Research was also needed into the early days of the Irish Youth Orchestra and I have been helped in piecing the story together by the recollections of Antony Lewis-Crosby and Honor Ó Brolcháin, who were on the original Ógra Ceoil committee. Sincere thanks are due also to Anton Timoney and Gerry Keenan, orchestra managers respectively of the Irish Youth Orchestra and the Junior Irish Youth Orchestra, who provided many fascinating insights; to Gearóid Grant, present conductor of the National Youth Orchestra of Ireland; to Joanna Crooks, former director of the NYOI; and to its present manager, Carol-Ann McKenna, and former administrator, Gillian Shiels.

I would also like to thank Eoin Garrett, Brían Howlett, David McConnell, Dinah Molloy, Rodney Senior, Carol Briscoe and Howard Freeman for additional information about the MAI, and in particular Teresa O'Donnell who has made the work of the MAI the subject of her PhD thesis. I am very grateful to Ian Fox who generously lent me his collection of *Counterpoint* magazines, and to William (Bill) Grimson who gave me some details about his late brother, Brian. Michael Dervan provided me with information about the magazine *SoundPost*.

So many musicians have shared their recollections of my mother, and to them all I extend my heartfelt thanks. I hope that this brief mention of their names will suffice as an appropriate acknowledgement: David Agnew, Colin Block, Alison Browner, Anne Cant Fitzpatrick, Jimmy and Pauline Cavanagh, Patricia Corcoran, Seamus Doyle, John Finucane, Gerard Gillen, Evelyn Grant and Gerry Kelly, Andreja Maliř, Rita Manning, Maighréad McCrann, Veronica McSwiney, Joan Mooney, Mary O'Brien, Fergus O'Carroll, John O'Conor, Cormac Ó Cuilleanáin, Niall O'Loughlin, Brian O'Rourke, Justin Pearson, Susan Proud, Jenny Robinson, Madeleine Staunton, Thérèse Timoney, Violet Twomey, Peter Whelan, Anne Woodworth.

Professor Barbara Wright and Susan M. Parkes have given me welcome insights into the workings of Trinity College Dublin; historical details of the Culwick Choral Society have come from Ann Simmons and Magdalen O'Connell; and information regarding the Dublin Feis Ceoil from Laura Gilsenan (Chief Executive Officer). I would also like to acknowledge the assistance of Natasha Serne (Collections Librarian of the Royal Dublin Society), Lynn Seguss (Associated Board of the Royal Schools of Music), and particularly Fiona Murdoch (Communications Officer of the Irish Girl Guides).

I am grateful to musicologists Dr Ita Beausang and Dr Laura Anderson for their empathy and encouragement, to John and Yvonne Carroll for information about Leon Ó Dubhghaill and their guidance on Irish spelling, to Roger H. Johnson for details of the bus belonging to his father Harold, and to Mrs P. MacManus (Mrs Mac) for her personal memories of my mother.

I consulted Canice Flynn for his recollections of my father's chemist shop; Maurice Brooks, Fred Yoakley and Jan Jefferiss for tales of their sailing exploits under my father's command; Joan Cowle who facilitated access to the records of Christ Church, Rathgar; and Anthony Warnock regarding the Warnock family.

At all stages during the writing of this book, I have been able to call on two guardian angels, both tolerant of my lack of computer literacy and able to extricate me from my latest technical confusion. They are Brendan Kealy and Colin Holman. Without their help it is possible that this book might never have been completed, and they have my undying thanks.

Ironically, I believe that the completion of the biography also owes something to an historical action of my mother's, some two years after her retirement from the MAI. The Council minutes for February 1978 record that she purchased a fire-proof filing cabinet for the office, to house the records of all her years of work. In March, she further requested that all past Minute Books should be lodged in the Bank. Indeed, had she not done so, this history might never have seen the light of day!

It is one thing to write a book, it is quite another matter to achieve its publication! Serendipitous advice led me to consult with my Ranelagh neighbours, Anna Farmar and her late husband Tony (publishers A&A

Farmar). Their reaction was encouraging and they effected an introduction to Jane and Andrew Russell of the Somerville Press. I find it difficult to express adequately my sense of indebtedness to Anna and Tony for their initial input, and to Jane and Andrew, for all that they have done to bring this book before the public. They have shown great tolerance of a novice author. The same sentiments apply to the wonderful designer, Jane Stark.

Two friends, Prof. Barbara Wright and Patrick G. Howard agreed to read the draft manuscript of the book. Their feed-back has been invaluable, and I can only express my most sincere gratitude for their willing involvement.

I am really delighted that Pat O'Kelly has agreed to contribute the Foreword.

Finally, to my long-suffering husband, Lindsay Armstrong . . . . Once he became accustomed to the idea that there was an author in the house, in place of the previously hard-working pianist and harpsichordist, his support and encouragement have been truly wonderful. This has made all the difference to me as I went on the long journey through my mother's life story and at least thirty years of musical history.

Gillian Smith

LIST OF ABBREVIATIONS

CAH . . . . . . Concert and Assembly Hall Ltd

CHAC . . . . Concert Hall Action Committee

CHF . . . . . . Concert Hall Fund

CIÉ . . . . Córas Iompair Éireann

CRC . . . . . . Cultural Relations Committee

DGOS . . . . Dublin Grand Opera Society

DOP . . . . . . Dublin Orchestral Players

DSO . . . . . . Dublin String Orchestra

ECYO . . . . . European Community Youth Orchestra

FÉ . . . . Fóras Éireann

GMB . . . . . Graduate Memorial Building, TCD

IAYO . . . . . Irish Association of Youth Orchestras

ICO . . . . . . Irish Chamber Orchestra

IYO . . . . Irish Youth Orchestra

IYWE . . . . . Irish Youth Wind Ensemble

JFK . . . . John F. Kennedy Memorial Hall

JIYO . . . . . . Junior Irish Youth Orchestra

LSL . . . . Lyall Smith Laboratories

LSQ . . . . . . London String Quartet

MAI . . . . . . Music Association of Ireland

NCH . . . . . . National Concert Hall

NDR . . . . . . Norddeutsche Rundfunk

NICO . . . . . New Irish Chamber Orchestra

NIWE . . . . . New Irish Wind Ensemble

NLSQ . . . . . New London String Quartet

NYOI . . . . . National Youth Orchestra of Ireland

NYOGB . . . National Youth Orchestra of Great Britain

ÓC . . . . Ógra Ceoil

OSC . . . . . . Orchestra of St Cecilia

PDA . . . . . . Photographic Dealers Association

RAM . . . . . . Royal Academy of Music, London

RDS . . . . . . Royal Dublin Society

RÉ . . . . Radio Éireann

RÉO . . . . . . Radio Éireann Orchestra

RÉSO . . . . . Radio Éireann Symphony Orchestra

RIAM . . . . . Royal Irish Academy of Music

R-S T . . . . . Richardson-Smith Musical Trust

RTÉ . . . . . . Radio Telefís Éireann

RTÉCO . . . RTÉ Concert Orchestra

RTÉ NSO . . RTÉ National Symphony Orchestra

RTÉSO . . . . RTÉ Symphony Orchestra

SFX . . . . St Francis Xavier Hall, Upper Sherrard St, Dublin

SMU . . . . . . Students' Musical Union of the RIAM

SRS . . . . Schools' Recital Scheme

TCD . . . . . . Trinity College Dublin

UCC . . . . . . University College Cork

UCD . . . . . . University College Dublin

WIT . . . . . . Waterford Institute of Technology

FAMILY TREE

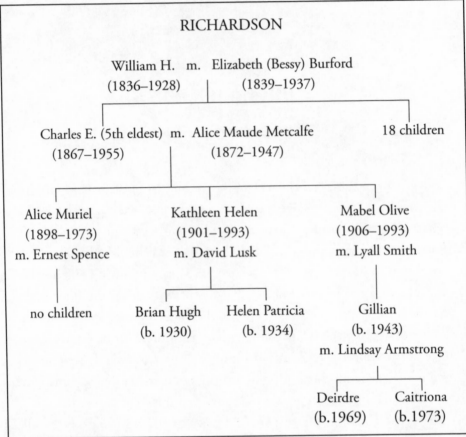

RICHARDSON

William H. m. Elizabeth (Bessy) Burford
(1836–1928)   (1839–1937)

Charles E. (5th eldest) m. Alice Maude Metcalfe   18 children
(1867–1955)   (1872–1947)

Alice Muriel   Kathleen Helen   Mabel Olive
(1898–1973)   (1901–1993)   (1906–1993)
m. Ernest Spence   m. David Lusk   m. Lyall Smith

no children   Brian Hugh   Helen Patricia   Gillian
            (b. 1930)   (b. 1934)   (b. 1943)
                              m. Lindsay Armstrong

Deirdre   Caitriona
(b.1969)   (b.1973)

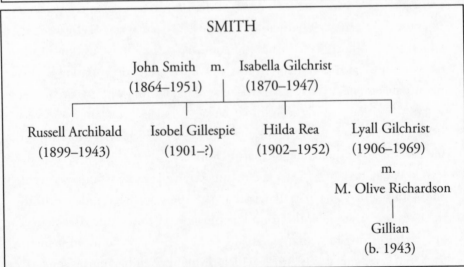

SMITH

John Smith m. Isabella Gilchrist
(1864–1951)   (1870–1947)

Russell Archibald   Isobel Gillespie   Hilda Rea   Lyall Gilchrist
(1899–1943)   (1901–?)   (1902–1952)   (1906–1969)
                                        m.
                                M. Olive Richardson

Gillian
(b. 1943)

PROLOGUE

29 September 1950 . . . The scene is set: a capacity audience in Dublin's Metropolitan Hall, on-stage the combined forces of the Culwick Choral Society and Cór Radio Éireann, together with the musicians of the Radio Éireann Symphony Orchestra and a distinguished quartet of vocal soloists. Conductor Otto Matzerath is just about to come to the rostrum to direct Bach's Mass in B Minor when, from the door high on the right-hand side of the gallery, the slight figure of Olive Smith emerges, wearing the white full-length concert dress of the Culwick, to take her place in the back row of the altos. This was a highly significant moment for my mother, indeed a turning point in her life, and she was undoubtedly filled with pride as she surveyed the scene before her.

This performance, the first to take place in Ireland using Bach's full orchestral forces, was the high point of the Bach Bicentenary celebrations organised by the newly-established Music Association of Ireland, of which my mother was Treasurer. She also held the same position in the Culwick, and had been involved in every detail of the organisation of this memorable event . . . advertising, ticket-selling, dealing with the orchestra, seeking hospitality for the soloists, engaging specialist trumpet players from England and obtaining permission from the National Museum for the use of one of their valuable harpsichords.

It was her first foray into the organisation of a major musical event and I think that she herself felt that she drew great confidence from this success. Always working under the aegis of the Music Association of Ireland throughout the 1950s and 1960s, she went on to implement the Country Tours programme, which brought chamber-music concerts

21

to venues throughout Ireland, to inaugurate the Coming-Out Recitals which launched the careers of so many Irish musicians, and to set up the Schools' Recital Scheme which involved Irish schools in regular concerts in their classrooms. Her crowning achievement, in 1970, was the creation of the Irish Youth Orchestra. In addition, through the body known as Concert and Assembly Hall Ltd, she campaigned tirelessly for a concert hall for Dublin, and though this effort did not bear fruit until 1981, it involved her in the organisation of a number of high-profile concert series with international artists.

In embarking on this account of Olive Smith's life and work, it has become clear to me that in fact her life divided into two halves. There was little in her first forty-four years to indicate the path that she would follow from 1950 onwards. But yet, in so many ways, her earlier years were an ideal preparation for what was to come. I hope, in the course of this book, to be able to clarify and expand on these points, whilst at the same time ensuring that there is a record of the ground-breaking work of the Music Association of Ireland, to which my mother dedicated so many of her extraordinary talents.

CHAPTER 1

The Early Years

My mother was born on 19 June 1906 at the family home at 7 Connaught Terrace in the Dublin suburb of Rathgar. Her mother was Maude Richardson (*née* Metcalfe) and her father Charles E. Richardson. It seems her birth was not an easy one. Her older sisters, Alice and Kay (Kathleen), then aged eight and five respectively, recalled spending some weeks away from home in the care of relatives and being greeted with the news of the arrival of a baby sister upon their return. There are even grounds for thinking that there may have been a twin sister who did not survive. It could be significant that my mother's baptism did not take place until 23 November, and even then the ceremony was performed in the family home. There is no doubt, however, that their mother was not in good health from that time forward, and a bout of the dreaded 'sleepy sickness' (encephalitis lethargica), which reached epidemic proportions after the First World War, left her in a semi-invalid condition until the end of her life.

Sometime between 1911 and 1915 the family moved just round the corner to 47 Kenilworth Square. This is a fine two-storey over basement Victorian house with a flight of granite steps to the front door, and spacious inter-connecting reception rooms off the entrance hall. There was an upright piano in the drawing-room and here my mother received her first piano lessons from her older sister Alice. Both Alice and Kay played and sang and so it was natural for my mother to do likewise. She found reading music very easy, and when she was put under the care of a local piano teacher, Miss Egan, she easily escaped with very little practice, just sight-reading her pieces at the lesson and being told 'that was very good, dear'! Later she went to a more demanding teacher, Miss Gertrude Coolahan, and her piano-playing flourished.

I sense that, due in some measure to her mother's poor health, and also the age difference with her sisters, there was an element of loneliness in my mother's young life. She spoke quite often of being unable to get to sleep at night, and of creeping downstairs, past the family rooms, to the basement where the kitchen was warm and she had the company of 'the maids'. They were Statia and Essie from Valleymount, near Blessington, Co. Wicklow. They were certainly good fun and taught my mother Irish dancing which she loved. They would have to say 'the rebels are coming! you'd better hurry up to bed' in order to bring the session to a close.

Both Alice and Kay remembered that my mother had a serious illness at about the age of four and they were again sent to their grandmother's house for some days. My mother always maintained that this was the first manifestation of her 'grumbling appendix' which finally resulted in quite a major operation when she was eighteen.

Possibly because of lack of company her own age at home, my mother loved school. All three sisters attended Norfolk College, also known as 'Miss Garrett's', a small private girls' school on the corner of Frankfort Avenue and Rathgar Road, which focussed on a surprisingly broad curriculum including science and a high level of mathematics. It seems that, from an early age, my mother had an extrovert, fun-loving personality, mischievous and at times rebellious, and with a sharp intelligence that found book-learning no bother. And there were other social outlets – the 'Guides' at Rathgar Presbyterian Church, tennis at the courts in Kenilworth Square, various church organisations, and friendships with a growing number of cousins.

Her father, Charles, came from a very large family. He was the 5th child of William H. Richardson and his wife Elizabeth (Bessy), and had seventeen brothers and sisters. Their home was at Mount Temple Terrace, Dartry Road, Rathmines, where three adjacent houses were joined to form one large unit. This was very much the central hub of the family and I can remember, as a small child, visiting the two or three remaining unmarried great-aunts there. For Alice, Kay and Olive, visits could be quite daunting if they had to sit beside their grandmother, a formidable woman who lived until her 99th year. She would poke them in the back and say 'sit up, child!' if they slumped in their seat. They preferred to spend time with their younger uncles who were fun and encouraged them to slide down the banisters! These uncles put on impromptu concerts and plays and taught their nieces to recite poetry.

Charles Richardson had his own business as a wholesale grocery and foreign produce merchant, unlike his father and some of his brothers who were chemical fertiliser manufacturers. His first premises were at Crown Alley, just off Temple Bar, near the Dublin quays. Later he moved to South William Street, first No.51 and finally No.55. This location gave him the idea of the name 'Sweet William Brand' for the packaged dry products he supplied to the grocery shops of Dublin. His emblem was a Sweet William flower and he also marketed goods under the name 'Charlie Richardson's'. He was undoubtedly an astute business man, and owned a number of grocery shops in the Dublin suburbs. I think that he passed this business acumen on to my mother.

There are no accounts of my grandfather Richardson having an interest in sports, but he was a keen and knowledgeable gardener, and also loved woodwork, finding this a means of relaxation from business, and possibly also from the cares of looking after my grandmother. She was the youngest daughter of Samuel Metcalfe and his wife Sarah and grew up in the town of Bray, Co. Wicklow, with three sisters and a brother. Her sister Anna's children were good friends with my mother, Kay and Alice, and her sister Eva's son, Arthur Franks, became a professional violinist. The third sister, Sara, moved to Canada following her marriage. It may have been his wife's connections with Co. Wicklow that led my grandfather to arrange for his family to spend the summer holidays each year at Crone, a farmhouse in the Glencree Valley, which they reached following an uphill journey by pony and trap from Bray railway station. My mother had the deepest affection for Crone, which was situated not far from the famous waterfall of the Powerscourt Estate. Surely those summer months in the countryside must have contributed to her love of nature, her knowledge of wild flowers and trees, and her lifelong determination to climb mountains! I recall her describing vividly an ascent of nearby Djouce Mountain to reach the summit in time for sunrise.

His Presbyterian faith was also important to my grandfather, following in the family tradition, and he and his wife and daughters were all very much part of the congregation at Christ Church, Rathgar. My mother and her sisters sang in the choir, and church attendance on Sunday was *de rigueur*, evening as well as morning service, plus Sunday School for the children. When they were older, the sisters became Sunday School teachers. My mother learned many passages from the Bible by heart, and also a big repertoire of hymns. Interestingly however, my grandfather had some reservations regarding the doctrine of predestination and never agreed to become an Elder. His chief focus was on the younger members of the congregation and he was very involved in the 'Band of Hope'. Founded in 1884, this was ostensibly a temperance organisation for young people, but at Rathgar it took on the character of a youth club and organised regular concerts with opportunities for members to sing, recite or play their instrument before a friendly audience. Once a year there were competitions for singing, elocution and piano. It was still in existence when I was old enough to take my first timid steps onto a concert stage! My grandfather's concern to encourage young people was shared by all three sisters – Alice assisted him in running the Band of Hope, and Kay led the Brownie Pack for younger girls. My mother developed a great interest in the Guide movement, of which more in later chapters.

All of this must be set against the backdrop of the First World War, the 1916 Easter Rising and the following Civil War of 1922-23. Rathgar was certainly close enough to the fighting in Dublin city centre for the Richardson sisters to see smoke from their bedroom window, though perhaps a childhood memory of bullets rattling off the railings in Kenilworth Square, causing them to hide under the bedclothes, was more imagination than fact. There were frightening accounts of shootings and executions, and later there was a nightly curfew whilst the dreaded Black and Tans' lorries patrolled the square and the surrounding streets. Sometimes an older cousin, caught out after curfew, would come hammering at the back door, having climbed the garden wall from the lane. And there were also some Canadian cousins, the sons of my grandmother's older sister Sara, who arrived *en route* to join the fighting forces in Europe. Two of them tragically never returned, and similarly neither did two sons of her other sister Anna.

Whilst peace treaties were signed in Europe in 1918-19, political instability and fighting continued in Ireland. The period from 1920 to 1922 saw the setting up of the Irish Free State and partition from Northern Ireland, with the Anglo-Irish Treaty being ratified by the Dáil in January 1922. Then followed the months of Civil War, which lasted until the cease-fire of May 1923. To have lived through this time at an impressionable age seems to have had a lasting influence on my mother. She often remarked that it was the executions of the leaders of the 1916 Easter Rising which swung public opinion behind the Republican cause, support having been quite luke-warm in the general population up to that, whilst the activities of the Black and Tans served only to consolidate anti-British sentiment. Her personal library in later life contained a considerable number of books on Irish Nationalism and the history of the IRA, as well as the Irish authors and playwrights of the time. She loved the writings of O'Casey, Synge, Joyce, James Stephens, AE, and particularly George Moore, whose complete works she collected over many years. Politically, in later years, she supported Fianna Fáil, and she had a high personal regard for Éamon de Valera, for Seán Lemass, and even for Charles Haughey, all of whom she regarded as men who could 'get things done'!

CHAPTER 2

University Days

In 1922 my mother won a scholarship to the highly-regarded Dublin girls' school, Alexandra College, where she took her final school and university entrance exams. She was preparing to follow her sisters Alice and Kay into university level study. They had both attended the Royal College of Science in Dublin, which was founded in 1867 to supply courses at degree level in science, engineering, mining and agriculture, and to train teachers of science. It occupied its own purpose-built college building on Merrion Street from 1911 until 1926, when it was absorbed into University College Dublin (UCD) as the faculty of Science and Engineering. This fine building was later taken over as the present Government Buildings. Both Alice and Kay became teachers of science in Dublin, Alice at Bertrand and Rutland girls' school and Kay at Norfolk College. Later on, Alice had a research post in the laboratories of the Royal Dublin Society.

My grandfather's modernity of mind, and his belief in the importance of education to the highest possible level, ensured that all his daughters obtained university qualifications. Amongst his own sisters only Norah (born 1883), who was a school teacher, had employment outside the home. His daughter Alice was born in 1898, so it is fair to comment that a sea-change in attitude to the education of women had occurred in the space of less than twenty years. The fact that women in Ireland were granted the right to vote in 1918 could also have been significant. The College of Science was an option, but my mother had set her heart on going to

Trinity College (TCD), which began accepting women undergraduates in 1904. Her school results were outstanding, having come first in Ireland in science and mathematics in the Senior School Certificate (the equivalent of the present-day Leaving Certificate). She entered the Faculty of Science in TCD in the autumn of 1924.

In the meantime, her musical interests and abilities had broadened, particularly when she became a piano and organ student of the renowned Turner Huggard, FRCO[1], a charismatic musician and inspiring choral conductor. Her piano technique improved to the extent of taking part in the Senior Piano competition in the Dublin Feis Ceoil, probably in 1925 – she told me that the winner was Frederick Stone, later to become official accompanist at the BBC in London. She also competed in the Senior Organ competition. Her membership of Turner Huggard's choirs, the Dublin Philharmonic Society and the Dublin Oratorio Society, laid the foundation for her own later expertise in choral conducting.

My mother's other big interest at this time was the Girl Guide company at Christ Church, Rathgar. The Girl Guide movement had been established in England in 1910 by Sir Robert Baden-Powell, the founder of the Boy Scouts organisation, with the intention of creating opportunities for girls in line with the aims and ideals of the Scout movement. The first Girl Guide Company in Ireland was formed in 1911 at Harold's Cross in Dublin and the company at Rathgar in 1914. It was known as the 4th South Dublin Company. My mother joined in 1920 when she was 14 – membership was open to girls between the ages of 11 and 17 – and was immediately like the proverbial duck in the pond! She loved the emphasis on outdoor activities, the comradeship and the opportunities to develop fresh skills. There were new friends and the excitement of her first camp at the Powerscourt Estate in Co. Wicklow, a location that was a wonderful home to Irish Scouts and Guides alike. By the age of 17 she was ready to assume more responsibility by taking 'Guider' training. She became a lieutenant in 1924 and Captain of the Rathgar Company in October 1927, at the age of 21. She revelled in bringing her wide range of interests into her Guide work. Former Guides thought her very knowledgeable and remembered her telling them about astronomy, birds, trees and wild flowers. She loved to have a 'sing-song' around the fire at night or to organise a group for Irish dancing. In fact she led an Irish-dancing team at a performance for Sir Robert and Lady Baden-Powell when they visited Dublin in 1928.

In 1924 it had seemed that all was set fair for a brilliant career at TCD, but during her first year it became clear that the situation at home was not at all settled. My grandmother's condition had worsened, and by this time both Alice and Kay were in teaching jobs. My mother was faced with the prospect that she might have to be the one to give up her university studies, in order to care for their mother full-time. This was a huge crisis for her, and though it was resolved fairly satisfactorily, she continued to refer to it for many years to come. Her saviours were, in fact, her Tutor and some of the lecturers. They were concerned that such a promising student should have her studies cut short and suggested to my mother that, by changing to a general Bachelor of Arts (BA) degree, she could attend lectures in the afternoon, by which time her sisters would be at home to care for their mother. They advised her to select areas of study that would be new and interesting for her, so she included French, Geology, Philosophy and Astronomy in her degree. They further suggested that she would have no difficulty in following the course for Bachelor of Commerce (B Comm) at the same time, as the lectures would also fit into this timetable. So the change was agreed and she switched courses.

However, she did have to deal with one further crisis towards the end of her first year. She was called to the study of her Tutor and asked to explain how she had quoted *verbatim* from a text book in one of her exam papers. She protested that she would never bring a book into an exam so the Tutor decided to test her. He gave her several pages to read and then asked her to write them out. This she did perfectly, the proof that she had a photographic memory! My mother had been unaware of this talent and told me that the Tutor advised her to be vigilant in future, and to be sure to use her own words in examinations.

I know that the enforced change in her course of study was very difficult for my mother, even though the B Comm degree was useful to her in years to come. There was always sadness, even resentment, in her voice when she referred to the opportunities she had to relinquish at this time, and probably regret that she was prevented from entering fully into student life.

Nonetheless, given her customary energy and enthusiasm, I suspect that she found ways around some of these restrictions. I certainly recall her telling me about going with other students to help the people of Grenville Street, part of the terrible tenement slums of inner Dublin. I also recall hearing of late-night escapades when some of the male students got locked out of their rooms in college. She made new friends such as Edward Solomons, then a medical student, and later to become a noted gynaecologist, and Lily Butler from Cork who became head mistress of a school in England. Easton Warnock, who was also a member of Christ Church, Rathgar, was in her year, studying for the BA and B Comm degrees. There were dances and tennis parties and one or two boyfriends who helped her to learn to drive their cars. Among these were my father, Lyall Smith, and Billy Stewart who was studying for the Presbyterian ministry. Billy gave her a present of a beautifully bound hymn-book, which she kept to the end of her life. But she told me that she didn't feel she was cut out for the life of a Minister's wife! My mother always loved dancing, as did her father, and when she was eighteen he took her on a memorable trip to London where they went to Tea Dances at some of the high-class hotels.

My mother graduated from TCD in 1928, but the year turned out to be very eventful. Her sister Kay had become engaged to David Lusk, originally from Ballymena in Co. Antrim, whom she met when they were both students at the College of Science. David had graduated with a degree in engineering and worked for a time in England, but was finding it difficult to get a suitable post. In early 1928 he was offered the opportunity of a government job in telecommunications engineering in Colombo, the capital of Ceylon (later Sri Lanka). The decision was made to bring the wedding forward so that Kay could travel with him. All three sisters were accomplished dressmakers, but nonetheless there was enormous pressure to have all Kay's trousseau ready by the deadline, and the making of the bridesmaids' dresses fell to my mother. At the same time, she was preparing to take the final exams of her two degrees, and she reminisced to me that she and Lily Butler took refuge in the peace and quiet of Crone in order to study. The only drawback was a madly insistent cuckoo, which kept them awake at night! Perhaps as the outcome of all this stress, by the day of her first exam my mother had developed a badly poisoned finger, and only managed to complete the papers with the help of my father's sister Isobel, who was a doctor. She came three times a day to the Exam Hall in Trinity to dress the finger. As it turned out, all the hard work paid off. My mother was awarded her B Comm degree 'with distinction' and also placed first in her year in the BA degree, in a special category known as 'Respondent'. This conveyed that her General BA degree had been upgraded, through the excellence of her results, to the equivalent of an honours degree. The final icing on the cake was the award of the King Edward Prize, which had been instituted to commemorate the visit of King Edward VII to Trinity in 1903. This was given each year to the 'best answerer' amongst the Respondents at the BA final exams.

Kay and David's wedding took place on 21 August at Christ Church, Rathgar, with the departure for Colombo following almost immediately afterwards. There was therefore not just the sadness of bidding farewell to Kay and David for some years, but also the readjustments to be made at home for the care of my grandmother because of Kay's absence. But my mother's graduation day seems to have been very special and she was delighted when her fellow students sang 'She's got eyes of blue, I never cared for eyes of blue, But she's got eyes of blue, She's the girl for me!' as she went up in cap and gown to receive her degrees and her King Edward Prize.

[1] See entry for Turner Huggard (1893-1944) in *The Encyclopaedia of Music in Ireland*.

CHAPTER 3

Marriage

In the preceding chapter, I mentioned briefly my father Lyall and his sister. Their parents were John Smith, a pharmaceutical chemist, and his wife Isabella (*née* Gilchrist). John Smith was born in Aberdeen in 1864 and came to Dublin in the mid-1890s, having qualified as a chemist in his native Scotland. He worked initially for Evans & Co., Dawson St, and in 1897 opened his own chemist shop in Rathgar. Isabella was born in 1870, also in Scotland, but came to Ireland as a child when her father, Andrew Gilchrist, became the owner of a farm at Grovedale, Kilternan, Co. Dublin. Her mother was Agnes (*née* Rea) and there was an older brother Archibald, born in 1867. Isabella married my grandfather Smith in 1898 and they made their first home in the rooms over the shop. Their eldest son, Russell Archibald, was born there in 1899. Two daughters followed – Isobel Gillespie in 1901 and Hilda Rea in 1902 – and then my father Lyall Gilchrist in 1906. It is not certain where the Smith family lived between 1900 and 1910, though a John Smith is recorded in the Dublin Street Directory of 1908 as living at 30 Mornington Road, Ranelagh. My grandfather must have been highly respected in his profession as he was elected President of the Pharmaceutical Society of Ireland from 1907 to 1910 – my father kept his medal of office and I have it still. Then about 1910 the family moved to a lovely house in the country, Ingleside, at Carrickmines, Co. Dublin, not far from Kilternan where my grandmother had grown up. My father had great affection for the neighbourhood and

33

used to relate how he could walk across the fields and a low ridge to reach Grovedale where his Uncle Archie and his grandmother Gilchrist still lived. My grandfather travelled to work each day by train from nearby Carrickmines station to Milltown on the Dublin to Bray railway, and my father also travelled by train to his school on St Stephen's Green.[1]

There must have been sadness for the family, however, as it became gradually apparent that both Russell and Hilda had some form of mental and physical handicap, and whilst they were able to attend school, and could read and write, neither was able to work outside the home as an adult. My father's other sister, Isobel, qualified as a doctor, later specialising as an anaesthetist, and practised in Dublin, London and South Africa. So it came about that my grandfather decided that my father should study pharmacy and be prepared to join him in the family business. It seems that my father had other ideas and tried to leave home to join the Merchant Navy, but this was not to be. He submitted to his father's wishes, began work as an apprentice in the shop and started to study for his pharmacy exams. But all his life he retained a great love of the sea and, in his spare time, became a skilful yachtsman and an expert navigator.

When my father was about 16, the family moved from Carrickmines to a large house with some 10 acres of land, Kilvare, on the banks of the river Dodder near Templeogue, then a small village on the outskirts of Dublin. Built about 1800, Kilvare is not a particularly graceful house, though it has a fine set of bay windows rising the full three storeys. Externally its most striking feature is an elegant sun porch, added at a later date, which is the setting for many Smith family photos. Internally there are still some lovely period ceilings and some fine marble fireplaces, thought to have come from the former Bishop's Palace at Tallaght. The famous steam tram which ran from Terenure to Blessington used to pass the side wall of Kilvare, and was something of a hazard when exiting the main gate by car.

The Smiths were Presbyterians, as of course were the Richardsons, and both families attended Christ Church, Rathgar. So it was as members of the same church community that my parents became acquainted. They shared a love of the outdoor life, of hiking in the Dublin and Wicklow mountains, and social pursuits such as tennis and dancing. My father was a gifted photographer and introduced my mother to this hobby; he also helped her to learn to drive, and supported her in her Guide activities. He was not particularly musical, though he enjoyed going to concerts, but at that time music only played a relatively small part in my mother's life. As it turned out, she never learned to share his enthusiasm for the sea and sailing.

Alice, my mother's eldest sister married Ernest (Ernie) Spence on 11 September 1929. He had been best man at the wedding of Kay and David, having become firm friends with David when they were both engineering students at the College of Science. After his marriage he went to work in my grandfather's business in an administrative position, but various family members have said that this was not an entirely happy situation for him. My grandfather was still active in the business into his eighties, so Ernie was never completely in charge, and perhaps my grandfather found it hard to delegate. Sadly, Alice and Ernie had no children, but he was very active in the Scout movement and also very kind to his nieces and nephew.

Alice's marriage, following just a year after Kay's, meant of course that even more of my grandmother's care would now fall on my mother's shoulders. However, a decision was taken that my grandmother should have a live-in companion, and this allowed my mother to start thinking about a full-time job. In 1931 she was appointed to an administrative post in TCD as Assistant to the Lady Registrar, Miss Christabel Godfrey. Even more significantly, the new situation at Kenilworth Square opened up the way for my parents to start planning their own wedding, which took place on 14 September 1932 at Christ Church, Rathgar. The marriage ceremony was performed by Dr J. J. Macaulay, Rathgar's highly-esteemed Minister, who had undertaken the same duty for Kay and Alice. The best man was Easton Warnock and the bridesmaid was Lily Butler. This joyful time was made even happier by the first visit home of Kay and David from Ceylon with their 2-year-old son, Brian Hugh, born on 24 August 1930. It was my mother's first opportunity to get to know her nephew. The marriage was followed by a honeymoon in the West of Ireland, returning to begin their married life (like my father's parents) in the rooms over the chemist shop, which now proudly displayed the words 'John Smith & Son' over the door. I still possess the little notebook in which my mother noted meticulously all the wedding presents they received – it makes fascinating reading!

Following graduation, my mother had done some part-time teaching at the school where Alice taught, but did not feel that this was really her *métier*. The position in TCD was much more to her liking and she remained there for the next 12 years. The Lady Registrar's office was in No.6 in Front Square and was the nerve-centre for everything connected with the activities of women students. Each girl had her own locker, there were toilet facilities and a lunch-room, open to both staff and students. Students even received their exam results from Miss Godfrey. She and my mother dealt with a wide range of administration, but also provided much-appreciated practical and emotional support for each year's cohort of female students. Women had first been admitted to Trinity in 1904, but even 30 years later they were still few in number and were subject to various irksome restrictions. Gowns had to be worn at all times and women were obliged to leave the College campus by 6.00 p.m. They were excluded from the Dining Hall and from membership of the two major college societies, the University Philosophical Society and the College Historical Society. They were allowed to join the Experimental Science Association, but had to be escorted by the Lady Registrar as the meetings were at 8.00 p.m.!

Women did have their own separate society, the Elizabethan – named after the College's founder, Queen Elizabeth I – which had rooms upstairs in No.6. This had been established in 1905 and was: 'intended to act as a social and literary centre for women'.[2] It offered the opportunity for weekly formal debates on political topics, current affairs and women's issues. By 1922 there were sufficient women graduates to found the Dublin University Women Graduates Association. There was also an increasing body of women staff members, the first female professor, Dr Frances Moran (Reid Professor of Law) having been appointed in 1925.

However, the really major step of appointing a woman as Fellow did not occur until 1968, long after my mother had finished her years in Trinity. By the 1930s, a significant number of women graduates had made their way into administrative posts. These developments are recorded in *A Danger to the Men? –A History of Women in T.C.D. 1904-2004*, edited by Susan Parkes. Indeed, it was said that: 'Trinity was a college for men, which was run by women'! Christabel Godfrey must have been a lovely person to work for. She herself had graduated in 1910, having been elected a Scholar in 1908. There is a passage about her in Susan Parkes' book: 'A gentle and caring person who was most concerned for the welfare of her students. Though always polite and at times deferential, she had a shrewd insight into the particular difficulties of College life, and she was prepared, when necessary, to defend the rights of women students.'

My mother enjoyed being in the thick of College life. In after-years she often referred to people she got to know at that time: Dr Thekla Beere (who became Ireland's first high-ranking female civil-servant), Prof. Frances Moran, whom my mother regarded as a role-model, the pianist, composer and poet Rhoda Coghill – one of the first women to receive the MusB degree, Owen Sheehy-Skeffington (lecturer in French), Dr Theo Moody, professor of modern history, and his wife Margaret, Dr A.J. McConnell (later Provost) and the flamboyant professor of Spanish, Walter Starkie. She became very good friends with Miss Helen Watson who, as secretary to Captain Shaw, the Assistant Registrar, had a key role in College administration for many years and (to quote from the same book): 'was known to hundreds of students for her helpful advice and knowledge of college procedures.' We will meet Helen Watson again later in this book. In the TCD Calendar for 1937-38 my mother is recorded with the degree of MA as well as B Comm. She had availed of the traditional facility offered by the College to upgrade her BA degree by the payment of a small fee.

My mother's musical outlets at this time were chiefly the choirs conducted by Turner Huggard. He became conductor of the Culwick Choral Society in 1929, following the sudden death of Miss Florence

Culwick. This was a remarkable mixed-voice choir, specialising at that time in *a capella* or unaccompanied singing. Special skill and training is required to develop beautiful tone and intonation, especially with such a large group of choristers. This tradition had been their hallmark since their foundation in 1898 by Dr James Culwick, and they continued to be exponents of this genre until about 1970. Each concert programme followed a similar pattern with a number of items for choir alone, ranging from music of the 16th century right up to contemporary works by Irish composers, as well as some instrumental items by a distinguished guest soloist. Given that Turner Huggard was my mother's former piano and organ teacher, and her great admiration for him, I can only imagine that she would have looked on membership of this choir as a dream come true! As far as I can ascertain, she became a member about 1930.

She took the Guides to camp in Powerscourt in 1929, and in 1930 was part of a group of Irish Scout and Guide leaders who attended an important Scout Jamboree in England. Later the same summer, she organised a Rathgar Guide camp at Castlewellan, Co. Down, and this was also the first camp attended by a young Guide named Patricia (Pat) McKnight, then aged 12. In spite of their age difference, Pat became one of my mother's closest friends, and remained so, right to the end of her life. Further camps at Kilquade, Co. Wicklow followed in 1931 and 1932, and that same year my mother took on the onerous role of 'Quartermaster', in charge of all supplies for an International Camp held in Powerscourt. This was organised in conjunction with the 31st International Eucharistic Congress, which took place in Dublin in June. Pat and other former Guides spoke to me of the respect they had for my mother. In their experience she was an inspiration and a role model. She had a deep interest in young people and identified with her Guides, and whilst she was a natural leader, she never looked on herself as being 'above' those in her care.

It is clear that in the crucial years of her late twenties my mother was continuing to develop her innate organisational ability through her work with the Guides, and that she was comfortable with positions of responsibility. She was very happily married, and my father was like-minded in his determination to develop his business – they shared a similar work ethic, as well as other interests. But with the benefit of hindsight, and knowing where her talents would eventually lead her, I think that the period spent working in the well-run and busy office in Trinity College was to prove the most valuable in the years to come. There she developed not only her ability to get on with all kinds of people, but also her considerable administrative skills.

[1] St Stephen's Green School, a Protestant boys' day school, headmaster Leonard R. Strangways, was at 75 St Stephen's Green.

[2] TCD Calendar 1926-27.

CHAPTER 4

From Crumlin to Ceylon

Quite soon after my parent's marriage they embarked on their first project together – the purchase of their own chemist shop. The Dublin suburb of Crumlin was in the throes of construction, intended as a means of re-housing the families from the worst of the city-centre tenements. My parents realised that a chemist shop could provide a much-needed service and purchased 199 Crumlin Road, which had good living quarters over the shop, plus a very welcome garden. The only drawback was that there was no space to set up a photographic business, developing and printing black-and-white and colour film, such as my father had already established at the rear of the Rathgar premises.

A pharmacist who lived over the business was reckoned to be 'on call', even through the night, and the night bell was quite often pressed for serious, or even minor emergencies. My father had a dog called Collie who was rather docile, so my mother determined to get a proper watch-dog. Thus Steven the Sealyham entered their lives: not only did he take enthusiastically to his job of protecting them, but gave them many hours of entertainment with his intelligent and characterful ways.

Crumlin is about 3 miles from the city centre and my mother was constantly on her bicycle – into TCD to her job, over to Rathgar to visit her parents and to attend Guide meetings, and to various halls for choir rehearsals. As mentioned in the previous chapter, she joined the Culwick Choral Society about 1930 but continued as a member of the Dublin Oratorio Society. She gave up her membership of the Dublin Philharmonic Society around this time, however her sister Alice continued to sing with them and is listed amongst the sopranos for a performance of *The Dream of Gerontius* on 25 November 1933.

In 1933 my mother was part of a team of twelve Guides who represented Ireland at a World Scout and Guide Dancing Festival in London. The following notice appeared in the *Sunday Independent*: 'I had the opportunity of seeing a charming and accomplished performance by the full Irish team; and I have no hesitation in saying it was one of the finest exhibitions of Irish National Dancing ever seen in London, and the loud applause at the close of the performance showed how highly it was appreciated. . . it is pleasing to record that the national garb of the twelve *cailíní* from Ireland with its saffron and blue was amongst the most beautiful and graceful of the feminine costumes.'[1] My mother was equally impressed by the two Irish pipers who played for them and who wore saffron kilts! Other Guiding activities in the 1930s included a camp in Powerscourt in 1935 and another at Ballycumber, Co. Offaly, in 1938. According to the records of the Rathgar Company, held by the archive of the Irish Girl Guides, during a short period from 1935 to 1937 my mother assumed responsibility for the Brownie Pack, but resumed duties as Guide Captain from September 1937. This archive has also revealed that she served on the Irish Girl Guides Training Committee from 1937 to 1943.

Meanwhile, in far-away Ceylon, a daughter was born to Kay and David on 18 March 1934: she was named Helen Patricia. The family's next home leave came in 1936 and Brian remembers that his great-grandmother Bessy Richardson was still in good health in her 98th year! His parents were concerned to make plans for him to commence his schooling in Ireland soon after his 9th birthday in 1939. It was agreed that my parents would be *in loco parentis* and that Brian would go as a boarder to Cabin Hill, on the outskirts of Belfast. The excitement for my mother was the proposal that she should sail to Ceylon in May 1939 and enjoy a holiday there until it was time to make the return voyage with Brian in

August. This was certainly the trip of a lifetime, and my father took the far-sighted decision to provide her with a ciné camera and a supply of the latest Kodachrome 16mm film. As a result, the family has a wonderful record in colour of life in Ceylon just before the Second World War. She sailed from Birkenhead on the Bibby Line vessel *Derbyshire* on 5 May, calling at Gibraltar, Marseilles, Port Sudan (via the Suez Canal), Cochin and arriving at Colombo on 29 May. This was leisurely travel, with time to go ashore in each port, and luxurious too, to judge by the eight-course dinner menus that my mother happily kept for posterity. Kay and David and the children lived at the Galle Face apartments in Colombo, near the sea and in an excellent position to view processions. An important event, shortly after her arrival, was the reception by the Governor in honour of the King's birthday, from which my mother retained a formal dance card, complete with miniature pencil!

Kay had established a reputation in Colombo as a singer, and my mother was quite surprised to find herself joining her sister for a radio programme of vocal duets. She remembered the occasion particularly because, during the live transmission, they were joined by a cat which proceeded to curl up on the top of the piano! My aunt and uncle made sure that my mother saw all the main sights of interest on the island, including the Temple of the Tooth and the Sacred Bo-Tree at Kandy, Sigiriya Rock, the Moonstone and statues at Polonnaruwa and the harbour at Trincomalee. Some time was also spent 'up-country' at a tea estate, and as all the travel was by car there were many opportunities to see how the local people lived, to learn the history and legends of Ceylon, and to appreciate the glorious scenery, flora and fauna. All this was recorded, not just on ciné film but also on lantern slides, and she was much in demand on her return to give illustrated talks about her trip. For these she prepared a spoken commentary, carefully written out in a notebook as an *aide-mémoire*.

Unfortunately this idyllic holiday had to be cut short as the political news from Europe was increasingly worrying, with talk that war might become unavoidable. My mother and Brian were to have sailed in late

August, however their booking was brought forward to 3 August. They were aboard the *Oxfordshire* but, compared with the outward journey, there were very few passengers risking the return trip at that time. There was increasing tension as they came through the Mediterranean, and in the English Channel they saw HMS *Ark Royal* and the aircraft carrier *Glorious* carrying out manoeuvres with an escort of destroyers. At night, searchlights played back and forth from the coasts of England and France, and the *Oxfordshire* observed a 'blackout'. The ship berthed at Tilbury Docks on Sunday 28 August and my father was there to meet them. They made haste to Euston station, just in time to catch the 'Irish Mail' train to Holyhead and were safely across the Irish Sea just five days before war was declared on 3 September.

This was the beginning of a new chapter for my parents, and I feel that the addition of Brian to their family was very enriching for them. Brian has told me that he was extremely fortunate to have such a wonderful aunt and uncle, who looked after him as his 'second parents' during his school years in Ireland. His stay at Cabin Hill lasted only two terms because my parents were increasingly concerned, as the Second World War progressed, that Belfast might be bombed, as indeed did happen just a year later. So it was decided that Brian should go instead to Aravon School, Bray, and he remained a pupil there until the summer of 1944.

The war years certainly made a difference to people's lives. Whilst Ireland remained neutral throughout the Second World War, a 'State of Emergency' had been declared by the Government on 2 September 1939 and the Emergency Powers Act was passed by Dáil Éireann the next day. Rationing of imported goods such as tea, sugar, tobacco, soap, clothing and shoes was gradually introduced, flour was of poor quality, and imported fruit such as oranges and bananas disappeared altogether. Petrol consumption was restricted to 8 gallons per month for a small car, and so by 1942 most cars were off the road. By 1943, gas and electricity were also severely rationed and newly-commissioned barges brought turf to Dublin by canal, where it was stored in great turf ricks in the Phoenix Park. German bombs were dropped, deliberately or accidentally, on the

North Strand area of Dublin on the night of 30/31 May 1941, leaving 28 people dead and almost 400 homeless, such was the destruction of houses.

All through the 1930s my parents had enjoyed holidays by car in Connemara, Donegal and Kerry, and had even made a memorable trip to Switzerland. But with petrol in short supply, holidays were taken nearer to home – Brian remembers very enjoyable summers at Crone (1941), at the seaside in Cahore, Co. Wexford (1942), and at Howth (1944) where my parents rented a house from the Bailie-Butler family. A lot of boating and swimming was involved and Brian got to know some of my parents' close friends – Philip Warnock (brother of Easton), his wife Connie and their little son, Antony, Alice and Harry Yoakley and their children Enid and Fred, Edward Solomons (Solly), Pat McKnight, Edgar Deale and his wife Ruth, and my parents' solicitor L.G.Carr Lett (also known as Tubby). My father took some hilarious ciné films of the antics of Tubby and Solly and also of Edgar, who was a very fine swimmer. Brian felt that he was treated as an adult by these friends, which pleased him a lot.

Another feature of the 'Emergency' years was that much entertainment had to be home-produced. The weekly recitals at the Royal Dublin Society (RDS) continued, as did concerts by local choirs including the Culwick, who performed at the RDS on 1 December 1941. On 13 April 1942, three hundred performers were on the stage of the Gaiety Theatre to give a bicentennial performance of Handel's *Messiah* – my mother and my aunt Alice both sang in this performance and their cousin Arthur Franks played in the orchestra. The D'Oyly Carte Company could not travel from England with their repertoire of Gilbert and Sullivan operas, so in 1940 a group of friends connected with the Culwick decided to try their hand at an amateur production of *Trial by Jury*. This was so successful that productions of *The Mikado* and *The Gondoliers* followed in 1941 and 1942. All the rehearsals and performances were in the large hall below Christ Church, Rathgar, which had a good stage. My father was in charge of scenery building and other practical matters such as lighting, Alice Yoakley was the musical director and played piano for the performances, along with Miss Agnes Paul. My mother sang the part of Pitti-Sing in *The Mikado* and was Tessa in *The Gondoliers*. Other parts were sung by Richard Midgeley, Edgar Deale and Olive McHugh. It seems to have been the greatest fun and there were numerous stories of the cast playing practical jokes on each other.

The nature of Guiding activities was somewhat altered by the war, and camping was certainly curtailed. The last record I have of my mother's participation in an official Guide event is a photograph of her carrying the flag in a colour-party for a special service to mark the death of the founder of the Guide and Scout movements, Sir Robert Baden-Powell. This was held in St Patrick's Cathedral, Dublin, in 1941 and, according to the Irish Girl Guide records, my mother ceased to be captain of the Rathgar Company in that year. However, she was persuaded in 1945 to establish an Irish Girl Guides choir and thus retained connections with many former Guide colleagues.

The shortage of petrol may also have been a factor in my parents' decision to place a manager, Christy Morrissey, in the Crumlin shop and to move, in 1941 or 1942, to an apartment on the top floor of 74 St Stephen's Green, next door to the building which had housed my father's school. It was very convenient for my mother's job in Trinity College, and there was the Terenure tram to take my father to work in Rathgar. Another factor was my father's membership of the Slua na Mara, a part-time auxiliary marine service which patrolled Dublin Bay right through the war years. Oddly enough, his commanding officer was the rather scatter-brained and humorous writer, Patrick Campbell. My father was often at sea at night and, even with Steven as protection, my mother felt somewhat vulnerable in Crumlin. The third factor was undoubtedly my father's growing interest in developing the photographic side of the business at Rathgar. In 1942, a local teenager named Vincent Trotman was looking for a summer holiday job and good fortune brought him to the doors of John Smith & Son. As it turned out, he never left. He quickly showed a great interest and aptitude for all the practical side of photographic developing and printing. Colour processing was the growing market, and Smiths held the franchise for Dufay Colour and also developed colour film for Dr Steeven's Hospital. All this was accommodated in cramped premises at the back of the Rathgar shop – the practical skills of both my father and Vincent were very much needed.

And then, early in 1943, came a big surprise – it became apparent that there would soon be another change in my parents' lives as, after eleven years of marriage and at the age of 37, my mother discovered that she was expecting a baby!

[1] *Sunday Independent* – 16 July 1933.

CHAPTER 5

Motherhood and Family Life in the 1940s

I was born on 19 November 1943 and, according to a letter from Brian to his father, I weighed 8 ¼ pounds. My place of birth was the Hatch Street Nursing Home, affectionately known to several generations of Dublin mothers as 'The Hatcheries'! The gynaecologist in attendance was the now illustrious Dr Edward Solomons, so mother and baby were in good hands. Enid Yoakley (later Mrs Jack Chaloner) remembers visiting my mother shortly after my birth. She was occupied with stitching and embroidering a baby shawl and said to Enid: 'I have waited ten years for this and I'm going to enjoy it!' But my arrival did highlight an immediate problem – the flat on the top floor of 74 St Stephen's Green involved the descent or ascent of three flights of stairs every time the weather was fine enough to wheel the pram into the Green across the road. However, wartime travel restrictions meant that a move to a more convenient house with a garden had to be postponed for the time-being.

In the early 1930s my father's parents had made a move of convenience when my grandfather built a fine modern house, which he called Corrybeg, in the grounds of the big Kilvare house at Templeogue. This became the new home of my grandparents, together with my father's disabled siblings, Russell and Hilda.[1] My father's other sister, Isobel, moved to a London hospital as an anaesthetist at the start of the Second

World War and never lived again in Ireland. She eventually settled in South Africa. It has to be said that she and my mother did not really get on, my mother in particular taking exception to Isobel's attitude to her siblings, especially my father. Her occasional visits home were rather dreaded by everyone. My grandfather Smith was 79 when I was born, but continued to work as a pharmacist into his eighties. Sadly, my Uncle Russell died on 10 September 1943, aged just 44 years. I know very little about him, except that he made beautiful hand-knotted wool rugs, several of which were in use in my home right up to the start of the 21st century.

Towards the middle of 1944 there was welcome news from Ceylon. Home leave had been completely put on hold during the first years of the war, and Brian had not seen his parents since 1939, but the situation in the Mediterranean was considered sufficiently improved for passenger ships to attempt the voyage. David and Kay and 10-year-old Helen started on a tedious train journey northwards through India to reach Bombay, from where they sailed under the protection of a convoy, one of the first to make it through the recently re-opened Suez Canal. A birthday telegram signed 'Ralph' was the secret signal that they were *en route*. The family were reunited in Dublin and Kay and the children never returned to Ceylon, though David did have to see out the remainder of his contract. Helen went as a boarder to the French School in Bray from 1944 to 1947, whilst Kay lived at Kenilworth Square and Brian started his secondary education at St Columba's College in Rathfarnham.

It was in the years immediately following my birth that my mother turned increasingly towards music as her main interest. She had given up her job in TCD before I was born, and had previously retired from the Guide movement. Around Easter 1945 the dream of a house of their own was realised and my parents purchased Clonard on Torquay Road, Foxrock, in Co. Dublin. This was a bungalow with three or four bedrooms, and my parents added a conservatory to one side of the sitting-room. It had quite a large garden to the front, and the back garden adjoined the tracks of the Harcourt St to Bray railway line.

The rattle of steam trains puffing and belching smoke are amongst my earliest memories. At first there was plenty to occupy my mother with the establishment of a flower and vegetable garden, curtain-making, and of course dress-making and knitting for herself and a growing daughter. She had some help in the house as Annie Gregan, who had also been at St Stephen's Green, came to live with us in Clonard. She came originally from Ashford in Co. Wicklow and I was very fond of her.

My mother had an upright piano and used to play and sing to herself, preparing for the weekly rehearsals of the Culwick. Turner Huggard died suddenly in November 1944 at the age of 51 and was greatly mourned. But my mother was delighted at the appointment of her friend Alice Yoakley as his successor and the choir continued to go from strength to strength, celebrating its Golden Jubilee in December 1948. Thursday night rehearsals could not be missed, and in addition my mother had taken on the role of Treasurer, a position she retained until 1956. Sometime in 1945 she was persuaded by some of her friends from the Guide movement to try her hand at choral conducting, and the Irish Girl Guides Choir came into being. This was her first opportunity to put into practice what she had learned from Turner Huggard and it turned out to be very successful. Ivy Kevelighan, who was the piano accompanist for the choir, reminisced that my mother was very good at explaining the technique of 'placing the voice' and knew how to get a choir to sing in tune.[2] The choir won the silver cup and gold medal for the Ladies' Choir competition in the Dublin Feis Ceoil of 1949, having been placed second the previous year.

The Monday chamber music recitals at the RDS were also a great source of joy. My mother was a member, so a concert was always combined with a visit to the Library. She was an avid reader, exploring all the most recent writers of fiction and keeping up with the subjects she had studied at Trinity. I remember her talking with excitement whenever something was published about a ground-breaking astronomical discovery; at the other end of the spectrum, as it were, she continued to read in French and delighted in the series of Georges Simenon stories about the fictional Inspector Maigret. Many of these appeared for the first time in the 1940s. She even embarked on a course of harmony and counterpoint lessons with William Watson FRCO. But in her own words, to quote from an article by Patricia Quinn in the music magazine *SoundPost*, 'she was going crazy with boredom'.[3]

Fortunately I was completely unaware of this build-up of frustration, and look back fondly on my early childhood, where I was made to feel important and cherished. My recollection is that we were outdoors a great deal, either in the garden or on hikes and visits in the countryside, and many of these expeditions were captured on film by my father, who seemed to have his ciné camera always with him. I knew the names of flowers and trees, of animals and insects, and helped my mother to plant bulbs and sweet-pea plants in the garden. I also remember being wrapped in an eiderdown very late one night and taken outside to see a comet! Pat McKnight's cottage was built around this period on a hillside overlooking Powerscourt, and Helen Watson had access to a little house near the Lead Mines Chimney at Ballycorus, so these were frequent destinations. We also visited Powerscourt waterfall very often, which my mother knew well from her childhood summers at Crone, and in the summer went to the seaside at Brittas Bay, Co. Wicklow, where Oonah and Gardner Budd (later Mr Justice Budd), old friends from College days, had a holiday house. I can only assume that by 1947 the wartime restrictions on petrol had been lifted. Then there was my grandfather's tradition of meeting on a Friday morning in Dublin at a particular coffee-house called FM's. He greatly enjoyed this, my two aunts Alice and Kay would often be there, and in the school holidays Brian and Helen also. We were each allowed to choose our favourite cake!

My parents both read aloud to me from the earliest time I can remember, and of course I loved this. As soon as I could read myself, my mother included me in her visits to the RDS library which had a good children's section. I think I started dancing classes at quite a young age, at Miss Catt's ballet school on Baggot Street, and certainly began piano lessons at about the age of six with Miss Alice Bryan, who taught in her home on

Leeson Street. I remained with her until I went away for third-level study in London and I am so grateful to have had such a wonderful teacher. In collaboration with her great friend from TCD days, Lily Butler, who was headmistress of a large school in England, my mother hatched another clever plan designed to broaden my education. Each year this school employed a French or German student teacher to give conversation classes, and my mother was able to solve the school's dilemma concerning the Christmas or Easter holidays by inviting the teacher to come over to Ireland. As a result we had a succession of charming visitors whose main task was to introduce me to their language in a playful, informal way, and this early initiation into German and French pronunciation has really stood to me. Also around this time I think that I became more aware of my father as a sailor. He was part-owner of a yacht in the Dublin Bay 17-Footer class, which raced out of Dun Laoghaire, and my mother and I would go down on a Saturday evening to see him finish his race. This boat was called *Bobolink* and he later became sole owner of *Echo* which had a red hull and beautiful blue sails. I think I inherited my father's sea-faring genes and was disappointed that I would not be allowed to go sailing with him until I could swim several lengths of a pool!

In January 1947 my mother's parents celebrated their golden wedding, but sadly my grandmother Richardson died the following August, having lived into her early seventies in spite of her poor health. I vaguely remember being brought to her bedroom before she died. There is one lovely picture of her as a young woman in a fashionable dress and stylish hat, but unfortunately most photographs show her with an expression of tired sadness. My father's mother also died in 1947, on 31 December, aged 78. I remember her rather better, particularly her beautiful short white hair, and although I have an impression of her as being a little sharp in manner, she was very kindly and always let me play with some favourite things whenever I visited Corrybeg. I inherited some of her lovely chairs.

Plans had to be made for the two widowed grandfathers, both of them in their eighties. Grandfather Richardson was quite happy to remain in his home with a housekeeper to look after his needs. After I started school in 1948, a new custom was established whereby my grandfather's driver, Mr Canavan, would collect me on Wednesdays and then my father and I would both go to lunch at Kenilworth Square. Canavan also figures in my cousins' recollections, driving them and our grandfather on holiday to Recess in Connemara and Laragh in Wicklow, probably in 1947 and 1948. Both Brian and Helen remember our grandfather as being very fond of his grandchildren, making toys and jigsaws with his wood-working tools, and showing them things in the garden. He found a way of giving Brian a little extra pocket money by paying him a penny for every earwig he could catch!

The situation was not so straightforward for grandfather Smith, as the ongoing care of Hilda, my father's handicapped sister, had to be considered. Reluctantly it was decided that she should go to live in a residential home, but my impression is that my parents regretted this, and I think they felt that if Russell and Hilda had been born in modern times, more could have been done to assist them to live a normal life. My grandfather stayed on at Corrybeg for a while, but matters were resolved when my parents decided to move house again in 1949 to another property in Foxrock, this time beside the golf course. This was Rockview and they rented it from Mr Benson who owned the Dartry Dye Works on the river Dodder. His wife had died and he no longer wanted to live there, but my mother had known Mrs Benson well and loved Rockview's beautiful and extensive garden. So a deal was done, and the outcome was that my grandfather Smith came to live in Clonard and my parents were able to oversee his care in the last months of his life. He died on 25 March 1951 aged 87. My recollection is of a gentle, quiet man, shorter and stouter than my father in build, but with a similar bald head. Photographs almost invariably show him smoking or holding a cigarette. I think he passed his patient temperament on to his son, but my father was altogether more lively and out-going and was well known for his repertoire of jokes.

[1] Kilvare was purchased in 1933 by a charitable committee from Clondalkin, with the financial assistance of Joseph McGrath of the Irish Hospitals Sweepstakes. This committee ran Cheeverstown convalescent home for children, and as their Clondalkin lease had expired they needed a new premises in which to continue their work. That is how my grandparents' home became the central building of the modern-day complex known as Cheeverstown which specialises in the care of handicapped adults.

[2] Interviewed by the author and Pat O'Kelly, 2001.

[3] *SoundPost* August/September 1983.

CHAPTER 6

Music in Dublin in the 1940s

The Music Association of Ireland (MAI) whose history forms the central core of this book, was founded in 1948. However it is interesting to note that an earlier body with an almost identical name – the Musical Association of Ireland – existed briefly from 1939 to 1941. This group presented a memorandum to a Government Commission on behalf of the music profession, advocating better organisation and safeguards regarding qualifications and standards, particularly referring to music in schools. Leading members of the profession – Prof. John F. Larchet (UCD), Prof. George H. Hewson (TCD), Prof. Aloys Fleischmann (UCC) and Mr W. S. Greig (St Patrick's Cathedral) – were involved in the compilation of the report and gave oral evidence. There was great disappointment when the Commission's report was pigeon-holed by Government.[1]

I feel it would be helpful at this point to give an overview of the live performances of classical music which were available to Dublin audiences in the 1940s, and which my mother might have attended. The most significant orchestral contributions came from the Radio Éireann Orchestra (RÉO) which, in 1937, numbered just twenty-eight musicians, but by 1942 had expanded to forty players. Its main duties were to broadcast live from the studio, but it also gave occasional public concerts. These programmes usually featured a large-scale work of the symphonic repertoire, or one of the major choral works, such as my mother would have performed with Turner Huggard's choirs. There was a long-standing practice of adding extra free-lance string players, with wind and brass from the Army No.1 Band. These players were under the direction of Colonel Fritz Brasé, and my mother and her fellow singers were greatly amused by his strong Germanic accent: 'You vill be seating on your stands at seven-surty sharp'!

In January 1941, Captain Michael Bowles became conductor of the RÉO and set about improving the group's artistic profile by organising a series of concerts in the Mansion House, which continued until the autumn of 1943. Such was the success with the public that it was necessary to move to the Capitol Cinema, where the concerts continued until early 1948. Joseph O'Neill, music critic for the *Irish Independent*, writing in *The Bell*[2] about the first concert in November 1941, commented that: 'With such a successful commencement we may look forward to Dublin justifying its phantom reputation as a musical city'. But the very next month, reviewing a performance by Rhoda Coghill of Brahms 2nd Piano Concerto, he describes the Mansion House as: 'the most unsuitable hall in the whole world!' Fortunately the Dublin public was hungry for performances of classical orchestral music so that, in January 1943, O'Neill's article in *The Bell* reported that: 'to secure a seat at any of the Radio Éireann (RÉ) symphony concerts you must be able to get up early the morning booking opens, have influence with some unknown person, or buy in the black market. It is now rumoured that the Ministry of Supplies is drafting a rationing scheme for tickets!' In the war years the soloists were mostly Irish, but the repertoire was cosmopolitan and wide-ranging. A fascinating selection of the programmes from 1941-1948 is contained in Pat O'Kelly's book *The National Symphony Orchestra of Ireland, 1948-1998*. It is likely that my mother and other family members were in the audience on 28 October 1945 to hear her first cousin, Arthur Franks, play Mozart's Violin Concerto in D.

During the 1940s, the Minister for Posts and Telegraphs occupied a position of considerable influence in Irish musical life, chiefly because all the musicians employed by RÉ came under the budget of his department. Fortunately P. J. Little, who held that position in the Fianna

Fáil Government (1932 -1948), was a cultured man with many visionary plans for music in Ireland. He even had a scheme to develop a concert hall on a site adjacent to the Rotunda Hospital and asked Raymond McGrath, an Australian architect with the Board of Works, to design the building. Equally importantly, his department head was Leon Ó Broin, father of the conductor Éimear Ó Broin. In 1946 Michael Bowles, who by this time was RÉ Music Director as well as conductor of the orchestra, proposed that the RÉO membership be increased to sixty-two musicians and that a Light Orchestra of twenty-two players also be established. These plans received Government approval and Michael Bowles was given leave of absence, encouraged to go abroad to recruit new players, and also required to seek out up-and-coming international conductors. He was successful on both fronts and returned to Dublin only to find that his own conducting contract would not be renewed. He promptly resigned as Director of Music. All this upheaval occurred just weeks before the launch in February 1948 of the newly-named Radio Éireann Symphony Orchestra (RÉSO), in the recently-refurbished Phoenix Hall, just off Exchequer Street. Fortunately Michael Bowles left a good legacy to the RÉSO in the calibre of the conductors he had successfully persuaded to come to Dublin. I clearly remember my mother and her friends discussing the concerts given by Jean Martinon, Sixten Eckerberg, Otto Matzerath and Hans Schmidt-Isserstedt with great enthusiasm and critical approval.

Unfortunately a new upheaval was on the way. Fianna Fáil lost the general election in 1948 and a coalition government was formed with James Everett as Minister for Posts and Telegraphs. He was completely against the resumption of public concerts by the RÉSO at the Capitol Cinema, largely for financial reasons, and was also against the employment of players who were foreign nationals. The Director of Music who succeeded Michael Bowles, Fachtna Ó hAnnracháin, established instead a regular pattern of broadcast studio concerts in the Phoenix Hall on Tuesdays and Fridays, to which the public were admitted. Whilst these were very well supported and much appreciated for the wide variety of works programmed, there was growing disquiet amongst the concert-going public that the newly expanded and renamed orchestra was being confined to studio performances.

The Dublin Grand Opera Society (DGOS) was founded in 1941. Previous attempts to establish an indigenous Irish operatic society had collapsed due to financial difficulties and, surprisingly, lack of public support. Dr John F. Larchet, Col. William O'Kelly and Col. J.M.Doyle were behind this new venture, creating a supporting subscription fund for patrons, and two regular seasons in Dublin each year. In spite of wartime restrictions and initial difficulties in recruiting an adequate orchestra, the DGOS directors persevered with works from the standard operatic repertoire. Fortunately the orchestral situation was resolved in 1946 when negotiations between the DGOS and the Minister for Posts and Telegraphs resulted in the RÉO becoming available to play for the opera seasons. Following the end of the war, international operatic stars were able to take roles in DGOS productions, and in Spring 1948 the cast of *Pelléas et Mélisande* (Debussy) from the Opéra Comique in Paris was hosted by the DGOS under the baton of Roger Désormière. This was an eye-opening experience for Dublin music lovers – I know that my mother talked about it for years afterwards.

P. J. Little was also involved, with the assistance of the Department of Education, in a plan to set up a Summer School of Music in Dublin for choral and orchestral conductors, pianists, violinists and composers. This was achieved in 1946. The tutors were of the calibre of Jean Martinon, Henry Holst and Arnold Bax, and there was a most encouraging participation of 167 students at Coláiste Mhuire, Cathal Brúgha Street. These Summer Schools became an eagerly-anticipated feature each summer up to 1952, with the venue alternating between UCD and Coláiste Mhuire and always attracting between 150 and 175 students. Their importance to Irish performers and listeners cannot be overstated, bringing an awareness of the musical world which existed outside Ireland, and a welcome breath of fresh air after the restrictions of 'the Emergency'. For some talented players, doors were opened to further study in Paris or London.

My mother attended the choral training and music appreciation classes given in 1948 and 1949 by Dr Thomas Armstrong of the University of Oxford.[3] She admired his work very much and a friendship was formed which would have lasting consequences. My parents took him to favourite scenic places by the sea and in the Wicklow mountains, and during his visits he came frequently to our house for a meal and conversation about music and musicians. We visited him and his wife Hester for a couple of nights in Oxford during our first holiday in England by car in 1949.

The Members' Recitals at the RDS, which had been inaugurated in 1886, continued right through the war years. These followed the long-established pattern of two recitals by the same artists at 3 p.m. and 8 p.m. on six consecutive Mondays in November/December and a further six in January/February, adding up to 24 concerts in each season. The greatest number were solo piano recitals, and in the decade leading up to the Second World War the celebrated performers included Alfred Cortot, Rudolf Firkušný, Myra Hess, Eileen Joyce, Frederick Lamond, Benno Moiseiwitsch, Artur Schnabel, Rudolf Serkin and Solomon. There were occasional recitals by violinists or cellists with piano accompaniment, and a fascinating international line-up of string quartets and piano trios from England, France, Germany, Italy, Hungary and Czechoslovakia. In the years between 1933 and 1942 Arthur Franks played in at least six recitals, giving the first performance in Dublin of the John Ireland Violin Sonata on 16 January 1933, partnered by Dorothy Stokes at the piano.

However, the report of the RDS Council for 1939 states that: 'Although the outbreak of the European War rendered it impossible for some of the artists already previously booked for the autumn session to fulfil their engagements, it was found possible to provide alternatives who worthily upheld the high standard required'. But the 1940 report was more downbeat, stating that the situation: 'rendered it impossible to obtain any artists from overseas'. So the performers during the war years were either Irish or London-based, but amazingly the recitals continued without a break. The Dublin String Orchestra (DSO), an accomplished semi-professional group conducted by Terry O'Connor, played four times between 1940 and 1944, each time including a work by an Irish composer. Charles Lynch played for the first time in 1940, Claud Biggs is mentioned and also the Trimble sisters from Northern Ireland. From London came the pianists Clifford Curzon, Moiseiwitsch, Moura Lympany, Denis Matthews, Cyril Smith and Phyllis Sellick. The instrumentalists included Léon Goossens (oboe), Lionel Tertis (viola), Henry Holst (violin), Douglas Cameron (cello) and the Griller Quartet; song recitals were given by Isobel Baillie, Astra Desmond, Heddle Nash and Robert Irwin. My mother attended as often as she could, but the shortage of petrol made this difficult and indeed the RDS recorded a significant drop in average attendances between 1938 (881 attended) and 1941 (520). From 1946 onwards continental artists were once again able to travel to Dublin and some exciting new names appeared: Paul Tortelier, Gina Bachauer, Arthur Grumiaux, Maurice Gendron, Yvonne Lefébure, Nikita Magaloff, the Czech Trio, the Hungarian Quartet and the Blech Quartet. There is no doubt that all through the 1940s the RDS maintained the highest quality of solo and chamber-music recitals for the Dublin public.

In addition to Terry O'Connor's DSO, which introduced many fine works to Dublin audiences, there were amateur organisations which were significant in promoting live music performances in Dublin during the 1940s. The Dublin Orchestral Players (DOP) were formed in 1939 to provide young players with experience in orchestral playing. Havelock Nelson, who later became such an important figure in Belfast's musical life, was the group's first conductor, succeeded by Brian Boydell in 1943. The DOP gave three concerts each year, which supplemented the wide repertoire of the RÉO's Capitol concerts. The DOP actually gave the first performance outside Russia of Prokofiev's *Peter and the Wolf* and were noted for promoting the work of Irish composers.

The Feis Ceoil, Ireland's oldest competitive music festival was founded in 1896 and continues to this day. Over the years it has provided an initial performance platform for countless Irish musicians. In the 1940s its competitions were held in May, attracting about 1,000 entrants. The festival ran for six days with large, enthusiastic audiences attending the major competitions. The Royal Irish Academy of Music (RIAM) ran fortnightly concerts organised by the Students' Musical Union (SMU), and there were also regular concerts given by the RIAM orchestra and choir. Similar concerts were promoted by the Dublin Municipal School of Music. The choirs which sang in the bicentenary performance of Handel's *Messiah* in 1942 included the Culwick, the Dublin Oratorio Society, the choirs of UCD and TCD and the chorus of the DGOS, and all these choirs also gave their own annual performances. It is important to note also that Cór Radio Éireann was formed in 1943 on the instigation of Michael Bowles and with the support of P. J. Little. Finally, the Rathmines and Rathgar Musical Society, founded in 1913, continued its productions of Gilbert and Sullivan operas at the Gaiety Theatre right through the war years, providing some much-needed light-hearted musical entertainment in those dark times.

[1] The complete text of this memorandum is printed on pages 91-94 of *Music in Ireland: A Symposium*, edited by Aloys Fleischmann (published in 1952).

[2] *The Bell* was an influential literary magazine, founded in 1940 by Seán Ó Faoláin and published monthly until 1954.

[3] Principal of the Royal Academy of Music, London, 1955-1968.

CHAPTER 7

The Foundation of the Music Association of Ireland – 1948

The MAI was the brain-child of four musicians – Brian Boydell, Edgar Deale, Frederick May and Michael McMullin. They were an interesting group. Both Boydell and May were already established composers, their works having been played by the RÉO at public concerts. Indeed, Brian had sung the solo baritone role in Fred's *Songs from Prison* at the first performance on 22 December 1946 in the Phoenix Hall with Michael Bowles conducting.

Other orchestral music by Fred May received first performances (1935 and 1937) by the Cork University Orchestra, conducted by Aloys Fleischmann, and by the DSO (1943) conducted by Terry O'Connor. Fred was Music Director at the Abbey Theatre from 1936 to 1948, and though he found the position troublesome it gave him the opportunity to compose incidental music for a number of plays. A very fine pianist and all-round musician, his career was ultimately limited by deafness and tinnitus. He benefitted from periods of study in London and Vienna and has been credited, together with Boydell and Fleischmann, with the spearheading of modernism in Irish music.[1] Certainly many of Fred's works were perceived as very dissonant at that time, receiving adverse critical comment which he found discouraging and lacking in understanding.

Whilst Fred May's early musical education was quite conventional for a Dubliner of middle-class background, comprising studies in piano, harmony and composition at the RIAM and graduation from TCD with the MusB degree and various prizes, Brian Boydell's early years followed a different path. Some 6 years younger than Fred, he was also from a Protestant family, but quite wealthy – his father ran a malting business. He attended public school at Rugby in England and went on to take a first in the Natural Sciences Tripos at Cambridge. But music was his great interest; in his own words he: 'spent far more time at music than I did at science.'[2] He was in fact a polymath, played the piano, organ and oboe, studied composition in London, was a trained singer and an accomplished painter. At the time of the foundation of the MAI he was conductor of the Dublin Orchestral Players (DOP), promoting his compositions through their concerts and other events that he organised, and was also on the staff of the RIAM as a singing teacher. In 1946 he was engaged by RÉ to give a series of music appreciation talks on radio, with illustrations by the RÉO – the beginning of a long career in broadcasting and lecturing on music, for which he had a wonderful aptitude.

Edgar Deale was also a man of many talents and interests. Born in 1902 in Dublin, he was the oldest of the MAI's founders. He was a chorister at Christ Church Cathedral from the age of eleven and as an adult possessed a remarkable bass voice, singing in choral groups (notably the Culwick) until his 80th year. His working life was with Zürich Insurance, and though he had some formal musical training, he tended to look on himself as a self-taught composer, not of the *avant-garde*. Much of his output is choral (published in England), but there are some instrumental pieces and his *Ceol Mall Réidh* had its first performance by the DOP in May 1947, Brian Boydell conducting. Edgar was a pioneer in many fields: he founded the Safety First Association in the 1930s because of his horror at the road accidents he encountered as an insurance manager. He was also a founder of the Irish Association for Civil Liberties, of the Irish Georgian Society, and was a governor of the RIAM. His interest in contemporary art found expression through his large collection of the ceramics of John ffrench, and he possessed a considerable number of autographed books, notably a copy of *Mein Kampf* signed by Hitler and Goebbels. Edgar brought a fondness for campaigning and a sound business perspective to the work of the fledgling MAI.[3]

Of the four founders, the least information is available about Michael McMullin. By his own account,[4] he studied composition at the RIAM with Dr Larchet, having returned to Dublin about September 1942 following travels in Sweden and Finland. He described himself as: 'a Sibelius enthusiast already in my schooldays.' He was friendly with Brian Boydell and was secretary of the DOP for a short time. At the time of the foundation of the MAI he was engaged to the noted piano accompanist, Dorothy Stokes, but this relationship did not last, and he eventually married a Miss Kelly and became involved in a furniture business with another music enthusiast, Brendan Dunne. It is likely that he was the youngest of the MAI founders, but already a confident critical commentator upon musical matters, as his article 'Music in Dublin' published in *The Bell* in May 1947 bears out.

Brian and Fred had also made a mark as music journalists, and both were contributors to Aloys Fleischmann's *Music in Ireland* (1952). Fred also wrote for the *Dublin Magazine*, but it is his article 'The Composer in Ireland' published in *The Bell* of January 1947 which is of particular interest in relation to the founding of the MAI. His initial thoughts sparked off expert, thoughtful responses and analysis from Brian, Aloys and Michael Bowles, and these appeared in the April issue. It is clear from their opinions that in early 1947 there was profound dissatisfaction with the state of music in Ireland.

Fred began his article: 'We have been governing ourselves for the past twenty-five years and this period is surely sufficiently long to have enabled us to hammer out certain minimum principles of musical policy which, once agreed upon, should infuse us with sufficient determination and energy to carry them to a successful conclusion. Up to the present, however, there has been no cohesive policy or platform of ideas which would encourage Irish musicians to develop their latent talent.' He went on to praise the Department of Education for the positive influence of their Summer Schools of Music, and to applaud the RÉ symphony concerts at the Capitol Theatre. For him, the provision of a fine purpose-built concert hall in Dublin, and the establishment of a music-publishing firm were essential. He also pointed out that: 'the three-fold aim of music education should be to produce composers, to produce performers, and lastly, to produce a lasting and constantly expanding public.'

Brian agreed that: 'appreciation of music should be regarded as an essential part of national education', and made the case for there being two RÉ orchestras, one to play light music and the other to bring symphonic repertoire to the whole country. As it turned out, RÉ established the Light Orchestra the following year, as well as increasing the number of musicians in the RÉSO. Brian also supported the idea of a concert hall in Dublin. Aloys dealt in considerable depth with the parlous state of music education in the schools and the disorganised nature of the music profession. He hoped that enlargement of the symphony orchestra would bring musicians from outside Ireland who would be willing to teach. Interestingly, he also proposed the foundation of an Arts Council for Ireland. His view is that *The Bell* articles are: 'timely expressions of the growing impatience with the backward state of music in this country. The public for good music has increased enormously within the past ten years. Through radio it has become aware of progress elsewhere, of the extent to which we are being left behind, and the demand for improvement is becoming ever louder.' Michael McMullin, in his article in *The Bell* the following month agreed that: 'in Ireland there are at last signs of a national awakening to the importance of music.' Even Michael Bowles, whose tone is perhaps understandably grumpy, concludes: 'I have confidence in the future of music in Ireland. Even now there is more work available than there are competent persons to do it. If we all work with a will, we may still make good the opportunity afforded to us by our neutrality during the recent world war.'

It has been established that the vision for the MAI arose from discussions amongst the four founders, meeting together in early 1948

1. My mother, Olive Smith (née Richardson) aged 3.
2. Olive, c.1916.

3. Olive's mother, Maude Richardson, around the time of her marriage (1897).
4. Olive's father, Charles E. Richardson, in his garden, 1930s.

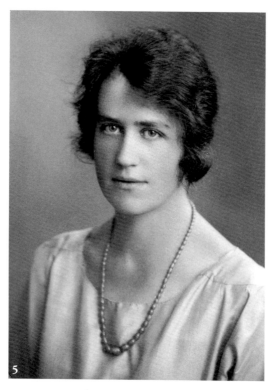

5. Alice Richardson (b.1898)

6. Kay Richardson (b.1901)   *7. Olive Richardson (b.1906)*

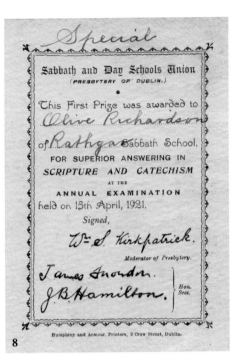

8

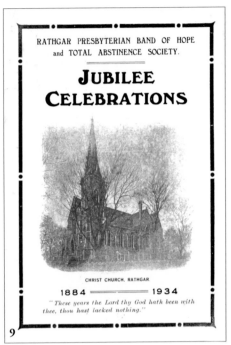

RATHGAR PRESBYTERIAN BAND OF HOPE
and TOTAL ABSTINENCE SOCIETY.

JUBILEE CELEBRATIONS

CHRIST CHURCH, RATHGAR.

1884 ════ 1934

"These years the Lord thy God hath been with
thee, thou hast lacked nothing."

9

10

10. Mount Temple Terrace, Dartry, Dublin, the home of the Richardson
family where Olive's father grew up with his seventeen siblings.

III

11 and 12. Olive as Guide Captain at camp with Rathgar Guides, c.1928.

13. The camp amongst the trees – Powerscourt Demesne, 1935.

14. *Pat McKnight, lifelong friend.*   15. *Olive as Irish dancer, 1933.*

16. *Olive (5th from left, back row) with the Rathgar Guide Company at camp, mid-1930s.*

17. Olive with Trinity College friends, Easton Warnock and Lily Butler.

18. Olive at the wheel of the Waverly car.

*19. Olive graduates from Trinity College, Dublin, with the
degrees of BA and B Comm and the King Edward Prize (1928).*

20. Rehearsal of the Culwick Choral Society, c.1930, Olive is on the right, front row.
21. J. Turner Huggard, conductor of the Culwick Choral Society, 1929-1944.

22. Bicentenary performance of Bach's B Minor Mass, 29 September 1950, in the
Metropolitan Hall, Abbey Street – the RÉSO, Cór Radio Eireann, Culwick
Choral Society, the vocal soloists and conductor, Otto Matzerath.

23. *My father, Lyall G. Smith,
late 1920s.*
24. *The chemist shop in Rathgar,
c.1900. My grandfather,
John Smith, is standing in the
doorway. Note* 'CHEMISTS TO
THE QUEEN' *over the door.*

23

24

25. Kilvare, the Smith family home near Templeogue, Co. Dublin.

26. The Smith family: SEATED AT REAR: *John Smith and Isabella Smith;* SEATED ON RUG: *Lyall, unknown guest, Isobel, Hilda and Russell.*

27. Olive and Lyall's engagement photograph.

28. Wedding photo (14 September 1932) in the garden of 47 Kenilworth Square.
SEATED (L TO R) *Charles Richardson, Isabella Smith, Maude Richardson, John Smith.*
STANDING (L TO R) *Easton Warnock (best man), Lily Butler (bridesmaid),*
the Groom and Bride, Revd Dr J.J. Macauley (minister), Mrs Macauley.

29. Honeymoon photograph.

30. Olive and Steven the Sealyham.

31. Lyall, Olive and Steven.

32

33

32. *The shop at 199 Crumlin Road.*
33. *Olive with her niece and nephew, Helen and Brian Lusk, 1936.*

34

34. *The Richardson family at 47 Kenilworth Square, Christmas 1939.*
SEATED ON FLOOR: *Olive, Brian and Lyall.*
SEATED BEHIND: *Charles Richardson, Ernest and Alice Spence, Maude Richardson.*

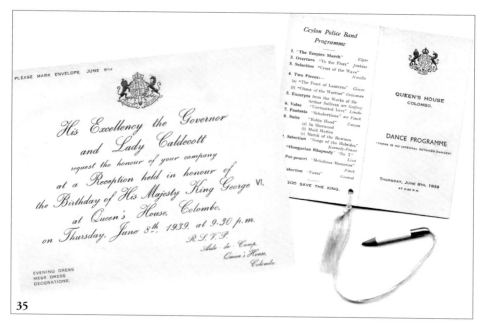

35. Reception and Ball at the Governor's Residence,
Colombo, Ceylon (later Sri Lanka), June 1939.

36. Typical street scene in Ceylon.

37. Olive relaxing on her Ceylon holiday, 1939.
38. A sculpture at Polonnaruwa, the ancient capital of Ceylon.

39. Sigiriya Rock (the Lion Rock).

40. *Paddy fields 'up country'.*   41. *The Moonstone at Polonnaruwa.*

42. *The magic of Ceylon.*

over lunch at the Unicorn Restaurant in Dublin's Merrion Row. It is easy to imagine the scene as they argued and developed their ideas on these musical matters which so exercised them. By mid-March they were ready to call a meeting, and I quote now from my mother's account of this event, written some thirty years later at the request of the MAI's magazine *Counterpoint*:

Thirty years ago this month the MAI was brought into existence at a meeting held in Dublin on Tuesday 30 March 1948. For some time Brian Boydell, Edgar Deale, Fred May and Michael McMullin had been discussing what steps could be taken to help the development of music in Ireland. Having come to the conclusion that a lot could be done by a voluntary association of musicians and music lovers they decided to call a meeting of people likely to be interested in such an idea.

The notice for the meeting, which was to be held in 16A Lincoln Chambers (by kind permission of Dorothy Stokes), set out six objectives for consideration:

1. To further musical education.
2. To improve conditions for composers and musicians generally.
3. To work for the establishment of a National Concert Hall.
4. To submit recommendations on musical policy to the authorities concerned.
5. To encourage the formation of musical groups, societies and choirs throughout the country.
6. To organise popular lectures, concerts and recitals and to awaken a musical consciousness in the nation.

It is worthy of note that these objectives still guide the work of the Association and are incorporated in its Constitution. At this meeting an association called the National Music Association came into existence. The main objectives were agreed and a further meeting arranged for Tuesday 13 April in 16 St Stephen's Green at which the formation of the Association was confirmed, the name altered to The

Music Association of Ireland and an executive committee elected. This first committee was : Brian Boydell, Edgar Deale, James Delaney, Brendan Dunne, Aloys Fleischmann, Joseph Groocock, Anthony Hughes, Fred May, Terry O'Connor, Joseph O'Neill, Dorothy Stokes, William Watt, Michael McMullin (Hon. Secretary) and Olive Smith (Hon. Treasurer).

This committee or council (as it came to be called) met on 22 April with Brian Boydell in the chair. A preliminary draft for a constitution (including the statement of the objectives) was discussed, circularised to all members and further discussed on 3 May. It was agreed to call an inaugural general meeting for Tuesday 18 May in the RIAM to ratify the proposed constitution, to elect or ratify the officers and council and to enrol members. The suggested subscription was ten shillings.

At the General Meeting, the aims as proposed were agreed, the constitution was passed, the provisional council and officers confirmed and a membership list opened. After the general meeting the Council met and a statement was issued to the press announcing the formation of the Music Association of Ireland, stating its six objectives, giving the names of the Council and officers and inviting those who supported the aims to become members. Press coverage was good both in Dublin and the country and we were off.[5]

The MAI Constitution is an interesting document, set out in six sections. It states that: 'The affairs of the Association shall be managed by a Council of 14 elected members in addition to the Honorary Officers, who shall be *ex-officio* members. There shall be five to form a quorum. At least seven members of the Council must be recognised professional musicians. The Council shall elect its own chairman, and shall have power to co-opt to fill vacancies, and to set up sub-committees. The Council may further co-opt not more than five other members to represent specific musical interests.' It further states that membership is open to those who support the objects of the Association, that the AGM shall be held in January and that a quorum of 25 shall be sufficient at any General Meeting. The first draft originally had seven sections, but one which provided for a termination of membership at a specially convened meeting, with right of appeal to a General Meeting, was deleted at the meeting on 18 May.[6]

One cannot fail to observe that many of the areas of concern, highlighted in their articles in *The Bell* by Boydell, May, Fleischmann and McMullin, were adopted as aims of the MAI. Its foundation should perhaps best be seen in the context of a growing appreciation of the arts, as the Irish Free State began to establish itself upon the world stage. The people who formed the first Council of the MAI were activists, innovators, citizens who thought deeply and argued intensely about the politics of their country and the importance of the arts in its future, especially regarding the role of music. The fact that there were so many composers amongst them, who were anxious to have their music more widely acknowledged, ensured that from the outset the MAI strove to be outward-looking and, whilst concerned with developing the classical music scene in Ireland, was also ready to embrace international influences.

The roles of Edgar Deale, Brian Boydell, Fred May, Dorothy Stokes and Michael Mc Mullin have already been touched upon. It is important to mention the other Council members briefly. Dr Aloys Fleischmann,[7] Professor of Music at University College, Cork, was a lifelong campaigner for music, not just in Cork but also nationally, whose contributions as a composer, conductor, professor and author have been universally praised. He represented Cork interests on the MAI Council for many years. Joseph Groocock, born in England, came to Ireland in 1935 as Director of Music at St Columba's College, Rathfarnham, where he was a much loved and respected teacher, organist and composer. In 1948 he held that position as well as conductor of the TCD Choral Society. Anthony Hughes, later to succeed Dr Larchet in the Chair of Music in UCD, was at that time just 20 years old, a piano student with a growing reputation. The violinist Terry O'Connor had a long and very distinguished career, having been the leader of the first instrumental group employed by 2RN, the Dublin Broadcasting Station in 1926, a position which she held until 1945. She was also the conductor of the

DSO, a group known for its high standard of playing and adventurous programming. Her colleague, Nancie Lord, succeeded Terry as leader of the RÉO, and was for many years a member of the RÉSO. Joseph O'Neill, a music teacher and music critic of the *Irish Independent*, also wrote occasionally for *The Bell*. William Watt was a business man in Waterford, the founder of the Waterford Music Club, whose beautiful tenor voice ensured that he was in constant demand throughout Ireland and England as an oratorio soloist. Mrs Madeleine Larchet, wife of Dr Larchet, was an accomplished musician in her own right, both as a pianist and a violinist; she was co-opted to the Council on 25 May.

Last but not least. . . Olive Smith (Hon. Treasurer). I suspect that Edgar Deale had some influence in her appointment, though she also knew Fred May and Brian Boydell. As mentioned in earlier chapters, Edgar and his wife Ruth were part of my parents' circle of friends. My mother had become treasurer of the Culwick some years previously, she always oversaw the financial side of my father's business, and she had of course a B Comm degree. The role of activist or campaigner was perhaps new to her, but it seems that in this, as in so many areas, she had a natural aptitude!

It is also worthy of note that quite a number of musicians, who were unable to attend the sequence of meetings that established the MAI, sent letters of support. These included the violinist Arthur Franks, the composer Ina Boyle, Ernest de Regge, the Belgian organist resident in Ennis, Co. Clare, Rhoda Coghill, pianist, composer and poet, Mrs Alice Yoakley, pianist and choral conductor, and Mrs Rita Broderick, Professor of Harmony at the RIAM.

There is an aspect of this first MAI Council which I feel is worthy of comment, namely that at least half of the 14 members were non-Catholic. In writing about my mother's formative years, I have of course described a middle-class Protestant upbringing, and this type of background would have been a common denominator amongst a number of the Council members. It occurs to me to wonder whether they identified with the leaders of the Irish Literary Revival of some fifty years earlier, many of whom were also Protestant, and that these musicians were hopeful of bringing about something similar for music. It certainly had occurred to Fred May, for he mentions this connection at the end of the first paragraph of his article in *The Bell*, though his notion is somewhat sharply rebuffed by Michael Bowles in his response. Other authors[8] have written in great depth about the conflict that existed between those who thought that Irish classical music should draw upon the richness of our indigenous musical heritage and those who favoured a more international approach. I am clear that, rather than entering into that particular discussion, my role is to document the practical steps taken by the Council and members of the MAI to implement their six stated aims.

[1] See Philip Graydon's article on Frederick May in *The Encyclopaedia of Music in Ireland*.

[2] Quoted from *The Life and Music of Brian Boydell* (Irish Academic Press, 2004).

[3] See article on Edgar Deale in *The Encyclopaedia of Music in Ireland*. He was interviewed at the age of 91 by Ray Lynott for a Lyric FM 'Profile' programme, broadcast on 2 May 1994.

[4] Letter from Michael McMullin to Mary Boydell, wife of Brian Boydell, 9 June 2004.

[5] *Counterpoint*, March 1978.

[6] Much of the documentation concerning the foundation of the MAI is in NLI – ACC 6000, box 7, green file 1.

[7] See *Aloys Fleischmann – A Life for Music in Ireland* (Mercier Press, 2000).

[8] Harry White, Marie McCarthy, Richard Pine, Axel Klein.

CHAPTER 8

The MAI – A good start
...and a crisis!

1948

The Council was very active right from the start, having held General Meetings on 30 March, 13 April and 18 May 1948, as well as Council meetings on 22 April, on three dates in May, and two in June. Apart from the intensive deliberations required for the agreement of the Constitution, another important project is mentioned in the Minutes as early as the first Council meeting on 22 April. This is the proposal from Michael McMullin: 'that a report on musical conditions, to be submitted to the Government, should be considered at the next Council meeting'. This document, largely written by McMullin himself, became known as 'The Memorandum' and deliberations over its various sections formed a recurring topic at Council meetings during 1948 and 1949. It was intended to urge, in particular, that music be adequately represented on the Council of Education, and that a competent musical advisory body be established in connection with RÉ. The document dealt with Music in Education, the Training of Musicians, the need for a National Concert Hall, and Broadcasting and the Radio Orchestra. On 30 June 1948, Council decided to send these two last-mentioned sections to the Minister for Posts and Telegraphs, James Everett, requesting that he would meet an MAI deputation to discuss their views and also address the pressing public concern at the cessation of public concerts by the RÉSO. As

70

it turned out, this meeting did not take place until 25 October, the MAI delegation consisting of Brian Boydell, Michael McMullin, Edgar Deale and Brendan Dunne. It is interesting to find, in a letter from Michael McMullin to P. J. Malone of the Irish Federation of Musicians, that representatives of the Union also met the Minister around the same time. Having exchanged copies of their respective documents, the MAI and the Union found that they had many objectives in common.

In the meantime, the Council was busy with other matters – I will let my mother's words resume the narrative:

The idea of a monthly news bulletin for members was discussed and the first *Bulletin* appeared in November 1948, edited by Anthony Hughes. In 1948 the Irish Congress of Trade Unions started their Adult Education Scheme and asked for assistance from the MAI. From October to December 1948 the MAI supplied lecturers in Music Appreciation to the People's College for 12 lectures. These lectures were continued throughout 1949 and for some years afterwards by members of the MAI.[1]

In fact the Council was teeming with ideas and a list of projects from this period includes affiliation with provincial Music Clubs, developing the interests of composers, a central bureau for concert dates, liaison with the Irish Federation of Musicians and the registration of music teachers. In addition to sending sections of the Memorandum to the Department of Education, there was also considerable correspondence with the Committee for Promotion of New Music in London, who were hoping for future co-operation with the MAI. An interesting letter from Edgar Deale to Michael McMullin, dated 9 June 1948, expresses his view: 'that the MAI should not turn into an association for giving performances of music … it will only be wasting our strength … an occasional lecture recital, particularly to young people, would be in accordance with our aims'. It is clear that Edgar, already a seasoned campaigner for other causes, saw the MAI as an important pressure group which, through various memoranda and meetings with Ministers, could make a difference to the future of music in Ireland.

The Minutes of 26 October record that, during his meeting the previous day with the MAI delegation, the Secretary to the Department of Posts and Telegraphs, Mr Leon Ó Broin, requested the Association to submit written comments on: '(a) the tone quality of music broadcasts and (b) cases of unfair engagements or neglect (*sic*).' There was also a proposal from his Department that the MAI might consider taking over the running of the public RÉSO concerts. This produced a flurry of letter-writing by Michael McMullin regarding possible performance venues, whilst my mother dealt with Leon Ó Broin and negotiations regarding the orchestra and conductor. Terry O'Connor warned that the players were unlikely to agree to perform as part of their regular duties without a special fee, but the Council did go as far as setting up a sub-committee to plan the programmes, and to identify four provisional dates. In the event, negotiations broke down in early 1949, but my mother may have learnt some useful lessons for the future regarding the complex relationship between RÉ and the Department.

1949

Almost at the year's end, on 21 December 1948, Francis J. Kelly, secretary of the Dublin Gramophone Society, was co-opted to the Council. Then at the AGM, on 18 January 1949, it was made known that Michael McMullin wished to retire as Hon. Secretary, due to anticipated absence from Dublin, and F. J. Kelly was appointed Hon. Secretary in his place, with my mother re-elected as Hon. Treasurer whilst also agreeing to act as Assistant Hon. Secretary. I will let my mother take up the story again:

In January 1949 the Minister for External Affairs, Mr Seán MacBride, appointed a committee to: 'advise him on schemes for the promotion and development of cultural relations with other countries, and to make available information on every aspect of our national life'. This became known as the Cultural Relations Committee (CRC). In May, Edgar Deale wrote to the secretary of this committee explaining how difficult it was for Irish composers to get their works published and therefore performed. He suggested that a sum of money might be set aside each year for the publication of a limited number of such works. This was followed in June by a memorandum from the MAI Council in the same vein and asking also for a subvention for arranging the performance of works by Irish composers abroad, possibly on an exchange basis. A reply from CRC in July suggested a meeting with its sub-committee on music. This meeting took place in November and the MAI was represented by Brian Boydell, Edgar Deale and Michael McMullin.[2]

It would appear that Mr McMullin was not absent consistently in 1949 as his presence is recorded at the April, May and June meetings, at each of which he read out part of his Memorandum. He also included a *resumé* of the text in his secretary's report for 1948.[3] By and large, it was very well received by the Council, and there was a unanimous vote of thanks to him at the June meeting. It was also agreed that he should be made a Life Member of the Association. In his letter to Mary Boydell,[4] he described reading out each section at Council meetings: 'for general discussion and approval' and also mentioned: 'a letter from Aloys Fleischmann about his attempts to publish it, but these were not successful'. The MAI did not have the financial resources for publication, and approaches to Cork University Press and *The Kerryman* came to nothing.

On 3 August 1949 quite an important event took place in the Organ Room of the RIAM – this was the inaugural MAI Members' Meeting, and it took the form of a lecture by Dr Thomas Armstrong entitled 'Music in a Present-Day Community'. This lecture came at the end of Dr Armstrong's 3-week sojourn in Dublin for the Department of Education's Summer School of Music, where his lectures on music appreciation attracted large audiences. As previously mentioned, he had become a good friend of my parents and of a number of Dublin musicians.

At the Council meeting on 26 September Michael McMullin resumed the role of Hon. Secretary. F. J. Kelly had written to my mother in May, and again in August, saying that he felt he was: 'not doing the job to my own satisfaction and am fervently hoping that Mr McMullin will return to his post of Hon. Secretary'.[5] It seems that Mr Kelly was not in good health and the September minutes note his resignation as Secretary. At the meeting on 10 October it was recorded that the suggestion of the Hon.

Secretary (McMullin) regarding the election of a President of the MAI should be deferred to the next General meeting. There are no minutes for the last two months of 1949, though in a letter to my mother, dated 2 November, Michael McMullin writes that a meeting is needed over the payment from the People's College to the MAI lecturers. He also says that his hopes for the publishing of his Memorandum are fading.

The next sequence of events is hard to understand, but certainly all was not well within the MAI Council. Michael McMullin called a meeting for 7 December at Dorothy Stokes' studio at 16A Lincoln Chambers with the following notice: 'At the last two Council Meetings there were not enough present to form a quorum and no business could be done. I have accordingly been requested to say to all members of the Council that the affairs of this Association cannot possibly be transacted if members are not prepared to put themselves to some inconvenience to attend in future. There are matters of urgency on the agenda. These include: i) Immediate and future policy of the Association; ii) *Bulletin*; iii) Composers and the Cultural Relations Committee'.

At this point I probably should remind readers that the quorum for a Council meeting was just 5 members. Mr McMullin's next notice, which was sent to all members, presumably issued at the end of December 1949, announces that: 'The last three Council Meetings having failed to produce a quorum, I have no alternative as Hon. Secretary but to call the Annual General Meeting, which will be held on Tuesday 10 January 1950 at 8.00 p.m. in the Organ Room of the RIAM, Westland Row, Dublin. As the future existence and policy of the Association are to be decided at this meeting, all members are asked to make a special effort to attend. The present Officers having announced their intention of resigning, nominations are invited for a Permanent Chairman, a new Hon. Secretary and Hon. Treasurer, and a Council of 13 members. These should reach me not later than 5 January. Agenda: i) Minutes; ii) Hon. Secretary's report; iii) Future existence or form of existence of the Association and discussion of policy; iv) Proposal to elect a permanent chairman of the Council, fixing of regular monthly Council meetings, election of Officers and Council.'

What was going on? My mother seems to have been very put out by this unsolicited announcement that she intended to resign. She must have written in protest to Michael McMullin, and so it is illuminating that his reply, dated 4 January 1950, still exists in the MAI archives.[6] In this he apologises for omitting the Treasurer's report from the AGM agenda and argues the point with her as to the need for a permanent Chairman. He continues: 'I understood you to say that you intended to resign . . . in connection with the fact that we could not muster a Council meeting. If this was a misunderstanding on my part, I apologise.' He also states that he thinks it likely that the MAI is not going to survive. It appears that my mother responded to this letter with a phone call on 9 January, the outcome of which was the following letter from Michael, dated the next day: 'I regret I shall be unable to attend the Council meeting at 7.00 p.m., but I shall be present at the General Meeting at 8.00 p.m. From the tenor of your remarks over the phone yesterday, I am convinced that no useful purpose would be served by my attending any preliminary meeting. As the Council is now sharply divided on almost every question, the only thing to do is to put the various issues to the General Meeting and let the members decide. I do not intend to discuss matters any further except in public, and it is only right that the meeting as a whole should decide. You will have ample opportunity to let the members hear your opinions. As regards the Report, I have not prepared a Council's Report, but a Secretary's Report, as clearly stated on the Agenda. As the Council has repeatedly failed to materialise I have come to the conclusion that it no longer exists, and therefore can scarcely produce a Report. If I read my Report to anyone beforehand I shall select my own advisors'.

So we have it, the classic split within a new Irish organisation[7] ... though not actually, as Brendan Behan wittily observed, the first item on the agenda! However, in spite of Michael's dire diagnosis, it appears that the Council did still exist! Brief Minutes in my mother's handwriting record that: 'A meeting of the Council was held on Tuesday 10 January 1950 at 7.00 p.m. in the RIAM. Mr Groocock was in the Chair. Present were Mrs Larchet, Mrs Smith, Messrs Boydell, Deale, Hughes, May and O'Higgins. Apologies for non-attendance were received from Miss Terry O'Connor, Miss Dorothy Stokes, Mr Dunne and Mr McMullin. As there was no report from the Hon. Sec. for consideration by the Council, the Council compiled a report of their work for the past year. This report and the Hon. Treasurer's statement of accounts were adopted. The Council arranged the Agenda for the General Meeting and there being no further business the meeting adjourned.'

Even at this remove, the vehemence in Michael's letter is palpable, and the telephone conversation alluded to must have been unpleasant for both him and my mother. I find myself wondering whether this was the first occasion on which she had to deal with a publicly hostile situation. Was she finding this very different from the more sheltered and genteel environment of the Irish Girl Guides or the Culwick Choral Society? Did she make the telephone call on her own behalf, or was she acting as a spokesperson for the Council members who took an opposing view to Michael?[8] Either way, it seems she handled the situation robustly, so perhaps she was selected for the task because her colleagues knew that she was capable of this?

1950

The extraordinary thing is that, if one were to judge by the Minutes of the AGM on 10 January 1950, this eruption of ill-feeling might as well never have taken place. F. J. Kelly took the Chair, Michael McMullin was particularly thanked for having written the Memorandum of some 40,000 words and was confirmed as a life-member of the Association. He was also re-elected to the Council. Dr Anthony Farrington was elected as Hon. Secretary, with R. W. McKeever as Assistant Hon. Sec., and my mother was re-elected as Hon. Treasurer. The only hint of the controversy which had raged so recently came from F. J. Kelly: 'who stated his belief that it would not be possible to carry on successfully unless a permanent Chairman of the Council was appointed to take some of the responsibility'. This is an interesting point. Mr Kelly had the experience of acting as Secretary and had found it too much. Michael had thrown himself whole-heartedly into the work of the fledgling MAI, producing well-written, clear Minutes each month, dealing with a great deal of correspondence and compiling the huge Memorandum of 40,000 words. In the Minutes of the 1949 AGM the Secretary's report contains this sentence: 'The limitations imposed by the amount of work devolving upon the Hon. Officers, in the absence of a paid secretary or staff, was reviewed and one or two recommendations made for the future'. The Constitution stated that: 'The Council shall elect its own Chairman', but in those early days this resulted in a different person chairing each meeting.

There was a good attendance at the next Council meeting on 1 February 1950, including several new names – P. J. Malone, John Miley and the organist William Watson. Dr Anthony Farrington, the new Secretary, was a keen music-lover and a noted geologist who did pioneering research on the glaciation of the Dublin and Wicklow Mountains. He was Secretary to the Royal Irish Academy and also to the Irish Geological Society. I remember him as a large, friendly man, whose house at Ticknock, on the edge of the Dublin mountains, was visited quite often by my parents and myself. The meeting dealt with a great deal of business including the submission of a memorandum to the new Radio Advisory Board, decisions on panels of judges for the compositions to be submitted to the CRC, the possible redrafting of the rules of the Association, the publication of the *Bulletin*, the need for co-ordination between the lecturers at the People's College, the possibility of setting up a Bureau of Concert Dates and concern at the customs duty on musical instruments. John Miley, a chartered accountant and member of the DOP, was well-known as a clarinettist and drummer. He made the wise observation that controversial issues should be avoided until such time as the Association felt itself established on a sounder footing, especially in view of the recent internal splits. Paddy Malone, the long-serving Secretary of the Irish Federation of Musicians, offered practical assistance regarding the *Bulletin* by arranging to have it copied on the duplicating machine in the Federation office on Lower Gardiner Street, and also preparing addressograph plates for the envelopes.

One other item was discussed on 1 February, namely the possibility of holding a Bach Festival in Dublin, to celebrate that year's Bicentenary. A sub-committee, whose members were my mother, Joseph Groocock, John Miley and William Watson, was set up to investigate ways and means and to report back to the next meeting. They were given power to co-opt other members of the MAI.

However, there was one more twist to come in the McMullin controversy, which begins with his letter of 27 March 1950 to Dr Farrington, asking that the MAI would pay for the publication of his Memorandum, and at the same time indicating that he intended to resign from the Council. Dr Farrington replied, on behalf of the Council, that it would not be possible to raise the funds at that time, but that they might be prepared to reconsider if the financial position became more favourable in time to come. He added that a future Council might wish to edit the Memorandum and enquired whether Michael would be agreeable to this. This was obviously the final straw and drew forth a furious riposte: 'Am I to take it that the present Council repudiates the memorandum, passed and adopted by the previous Council? Kindly inform the Council that any appropriation or use by the present Council of any part or parts of the Memorandum is forbidden, and that all copies may be returned to me'. This was written on 10 April 1950 and on the same day F. J. Kelly wrote to tender his resignation from the Association. In his letter to Mary Boydell, Michael McMullin mentioned that he married F. J. Kelly's daughter. It is thought that the Memorandum was amongst his papers at the end of his life.

¹ *Counterpoint*, March 1978.

² *Counterpoint*, May 1978.

³ NLI – ACC 6000, box 20.

⁴ Letter of 9 June 2004.

⁵ NLI – ACC 6000, box 7, green file 2.

⁶ Ibid. box 7, green file 3 – for this letter and other correspondence with Michael McMullin.

⁷ The whole episode is covered in some detail in Brian Boydell's diary for 1950, published in *Rebellious Ferment* (ed. Barra Boydell, publ. 2018), pages 123-129 &145.

⁸ It is clear from the Boydell diary entries that other Council members engaged with Michael McMullin during the crisis, notably Edgar Deale and Aloys Fleischmann.

CHAPTER 9

The Bach Bicentenary – 1950

The sub-committee appointed on 1 February to progress the idea of a Bach Bicentenary celebration in Dublin reported back to Council on 1 March, bringing the good news that RÉ had offered the services of the RÉSO. It was decided to spread the scope of the Commemoration as widely as possible, encouraging other bodies to include works by Bach in their concert plans, and in particular eliciting the participation of organists. Such concerts would then be advertised as being part of the Commemoration. The Council was happy with the work of the sub-committee and directed them to proceed. It is probably fair to say that a number of the Council were very wary of this whole project. There were those who thought that the MAI should stick with its campaigning and lobbying role, and others who felt that attempting the organisation of such high-profile concerts would be beyond them. The planned performance of the Mass in B Minor would, of necessity, involve the RÉSO, and perhaps people were apprehensive, given the breakdown of negotiations the previous year over the revival of public symphony concerts. My mother, however, seemed undaunted, perhaps spurred on by her great love for the B Minor Mass and the fact that the Culwick Choral Society would be one of the participating choirs.

Many years later, my mother contributed her own account to the MAI magazine *Counterpoint*[1] and in quoting this *verbatim* I feel that readers will become very aware of the unusual scale of this venture:

At the first meeting of the Council in 1950, it was suggested that the Music Association should take the initiative in promoting a commemoration of the Bicentenary of the death of J. S. Bach during the year. Doubts were expressed about the MAI promoting large-scale concerts and there was some opposition to the idea. But a proposal to establish a guarantee fund to cover the financial commitment, and the offer by the Department of Posts and Telegraphs to co-operate in the venture, by making available the RÉSO and their conductor for two public concerts, made the undertaking more feasible and the Council agreed to go ahead.

A letter was sent to MAI members, and to others likely to be interested, in early May and later released to the press, announcing the planned commemoration, and giving details of the two subscription concerts to be given in the Metropolitan Hall. The first concert, on 29 September, was the Culwick Choral Society, Cór Radio Éireann and the RÉSO in the B Minor Mass, with Margaret Field-Hyde (soprano), Anne Wood (contralto), Ronald Bristol (tenor), Owen Brannigan (bass) and conductor Otto Matzerath. The second concert was announced for 20 October – a choral and orchestral concert with two Cantatas, 104 and 65, the Suite No. 3 in D and the *Brandenburg* Concertos Nos. 3 and 6 (note: No. 6 was actually changed to No. 4). This concert was with the Clontarf Choral Society, Richard Lewis (tenor), Richard Standen (bass) and the RÉSO, conducted by Sixten Eckerberg. Recipients of the letter were asked to support the venture by agreeing to guarantee a sum to cover possible loss. The response was immediate and generous. By 15 May over £200 had been guaranteed and plans could go ahead.

Other events were added to the programme: Sylvia Fannin offered to arrange and conduct two recitals in the Centenary Church, St Stephen's Green, with her church choir and organist Ethel Graham. These took place in October and included four cantatas and vocal and organ solos, with Anne Wood, Ronald Bristol, Reginald Hall, Dorothy Graham, Molly Dunlop, William Watt, Richard Standen, Joseph Groocock and William Watson. Two organ recitals were given by Joseph Groocock, F. C. J. Swanton and William Watson in November and included two Preludes and Fugues in B and E minor, the Toccata and Fugue in F, the Fantasia and Fugue in G minor, and 8 Chorale Preludes. As an introduction to the whole series, two lectures were given by Joseph Groocock and Brian Boydell on the B Minor Mass, and the Cantatas and Organ works.

Early in June we realised that not only did RÉ not possess a harpsichord but there was not one available for hire anywhere in Ireland, North or South. Enquiries were made from firms in England, also without success. Finally, in desperation, 'Quidnunc' of the *The Irish Times* was asked if he would enquire through his column whether anyone in the country had one which they would be willing to lend. Under the heading 'IF . . .' the following appeared in 'An Irishman's Diary': 'If you are one of those soulless scoundrels who is at present using great-aunt Agatha's harpsichord as a repository for the assegais carried home in triumph from the Zulu war by great-uncle Egbert, I am requested to beg you to desist at once, extract the assegais . . . get great-niece Millicent to try out the harpsichord with one of the late Herr Kuhlau's Sonatinas . . . If Millicent's virtuosity sounds reasonably like whatever she is trying to play, and if you are of a disposition to reverence the memory of Johann Sebastian Bach more than that of great-uncle Egbert, you will then telephone 83968 at once, ask for Mrs Lyall Smith and say to her: "Sleep in peace – your quest is ended, when do you wish to pick up a harpsichord in playable condition?" ', and so on for two more paragraphs, ending with a serious account of our plans for the Commemoration.[2] This did not produce a harpsichord but it was excellent publicity for the festival!

It was now decided to investigate the harpsichords in the National Museum. One of them, made by Ferdinand Weber of Dublin (c.1780), seemed promising and John Beckett and Paul Egerstorff[3] were asked to examine the instrument. They reported that: 'it is our opinion that the instrument can be used for these performances' adding that: 'even after necessary adjustments have been made to the action and the quills, and when necessary new strings have been fitted, the player will have to transpose his part up one semitone'! The Minister for Education gave his permission to use the instrument and to make the necessary adjustments. So the quest ended. The necessary strings and some advice were obtained from Alan Hodson, the harpsichord maker in Suffolk. The adjustments were carried out. John Beckett played the instrument, or perhaps I should say 'coaxed the instrument along' in the two performances successfully. It was a considerable achievement. George Eskdale, principal trumpet of the LSO, and his second trumpet Bramwell Wiggins were engaged to play the D trumpets in the B Minor Mass and all was now in readiness.

As will be evident from the foregoing, the organisation of this commemoration was a remarkable exercise in co-operation and dedication by all those intimately concerned in the performances and their presentation. Also by the members of the MAI, who provided hospitality for all the artists from outside Dublin, and who formed the majority of the guarantors. We also got helpful co-operation from the press. The reaction of the musical public was very encouraging, all the concerts and recitals being well attended. It was the performance of the B Minor Mass which aroused the greatest interest and drew an audience of almost 1,000. I shall never forget the wonderful atmosphere of expectancy and excitement in the over-flowing hall that night as the audience awaited the entrance of the conductor. It was electrifying and the tension was maintained right through the performance (during which, be it noted, there was no interval). It was a rewarding and thrilling experience for all who had come together to honour the memory of J.S. Bach.

The experience gained by organising this commemoration was very important in the life of the MAI. In his report for the year 1950, the Hon. Secretary Anthony Farrington said: 'The advertisement and credit which the MAI has gained, and the confidence which the success has inspired, has gone far in strengthening the Association's position.' This quotation from the *Bulletin* of July 1950 offers a telling insight as to how the Council was feeling in the run-up to the whole project: 'The B Minor Mass will probably not be sung again in Ireland in our lifetime owing to difficulties such as expense'.

My own recollection of this time was of unusual excitement in the house and talk of strange instruments such as the harpsichord and the D trumpets. My father was involved in the visit to the National Museum on the day when Otto Matzerath was taken to hear the harpsichord being played by John Beckett. My mother and Brian Boydell were there also, and my father produced an historic set of photographs of the occasion which have been reproduced in a number of publications. The Bach Commemoration was the first project for which my mother became involved in booking soloists through the various concert agencies in London, and I do find it amazing that such distinguished singers were all happy to accept hospitality in Dublin in lieu of a hotel room. At different times we had Owen Brannigan, Ronald Bristol and Richard Standen staying with us. Mr Brannigan even agreed to baby-sit for me on one occasion . . . this I remember as being highly entertaining, as he thought that the best way to get me to sleep was to sing to me, which of course had the opposite effect!

Regarding the orchestral conductors, the Swedish maestro Sixten Eckerberg had already conducted the RÉSO in 1948 and '49, and the German Otto Matzerath had engagements with the orchestra earlier in 1950. My mother thought very highly of their musicianship. It is, of course, very interesting to see the name of John Beckett[4] coming to the fore, a musician whose reputation became almost synonymous with the performance of Bach's music in Dublin in the 1970s. He was already a supporter of the MAI and was involved as one of the lecturers at the People's College. In 1950 there were no professional harpsichordists in Dublin, but John had taken lessons from Gertrud Wertheim, a former student of Wanda Landowska, at Morley College, London, as a form of extra-mural study whilst he was a composition and organ student at the Royal College of Music. He later developed his own very individual style of playing. My mother's remark in her article, that John had to transpose every note of the B Minor Mass up a semitone, gives only a very superficial idea of the skill that this involved. John would have played from the figured bass line of the score, written out in keys a semi-tone higher, probably in John's inimitable music manuscript. It is also worth noting that, in fact, not all the orchestral instruments required by Bach were used. Some of the writing for oboe d'amore was played on cor anglais, and the difficulties of the notoriously demanding horn solo were solved by playing it on a euphonium! This information comes from a letter written by the principal oboist, Roland Dufrane, to my mother in early 1951.[5]

Following his initial comical plea to non-existent harpsichord owners, 'Quidnunc' of the *The Irish Times* became interested in the provenance of the National Museum's instrument and, with my mother's help, tracked down a direct descendent of Ferdinand Weber, Mrs Cathleen Sealy, who was living in Dublin. She supplied many interesting details, which appeared in 'Quidnunc's' column during the week preceding the performance.[6] He was also invited by my mother to attend at the Museum for the official inspection of the instrument by the conductor, Otto Matzerath, at which John Beckett played and my father took photographs. His column the next day contained this passage: 'At the keyboard, John Beckett impassively permitted the instrument and himself to be photographed, rippling from time to time through the plangent gaiety of a Scarlatti sonata, with a delicacy of touch that belied his bulk. The music and the setting obviously demanded wigs and knee-breeches; but Mr Beckett wore a sombre lounge suit.'[7] The writer of 'An Irishwoman's Diary',[8] not to be outdone, contributed a piece on the participating choirs, obviously fascinated by the number of female conductors involved. Her column contributed to the considerable press build-up, as did an article in the *Irish Press* on the day of the concert which focussed on the harpsichord and John Beckett, and also on George Eskdale, the famous principal trumpet from London.

Unfortunately, *The Irish Times* review following the performance was somewhat ambivalent: 'This monumental work of Bach's involves so many players and singers and presents so many difficulties, both in the performance itself and also in the organisation of the concert, that the Association must be congratulated upon a successful venture. Of the standard of performance, it may fairly be said that, if one judges by professional achievements it was mediocre; if one compares it with amateur performances, it was magnificent'.[9] But the *Irish Press*, the *Irish Independent* and the *Evening Herald* were more generous, particularly in praise of the violin solo of the leader, Renzo Marchionni, the singing of Owen Brannigan, the responsiveness of the choir and the fine interpretation of the work by the conductor. There does seem to be a consensus, however, that the choir would have benefitted from additional choristers. Following the second concert on 20 October, there was critical acclaim for the instrumentalists, particularly the soloists in the 4th *Brandenburg* Concerto (Marchionni, with flautists André Prieur and Tom Browne), and for the singing of Richard Lewis and Richard Standen.

The Council and members of the MAI were united in their thanks to one person in particular. The *Bulletin* for October recorded: 'The undertaking has been a stupendous task, and great attention has been given to the minutest detail, to ensure as great a performance as possible of this magnificent work. Mrs Lyall Smith, our Hon. Treasurer, has had almost all the responsibility on her shoulders, and through her enthusiasm and determination she has made this performance possible'. The following is an extract from the Council's report to the AGM, held on 23 January 1951: 'A sub-committee had been formed to report on the possibilities of promoting a commemoration of the bicentenary of the death of Bach, and subsequently to organise such a commemoration, which was done with outstanding success and credit of the Association. It was stressed that this was due in very large measure to the initiative and energy of the Hon. Treasurer, Mrs M.O. Smith. It was only right that her name should be especially associated with the venture.' At the AGM itself, a bound and autographed score of the Mass was presented to my mother as a token of appreciation: 'of the very valiant work and enthusiasm with which she inspired and led, to supreme success, the organisation of the

Bach Bicentenary Commemoration.' I still have this special score in my possession – my mother treasured it throughout her life – it is the Eulenberg miniature score, bound in dark blue leather with a gold trim and the title of the work in gold also. At the lower RH corner, picked out in gold, are the initials 'O.S.' Inside it is signed by Otto Matzerath '*Mit alle warme Liebe*' and by Anthony Farrington, Brian Boydell, William Watson, Dorothy Stokes, Joseph Groocock, Michael O'Higgins, Patrick Malone, John Miley, Robert McKeever and Edgar Deale.

One might suppose that the Council would have taken a little time to bask in the glow of their success, but it is clear from the Minutes of 4 October 1950 that a larger and more momentous project was on their minds. Edgar Deale raised the topic by reminding the Council that working for a Concert Hall was one of the primary objects of the Association, and P. J. Malone suggested the formation of a National Concert Hall committee. Ironically, I cannot help wondering whether the limitations of the Metropolitan Hall, experienced during the Bach concerts, had served to bring the need for a purpose-designed concert hall back into sharp focus. The hall in Abbey Street had a capacity of over 1,000 seats including a balcony, with a high stage capable of seating a small orchestra such as was used for the Bach Mass, and tiered with several rows of choir seats. It had a good acoustic but the audience seating was uncomfortable and the *décor* bare. It belonged to the organisation known as the Young Men's Christian Association (YMCA) and, being used frequently for religious meetings, had a large biblical text over the stage. Over many years it was the venue for the major competitions of the Dublin Feis Ceoil, but was finally razed to the ground at the hands of a developer in the 1970s. With a capacity of more than twice that of the Metropolitan Hall, the other main concert venue in Dublin was the Theatre Royal, also later demolished in favour of an office block. It was used for variety performances and for certain celebrity concerts that were guaranteed to attract a large audience.

At their October meeting the MAI Council agreed that Lord Moyne, Mr Seymour Leslie and Mr Leon Ó Broin should be invited to attend the next meeting, to open a preliminary discussion of the matter. These three names are interesting. Lord Moyne was a senior member of the Guinness family, the younger brother of Lord Iveagh, and well-regarded for his philanthropy and support for the Arts in general. He had a reputation as a poet, publishing under the name of Brian Guinness and was very fond of music. Seymour Leslie was a son of the family who owned Castle Leslie in Co. Monaghan and was known as a promoter of celebrity concerts at the Theatre Royal and for his work in raising money for various charities. Leon Ó Broin's name has already appeared frequently in this narrative, being the Secretary to the Department of Posts and Telegraphs under whose authority were RÉ and the RÉSO. The suggested meeting did not happen, but Lord Moyne replied by letter with some suggestions, and at the December meeting Edgar Deale reported that he, my mother and P. J. Malone had met Mr Ó Broin and found him in agreement in principle with their proposals. It was decided to refer the whole matter for discussion at the AGM in January.

It is worth noting that in October 1950 another music organisation was launched in Dublin. To quote from the *Bulletin*: 'A new society to encourage an appreciation of good music, and to bring music lovers together, has been formed called the Irish Musical Arts Society, Dr Larchet being President.' Six Sunday afternoon concerts, each a month apart, were announced in their first season, with admission to members only, on payment of a subscription of £1.10s.0d. The inaugural recital was given at the Mansion House by the English mezzo-soprano Flora Nielsen, accompanied by Kitty O'Callaghan. These recitals continued until 1953 with a mixture of international and Irish artists, moving on occasion to the Gresham Hotel or the Archbishop Byrne Hall.

One or two other matters of interest came before the Council before the end of 1950. A letter was sent to the Department of Posts and Telegraphs recommending that a suitable permanent conductor be engaged for the RÉSO. It was agreed that a Music Diary should be kept at McCullough's music shop, to facilitate concert promoters in avoiding a conflict of dates. The main performing groups in the country were contacted to inform them of this new facility and encourage its use. And finally, Brian Boydell wrote an article for *The Bell* entitled 'The future of music in Ireland' which was published in the January 1951 issue. He encouraged members of the Council to reply to this, which resulted in a letter from Anthony Farrington in the issue of February 1951, and three articles by Aloys Fleischmann, P. J. Malone and Joseph O'Neill in April. Members of the MAI had not lost sight of the need to keep the current issues concerning 'serious' music as a live topic. Another good development in *The Bell*, though short-lived, was a regular contribution by John Beckett of several pages of music criticism in the four months May to August 1951. These covered some Phoenix Hall concerts by the RÉSO, one or two radio broadcasts, a piano recital by Solomon at the Theatre Royal and the performances of *The Barber of Seville* and *Il Seraglio* by the Hamburg State Opera at the Gaiety Theatre. My mother, who was not very fond of 'grand' opera, waxed lyrical over these productions, as indeed she had also when the same company presented *Don Giovanni* and *Così Fan Tutte* in May 1950.

[1] *Counterpoint*, April 1978.

[2] *The Irish Times*, 29 June 1950.

[3] Paul Egerstorff, Irish painter (1906-1995) – an amateur musician, with a particular interest in early instruments.

[4] See *John S. Beckett: the Man and His Music* (Lilliput Press, 2016)

[5] National Library of Ireland (NLI), ACC 6000, box 42, beige folder 2 – this folder contains all the archived material concerning the 1950 Bach Festival.

[6] *The Irish Times*, 26 September 1950.

[7] *The Irish Times*, 21 September 1950.

[8] *The Irish Times*, 15 September 1950.

[9] *The Irish Times*, 30 September 1950.

CHAPTER 10

The Concert Hall:
Part 1 – 1951 to 1953 –
The MAI leads the way

The Annual General Meeting of the MAI on 23 January 1951 was unusual in that the Council invited as guest chairman the Minister for External Affairs, Mr Seán MacBride. It is possible that the invitation was issued as a means of raising the public profile of the MAI, but undoubtedly it was chiefly in recognition of the close co-operation between the CRC and the MAI regarding the scheme to promote the works of Irish composers. This had been ongoing since mid-1949, and was referred to by the Minister in a short address in which he thanked the Association for their assistance. I think that my mother was intrigued by Seán MacBride. She told me about his early life in Paris (which explained why he spoke English with a French accent), his mother Maud Gonne and her relationship with Yeats, and about his father Major John MacBride, who was executed in 1916. But I actually did not realise until researching the MAI minutes that she had met him. The politics of the Inter-Party Government were of great interest to my parents, covering the declaration of the Irish Republic in 1949, the decision to leave the Commonwealth, and especially the crisis in 1951 over the Mother and Child Scheme. Of course Seán MacBride went on to enjoy a most illustrious international career in Europe, working with the United Nations and

Amnesty International. He received the Nobel Peace prize in 1974 as a man who: 'mobilised the conscience of the world in the fight against injustice'.

1951

The major item on the AGM agenda on 23 January was a discussion about the concert hall, followed by the film *The Young Person's Guide to the Orchestra* which my father had agreed to show. Brian Boydell and my mother introduced the topic, putting forward the view of the Council: 'that the necessity for a National Concert Hall to be located in Dublin was all too apparent; that the building should consist of a major Concert Hall to seat around 1,200, a smaller Hall for such items as Chamber Music Recitals, and adequate rehearsal facilities. It was felt that the scheme previously considered by the Board of Works for the rehabilitation of the Rotunda buildings should be re-investigated, together with other sites for a new building. It was suggested that the money could perhaps be raised by means of a 'three-way split', part by Public Subscription, part to be subscribed by the Government and part by Dublin Corporation. The possibility of participation in any scheme by RÉ must also be considered'.[1] There was good participation from the body of the meeting in the discussion which followed, including the Minister who commented that most members of the Government would be in agreement regarding the need for a concert hall. He suggested that the Council should be authorised to appoint a committee to investigate the whole question, and this was approved by the meeting.

The Council lost no time and at its next meeting on 7 February a committee was elected, including a number of people who were involved in the MAI but were not on the Council. Its members were:- Leon Ó Dubhghaill – a school-teacher and secretary of An tOireachtas; Michael Scott – an architect with a growing reputation; Seymour Leslie – already mentioned in connection with the Theatre Royal; Revd Dr McNevin – administrator of Our Lady's Choral Society; P. J. Malone – secretary of the Irish Federation of Musicians; Edgar Deale; Mr T. S. C. Dagg – who had been involved in the building of the Dagg Hall at the RIAM; and my mother (now apparently known by two names, Mrs Lyall Smith or Mrs Olive Smith). Their terms of reference were:

1) The Committee has been elected to consider ways and means of providing a suitable National Concert Hall building in Dublin.
2) The Committee is urged to seek the co-operation of other concert-promoting bodies, and other interested parties.
3) The Committee shall report back its findings and shall submit all recommendations to the Council of the Music Association of Ireland.
4) The Committee shall appoint its own Chairman and Secretary and shall have power to co-opt further members as it may consider desirable.

The committee gave an Interim Report to the Council on 27 June 1951, detailing their four meetings since their appointment and their interviews with Leon Ó Broin regarding the Rotunda plan, and with the City Manager, Dr P. J. Hermon, about various sites which included the Rotunda, the Blessington Street Basin and the Iveagh Gardens. Mr J. J. McCann, after whom the hall at the College of Music was named, and Mr P. J. Little, former Minister for Posts and Telegraphs, had been co-opted and my mother had agreed to act as secretary. The committee was hoping to send a deputation to discuss potential sites with the Taoiseach as soon as possible. In fact, a large number of sites are mentioned in various documents held in the MAI Archive, including possible rebuilding at the Antient Concert Rooms, the Metropolitan Hall, the Mansion House, and the Royal Hospital, Kilmainham, as well as derelict sites at Parnell Square, Golden Lane, Cuffe Street and on the Quays.[2] In general, Dr Hermon was not encouraging. At a meeting on 18 June 1951 with an MAI delegation of Edgar Deale, Dr McNevin, Michael Scott and my mother, he said that he saw no need for a concert hall and that the priority for derelict sites would be housing. He also said that he did not think there would be money available from the Corporation and that the Rotunda plan, as proposed by P. J. Little in the 1940s, would be their best option.[3]

At this time, the committee also sought and received expressions of support for their aims from other bodies such as the Feis Ceoil, the Dublin Grand Opera Society, the Culwick Choral Society, the Dublin Orchestral Players, Conradh na Gaeilge, the Irish Federation of Musicians, the Trades Union Congress, an tOireachtas, the Royal Irish Academy of Music and the Vocational Education Committee of the City of Dublin. At the next Council meeting on 25 September, my mother reported that the disastrous fire at the Abbey Theatre had delayed their meeting with the Taoiseach, Dublin Corporation had turned down the idea of Blessington Street, but other sites at Cuffe Street and Parnell Street were under discussion. The year ended with another Interim Report which contained the encouraging news that Hilton Edwards of the Gate Theatre was well-disposed towards a joint project at the Rotunda site, and also noted that P. J. Little had been appointed Chairman of the newly-established Arts Council, a development which the committee felt could be very favourable. In this they may have been unduly optimistic, as it is clear from the debate on the Arts Bill, which took place in the Dáil on 24 April 1951, that music was not considered to be a great priority for the Arts Council.[4] Ultimately the committee decided against rebuilding at the Rotunda, preferring to set their sights on a new purpose-built hall.[5]

1952

The next AGM on 30 January 1952 brought another opportunity for MAI members to discuss the proposed concert hall. The architect Patrick Delany was asked to speak on the topic and, as the Minutes describe: 'delivered himself of a most interesting and controversial address on this subject, with particular reference to the question of design, from the points of view of Acoustics, Comfort, Facilities and Seating Accommodation'. The ensuing contributions from the membership were certainly lively, various speakers disagreeing as to the ideal seating capacity, the exact nature of the hall and the pitfalls of an 'all-purpose hall', commenting on the Royal Festival Hall in London, and speaking of the need to grow audiences and make some seats available at cheap prices. The meeting was chaired by the writer Seán Ó Faoláin, who at that time was editor of *The Bell*. He made the point that, whichever type of hall was finally built: 'it must be a good one, worthy of the Nation'. The connection with Ó Faoláin was a fruitful one as the January 1952 issue of *The Bell* saw the publication of an article by Patrick Delany entitled 'A Concert Hall for Dublin?' with a short foreword by John Beckett, encouraging further contributions on the subject. The February issue printed responses from Edgar Deale, James Chapman (violinist with the RÉSO), Walter Beckett (composer and professor at the RIAM, a cousin of John) and Aloys Fleischmann. These articles, with their diverging and, at times, outspoken views undoubtedly helped to keep the topic in the public consciousness.

During the spring of 1952 it became generally known that plans were under way for a large scale arts festival in Dublin during 1953, to be known as An Tóstal. The MAI saw this as an opportunity to lobby for support and compiled a memorandum, with the help of the Concert Hall Committee, pointing out the benefits a concert hall would bring to such a venture, which was envisaged as being a multi-annual event. The Irish Tourist Board was the organisation in overall charge of the plans for An Tóstal, so my mother wrote to the chairman on 24 March, drawing attention to the memorandum and seeking a meeting. But the only outcome was an invitation for the Association to attend a preliminary planning meeting. Although my mother did represent the MAI at this, it seems that no co-operation developed.

However, in the summer of 1952, as a means of raising the profile of the campaign, the committee sent letters seeking support to a number of prominent musicians, in particular conductors who had worked with the RÉSO in the preceding five years. They were justly rewarded and it is fascinating to read the encouraging letters in the MAI file, signed by Arnold Bax, Jean Martinon, Hans Schmidt-Isserstedt, Sir John Barbirolli, Sir Adrian Boult, Sir Malcolm Sargent, Carlo Zecchi, Sir Hugh Roberton and Margaret Burke-Sheridan.[6]

The next positive news appeared in the June minutes of the MAI, the Concert Hall Committee reporting that a site mutually agreeable to them and to Dublin Corporation had been identified. This was on Merchants' Quay, opposite the Four Courts and near the old city walls and St Audeon's Gate. The committee were advised to consult with Fr Cormac O'Daly, Guardian of the Franciscan Church on the Quays. But at a meeting on 29 May 1952 the Corporation made their position clear – a concert hall could not be regarded as a municipal purpose unless they controlled it. So the site would have to be acquired or purchased by the MAI and planning approval sought in the usual way. On 3 July a letter was received which stated that: 'the City Manager, on the recommendation of the Town Planning & Streets Committee, had made an order approving in principle the Association's scheme'.

On 24 July the committee hosted a drinks party at the Shelbourne Hotel at 5.30 p.m. to which they invited a number of prominent business men, hoping to interest them in the project. Unfortunately very few of those invited turned up, but a seed for the future must have been sown because in September 1952 my mother informed the Council that a proposal had been put to the Government that a company should be floated to acquire the site, financed by eight business men who would contribute £200, and that the Government had undertaken to guarantee the interest on a loan. She suggested that the MAI should try to raise £500, including a possible contribution of £20 from the Association's funds, and the Council instructed her to proceed.

The really significant decisions were taken at the October Council meeting. My mother reported: 'that the Concert Hall Committee, acting in accordance with legal advice, thought that a small promoting Company would suffice, and had passed the following Resolution at a meeting held on Monday 27 October 1952 : "Consultations having taken place with a number of business men, this Committee has unanimously agreed:

a) That it is necessary to form a limited company to find ways and means of financing the new Concert and Assembly Hall;

b) That there should be a small number of Directors and that the Council of the Music Association should nominate two members;

c) That the Concert Hall Committee be given authority by the Council to form such a Company;

d) That the Concert Hall Committee will continue in an advisory capacity."'

My mother explained that Lord Moyne would contribute £25 and that the rest of the Company Members would give £200 between them, including £50 from the MAI. On the advice of Arthur Cox & Co., solicitors, a small Company Limited by Guarantee would be formed, and the Council agreed that my mother and Edgar Deale would be the Directors representing the MAI.

Concert and Assembly Hall Ltd (CAH) was incorporated on 8 December 1952 and a formal press statement was issued which resulted in coverage in the *The Irish Times* and *Irish Independent* and a leading article in the *Evening Mail* of 10 December. The first meeting of the Directors was held on 17 December at the offices of Arthur Cox & Co. on St Stephen's Green. Six of the seven Directors were present: M. Olive Smith, Alexander W. Bayne, Lawrence P. Kennedy, Augustus P. Reynolds, Edgar M. Deale and Michael Scott – only Lord Moyne was absent. At their first meeting, resolutions were passed appointing A. P. Reynolds as Chairman and my mother as Secretary of the Company. Arthur Cox & Co. were appointed as solicitors and J. A. Kinnear & Co. as auditors. Kinnear's offices at 1 Leinster Street were designated as the Company's registered office, and following the date of incorporation were used for all meetings of CAH and as the correspondence address.

The Memorandum and Articles of the Company state, as the main object: 'to promote, build or acquire a public concert hall and assembly rooms and to conduct and carry on the same for the use and enjoyment of the public, and to promote public knowledge and appreciation of music, drama, ballet and like arts'. There followed another 24 clauses which set out all possible uses for the hall, foresaw the need for catering and bar-keeping, for legal matters such as copyright and performing rights, and for the huge spectrum of financial and administrative matters which could arise in the management of such an enterprise.

1953

Two more Board meetings were held in quick succession. On 1 January 1953, it was decided that there should be 20 Founder members who would each contribute £25, and two more categories – Ordinary members (£1 per annum) and Associate members (10/- p.a.). This structure never actually came into being. The seven Directors already named were in fact the Founders, being known also, rather confusingly, as Subscribers. There were three additional Subscribers, whose names appeared in the CAH accounts for the year ended 31/12/1953, making a total of 10 Founder members. These were Fr Cormac O'Daly, W. H. Freeman and C. B. Creede. At the next meeting on 12 January, Michael Scott's elegant lyre design was accepted as the logo of CAH.

The members of the MAI were officially informed of the incorporation of CAH at the AGM on 28 January 1953 and a fitting tribute was paid to the work of the outgoing Concert Hall Committee: 'The Council must take the opportunity of expressing gratitude to its Committee, which has been unrelenting in its efforts. Future generations of musicians in Dublin will have cause to be very grateful to this Committee'. Just three names were carried over as Directors – Michael Scott,[7] Edgar Deale and my mother. The additional Directors/Subscribers are interesting. Lord Moyne has been previously mentioned – as a member of one of Ireland's most influential families his support was very important; A. W. Bayne was managing director of the Irish Assurance Co. Ltd and had already offered a considerable sum to the Arts Council with the aim of acquiring the Rotunda for conversion to a concert hall, a scheme also originally favoured by Lord Moyne; Lawrence Kennedy was a successful business man, owner of Kennedy's bread company; Fr Cormac represented the Franciscan Order, because of the site at Merchant's Quay; C. B. Creede represented Our Lady's Choral Society, but there is no information to hand concerning W.H. Freeman.

A. P. Reynolds, chairman of Córas Iompair Éireann (CIÉ), knew Michael Scott through his work for CIÉ. Scott also renovated Mr Reynold's home at Abbeville, Kinsealy, later the home of Taoiseach Charles J. Haughey.

A. P. Reynolds was a business man and accountant, and a successful owner and breeder of horses. He was also fond of music and his interest in the CAH project was very genuine. My mother respected him greatly and regarded him as an excellent chairman. Being a company limited by guarantee, none of them received any remuneration. One wonders whether they could have foreseen the nature of the long uphill battle that lay ahead.

The Board of CAH engaged Good & Ganly, property valuers, to obtain accurate information on the Merchants' Quay site. They reported on 17 February 1953 that there were a number of property and business owners involved who would not be willing to sell unless for a substantial figure, and suggested that the site of the Mendicity Institute on nearby Usher's Island might be easier to clear, as there were more buildings in poor condition. The Board finally decided against Merchants' Quay on 9 April on financial grounds, and wrote to Dr Hermon on 22nd to give him this decision and to ask whether a site might be available in the High St area. A reply dated 9 May stated that Dr Hermon: 'has no objection in principle to the siting of a hall in the area proposed' but that site clearance would have to proceed before a precise location could be identified.

Then followed a frustrating period during which the Board tried to make contact with the Corporation, having heard that the proposed High St site might be allocated to Civic Offices instead. A lengthy report gives quite an insight into my mother's tenacity in refusing to be fobbed off with excuses and postponements as she threatened to telephone twice a day until she got an answer! The result was a meeting between a delegation from CAH (A. P. Reynolds, A. W. Bayne and my mother) and three Corporation officials including the City Manager, which took place on 17 August 1953, but only an undertaking to refer the matter to the Town Planning Committee was forthcoming. A delegation from CAH, including Michael Scott and my mother, was invited to view the site on 8 September, and then progress stalled for several months. In December there was a rumour that the Planning Committee's decision was in favour of the Civic Offices and a TB clinic, but this information was not conveyed to CAH by letter until 5 February 1954. It seems that they were being treated like pawns in a game, but nonetheless my mother replied politely to the City Manager on 18 February, saying that the Board had decided to consider other ways and means of securing a site.

My recollections of this period are of quite a lot of tension, of papers overflowing from my mother's desk and onto the dining-room table, and of a great number of telephone calls. Some of these appeared to be top secret and I was expected to 'make myself scarce'! The word 'Montrose' in particular seemed to be connected with these hush-hush conversations, but at that time it was not clear to me whether it was a house or a possible site.

[1] Minutes of AGM of the MAI, 23 January 1951.

[2] NLI – ACC 6000, box 11, blue file.

[3] Ibid. box 47, beige file 4 – dealings with Dublin Corporation, 1951-52.

[4] The Arts Council was established under the terms of the Arts Bill 1951. During the debate the Taoiseach gave the view that 'music and drama may come later'. Maurice Dockrell TD picked up on this point, saying that the Taoiseach's words 'had shocked me to the core . . . we should have started off with music and drama, especially music'.

[5] NLI – ACC 6000, box 11.

[6] Ibid. box 11, blue file 1951-53.

[7] Michael Scott (1905-89) designed the Irish Pavilion at the New York World's Fair in 1938. In the early 1950s he undertook work for CIÉ, creating contemporary designs for Donnybrook Bus Garage and Busáras in Dublin. He was also the architect for the re-built Abbey Theatre (1966).

CHAPTER 11

The Concert Hall:
Part 2 – 1953 to 1956 –
Montrose versus High Street

Montrose was in fact a period house with more than 20 acres of land on the main Stillorgan Road, just past Donnybrook. It was earmarked as the site for the expansion of RÉ, presumably looking forward to the time when Ireland would have its own television service. In the MAI archive there is a letter to Michael Scott, dated 4 August 1953, from a contact in the Office of Public Works which suggests that CAH should consider raising the possibility with the Minister for Posts and Telegraphs, Erskine Childers, that a small corner of the site could be allocated to the Concert Hall. A meeting took place on 3 September which seems to have gone well, as a sketch plan of the Montrose site, including the Concert Hall and all the proposed RÉ buildings, was drawn up by the Office of Public Works, dated 21 September 1953.[1] My mother wrote back to the Minister on 1 October, following receipt of the plan, saying: 'my co-directors are inclined to favour Donnybrook, as no capital expenditure would be involved in securing the site there, whereas the city site would involve such expenditure'. She requested a further meeting and listed a number of points for discussion before a decision could be taken. These included the size of the site for the Hall – three acres being suggested – and the cost of the lease; the amount of usage of the Hall by the

RÉSO and the financial implications of this; and further consideration of the size of the Hall and its ancillary accommodation. A long and detailed letter of 6 November, signed by the Minister's secretary, addressed all these questions in a very satisfactory manner, agreeing to the allocation of three acres and anticipating 20 full-scale symphony concerts per year, for each of which the Hall could charge a letting fee of £100. In addition RÉ wanted to explore the possibility of giving short weekly concerts at nominal prices. RÉ was happy with the projected seating for 1,500 to 2,000 and pointed out that there would have to be ample storage space for instruments, good dressing rooms and 'booths for Announcer and Control Officers'. RÉ did not envisage making much use of the smaller ancillary hall, which was part of the CAH blueprint.

1954

I can only imagine that the CAH directors must have been overjoyed to receive such a promise of support and good faith. My mother replied on 10 November 1953, enclosing a brochure about the Royal Festival Hall, which Minister Childers acknowledged on 12th, saying that he would return the brochure at their next meeting and hoping that my mother had completely recovered from an attack of lumbago! It seems that relations were very cordial at that time, but the next couple of letters (22 February and 10 March 1954) indicate a delay in the completion of the lease of Montrose between the Government and the ground-landlords, the Pembroke Estate.² The CAH board were hoping for a clear response concerning Montrose in time for their first AGM on 18 February 1954, but this did not materialise. As already noted, neither did they have good news regarding the High Street site. They even investigated the site of the Greenmount Oil Refinery at Harold's Cross, and followed up a rumour that the High School might be considering selling their building on Harcourt Street. A pattern of hopes being raised, only to be very swiftly dashed, was becoming recurrent.

The next set-back emanated in political circles. Éamon de Valera, having lost his overall majority, called a general election for 18 May 1954.

The CAH board busied themselves during the election campaign, seeking and receiving a number of expressions of support from various candidates, but on 5th May, in the dying days of the Fianna Fáil administration, the Minister for Finance Seán MacEntee wrote to my mother, stating that while he had long been in favour of the idea of a concert hall for Dublin, as regards funding he could not commit this or any other future Government due to: 'the very numerous and varied demands upon our country's resources'. Another letter, dated 20 May, from the Taoiseach's private secretary, only served to reinforce this decision taken prior to leaving office.

The election resulted in the second Inter-Party Government, comprising Fine Gael, Labour and Clann na Talmhan, who took office on 2 June with John A. Costello as Taoiseach. In spite of the rebuff from the outgoing administration, the CAH board lost no time in writing to the new Minister for Posts and Telegraphs, Mr Keyes, to acquaint him of the progress already made regarding the Montrose site, and seeking a meeting at his earliest convenience, to be attended by my mother, Edgar Deale and Mr Bayne. This was scheduled for 7 July 1954. The CAH minutes for the Board meeting on 9 September record: 'Mr Bayne reported on the interview with the Minister for Posts and Telegraph on 7/7/54, when the Minister confirmed the understanding re the Montrose site and indicated that he was favourably disposed to the project'.

This was followed by a meeting with the Taoiseach on 12 November, at which the same three Directors, A. W. Bayne, Edgar Deale and my mother sought to ascertain the level of support that might be forthcoming from the Government. Mr Bayne seems to have very much taken the lead in presenting the CAH case and in putting forward ideas as to how the Government's contribution might be raised. The Taoiseach asked how much support might be expected from the general public and Mr Bayne suggested that this could come in the shape of a guarantee fund to cover the expenses incurred in the early stages, before the hall was running at full capacity. The deputation stressed that Montrose was their favoured site, but Mr Costello noted that two successive Ministers for Posts and Telegraphs had given an undertaking about the site without any reference to the Government. Nor had the project come up at any time for discussion by Government, so he asked CAH to send in a definite financial proposal which he undertook to have considered along with other capital projects. All this was reported to the CAH Board on 18 November in a written report from Mr Bayne, who also agreed to draw up the memorandum required by the Taoiseach.[3] This was discussed at Board meetings on 2 and 16 December. The final agreed version was delivered to the Taoiseach's office on 24 December. The amount of Government finance sought was £450,000.

1955

On 17 February 1955, the Board decided to send the memorandum also to the Minister for Education, the Minister for Posts and Telegraphs, the Director of the Arts Council and the former minister, Erskine Childers. My mother received a hand-written reply from Mr Childers, offering to speak about the concert hall during the debate on the estimate for the Arts Council. This was gladly accepted, my mother noting that the Arts Council were planning to send a recommendation on the CAH proposals to the Taoiseach. On 24 March she wrote to the Taoiseach's private secretary, enquiring whether there was any Government response to the memorandum and received a reply stating that it had been given to the Minister for Finance. In fact, nothing was heard until May 1956.

Also in the early months of 1955 the CAH Board were surprised to learn that Dublin Corporation had set aside a site at Waterford Street for a concert hall, to be built by Our Lady's Choral Society. Waterford St no longer exists, but the site was almost opposite the Pro-Cathedral in Marlborough St, next to the Model Schools, now the Department of Education. The announcement was made by the Lord Mayor at a dinner in the Gresham Hotel in honour of Sir John Barbirolli. There is some correspondence about this in the MAI archive, with CAH pleading that Archbishop McQuaid would consider calling it 'Our Lady's Hall' thereby omitting the word 'Concert' altogether. The Board feared that two 'Concert Halls' would cause public confusion! However, it appears that the project was short-lived.[4]

During April, CAH was made aware of a rumour that the planned Civic Offices might not be built at High St after all, and that the site could become available again for a concert hall. This was confirmed in a letter from the Corporation, dated 13 June 1955, which stated that the City Manager, on the recommendation of the Town Planning Committee: 'directs me to inform you that there is no objection in principle to the siting of a Concert Hall on the High Street frontage'. Information on the amount of ground needed was requested and some idea of the size of the building. Michael Scott was asked to do some sketches.

It is not clear how this latest development came to the attention of journalists, but a curt letter from Leon Ó Broin to my mother dated 14 June states: 'I have been reading in the papers about the site the Dublin Corporation is said to have given for a concert hall at the junction of Nicholas and High Streets. How much of this is true? And has your Committee yet accepted the offered site which, I take it, would mean that you were no longer interested in the Donnybrook site?' For CAH, this was not a welcome development and it was probably unfortunate that, because there had been no Board meeting, my mother's reply was delayed until 20 July 1955. From her letter I get the impression that the Board were trying to stay on good terms with both the Department of Posts and Telegraphs and the Corporation, but can only conclude that this did not go down well with the Department as there is no further correspondence about Montrose.

In my view, and with the benefit of hindsight, this was actually a major calamity. The opportunity to build a purpose-built hall on a 'green-field' site was lost, also the chance to provide a permanent home for the RÉSO on the same campus as the rest of the broadcasting services. And sadly, CAH found itself dealing yet again with the unpredictability of the planners of Dublin Corporation.

Michael Scott wrote to Arthur Cox on 21 July 1955 enclosing two site plans, which unfortunately are not in the archive. One showed the proposed space allocated by the Corporation. The second showed the area required by CAH, taking into account 'the odd shape of the site'.

The building envisaged 'will incorporate a large auditorium to hold 1500 to 2000 people, a smaller hall for 500 people, a restaurant and the usual cloakrooms etc.' Arthur Cox & Co. were retained to deal with the legal aspects of the Corporation proposals and in this capacity received a letter from the Town Planning Department, on behalf of the City Manager and Town Clerk, dated 24 November 1955. This brought the news that an order had been made approving the leasing of the site to CAH. The writer continued: 'I would point out, however, that the site required is at present not wholly in the possession of the Corporation . . . A considerable area remains to be acquired and it is not possible at this stage to indicate what the final cost of acquisition will be . . . The question of the rent to be charged could not be indicated until the remaining sites will have been acquired.'

1956

There follows a number of letters between the CAH Board and Arthur Cox. It seems that the Board, rather unrealistically, wanted the Corporation to proceed quickly towards the acquisitions and were prepared to embark on public fund-raising without a definite financial agreement with the Corporation. Cox offered some advice as to how CAH might go about raising the capital required, including an approach to the Industrial Credit Company and the Irish Assurance Company, but also raised the question as to whether the site was completely suitable. On 9 January 1956 he informed the Board that Lisney's Auctioneers were offering some of the premises at Christchurch Place (High Street) for auction. He continues: 'I do not think that there is anything that we can do as to this. Even if you were advised that it is the best possible site and suitable in other ways, we would not have the money available to bid for them and buy at auction. I have had no further word from the Corporation.' His concern at the Board's possible foolhardiness is clear from his letter of 21 January in which he asks: 'You say: We have now been granted a site by Dublin Corporation. Is this really true?'

On 18 May, CAH finally received a response from the Government to their memorandum of December 1954. It stated: 'The Government could not, under the existing conditions, undertake such a financial commitment.' This was reinforced by a private letter from the Taoiseach to Arthur Cox, dated 17 May 1956, in which Mr Costello writes 'I am afraid that the financial difficulties presented by the proposal submitted by CAH have proved insurmountable.' Given the deterioration in the Irish economy, it was not a good time to launch a fund-raising campaign, even though the visit of the Vienna Philharmonic to Cork on 13 May had occasioned some letters to the papers lamenting that there was no suitable hall in Dublin to accommodate the orchestra, the Theatre Royal being unavailable.

A. W. Bayne suggested that he might try to meet the City Manager and the Town Planning Officer, and did so on 22 May. He submitted a closely-typed, 2-page report following the meeting which makes very interesting reading.[5] The whole question of the type of lease CAH might expect from the Corporation for the High Street site was discussed, also the method by which it would be calculated and at what point CAH could be expected to take it up. The Corporation officials revealed that about 9/10ths of the total area had already been acquired, and that they might be prepared to use compulsory purchase orders for the remainder.

My mother, reporting to the MAI Council on 7 November 1956, could only repeat CAH's hopes for the High Street site and possible Government funding in the future. Nonetheless, according to the Minutes: 'The Council asked Mrs Smith to convey to the Directors of CAH their desire for the project to continue.'

[1] NLI – ACC 6000, box 18, grey folder 7.

[2] Ibid. – correspondence re Montrose in box 18, grey folder 7.

[3] Ibid. box 47, blue file 2.

[4] Ibid. box 11, beige file 2 – also contains correspondence with Dublin Corporation and Arthur Cox (solicitors) during 1955 and early 1956.

[5] Ibid. box 47, beige file 4.

CHAPTER 12

The Development of the MAI
– 1951 to 1954

1951

With the establishment of CAH Ltd, the immediate pressure of work towards a National Concert Hall was removed from the MAI Council, and they were able to concentrate on other matters. The monthly *Bulletin*, which carried musical news to the MAI members scattered throughout the country, was proving a success. Madge Clotworthy (née Bradbury), a fine pianist who had a unique gift in singing to her own accompaniment, took over as Editor from Dorothy Stokes and Edgar Deale in the autumn of 1951. Its printing and distribution were handled by McCullough's Music Shop, in return for a small advertisement in each issue, and McCullough's also kept the MAI Diary of Musical Events into which concert promoters were encouraged to enter their upcoming plans. At this stage the MAI had no office of its own, the headed notepaper carrying just the private addresses of the Secretary and Treasurer. Council meetings were mostly held in Edgar Deale's office at the Zürich Insurance, 8 Dawson Street, or occasionally at Dorothy Stokes' studio in Lincoln Place.

In October 1950, P. J. Malone, conscious, one assumes, of the enthusiasm with which the MAI membership had supported the Bach Commemoration, proposed that the Association should arrange some Members' Meetings each year. The idea was to offer a lecture recital on the lines of Dr Armstrong's talk in August 1949, or a film or a performance of a specialised nature – the Council was anxious not to be perceived as encroaching on other well-established music organisations. The first of these took place on 23 April 1951 when a performance of the *St Matthew Passion* by Heinrich Schütz was given by a chamber choir, Cór Laoídheagach, conducted by Dr Hans Waldemar Rosen. This was held in the upstairs room of the Presbyterian Association, 16 St Stephen's Green, and attracted an audience of 83, of whom 23 were members. The second Members' Meeting of 1951 on 8 October took advantage of the good relationship that had developed between the MAI and the National Museum in the course of the Bach celebrations the previous year. The Minister of Education gave permission for a concert of Medieval and Renaissance vocal and instrumental music, limited to an audience of 50 MAI members. John Beckett played the Weber harpsichord with Betty Sullivan as continuo cello. The lute was played by Michael Morrow, the Irish-born musician who went on to become the founder of Musica Reservata, the ground-breaking Early Music ensemble based in London in the 1960s and '70s. By way of introduction Liam Gogan, keeper of the musical instrument collection of the Museum, gave a short talk.

1952

The Council and members were well pleased and two more events were planned for 1952, though there was an on-going search for a suitable venue for these events. With the assistance of Dr Edward Solomons, a very good friend of both my parents and of Edgar Deale, permission was obtained to hold a recital on 8 March 1952 in the hall of the Royal College of Physicians on Kildare Street. This beautiful room proved to have a lovely acoustic for chamber music, and the programme, given once again by Cór Laoídheagach under Dr Rosen, with instrumental music directed by John Beckett, was very well received. Members were admitted free of charge to these Meetings and could bring one guest; non-members were charged 3/6d and 2/- for students. The venue for the November meeting moved again, this time to the Organ Room of the

RIAM. Joe Groocock suggested that members might like to entertain themselves in singing madrigals and part-songs under his direction, which proved most enjoyable!

In late 1952 the first of the MAI's 'Satellite' organisations was formed – this was the Chamber Music Group. John O'Sullivan informed the Council that a meeting had been held at Brian Boydell's house on 6 December, attended by some 60 people, who had formed themselves into a society for the promotion of chamber music, with a subscription of one guinea. The Council felt that there should be a definite relationship between this group and the MAI, especially as there had been an anonymous donation of funds for the formation of a lending library of chamber works, and asked Anthony Farrington to meet with the appointed secretary of the Group. He was James Plunkett Kelly, a keen amateur viola player, writer and radio producer, later to become a household name for his book *Strumpet City*.[1] Here it is also important to identify John O'Sullivan, elected to the Council in 1952. He was an excellent organist, harpsichordist, pianist and choral director, who became deeply involved with MAI activities for several years.

1953

During 1953 the Chamber Music Group met on a number of occasions to listen to prepared performances by members and also to enjoy sight-reading repertoire. My mother was a member, occasionally taking part as a pianist, and the Group met from time to time in our house. One such occasion was the Members' Meeting on 20 June 1953 when the players were Shirley Pollard (viola), Henry Dagg (clarinet) and John Beckett (piano).

The November Members' Meeting in 1953 was held at the home of Brian and Mary Boydell and was part of the lead-in to the formation of the Composers' Group, another 'Satellite' body of the MAI. At this event, recordings were played of compositions by Seóirse Bodley, Brian Boydell, Edgar Deale, Frederick May and A. J. Potter. It is hard to overstate the importance of the Composers' Group. Right from the outset, so many of those who drove the vision of the MAI were composers and there was total support for the second of the MAI's stated objectives: 'To improve conditions for composers and musicians generally.' Some progress had been made on behalf of Irish composers during 1949 and 1950 through co-operation with the CRC, but there was general recognition that working together under the umbrella of the MAI could greatly strengthen their cause and hopefully lead to the establishment of a Composers' Centre.

Other preoccupations of the Council in this period included ongoing dialogue with the Department of Posts and Telegraphs concerning the RÉSO, its lack of a permanent conductor, and the status of music in broadcasting in general. The MAI also assisted with the foundation of a Music Teachers' Association. In October 1953 Anthony Farrington indicated that he would be resigning as Hon. Secretary and John O'Sullivan agreed to take over from him following the AGM in January 1954. Dr Farrington had been a stabilising influence during those early days of the MAI. His minutes were exemplary, especially those written by hand for the AGMs, and he dealt efficiently with a great deal of correspondence. Most importantly, he and my mother had a very good working relationship, each having great respect for the other, and being on friendly terms outside the work of the MAI. He was presented with an inscribed pen and pencil set at the AGM as a token of appreciation. His minute records: 'The outgoing secretary, being somewhat nonplussed by the unexpected presentation, replied very inadequately. Nevertheless he most gratefully accepted it as indicating the Council's good opinion. He is also a bit embarrassed at having to write this minute himself.'

1954

The organisation of the Members' Meetings was usually in the hands of several council members, my mother participating as required by her role as Treasurer. However she was much more involved in the first Meeting of 1954, which turned out to be another landmark occasion for her. In December 1953 the pianist Charles Lynch[2] and Fred May had made the suggestion to the Council that the MAI should organise a memorial concert for Sir Arnold Bax, Master of the Queen's Music, who had died in Cork on 3 October 1953. Although English-born, and the occupant of the highest position for a British composer, he had very strong connections with Ireland, both literary and musical, writing stories and poetry under the pseudonym Dermot O'Byrne and also a number of musical works with Irish titles. He visited the West of Ireland frequently from 1902 onwards and also lived for a while in Rathgar, where he was part of AE's literary circle. It is said that he was able to speak Irish. Following a visit to Cork in 1927 he became a close friend of Aloys Fleischmann and his wife, and from 1945 onwards was External Examiner in Music at both UCC and UCD. Máire and Sheila Larchet, daughters of Prof. John F. Larchet, recall that he stayed at their parents' house in Ballsbridge in the late 1940s, describing him as a rather taciturn man, in contrast to the high romanticism of his music. According to Edgar Deale, who had some lessons from him, he 'suffered from shyness'. He actually died in Aloys Fleischmann's home and is buried in Cork.

The Council took up the suggestion of the memorial concert and my mother was asked to proceed with the preliminary arrangements. It seems that Charles Lynch already had the outline of the programme in his mind. He was very anxious to include Bax's Piano Quintet in G minor (1915) which had never been performed in Ireland, and was aware that there had been a BBC broadcast of this during 1953 by Colin Horsley with the New London String Quartet. Charles had ascertained that the Quartet would be willing to perform it in Ireland with him, and was proposing two concerts in Dublin and Cork on 30 and 31 March 1954. The Quartet had already played at the RDS on 9 November 1953, so they were known to Dublin audiences, which was an advantage. The rest of the programme would consist of Bax's 2nd Violin Sonata with François D'Albert, violin professor at the RIAM, some piano pieces and a short piece for cello[3] and piano entitled *Folk Tale*. It was decided to hold the Dublin concert in the lovely octagonal room in the Civic Museum, by kind permission of Dublin Corporation, whilst the Cork concert was held in the Aula Maxima of UCC. My mother was successful in procuring financial support from both the CRC and the Arts Council.

110

The New London String Quartet (NLSQ) was an interesting group. Three of the players, 2nd violin Lionel Bentley, viola Keith Cummings and cellist Douglas Cameron had been members of the Blech Quartet which had famously played to entertain the Heads of State at the Potsdam Conference in 1945, at the end of the Second World War. This group had played at the RDS in 1946, 1948 and 1949, but the leader Harry Blech, founder of the London Mozart Players, retired in 1950 to devote himself to conducting. The three remaining players regrouped with the young Austrian-born violinist Erich Gruenberg under their new name. They arrived at Dublin airport on Sunday 28 March and my mother went to collect them. I remember that she was very nervous at meeting such renowned musicians – she had become quite comfortable in the company of the famous soloists who had sung in the Bach Bicentenary concerts, but was apprehensive as to how she would get on with these well-known instrumentalists. When she returned home she was delighted – they were so friendly, so easy-going about the arrangements for rehearsals – a good relationship was established from the outset. The rehearsals for the Quintet took place in our house and I was allowed to listen quietly in the corner of the room. I did not attend the concert which, by all accounts, was very successful with a large audience and very good reviews. The journey to Cork next day was in two cars, driven by my mother and Mairtín McCullough.

For some reason it was arranged that my father would collect Charles Lynch, who was staying at a hotel in Dún Laoghaire, and bring him into Dublin to meet up with Mairtín and François D'Albert. When he arrived at the hotel, the porter told my father that Mr Lynch had gone for a walk down the East Pier, so with the deadline of the journey to Cork foremost in mind, my father set off down the pier, fully expecting to meet Charles at least half-way. But there was no sign of him until my father thought to look over the wall at the very end. Charles was sitting out of sight, gazing out to sea and quite reluctant to leave. He explained that the previous night's concert had been so wonderful that he really doubted whether he was capable of playing the programme again! Fortunately my father was able to persuade him that it was worth trying, especially as there were five other musicians depending upon him, and so the Cork concert did in fact take place.

However, it was the conversations that my mother had with Douglas Cameron and Keith Cummings during the car journeys which were of real significance for the future. They explained to her how chamber groups such as theirs made a living in the UK, describing the network of music clubs all over the country and how short tours could be arranged that worked well financially for both the promoter and the performers. These concerts were the 'bread-and-butter' of their work as a string quartet and they felt that the same system could work in Ireland. By the time they got back to Dublin from Cork they had almost persuaded her to try organising a short 'pilot-project' tour for them in the Autumn. My mother was excited because the concept fitted so well with two of the original aims of the MAI: 'To organise popular lectures, concerts and recitals and to awaken a musical consciousness in the nation' and 'To encourage the formation of musical groups and societies throughout the country'.

From the end of 1953, and particularly after the 1954 AGM, the Council had been exercised about the establishment of a Federation of Irish Music Clubs as a means of strengthening co-operation and support amongst musical bodies throughout the country. A special General Meeting of the MAI was called for 1 June 1954 at which the following resolution was passed: 'That Rule 4 of the Constitution of the Association be amended to read as follows: Membership is open to those, including music societies, who support the objects of the Association.' These music societies came to be known as the Corporate Members of the MAI, at an annual subscription of £1. The Hon. Secretary was asked to begin a process of circularising groups and inviting them to become Corporate Members.

Following that special General Meeting on 1 June, an unusual programme of Medieval and Renaissance music for voices and instruments, dating from 1200 to 1500 AD, was organised by John O'Sullivan. At the other end of the historical spectrum, as it were, A. J. Potter, as secretary to the MAI Composers' Group, reported to the Council in September that sixteen composers had joined the Group. In October, they undertook to organise a series of Lunchtime Concerts of contemporary Irish music in the Graduate Memorial Building (GMB) of TCD. These took place in November and December 1954, and featured music by a number of members – Fred May, Rhoda Coghill, Daniel McNulty, A. J. Potter, John Reidy (Seán Ó Riada), Seóirse Bodley and Brian Boydell. The Council agreed to bear the deficit on the series, which amounted to £9.7s 0d.

Meanwhile, my mother had been busy investigating the possibilities for a tour by the NLSQ in late October and early November 1954. No time was lost following the Quartet's return to England after the Bax concerts – Douglas Cameron's first letter is dated 17 April – and he reported that RÉ had offered them a broadcast of Fred May's String Quartet on Wednesday 27 October, so the tour could commence on Thursday 28th. Patiently, my mother compiled a list of possible towns and dates and approached the Arts Council for a guarantee against loss, which was granted. My father put forward a very good solution to the practical difficulties of transporting instruments, luggage and four musicians, namely the purchase by my parents of a handsome dark-green Commer station-wagon, which was so roomy that only one vehicle and driver (my mother) would be needed, thereby halving the transport costs. The final itinerary was: **Sligo**, promoted by the Sligo Singers at the Assembly Room in the Town Hall; **Galway**, organised by Arthur Healy, Cáirde an Cheoil, at the Taibhdhearc Theatre; **Cork**, University Arts Society at the Aula Maxima, UCC; **Limerick**, organised by the Limerick Symphony Concerts Society at Cruise's Hotel; **Carlow,** promoted by the Carlow Arts Council at the Town Hall, and followed by a Children's Concert the next morning; **Waterford**, the Waterford Music Club at the Municipal Theatre; **Wexford**, afternoon recital at the Wexford Opera Festival; **Kilkenny**, promoted by the Kilkenny Music and Arts Council at the Art Gallery of the Vocational Education School; and lastly **Clonmel**, organised by a local committee at the Municipal Theatre. The tour ended with a concert in **Dublin** at the Provost's House, TCD. The Quartet's fee was an all-inclusive £350, which worked out at £35 per concert or just under £9 per player!

The Council minutes for 5 October note the decision to ask members to wear evening dress for the concert in the Provost's House. The beautiful salon upstairs was a new location for a recital, and it was helpful that my mother knew Provost A.J.McConnell from her days at TCD, and could also enlist Helen Watson's knowledge of College protocols in arranging this event for the MAI.

Regarding the preceding Tour, each centre had a choice of programme from a rich selection of major works including Mozart – 'Dissonance', Haydn – 'Lark', Schubert – 'Death and the Maiden', Dvořák – 'American', Beethoven – Op.18 No. 4, Brahms – No.1 in C minor, Wolf – *Italian Serenade* as well as Debussy. The Dublin programme consisted of two *Fantasias* by Purcell, the Schubert *Satz* (first performance in Ireland) and quartets by May and Bartók. The May was also played in Cork where Fred was in the audience. Three of the venues had never hosted a string quartet concert before. Carlow, having been very cautious at first, was encouraged by the guarantee, and suggested a children's concert as well which drew a large audience. Charles Ryan of Kilkenny reported that: 'There has been a considerable amount of talk since the recital and I feel that a great deal of good has been done by the presence here of such a distinguished group' and the Cork review stated: 'Listening to the tonal balance attained by the quartet last night it was clear that these fine musicians know their work intimately'. Arthur Healy of Galway wrote that Cáirde an Cheoil would become Corporate Members of the MAI: 'with whose objects I am in complete agreement' and added: 'The recital here was regarded as a tremendous success and will be a great help in improving the attendance at our future functions'. The only discordant note was struck by Wexford, who allowed latecomers to enter during the music and failed to quell distracting noise outside the recital room – correspondence shows that the Festival organisers did apologise for this afterwards.

My mother was overjoyed at the success of the whole venture and, unusually for her, wrote a daily journal of the tour.[4] It is no wonder that the Quartet also enjoyed the trip for she took them by the most scenic routes where possible, visiting the Cliffs of Moher, Pontoon and Ashford Castle and passing through the lovely scenery of the Barrow and Nore valleys. Apparently there were frequent stops for Keith to take photos. There were also parties after most of the concerts and these late nights resulted in quite a bit of snoozing during the journeys, though my mother did say that one member of the quartet was always delegated to chat to her, so that she wouldn't fall asleep! Douglas Cameron wrote afterwards: 'We feel it has been so much worthwhile, thanks entirely to your foresight and organising ability. Your ears must often burn – for we are continually singing your praises'. The success was also noted in the Council's report for 1954: 'Our special thanks are due to the Hon. Treasurer, with whom the idea originated and whose subsequent work made the tour possible'. The whole venture was undoubtedly of seminal importance, as not only did it enable the MAI to begin the work of fulfilling two of its original aims, but the manner in which the tour was organised created a template for the future organisation of country-wide concerts outside the Dublin area.

[1] Written under the name James Plunkett.

[2] Charles Lynch (1906–1984) was regarded in the 1950s and 60s as Ireland's foremost pianist; he was a friend of Arnold Bax. See entry in *The Encyclopaedia of Music in Ireland*.

[3] Played by Douglas Cameron.

[4] This journal and many other details of the NLSQ tour in 1954 are in NLI – ACC 6000, box 20, green folder 2.

CHAPTER 13

The Continuing Development of the MAI – 1955 and 1956

1955

The spring of 1955 brought a new MAI venture – following the concerts organised the previous autumn by the Composers' Group in the GMB of TCD, four Lunchtime Concerts devoted to the music of Schubert were held in the same venue, with some financial help from the Arts Council. The programmes were devised by John O'Sullivan and Fred May, who also took part as performers in the 'Grand Duo' for piano duet in the first recital. The other programmes featured songs and chamber music, including the 'Trout' Quintet. Lunchtime concerts were a rarity at that time, so once again the MAI was leading the way in this respect. Further series, all organised by John O'Sullivan, took place in the autumn of 1955 and spring of 1956, each focusing on either a single composer or works from a common period, and offering the increasingly supportive audience music by Fauré, Monteverdi and Dufay, Telemann, Mahler and Berg, Byrd and Tallis, Beethoven and finally Mozart.

The first Members' Meeting of 1955 also broke new ground with a talk by Caoimhín Ó Danachair (Kevin Danaher) of the Irish Folklore Commission, held on 19 March at the RIAM, which was illustrated with gramophone records and also with performances by three traditional musicians, notably Leo Rowsome on the uilleann pipes. On 16 April, the

Composers' Group arranged a visit to the Co. Wicklow home of one of their members, Ina Boyle, at Bushey Park, Enniskerry. My mother brought me along with her and the occasion made an impression upon me – a beautiful spring afternoon, the long driveway up to the period house, the concert in an elegant drawing-room and tea served afterwards. Ina Boyle had been a student of Vaughan Williams and retained connections with a number of English musicians. At that time considered to be rather on the fringe of Irish music, the significance of her compositional output has been better recognised in the 21st century.[1] Ina Boyle's friend of many years, the composer Elizabeth Maconchy was there and also the Macnaghten String Quartet, who performed the 4th String Quartet of Maconchy as well as *Fantasias* by Purcell, *Landscapes* by Bloch and Vaughan Williams' Quartet No. 2 in A minor.

During 1955 the Minutes record increasing co-operation between the MAI and Fóras Éireann (FÉ).[2] This body's principal object was: 'to assist and promote the social, cultural and economical development of rural Ireland in accordance with our national ways of life'. It was set up in 1949 as a permanent conference of voluntary organisations with a secretariat funded by the Carnegie UK Trust. It also acted as an agent for the administration of grants from the Carnegie Trust and the Charlotte F. Shaw Trust to a wide spectrum of Irish organisations. Its members included Conradh na Gaeilge, the Irish Country-Womens' Association, the Irish Farmers Association, the Amateur Drama Council of Ireland, the Royal Irish Academy of Music, Muíntir na Tíre, the Irish National Teachers Association and the People's College. There was a Council of ten members, elected at the AGM from candidates proposed by member organisations, and this Council appointed an executive committee with a chairman, secretary and treasurer. In addition there was a paid administrator. My mother and Edgar Deale attended a meeting held by FÉ in April 1955 at which a scheme for the appointment of Area Music Advisors, partially funded by the Carnegie Trust, was discussed. Following this meeting, FÉ set up a sub-committee to prepare a plan for rural music and considered that the MAI had expertise to contribute. It was decided in July that the MAI should become an affiliated organisation of FÉ, thereby contributing its knowledge of the state of music in rural Ireland, accumulated through the newly established system of Corporate Members. My mother, Brian Boydell and Edgar Deale were all appointed to this FÉ sub-committee and other members were co-opted including Aloys Fleischmann (Cork), Mrs Mercedes Bolger (Wexford), Charles Ryan (Kilkenny) and Arthur Healy (Galway) with John O'Sullivan acting as secretary. Mrs Esther Bishop was the link to the council of FÉ. The sub-committee met during the summer months, completing an important memorandum by the end of August, which was then submitted to the Carnegie Trustees for their consideration.

In the meantime, my mother was also busy with more concert plans. The first concerned a visit to Dublin by the distinguished American harpsichordist, Ralph Kirkpatrick. This is first mentioned in the Council Minutes of 8 March 1955, but I am not clear as to the exact provenance of the idea. Certainly RÉ was involved as they had recently purchased a double-manual Dolmetsch pedal harpsichord and offered Kirkpatrick two broadcasts. From the correspondence between my mother and the American Ambassador, William H. Taft, it is also clear that the Embassy was very much party to the arrangements, and indeed assisted financially. We knew the Ambassador's family socially because Maria Taft was in my class at school. Her father had been on the embassy staff from 1949, and then served as ambassador from 1953 – 57. This acquaintance helped to smooth the way in preparation for the eminent visitor. Grove's *Dictionary* states that Kirkpatrick, who had studied with Landowska and Boulanger in Paris, had all of Bach's output for harpsichord in his repertoire as well as a great many sonatas of Domenico Scarlatti. He was a musicologist as well as a performer and published what was recognised for many years as the definitive performing edition of sixty of Scarlatti's Sonatas. His Dublin concert on 10 September 1955 at the College of Physicians was recorded by RÉ and included the *Italian Concerto* and *Chromatic Fantasy* of J.S. Bach, pieces by Byrd, Sweelinck, Couperin and Rameau, and six Sonatas by Scarlatti. Kirkpatrick also broadcast a second programme from the RÉ studios during his visit. It is interesting to note that Raymond Russell travelled with Kirkpatrick on this visit to Dublin. The author of one of the standard books on the harpsichord, he was also the founder of the famous Russell Collection of period keyboard instruments, most of which were donated to the University of Edinburgh following his death. The MAI Council was understandably nervous at hosting such a prestigious concert and decided to ask each member to try to sell two tickets. In the event there was a large and enthusiastic audience, the Embassy were delighted and the MAI's reputation enhanced.

My mother's other project for 1955 concerned a return visit by the NLSQ, which involved two Dublin concerts and a more extensive Country Tour than the one in 1954. Knowing that she would spend time with the Quartet in Newcastle at the end of January 1955,[3] my mother brought the idea to the Council on 11 January and was given approval in principle to make preliminary enquiries. There were opportunities for some discussion during the Newcastle visit and the period from 19 October to 2 November was set aside. There was a 45-minute broadcast from RÉ in its Wednesday Recital Series on the 19th and then the tour began on 20th with my mother once again driving the big green station wagon. In the meantime, there had been a change in both the Quartet's name and personnel. Erich Gruenberg, later to become leader in turn of the Stockholm Philharmonic, the London Symphony and the Royal Philharmonic Orchestras, resigned in the spring of 1955 and was replaced by Canadian Frederick Grinke, professor of violin at the Royal Academy of Music (RAM), London. To mark this appointment the word 'New' was dropped from the Quartet's name and they were henceforth known as the London String Quartet (LSQ). On this tour[4] emphasis was placed on the four wonderful and historic instruments played by the group and this proved to be a point of very popular interest with the audiences. Fred played the Maurin Stradivarius (1718), Lionel an earlier Strad (1684), Keith had a Guadagnini viola (1757) and Douglas a Montagnana cello (1733). 'Quidnunc' of the *The Irish Times* wrote in his 'Irishman's Diary': 'Mrs Lyall Smith, of the Music Association, drives the station-wagon – a job which would turn my hair white, with such a precious cargo of artists and instruments aboard'. The towns visited were Mullingar, Sligo, Birr, Galway, Limerick, Tralee, Waterford, Kilkenny, Carlow and Wexford. In addition there were two evening concerts in Dublin – on 29th in the Provost's House for MAI members, and on 31st a public concert in the Hibernian Hotel. On the morning of 31st a concert for 400 schoolchildren was organised in the Metropolitan Hall by James Blanc of Ceol Chumann na nÓg. This body, founded in 1952, had excellent connections with the Dublin schools, as it organised the Schools' Concerts given by the RÉSO, but a chamber-music concert was a new venture. It turned out to be a great success, with Douglas making the introductions to the music from the stage. There were also schools' concerts in Mullingar (200 children) and Kilkenny. It was the first time for Mullingar to host a string quartet, but an old school-friend of my mother, Mrs Beryl Hutchinson, lived there and she helped to smooth the path with the arrangements. I remember that we went to lunch at her house overlooking Lough Owel so that my mother could meet the organisers. It was also a first time for Tralee, hosted by the local Gramophone Society. They were very pro-active with publicity and there are a number of lovely press photos in the MAI archive of the players surrounded by enthusiastic audience members. The promoter in Birr was Patrick Trench of Cloughjordan. He was pessimistic about attracting an audience at first, but gradually became more positive and offered lunch and a tour of Birr castle. In Galway there was an unexpected highlight for the quartet – they heard *sean-nós* singing for the first time at the party after their concert. The great Máire Ní Scolaí was the singer and I remember that when the quartet got back to Dublin they could talk of nothing but the haunting beauty and purity of her voice and her impeccable intonation. I also remember their Dublin recital very well, because of their performance of the *Voces Intimae* quartet by Sibelius. Being more used to Mozart and Haydn, I was quite astonished at the tonality, power and energy produced by the quartet in this masterpiece.

The year 1955 was the busiest for the MAI in the short time since its foundation, and it must have been increasingly difficult for the Hon.

Secretary and Hon. Treasurer to store all their paperwork at home. It was felt that an office in town would be a great help, so the Council was very supportive when my mother reported in October that a small back office belonging to the Feis Ceoil at 37 Molesworth St was available for a rent of twelve guineas per annum. The Council was able to announce to the AGM in January 1956 that this was now the official address of the MAI, though Council meetings continued to be held at Edgar Deale's office. Their report also contained the welcome news that during 1955 membership had increased substantially to about 330 members and that seventeen music societies had become Corporate Members. An initial meeting of these groups was organised on 19 January 1955, and from 1956 onwards representatives of these societies held their own annual meeting on the same evening as the AGM of the MAI, each submitting a report of their activities during the previous year.

1956

Two major musical centenaries were marked at Members' Meetings during 1956. On 19 March, the bicentenary of Mozart's birth was celebrated at a recital given in the College of Physicians by the Prieur Ensemble. This was a fine group of principal players from the RÉSO including Máire Larchet (viola), Maurice Meulien (cello) and Albert Solivérès (oboe) under the direction of the French flute player, André Prieur. On this occasion they were joined by violinist Jaroslav Vaneček for a programme that included the Oboe Quartet and two Flute Quartets by Mozart, as well as his String Trio and a duo for Violin and Viola. Vaneček, a remarkable Czech musician who settled in Ireland in the late 1940s, featured again in the recital on 7 July to mark the centenary of the death of Schumann. This was also at the College of Physicians, preceded by a short talk by Hans Waldemar Rosen. The noted Irish pianist Rhona Marshall, MAI Council member and professor of piano at the RIAM, contributed a group of piano pieces and joined Vaneček in the A minor Violin Sonata. The distinguished singer, Flora Nielsen, sang the *Frauenliebe und Leben* cycle and some other songs, accompanied by Kitty O'Callaghan. This recital was sponsored jointly by the MAI and the Irish German Society.

Midway between these two recitals, on 13 May 1956, a large party of 125 MAI members set off on a special train to hear the Vienna Philharmonic Orchestra play at the Savoy Cinema in Cork. It had not been possible to arrange a concert in Dublin as the Theatre Royal was unavailable, so the prospect of hearing them in Cork instead was very exciting. Mairtín McCullough took charge of all arrangements which included high tea on the train at 5.30 p.m., a bus transfer in Cork, a ticket for the concert, a 3-course supper on the return journey and projected arrival at Kingsbridge at 2.10 a.m. – all this for 63 shillings (3 guineas). There is an interesting and humorous description in the MAI archive, written by none other than Michael Yeats, later Senator, son of W.B. Yeats.[5] 'Long before the concert was over we realised that we had been brought by the MAI to one of the great Irish musical occasions of our time . . . we were left almost breathless with excitement . . . Mairtín McCullough deserves the thanks and congratulations not merely of the MAI but of the Dublin musical public at large'. Of course my mother was one of the participants and was totally delighted with the whole experience.

She was involved on the periphery of the next Members' Meeting on 5 September, chiefly because Ambassador Taft and the American Embassy lent their support, both organisational and financial. The event was an illustrated talk by the American composer Henry Cowell, organised by the Composers' Group of the MAI, and held in the Organ Room of the RIAM. Cowell was at the forefront of experimentation with 'prepared piano' techniques and he demonstrated some of these. At the end of his talk he showed me how to hold down a chord and simultaneously stroke the strings of the grand piano, creating a harp-like effect. Needless to say, I was charmed!

My mother's main concern in the autumn of 1956 was another project involving Douglas Cameron. He had formed an all-female string orchestra, with himself as conductor, and was very keen to bring them to Ireland. Logistically this was of a different order to the preceding string quartet tours. The Douglas Cameron String Orchestra comprised sixteen players and the conductor, plus all the instruments and luggage. But to someone with years of experience of taking Girl Guides on camping trips perhaps it was not all that daunting! The first breakthrough was my father's brilliant suggestion that the small bus belonging to his friend Harold Johnson could solve the trickiest part of the transportation problem, and that he (my father) would be prepared to drive it. Harold Johnson's son Roger told me that this vehicle was a green Ford V8 former Post Office van, converted by Harold into a holiday bus for his own family and groups of young Quakers. It had windows, seated eight or nine comfortably and had a roof-rack with a canvas cover. Our station-wagon was driven by my mother and Mairtín McCullough very kindly drove his car. Initially there was disappointment that some of the usual centres felt they could not accommodate an orchestra, but plans went ahead with Waterford, Cork, Tralee, Clongowes College and Birr. I was amazed to discover that the group were able to travel by train from Paddington to Fishguard and then by the British Rail steamer *Great Western* direct to Waterford, mooring at the city centre quay just a few yards across the road from the Adelphi Hotel where they stayed. The entire fare for the whole group was £66.7s.6d.[6]

Mozart was well-represented in the repertoire for the tour, including the Piano Concerto in E flat, K.449, played by Jean Harvey who also doubled up as one of the violinists. There were works by Sibelius and Dag Wirén, and Seóirse Bodley's *Music for Strings*, written just four years earlier. Douglas had been insistent that a contemporary Irish composer should be included. Seóirse met the orchestra in Waterford on 2 October and attended the concert. The next day the bus and two cars departed for Cork, stopping to visit the Waterford Glass factory on the way. The review for the Cork concert on 3 October, held in the City Hall, was very positive: 'a programme that gladdened the hundreds of real music lovers who flocked to hear, to be charmed and to applaud, for it is not often that the true beauty of a string ensemble is so displayed'. The only disappointment was that the children's concert next morning had to be cancelled because of the serious polio outbreak in Cork at that time. It was decided to travel to Killarney via Glengarriff, complete with picnics, and to spend the night of

4 October at the Lake Hotel, where the players relaxed with boating, riding, walking (and some practice!). At Tralee on 5 October there was an audience of over 300 'spellbound by the artistry of the performers'. Apparently there was a good party afterwards, at which some of the players gave impromptu performances. A long journey followed the next day, with a lunch-stop at Limerick, arriving at Clongowes College, Co. Kildare in time for a meal before the concert, which was greeted with great enthusiasm by the boys and a few outside visitors. A late-night journey brought everyone to Dublin where hosts and hostesses were waiting to whisk tired players off to comfortable beds. One player reported that she was given breakfast-in-bed the next morning! It was awkward but unavoidable that the Birr concert on 7 October involved a re-tracing of steps, but it was worthwhile for the visit to Birr Castle and the review: 'So spontaneous and prolonged was the applause . . . an audience avid for more of the glorious, warm-toned music which had held it enthralled for close on two hours' – an encore was given!

This orchestra tour was the first for which the MAI had funding from the Shaw Trust, as a result of their recent affiliation to FÉ. This amounted to a guarantee against loss of £35 for each local promoter. In addition, the Arts Council gave a grant of up to £200 towards the travel costs. The remaining days were spent in Dublin, with an evening concert for MAI members and friends on 8 October, which experimented with a brand new venue, the Philips Hall in Clonskeagh. This hall, which seated about 400, was actively promoted by the Philips Company as: 'well-lit and appointed . . . a delightful place for chamber music'.[7] As it turned out there was always disagreement about its acoustics, some musicians judging it to be too dry. I should also mention that the Shaw Trust could not fund the Dublin concert directly, but bought 120 seats which they allocated to visually impaired people through the Council for the Blind.

On the morning of 9 October, at the Metropolitan Hall, a children's concert was organised by Ceol Chumann na nÓg and with Douglas making his delightful introductions to the huge audience of 1200, it was another big success. The remainder of the day was spent at the Phoenix Hall where the orchestra recorded a 45-minute programme for future transmission and gave a live 60-minute broadcast during the evening. On 10 October the entire day was free for sightseeing and shopping in Dublin and all departed from Dún Laoghaire on the evening boat. The archive file contains a number of lovely thank-you letters to my mother and a hand-written diary of the tour by one of the players, unfortunately anonymous. This lady went in for eloquent descriptions of the scenery and the Irish friendliness she encountered everywhere. She mentions my father: 'who drove the bus nearly 600 miles, constantly clambering up and down from the roof with our luggage – he will certainly never want to lift another cello or double-bass in his life again'. Also my mother: 'Mrs Smith was the prime mover and organiser and arranger of the tour (and what an organiser!) as well as chauffeuse, general hostess, comforter and encourager'. I think that for my parents one of the bonuses was getting to know Douglas's wife, the cellist Lilly Phillips, a wonderful character and a very fine musician, who also became a much-loved friend of our family. Another member of the group was viola-player Ruth David who came to live and work in Ireland in the 1970s as the partner of John Beckett. Finally I should mention the one Irish member of the orchestra, violinist Mary O'Brien, who will be an important figure in the next chapter.

Regarding the project to appoint Area Music Advisors, a joint initiative of the MAI and FÉ, considerable progress was reported by the end of 1956. The MAI sub-committee of Brian Boydell, Edgar Deale, John O'Sullivan and my mother had committed a great deal of time to this work, so there was considerable relief and satisfaction when it was decided to appoint, in the first instance, a National Music Organiser supported by funding from the Carnegie Trust and the Mayer Foundation. The closing date for applications was 8 December 1956. It was decided that either Sir Robert or Lady Mayer would sit on the interview board, together with Brian Boydell. It is clear from the job specification for the post that the initial priority for the Organiser would be an in-depth survey of the state of music in the country. It was noted that outside the larger centres there were very few competent teachers of instrumental music and choral singing to be found. The Organiser's task was to make personal contact with educational bodies, with music societies, teachers and music enthusiasts, with the aim of completing the survey within a year. After that the Organiser was expected to make recommendations, and during the second and subsequent years to begin more detailed activities, such as the formation of new music-making groups. Music appreciation classes would be encouraged and a much expanded range of live music performances, made possible by grants from the Shaw Trust or the Arts Council. It was envisaged that the Organiser would be someone with enthusiasm and a thorough approach to the work. The salary was £1,000 per annum, including expenses, for a period of up to five years.

The choice of Joseph Groocock for this position was a very good one. With more than twenty years of experience as music master at St Columba's College and a fine reputation as a choral conductor, Joe radiated his love of music. His enthusiasm and conviction that music should be enjoyed by everyone were boundless. Many generations of students would attest to this – to me, personally, he was the soul of kindness, encouraging myself and his eldest daughter and son, Stephanie and Richard, to play simple pieces of chamber-music, even writing something for us to while away a wet afternoon at their house at Tibradden, Co. Dublin. He published his completed work for FÉ as a book *A General Survey of Music in the Republic of Ireland* in 1961.

[1] See *Ina Boyle – A Composer's Life* (Cork University Press, 2018).

[2] NLI – ACC 6000, box 8.

[3] The NLSQ performed all the Beethoven String Quartets at Newcastle-upon-Tyne from 24 – 29 January 1955.

[4] Ibid. box 14, green file, for details of this tour.

[5] Ibid. box 19, pink file 1.

[6] Ibid. box 19, beige file 6, for details of this tour.

[7] Ibid. box 5, folder of correspondence.

CHAPTER 14

The MAI – Coming-Out recitals and other events – 1957 and 1958

The following is a minute from the Council meeting held on 7 November 1956: 'It was generally agreed that the MAI should try the experiment of sponsoring recitals by young soloists, since the Schools of Music did not appear to provide such opportunities. It was agreed that a series, rather than one isolated recital was essential. The possibility of having a joint recital, shared by two performers was suggested – especially in the case of a singer. It was agreed that a recital should be organised for Mary O'Brien, as the first of the series. The following sub-committee was appointed to pursue this matter: Mrs Clotworthy, Mr McCullough and the Hon. Treasurer.'

1957

My mother had already suggested, at the Council meeting on 15 October 1956, that Mary O'Brien might give a short violin recital following the AGM due to be held on 15 January 1957. As mentioned in Chapter 12, Mary was a member of Douglas Cameron's orchestra (whose tour had finished on 9 October) and I suspect that Douglas had yet again sown the seed of a good idea in my mother's mind. Douglas became aware of Mary's talent during her short period of study at the RAM under David Martin, following five years at the Paris Conservatoire where she was awarded the Premier Prix. Her teacher in Dublin was the renowned

Michael McNamara at the Municipal School of Music, where her father Joseph O'Brien was the Director.

As it turned out, the AGM was brought forward to 5.45 p.m., and the full-length Coming-Out recital was held at 8.00 p.m. It was a great success, with an attendance of about 350. The *Evening Mail* of 16 January reported: 'It was "standing-room only" in the Hibernian Hotel last night for the first of a series of Coming-Out recitals, sponsored by the MAI for young Irish musicians who have not yet been launched before the public. This new facet of the society's work is very laudable and it is encouraging to be able to report that it received excellent support'. Other Dublin papers were equally appreciative and all published critiques. For the debutant musician these reviews were an important asset, providing quotes that could be used in publicity material and in efforts to secure future engagements. At that time each Dublin paper had a music critic whose column appeared at least several times a week.

Mary was partnered in the recital by the distinguished accompanist, Kitty O'Callaghan, and her programme included the Brahms D minor sonata and Ravel's *Tzigane*. For me, her playing of the 3rd Sonata for Unaccompanied Violin by Ysaÿe was particularly memorable. Interviewed in 2016,[1] Mary's assessment was that the concert was: 'a big event, a big challenge, and gave me great confidence'. The second young musician to give her debut recital was the pianist Florence Ryan, on 30 April 1957, with a programme that included major works by Mozart, Mendelssohn, Ravel and Chopin. The third was on 14 October 1957 when violinist Margaret Hayes, again with Kitty O'Callaghan, played music by Mozart, Bach, de Falla and Glazounov. An important template for the future had been established. In one of the articles in her 'History of the MAI' series, in *Counterpoint* in November 1978, a full 21 years after the series was inaugurated, my mother commented that the names of the artists who participated:

read like a successful impresario's list. Some of them have achieved international acclaim, some are working in London or elsewhere abroad. Very many are living and working in Ireland as soloists and in chamber music groups, in orchestras and as teachers, and

128

are contributing in an important and vital way to the musical life of the country.

The full list makes fascinating reading and can be perused in Appendix 4.

From the point of view of the young performer, these MAI Coming-Out recitals were invaluable. All the expenses – hire of the ballroom in the Hibernian Hotel, hire of the piano, printing and publicity costs – and all the organisational details, such as seeking press 'write-ups' prior to the concert, were paid for by the MAI and looked after by the special sub-committee. A good attendance by MAI members was almost guaranteed and the recitalist had peace of mind to concentrate on their practice and preparation for this most important event in their career. Having been the prime motivator during the initial series, my mother reverted to a supporting role in the second year and her place on the sub-committee was taken by Fr Oliver O'Brien. As Mary O'Brien's brother, he became interested in the work of the MAI at the time of her recital, and was elected to the Council at the AGM in early 1958.

Mary was the first recitalist to benefit from another opportunity devised by my mother as a follow-up to the Coming-Out concert, namely the chance to participate in an MAI Country Tour. In October 1957 she joined the South African tenor, Lloyd Strauss-Smith, for a tour which visited Tralee, Cork, Kilkenny, Nenagh and Limerick. Mary Lees played for Strauss-Smith and Mary O'Brien was accompanied by Ivy Kevelighan (of the Culwick and Guide Choirs). Their partnership received warm reviews in Cork: 'a thorough understanding of the music, work of outstanding merit'; and Kilkenny: 'Miss Kevelighan nearly stole the show!' It is interesting to read in the MAI Corporate Members report for 1957 that this tour was largely arranged by Dr Maureen Carmody of Nenagh (mother of David Carmody, later principal horn in the RTÉCO), who: 'took the artistes around in her own car and gave them hospitality for a considerable part of the tour'. My mother had a very high regard for Dr Carmody who, almost single-handedly, promoted the cause of classical music in her part of Co. Tipperary. Another venture for the younger generation, with MAI support, was the concert organised by Mairtín McCullough under the auspices of the 1957 Wexford Festival at which the performers were Mary O'Brien, Florence Ryan, Maeve Broderick (violin) and Fergus O'Kelly (tenor) with accompanist Kitty O'Callaghan.

The year 1957 was very active for the MAI, so my mother was delighted when her workload was considerably lightened by the appointment of Alan Cowle as Assistant Treasurer. Alan came from a very musical family – his father was the highly-regarded singing teacher, Frank Cowle, and his aunts Helen and May sang in my mother's Olivian Singers; Alan himself was an organist. The year began with a return visit from the singer Flora Nielsen who, with Kitty O'Callaghan, gave well-received lecture recitals entitled 'The Charm of Song' in January, visiting Limerick, Nenagh, Galway and Gorey. Miss Nielsen was a frequent visitor to Ireland, having taught at the Summer Schools for a number of years, given recitals at the RDS and taken part in the MAI's Schumann commemoration in 1956. Her choice of songs for these lectures embraced Schubert, French song (Fauré, Duparc) and Folk Songs. The correspondent from Limerick described her as: 'a delightful artiste and a very charming person'[2] and my mother noted that she was very accommodating regarding travel, electing to come by boat and train for fear of fog and also to save costs. There were young people at the recital in Gorey and Mrs Bolger wrote to my mother:[3] 'Miss Nielsen said she was delighted to see how intently the children listened, both to the music and to her explanations.' P.D., the very enthusiastic reviewer for the local Gorey paper wrote: 'She could let a phrase fade almost to a whisper and still have it clear and distinct, and carried her audience in imagination through a variety of scene and situation, grave and gay, hopeful, tender and sprightly.' These recitals must have been a marvellous experience.

On 22 February the Quarterly Members' Meeting at the Philips Hall was a lieder recital by the renowned German baritone, Gerard Hüsch, with pianist Geoffrey Parsons. Hüsch had given memorable recitals at the RDS on 6 February 1956, singing the *Dichterliebe* song-cycle of Schumann in the afternoon and Schubert's *Winterreise* in the evening. Not surprisingly, a return visit was proposed almost immediately, to be funded jointly by the MAI, RÉ and the German Legation in Dublin. A considerable delay in obtaining a commitment from the Legation is recorded in the Minutes, but this was resolved in time. I am amused by an instruction to my mother (minutes of 6 September 1956) that she was to: 'try to arrange that the recital did not consist entirely of songs by Hugo Wolf'! In the event, Hüsch presented a most interesting programme of Wolf and the Finnish composer Henrik Kilpinen. In his *Irish Times* review, Charles Acton wrote: 'Among all its activities, the MAI continually provides us with programmes of a quality of musical interest that no commercial management would dare to put on. Gerard Hüsch and Geoffrey Parsons gave an entirely new and marvellous significance to all these songs'.[4] There was much public interest in the recital, 40 new members joined the MAI as a result, and my mother was congratulated at the March meeting of the Council for her organisation of the event.

The Summer Quarterly Meeting was held on 1 June at Carton House, Co. Kildare, by kind invitation of its occupant, the Hon. Desmond Guinness (the owner was actually Lord Brocket). This was a special event as the MAI members and guests were given the opportunity to view the house and grounds, in addition to a recital by the New Dublin Quartet who were joined by the singer Cáit Lanigan, Peter Schwarz (recorder) and John O'Sullivan, playing the charming chamber organ in the Carton Music Saloon. This group performed music by Telemann and Purcell and there were string quartets by Haydn and Beethoven. The Quartet players were Max Thöner (who was my violin teacher at the RIAM), Jan Magna-Bobak, Archie Collins and Erich Eisenbrandt – all members of the RÉSO. This group also undertook a Country Tour during 1957, visiting Clongowes, Cork, Galway, Gorey and Nenagh. They played works by Haydn, Beethoven and Dvořák, but unfortunately the audiences were reportedly small, though any losses were offset by a grant from the Shaw Trust.

At the meeting on 7 November 1956, the Council had been informed of the MAI's election to represent Ireland on the International Music

Council of UNESCO. This was felt to be a great honour, but it carried with it a requirement to pay an annual subscription of 100 dollars, the amount for 1956 being due before the end of the year. This was a considerable sum and the Council took the view that official help should be forthcoming. Approaches during 1957 to the Departments of External Affairs and Education were unsuccessful, so in July it was decided to have a fund-raising concert in the autumn which Brian Boydell offered to organise. With the fascinating title 'Music in Dublin – 1597 to 1957' it took place in the College of Physicians on 21 October, but disappointingly raised just under £10 of the £35 needed, leaving the MAI to pay the balance of the UNESCO subscription out of its own funds. Brian Boydell, on behalf of the Council, persevered in maintaining the MAI's position with the International Music Council during most of 1958, but in October it was decided, following consultation with RÉ, that the MAI was not getting value for the subscription paid and should withdraw from membership.

A number of other matters of significance concerned the Council during 1957. Firstly, the MAI's sub-committee on education, led by Mrs Rhona Marshall and Dr Archie Potter, received 34 replies to a questionnaire sent out to members. From these a memorandum on the state of music education in Ireland was drawn up and sent to the Council for Education. Secondly, RÉ was approached with specific points regarding the employment of Irish and foreign nationals in the RÉSO, namely: 1) the statement by the Minister in December 1953 that all suitable Irish applicants for positions in the RÉSO would be accepted; 2) the large number of Irish permanent deputies; 3) the suspected existence of special contracts between RÉ and some of the foreign members of the orchestra; 4) one or two cases of excellent Irish musicians who had been unable to gain permanent positions. And thirdly, the Council offered continuing support, both written and verbal, to Aloys Fleischmann's campaign to secure the transfer of one of the RÉ orchestras to Cork. This last matter had a rewarding outcome as acknowledged in Prof. Fleischmann's letter to the MAI in early December, thanking them for their representations to the Radio Council, which had resulted in the agreement of RÉ to establish a String Quartet in Cork.

For my mother also, the year ended on a positive note with a Country Tour by the Amici String Quartet in December. This was a relatively new group, led by Lionel Bentley who had been in the LSQ up to 1955. The other members were Marta Eitler (violin), Harold Harriott (viola) and Joy Hall (cello). Their visit began with two RDS recitals on 9 December and then my mother was on the road again, driving them to Gorey, Kilkenny (an audience of 100), Birr and Waterford. A most enthusiastic report was written by Mrs Bolger of Gorey, where there was an audience of 200: 'From start to finish the audience and players seemed to be friends and it was difficult to know whether the players or the audience enjoyed the evening most. The short explanations given by Harold Harriott were much appreciated and added to the easy friendly atmosphere. It is difficult to express the value of these recitals in Gorey, and on each occasion there were people present from Wexford, Enniscorthy and Arklow'.

1958

The year 1958 began with some significant changes in the MAI administration. John O'Sullivan tendered his resignation as Hon. Secretary in early January, having been absent at times during the previous two years. Nonetheless, he had contributed greatly to the Association's work. As has been said before, he was a very fine musician and his gently humorous and self-deprecating personality would be missed. It was decided that my mother and Mairtín McCullough would become Joint Hon. Secretaries, whilst my mother remained as Hon. Treasurer with Alan Cowle as Assistant. Edgar Deale had been appointed Chairman in 1957 and was re-elected to this role for 1958. The arrangement regarding Mairtín McCullough pleased my mother. She had a very high regard for him as a business man, they had already worked together on a number of projects, and she was also very fond of his wife Mary. The admiration was mutual – interviewed in 2003, Mairtín referred to my mother's business acumen as extraordinary and her organisation of concerts as both practical and sensible, meticulous in every detail.[5] He also described her as having immense moral courage. As 1957 came to a close, she was thinking ahead about the MAI's finances and the running of the Office. The Council agreed to her proposal that the members' subscriptions should be raised to £1 (students 10 shillings). There were currently 450 members and the workload was getting too heavy for the Honorary Officers, so it was also decided that a part-time paid secretary should be sought and Mrs A. N. Pellew was appointed in January 1958.

At the close of the AGM on 29 January 1958, a rather touching tribute was paid to my mother. To quote from the AGM minutes: 'The Chairman then asked Mr Boydell to speak on behalf of the Council to the meeting. Mr Boydell disclosed that it was the wish of the Council to make a presentation to the Hon. Treasurer, Mrs Lyall Smith, in recognition of the excellent work she had done for years in organising tours and members' recitals. Mr McCullough supported this and the Chairman suitably endorsed what had been said, then making the presentation amid scenes of enthusiasm'. The gift was, in fact, a record token.

As regards concerts, a Coming-Out recital by Julian Dawson (piano) and Hazel Morris (contralto) followed the AGM. The MAI Lunchtime Concerts at the GMB in Trinity College were resumed in February, this time with a focus on the music of Haydn. Organised jointly by Alan Cowle and David Lee, they were supported by a guarantee of £2 per concert by the Council. On 3 March, the Quarterly Meeting concert at the Royal College of Physicians was given by Jaroslav Vaneček and Margaret Hayes (violins), with Rhona Marshall (piano), in an interesting programme that included works for two violins by Martinů and Scriabin. The Council was already looking ahead to two major projects – the staging of a production of Benjamin Britten's *Let's Make an Opera* just after Christmas in 1958 and the marking of the bicentenary of Handel's death in 1959. Sub-committees to deal with both projects were set up with, of course, funding being the major concern.

But there is no doubt that the project which was exercising my mother most in those first few months of 1958 was the impending visit to Ireland of the National Youth Orchestra of Great Britain.

1 Interviewed by the author, 15 August 2016.

2 NLI – ACC 6000, box 46, beige file 1.

3 Letter from Mrs Mercedes Bolger, 26 January 1957.

4 *The Irish Times*, 23 February 1957.

5 Interviewed by Pat O'Kelly, 3 February 2003. Proprietor of McCullough's Music Shop, Dawson St, and later McCullough/Pigott's on Suffolk St, Mairtín McCullough was a very active member of the MAI Council for about thirty years, willingly undertaking a number of different roles and always very supportive of the work of the Association.

CHAPTER 15

The Visit of the National Youth Orchestra of Great Britain – 1958

Apart from the setbacks involved in the search for a site for the Concert Hall, no other project in the 1950s caused my mother as much frustration as the visit to Ireland of the National Youth Orchestra of Great Britain (NYOGB) in April 1958. Yet paradoxically it was a stimulating and highly significant event for her, sowing seeds that would bear fruit some twelve years later with the foundation of the Irish Youth Orchestra.

My mother had heard about the NYOGB from Douglas Cameron and Keith Cummings, both of whom were orchestral tutors for their respective instruments. She first mentioned a possible visit by the Orchestra to Ireland at the MAI Council meeting on 8 February 1955 (just a couple of months after the first Irish tour by Douglas Cameron's quartet) and received support for her suggestion of a concert in the spring of 1956. But the minutes of 5 April 1955 record that this would have to be deferred due to a visit of the BBC Symphony Orchestra to Dublin around the same time. However, I am intrigued to have found a letter to my mother from Aloys Fleischmann amongst the MAI archives, dated 14 March 1955, in which he says that he is delighted to hear that the NYOGB will be visiting Dublin in 1956 and that he hopes Cork will be included in the visit, especially as it was he who 'started that ball rolling' in 1954!

My mother heard the orchestra 'live' for the first time in April 1956 when, during a visit to London, we attended their Royal Festival Hall concert. It created a huge impression for both of us; in my case particularly as it was the first time I had heard Brahms' 4th Symphony, and I was also captivated by the brilliant playing of the cello soloist, Rohan de Saram. The conductor was Jean Martinon. Apparently she lost no time in renewing the invitation to Dublin as the Director, Miss Ruth Railton, wrote on 3rd May 1956 to explain that their plans for 1957 were already in place, being the Orchestra's 10th anniversary, but that they would love to come in 1958. A further letter from Aloys, dated 24 June 1956,[1] explains that he has been talking to Ruth Railton on the phone and that the NYOGB would gladly consider doing the course in Dublin with concerts in Dublin and Cork. He wonders if my mother could find accommodation in a hostel or school that would be available during the Easter holidays, though there could be a difficulty if the dates of the English and Irish holiday periods did not coincide. He further states that: 'they would apparently be prepared to pay all the expenses involved' and suggests that my mother should go to see Ruth Railton during a visit to London in July. There are no records to suggest that my mother did this, but she informed the Council meeting on 24 July of the plans as outlined by Aloys, of the possibility of a concert in the Theatre Royal and of the need to find suitable accommodation. The Council approved my mother's suggestion that the course could be held under the auspices of the MAI, and she undertook to make some preliminary enquiries in September.

In February 1957 Miss Railton came to Dublin and had a meeting with my mother, at which plans to hold the week-long training course and rehearsals in Dublin were discussed. The best date for the concert was 19 April 1958 and my mother agreed to approach the Theatre Royal. She was also given the size of the orchestra, the number of sectional rehearsal rooms needed, the minimum dimensions required for the large rehearsal room, plus a rough outline of accommodation and transportation requirements. There was talk of a second concert in Cork and a final one in Liverpool. The Theatre Royal had a provisional booking for the Leipzig Gewandhaus Orchestra on 19 April, but fortunately they decided to postpone and the date was confirmed for the NYOGB. My mother reported on her negotiations at the Council meeting on 5 March, stressing that the chief problem would be one of accommodation, and received offers of help from Council members in contacting suitable schools. No further mention occurs in the Council minutes until 27 January 1958 but it is clear from the correspondence in the MAI archive that plans were not proceding smoothly.

It appears that from the outset the NYOGB stipulated that the cost of a week's accommodation should be no more than 5 guineas per person, stretching to an absolute upper limit of £6 should the lower figure prove impracticable. As it was not going to be possible to make use of a boarding school, owing to the discrepancy between the dates of the Easter school holidays in Ireland and England, my mother began to look at hotels, enlisting the assistance of Bord Fáilte, but finding that very few were interested at less than 7 guineas. These searches continued over the months from March to September and on 30 September Miss Railton came to Dublin, held some auditions, and visited hotels in Bray and Greystones with my mother. There was one in Greystones that was felt to be the best option, though there were some doubts concerning the availability of the ballroom for the full orchestra rehearsals. In a letter of 3 October, Miss Railton raised the possibility of holding the course in Cork, or alternatively in Belfast or Liverpool.

The archived correspondence is very incomplete, but it seems that by November my mother had put together another proposal and hoped that Miss Railton would have time to come to Dublin before she left for a trip to South Africa. As this proved impossible, Miss Diana Scholefield, the NYOGB secretary, came instead but was unable to reach a decision as the hall had problematic pillars. The situation remained unresolved, awaiting a visit from Miss Railton on Monday 3 February 1958. I can imagine that this delay, given the commencing date of the course was only 10 weeks away, must have been almost intolerable for my mother, who liked to have everything in place in good time, especially for such a high-profile undertaking. On 3 February she took Miss Railton to view the hall of the Dominican Convent in Dun Laoghaire and the accommodation at the Killiney Court Hotel, already provisionally booked. Miss Railton was unhappy at the number of bus transfers involved, the consequent loss of rehearsal time and increase in transport costs. During the course of the day it appears that Miss Railton told my mother of her visit to Cork two days previously, where the organisers could provide accommodation, rehearsal rooms and the concert venue, all within walking distance. Though the charge for accommodation would be £9 per person, there would be savings on transport.

My mother digested this information overnight and on 4 February sent a bitterly angry letter to Miss Railton, pointing out that she could have obtained completely satisfactory accommodation months earlier in Bray, including a huge ballroom for rehearsals, had she been allowed to settle a deal at 7 guineas! She did agree that Cork might be the best option from a transport point of view, but was obviously totally affronted that the accommodation cost might be £9 or 9 guineas. She was also very anxious that there should be no impression given that accommodation was unavailable in Dublin and stated that the MAI Council would be very disappointed that months of negotiation had come to nothing. The odd thing is that the Minutes for the months April to December 1957 record nothing of her struggles, the entry for 27 January 1958 merely recording that the NYOGB concert date in Dublin would be 19 April in the Theatre Royal with Jean Martinon conducting. The prospect of failure to secure the course for Dublin, in spite of her acknowledged negotiating skills, must have been a hard blow and the wasted hours of precious time rankled deeply.

Miss Railton's response of 5 February stated that she was very surprised at my mother's 'very unhappy and hurt letter', maintaining that a final decision still had to be taken in consultation with the NYOGB Treasurer, stressing that transport costs were a major issue, and that the complicating factor of Belfast was still unresolved. She thanked my mother several times for all her work over a period of years and recognised her aspiration that a visit by the NYOGB would offer great stimulation and encouragement to young Irish musicians, whether in Dublin or Cork. Nonetheless the decision went in favour of Cork, this being communicated to my mother by Aloys Fleischmann in a letter dated 11 February. As I was lucky enough to play in the Orchestra, in the very back desk of the second violins, I know that we stayed in the Imperial Hotel, that the sectional rehearsals were held in the Cork School of Music and that the final full rehearsals were on the stage of the City Hall, which was also the venue for the concert on 17 April. These are indeed all situated within easy walking distance.

The programme was the *Oberon* overture by Weber, Mozart's Violin Concerto in A major with soloist Sidney Mann, the *Fair Day* movement from Hamilton Harty's *Irish* Symphony, Borodin's 2nd Symphony and *Capriccio Espagnol* by Rimsky-Korsakov. I had only played before in the RIAM student orchestra (strings plus an oboe and a horn), so the sheer excitement of the full orchestra sound was overwhelming, and I felt almost literally blown away by the brass and percussion sections! There were a number of other Irish players – Maeve Broderick and Sheila O'Grady (Dublin) and Olivia Cafolla (Derry) in the first violins, and James Beck (Dundonald) in the horn section. Another horn player was Tom Briggs who later settled in Dublin as a member of the RÉSO. My delightfully comical desk partner was Michael Vyner from Leeds who, in later life, became Artistic Director (1973-1989) of the London Sinfonietta. I was also reassured by the familiar and kindly presence of Douglas Cameron, who was coaching the cellos. Following a most successful concert in Cork the Orchestra travelled to Dublin by train on 18th and then visited the Zoo, where lunch was arranged. Accommodation on 18 April was at two hotels on the Quays, the Ormonde and the Four Courts. A morning rehearsal in the Theatre Royal on 19th was followed by the concert in the afternoon, a meal at Clery's Restaurant hosted by the British Ambassador and Lady Clutterbuck, and then an overnight sailing from Dublin to Liverpool, where the final afternoon concert took place on Sunday 20th.

In picking up the pieces from the disappointment over Cork, the MAI Council determined to make the visit of the NYOGB to Dublin a memorable one, inviting distinguished guests such as the President of Ireland, the two Archbishops and the British Ambassador. Members of the MAI were offered priority booking and there was a good build-up of press coverage before the concert. My parents travelled down for the Cork concert and, to my surprise, I learned from them that a problem was brewing over the National Anthem. It was customary at that time for orchestral concerts, operas, ballets and plays to be preceded by the playing of the Anthem and the Theatre Royal had a set of parts of the arrangement by Dr John F. Larchet, for use by visiting orchestras. These had been collected by Diana Scholefield on her way to Cork and indeed I can recollect the Orchestra rehearsing the Anthem there, because I had never played it before.

The dispute arose, apparently, because Miss Railton and the NYOGB administration were expecting to play both the British and Irish anthems, but it was explained to them in Cork that there might be objections if the Orchestra played 'God save the Queen' in the City Hall, so they decided not to play either. In a newspaper interview, Diana Scholefield is reported as saying: 'We were told that there would be a row if we played the British Anthem. We were advised by the Music Association of Ireland not to play it. We would play both or neither'. In the same newspaper, Mr Anderson of the British Embassy commented: 'The orchestra's visit was not an official one in any way . . . He had been contacted and had told the orchestra that the proper thing to do was to play the Irish National Anthem, and that it was not in accordance with the customary procedure to play the British Anthem'. The same diplomatic protocol was later confirmed to Aloys Fleischmann in a letter (28 April 1958) from Miss Mary Tinney of the Department of Foreign Affairs, in which she clarified that the foreign anthem should be played only if the occasion is an official visit, and would not be appropriate for this visit of the NYOGB.

My mother was extremely upset that the Orchestra's visit, which had been successful up till then, looked like ending in a diplomatic incident. She could see that although there were people who would be upset if the British Anthem were played, there would be many times more who would be outraged if the Irish Anthem was not played. She certainly explained this to Miss Railton, but it had little effect as she was told that Miss Railton had telephoned Mr de Valera and that he had said he did not mind! So unfortunately, in the immediate aftermath of the two concerts, there were adverse press comments, and my mother did not help matters by saying that the Anthem was omitted because there were not enough orchestral parts! I can only suppose that this slip was occasioned by the stress of the whole situation. She did receive a well-worded personal letter of apology from Mr John Newsom, Vice-Chairman of the Executive Committee of the NYOGB, who had been present at the Theatre Royal and, it would seem, had understood the advice of the Ambassador. He also expresses his 'very great gratitude' for all that my mother did to make the concert a success.[2]

Fortunately, the Orchestra's playing was so outstandingly good that the reviews were uniformly complimentary. John O'Donovan of the *Evening Press* wrote: 'Here is no bunch of teenagers claiming our indulgence while they try to chew more than they should have been let bite off; but a body of proficient players who in some respects could give the RÉ Orchestra points. They did an excellent job on Borodin's 2nd Symphony, turned out the best reading of Harty's *Fair Day* scherzo I've ever heard, and as for the *Capriccio Espagnol*...! Oh, but it did my heart good to hear them blaze away in this showpiece of showpieces'.[3]

As far as Cork was concerned, there was an immediate follow-up to the NYOGB's visit with the establishment, in April 1958, of the Cork Youth Orchestra under the baton of Michael O'Callaghan, which was achieved with the wonderful support of the Cork Soroptomist Club. This group was Ireland's first Youth Orchestra. In 1970, some twelve years later, my mother went on to found the National Youth Orchestra of Ireland.

[1] NLI – ACC 6000, box 19, beige file 6.

[2] Ibid. box 19, beige file 4 – contains the relevant documents for this chapter.

[3] *Evening Press*, 21 April 1958.

CHAPTER 16

Family Life in the 1950s

Of all the houses my mother lived in, I believe that she loved Rockview the most – I have already referred to it at the end of Chapter 5. A spacious bungalow with a south-facing verandah, it was set in almost two acres of garden which included an orchard, a vegetable garden, a copse of larch trees, a natural rockery with a pond, and extensive lawns. Even though a gardener came several days a week my parents, being practical people, liked to be involved too, especially with the produce of the vegetable garden and the orchard. My mother knew how to preserve plums, raspberries and green beans in glass Kilner jars, whilst my father was in charge of storing the apples on special trays so that they would last right through the winter.

Rockview was the backdrop to the MAI's activities in the early 1950s – this being the Treasurer's address prior to the setting-up of the Office at 37 Molesworth St – and I was quite intrigued with the comings-and-goings of well-known musicians. These included not only string quartet members from England but many local musicians as well. Shortly before we moved to Rockview my mother sold her upright piano and bought a Bechstein boudoir grand with a most beautiful rosewood case. It came from Kilkenny and I understood that its previous home had been Kilkenny Castle. It was her pride and joy, though personally I always found its action a bit stiff and difficult to control – perhaps it had been in a damp room in the Castle. This was the piano used by Charles Lynch for the Bax Quintet rehearsals, and also by members of the MAI Chamber Music Group when they met in our house. My mother was an excellent cook, producing meals for visitors without any apparent stress, though all through this period we did have what was euphemistically called 'help in the house'. Nellie came to us every day, did the housework and cooked basic meals. She was also there for me if my mother was out when I came home from school. These were the early days of my own musical activities, having won my first piano competition in 1953, and commenced violin and theory lessons that same year at the RIAM. When I became sufficiently proficient on the violin to play pieces with piano accompaniment my mother would play with me, and we also played piano duets. I suspect that the latter may have been a ruse on her part to make me improve my sight-reading! I remember that we became a two-car family about this time, and the acquisition of a small blue Fiat 600 with a fold-down roof certainly gave my mother greater independence. CAH meetings were usually held in the daytime, but the MAI Council met in the evening, as did the Culwick, and of course concerts were almost always at night. Otherwise my mother worked from her desk and telephone at home. I have been intrigued to discover, from the archived MAI and CAH correspondence in the National Library, that all through this period my mother continued to use the name Mrs Lyall Smith (and occasionally Mrs Olive Lyall Smith) rather than Olive Smith.

My father's photographic business was undergoing significant expansion at this time. Vincent Trotman (whom I mentioned in Chapter 4) described the rapid rise to popularity from 1950 onwards of the colour photographic print, through innovations brought in by European firms such as Gevaert, Agfa and Kodak.[1] My father secured the Agfa agency for Ireland which involved the installation of new processing machinery and the renting of additional space at the rear of the chemist shop. There were close links between the Agfa Company and my father's photographic works, which meant that he travelled frequently to Leverkusen in Germany, flying to Düsseldorf and often accompanied by Vincent. There were also regular inspections in Dublin and my father developed a very good working relationship with the Agfa representatives. As the owner of one of the leading photographic businesses in Ireland, he was invited to become a member of the Photographic Dealers

Association (PDA) in the UK, where he served on the executive Council. He was elected President of the Association in 1953 which involved, amongst other duties, the glamorous Annual Dinner Dance at the Grosvenor House Hotel on Park Lane in London. I still have the menu and the guest list for the occasion – my parents' photo is on the opening page, both in full evening dress – and by all accounts my father gave a most entertaining President's address. The following year, as Past President, he received a handsome medal on a blue riband which I am happy to possess to this day. All this involved a great deal of travel back and forth to London, mostly by mail-boat from Dún Laoghaire and night-sleeper on the train from Holyhead. But occasionally, anticipating a rough crossing in mid-winter, he would go by air. One of his closest friends on the PDA Council was Jim Caithness from Kirkaldy, who occasionally flew home to Scotland. On 10 January 1952 they were so deep in conversation at Northolt Airport that my father missed hearing the call for Aer Lingus flight EI 165. This ill-fated plane never made it to Dublin – it crashed in the Welsh mountains with the loss of all souls on board.

From the time of my grandfather's retirement, my father had overall charge of the chemist shop, with the assistance of Christy Morrissey who moved to Rathgar from the Crumlin shop. On the financial side he was assisted by my mother who oversaw the accounts each month, although there was a full-time book-keeper. It was still customary for pharmaceutical chemists to make up prescribed medicines at a bench to the rear of the premises – to me it was like a sorcerer's cave with rows of little wooden drawers, each carefully labelled with the substance it contained, and special elegant glass bottles of various liquid preparations. My father and Mr Morrissey worked there in their white coats and sometimes there would be an apprentice, learning hands-on the trade of the dispensing chemist. It was essential for my father to employ another qualified dispenser as the shop was equally well-known for its range of cameras and photographic equipment, and my father would often need to take time with potential purchasers of these expensive items. His reputation as a photographic dealer was supported by his profile as a noted amateur photographer, so he was always in demand as a lecturer to camera clubs and as a judge at exhibitions and competitions. My mother was a good photographer too, and I was initiated into this hobby at quite a young age with the gift for Christmas of a Box Brownie camera.

My father had two main hobbies, wood-working and sailing – one activity for winter and one for summer! From 1953 onwards I was allowed to go out with him on *Echo* on Sunday afternoons, thus starting to learn how to crew and handle the boat. From the age of about twelve I became a regular crew member, which meant that I took part in the weekly races in Dún Laoghaire harbour on Thursday evenings and Saturday afternoons. Prizes were given out at the end of the year, which took the form of genuine silver teaspoons engraved with the name of the boat and the year. I have a collection of at least a dozen of these. It has occurred to me that, even though I was an only child, I was very lucky to be able to share both in my father's love of yachting and photography and my mother's passion for music. Looking back, I can only describe the Smith household as being very busy and positively brimming with energy and creativity.

I find my parents' relationship very interesting. Their temperaments were very different, but I feel that nonetheless they complemented each other splendidly. My mother could identify with almost all of my father's interests – the notable exception was sailing, with which she was really uncomfortable – as far as I know she never set foot in any of his yachts. My father liked to switch onto 'light music' on his radio whilst making things in his workshop, but found it hard to hold a melody in tune. He was very supportive of my mother's activities, as can be seen from his readiness to drive the bus for the Douglas Cameron Orchestra in 1956. Being a friendly and affable man with a good store of jokes, he got on well with the musicians who stayed with us or visited the house. He shared his interest in photography with Brian Boydell, and also with Keith Cummings of the LSQ. With Douglas Cameron there was a common Scottish heritage. Edgar Deale had been a friend of both my parents for many years, though Pat McKnight confided to me in latter years that she felt Edgar's opinions had contributed to my mother turning away from her Presbyterian faith! I am actually inclined to doubt this as my mother was interested in philosophy from her days at TCD and her religious scepticism was a very deep-seated matter. If the topic of religion arose, my mother would say that she had attended church so much when she was growing up that it would 'do her for the rest of her life'! I think that perhaps Pat regretted my mother's transformation from Girl Guide leader to high-powered music organiser and campaigner, but in spite of these reservations she remained the most loyal of friends and, to the end of her life, my mother loved visiting Pat's cottage in Co. Wicklow.

As regards the strong musical influences in my mother's life, I have noted a recurring pattern. The first to inspire her was the charismatic Turner Huggard, whom she encountered in her late teenage years, and whose name came up whenever choral matters were discussed. The second was probably Edgar Deale and the third was Thomas Armstrong. Undoubtedly the fourth was Douglas Cameron and in times not yet discussed the fifth would be Hugh Maguire. I think that these people supplied, at different stages of her life, a certain musical stimulus and fulfilment that she craved. My assessment is that my mother was an exceptionally musical woman, but that her particular family background missed out on developing this. She grew up as an all-rounder, very good at all subjects at school, a capable Guide leader, good at tennis, fond of dancing, able to sing, to play the piano and the organ, and fully enjoying a good social life. She was so intelligent that everything came easily to her with her photographic memory, but as a result there was no incentive to put in the long hours of piano or organ practice that would have really brought out the depth of her musicality in a way that satisfied her. Some of this intensity came through in her choral conducting. Having sung in choirs that she directed, I did experience this profound musicality at first hand. So there was a hunger there that came to the fore and responded when a musician with similar gifts crossed her path. I am certain that the excitement that she felt at such musical encounters was an all-important factor in the path that she chose to follow. It was a stimulus that enabled her to persevere with new ventures and a significant explanation of her devotion to the cause of music over so many years.

Did she suffer any ill effects from the extraordinary workload that she shouldered at this time when she was running so many events for the

MAI, as well as battling over concert hall sites on behalf of CAH, acting as treasurer for both the MAI and the Culwick, and also finding time for husband, daughter, home and garden? My recollection is that she was prone to what she called a 'strep-throat', in other words a streptococcal infection that afflicted her whenever she became seriously overtired. This would be treated with a course of penicillin. She also suffered with rheumatism in her hands, which eventually hindered her piano playing, and particularly in her neck and shoulders and lower back. For this she attended a rheumatism clinic in Upper Mount St where she underwent rather severe injections into the sorest points. Episodes of lumbago seemed to occur mostly in the autumn and I remember that at several of my birthday parties in November my mother was unable to sit and could only kneel in front of the open fire with a little table before her from which she directed our party games. This was so typical of her determination to carry something through, even though she was not feeling well. I do have the sense too, that from about 1953 onwards she became less tolerant of any little misdemeanours on the part of myself or my father. Of course I was nearing my teenage years, so might have become more annoying, but I learned by experience that there were times to keep out of the way! With hindsight, this loss of equanimity on her part must have indicated that my mother was stressed and, at times, under considerable pressure from all her commitments. There were certainly occasions on which she expressed irritation about people with whom she was working, and frustration at slow progress or difficulties in some of her projects. Her reputation as an organiser and campaigner grew, but at the same time she became known as someone who did not suffer fools gladly!

As soon as my mother heard that the NLSQ had been engaged to perform all the Beethoven String Quartets under the auspices of Newcastle University, from 24–29 January 1955, she became absolutely determined to attend. It involved quite a complicated journey to the North of England in the depths of winter but she returned really elated, having experienced so much extraordinary music in six intense days. She brought back with her a bound score of the Beethoven Quartets, autographed for her by the four players. I feel that my mother related very particularly to the medium of the string quartet, and I wonder whether this was connected to her ability as a choral conductor, which required her to follow four lines of music in much the same way as she appreciated the scoring of a quartet. I know that she was always delighted when audiences in rural Ireland reacted with enthusiasm to a quartet programme, confirming for her the importance of bringing this music to as wide an audience as possible.

Personally, I owed the members of the LSQ a great deal. They sourced my full-size violin in one of the London instrument dealers and brought it over with them in October 1955. On a later visit, Lionel brought me a beautiful Lamé bow. All of the members of the quartet were extremely kind to me when I went to study in London, allowing me to practice on their pianos and giving me opportunities to partner their students which meant, of course, that I attended their lessons and benefitted from their coaching for competitions and concerts.

Also in 1955, my mother took on a new role, but unconnected with her work for the MAI or the Culwick – she was appointed Local Representative for the music examinations of the Associated Board of the Royal Schools of Music, a position which she retained until 1958. This involved handling all requests for application forms and syllabi, making arrangements for the period of practical and written exams three times a year, booking accommodation for the examiners, being in attendance at the exam centre, and generally dealing with all sorts of queries. She had several desk drawers full of Associated Board materials, and went to London each year for an annual meeting of representatives. I think she rather enjoyed the three years' involvement.

Towards the end of the 1950s, my mother developed an interesting, and perhaps unexpected, friendship with the Jesuit priest, Fr Oliver O'Brien. This connects with my earlier comments about my mother's attitude to religious matters. His sister, the violinist Mary O'Brien, confirmed to me that he and my mother shared an interest in books, plays and philosophy.[2] She described him as having: 'a passion for the best in music; like Olive Smith, he would never settle for second best'. He was a very good pianist with a music degree from UCD in addition to degrees in theology and philosophy. Mary also said that his vocation shone through in the loving care he gave to the sick, down-and-out and disadvantaged. I know that around this period my mother developed a great interest in the life and writings of Pierre Teilhard de Chardin, the French philosopher, palaeontologist and Jesuit priest. She owned a number of books by him, notably *The Phenomenon of Man* (published 1959), *The Divine Milieu* (1960) and *Letters of a Traveller* (1962) and it seems likely that she was introduced to these by Fr Oliver. They were not published until after de Chardin's death in 1955, as he had been censored by the Catholic Church and forbidden to teach. This public silencing of a great mind was something that my mother found hard to take, and I recall her speaking about it quite emotionally. She felt that that same spirit was at work when the Jesuit order required Fr Oliver to move from Belvedere College in Dublin to the Crescent College in Limerick in 1962 and then again to Australia in 1965. My recollection is that he enjoyed coming to our house for a meal when there was MAI business to be discussed, and that he was always very encouraging to me, giving me some coaching for the Senior Piano competition in the Feis Ceoil in 1960 when my own teacher, Alice Bryan, was seriously ill. I found him very perceptive and helpful with a difficult piece by John Ireland, and indeed Lindsay (my husband) recollects that I continued to consult him whenever I came home from London. It is good to add that he had a period of musical fulfilment in Australia, where he became the conductor of the professional chamber choir of the Adelaide radio station, in addition to his work as a hospital chaplain. He died in 1994.

I also remember that my mother was very inspired by the story of Dr Albert Schweitzer, organist and Bach scholar, philosopher and theologian, medical doctor and friend of the sick in Africa. On her bookshelves, a copy of his book *The Quest of the Historical Jesus* sat alongside those of Teilhard de Chardin, and she spoke frequently of how he had turned his back on his academic career in order to devote the rest of his life to the hospital he had built at Lambaréné in present-day Gabon. Her admiration for the writings of Schweitzer and de Chardin, juxtaposed with those of the philosopher, mathematician and social activist Bertrand Russell and the latest publications about radio astronomy, indicate how much my mother's mind was drawn to existential matters. Her rejection of formal religious practice was her outward position, but inwardly it appears that she continued to search on a deeper level.

In 1957 the Smith family was on the move again. From time to time my father voiced to me his concern at the costs involved in the upkeep of Rockview, and he must have convinced my mother of this because they decided to buy Garryknock, a dormer bungalow with a much smaller garden, on the main Bray Road. From the point of view of transport it was a practical decision, as this had a good bus service and gave me growing independence as a teenager. By this time my mother worked every day in the MAI office in 37 Molesworth St, so Anne Coleman was engaged as the very efficient full-time cook-housekeeper. At this point it is worth mentioning that all the work my mother did in the cause of music was unpaid. Following the death of her father in December 1955, I have to assume that she inherited sufficient money to enable her to follow what was, in effect, the career path of a chief executive. It would be unthinkable nowadays that a person at this level would not have a salary. And of course her position within the MAI was still merely that of treasurer, but yet her energy, vision and determination must have been very much recognised by her fellow Council members as it seems she had their support.

My mother ceased to be treasurer of the Culwick in 1956. In 1957, perhaps having a little more leisure time, she conceived the idea of establishing a Ladies' Choir which she named The Olivian Singers. This was really a hand-picked group. She was building on the experience already gained from her Girl Guide Choir, and indeed some of the membership overlapped, but she also had a particular sound in her head and chose voices that would allow her to realise this. She loved the *Stabat Mater* of Pergolesi and performed it often, but she also wanted to explore recently-published music so Bartók, Martinů and Britten featured in a number of programmes. In the MAI *Bulletin* for December 1957, a performance of Britten's *Ceremony of Carols* was announced for 6 January 1958 with Mercedes Bolger (harp). This concert, in the Jellicoe Hall at Alexandra College on Earlsfort Terrace, was the Olivians' first public performance.

Charles Acton, who did not always see eye to eye with my mother on a range of matters,[3] was on this occasion very gracious in his praise, congratulating her 'on her outstanding choice of programme' and commenting: 'the choir sang extremely well. Olive Smith has obviously worked them very hard, with musicianliness and intelligence, and they have responded fully.'[4]

In 1960 The Olivians gave the first performance in Ireland of Britten's *Missa Brevis*. For their prize-winning entry at the 1958 Cork Choral Festival my mother commissioned a setting of 'O Breathe not his Name' by Frederick May. Having won the international competition for female choirs in Cork, my mother brought the choir to the Belfast Festival in 1959 where, again, they swept the board. The Olivians were still in existence in the late 1960s, so this was a significant musical outlet in my mother's otherwise rather administration-centred life. During 1959 she also acted as chorus-mistress for the Culwick, preparing a programme of Bach, Vaughan-Williams, Kodaly, Bartók and Britten for their concert on 12 February at the SFX Hall, which was conducted by Frederic Jackson. She also took all but the final rehearsals for the Handel oratorio *Samson* which was the Culwick's contribution to the 1959 Handel Festival.

With such busy lives, holidays were important. My father travelled a great deal to London and Germany in the course of business, and my mother and I certainly went to London at least twice a year, keeping in touch with her sister Kay's family and also her friend from TCD days, Lily Butler. My cousin Helen was married in 1957 and I was very proud to be bridesmaid. Otherwise, holidays were mostly in the West of Ireland or Donegal, though my parents did make a special trip to Italy in the early 1950s, visiting Venice, Florence and Portofino on the Ligurian Riviera. My first continental holiday was in 1958, following my Intermediate Certificate exams, when we all went to the Engadin region of Switzerland, walking in the mountains, hiking close to glaciers and experiencing the amazing Swiss mountain railways. Also in 1958, my parents took the innovative step of booking into a hotel in Connemara for Christmas, but this plan was almost sabotaged when RÉ offered the Olivian Singers a live broadcast of the *Ceremony of Carols* at 9.30 p.m. on Christmas Eve! The problem was solved by driving as far as Athlone after the broadcast and then on to Connemara on Christmas morning. I feel that this unusual winter visit re-awakened for my parents something of the magic of the West that they had known when they were younger. At various times over the next two or three years they rented a holiday property near Carna and invited Kay and David, and also Douglas and Lilly Cameron, to join them there.

In the summer of 1960, having just taken German as one of the subjects in my Leaving Certificate, my parents arranged a student exchange for me with Ulrike, daughter of Herr Dr and Frau Bier, who lived near Frankfurt. This arose from the connection, made at least a decade earlier when Ursula Bürgel came to stay with us during the school holidays whilst she was a student teacher at Lily Butler's school. My mother developed a long-standing friendship with Ursula and sought her advice as to whether one of her pupils might be interested in an exchange. The trip to Germany included a delightful reunion with Ursula, a pleasant week's holiday for my parents, and a totally memorable three-week stay at the Bier's home for me. Ulrike and I returned by boat and train, stopping for a few days' sightseeing in London under the care of my aunt and cousins, and completing the six weeks of the exchange in Dublin. My enduring relationship with Ulrike, her parents, her husband Wolfgang, her daughters and grandchildren, has included many visits and holidays and has been a great richness for me and my family. For all this, I am greatly indebted to my parents.

---

[1] Interviewed by the author and Pat O'Kelly, 5 November 2001.

[2] Interviewed by the author, 15 August 2016.

[3] An old disagreement, dating back to the Handel Festival of 1959, was apparently still a source of annoyance to Mr Acton some twenty-three years later. He wrote, on 22 March 1982: 'I suggested to a council meeting of the MAI that, as well as Handel and Purcell, the MAI might devote an evening to the 150th anniversary of Haydn's death; but was fiercely derided by Olive Smith for thinking that anyone would ever want to listen to a whole evening of Haydn, apart from *The Creation*. Ah well....'

[4] *The Irish Times*, 7 January 1958.

CHAPTER 17

The MAI – 'Let's Make an Opera' and the Handel Festival, 1958 and 1959

1958

Meanwhile, MAI projects were progressing as usual. A short Country Tour by Patricia O'Keeffe (soprano) and Patricia Herbert (piano) took place in the spring of 1958, visiting Carrick-on-Shannon, Gorey and Cork. The violinist Brendan O'Reilly gave his Coming-Out recital on 28 April, accompanied by Kitty O'Callaghan, the Chamber Music and Vocal Groups continued to meet regularly, and the Council had a positive response from Sir John Barbirolli concerning the performance of Irish compositions by the Hallé Orchestra. September had two events – a lecture on 15th in the Oak Room of the Mansion House entitled 'Aesthetics and Criticism' by Frank Howes, music critic of *The Times* of London, and a Coming-Out recital by Valerie Walker (piano) on 29th.

On 20 October the Quarterly Members' Meeting was given by the Gordon Clinton Singers, a group of five singers whose visit was initiated by Brian Boydell. Their Dublin recital at the Philips Hall, Clonskeagh, included madrigals and one of the Byrd Masses and came at the end of an extensive Country Tour which visited Boyle, Portarlington, Waterford, Gorey, Kilkenny, Tralee and Cork. Brian was particularly interested in this genre of vocal chamber-music – his own specialist group The Dowland Consort was formed in the autumn of 1958. Regarding the tour of the Clinton Singers, unfortunately there was a rather inauspicious beginning as there seems to have been a misunderstanding concerning the financial arrangements. Gordon Clinton wrote that the singers would make the best of it, but that some had turned down other work. However, in order to keep costs down, they were happy to accept hospitality wherever possible, and were quite delighted with the reception they received. One of the group, Philip Todd, wrote to my mother on 26 October 1958: 'We had a wonderful trip . . . the tour of the Ring of Kerry I shall never forget.' And Gordon Clinton wrote a lovely personal letter to my mother, telling her that the whole group: 'had taken an immediate fancy to her!'[1]

In November, there were four Organ Recitals at the RIAM under the auspices of the MAI, which featured Joe Groocock, John O'Sullivan and David Lee, who also organised the series. Finally, there was a Country Tour in December by the celebrated English oboist, Léon Goossens, with Charles Lynch (piano), mainly organised by Dr Maureen Carmody of Nenagh with a grant from the Shaw Trust. They visited Limerick, Birr, Kilkenny and Tralee.

There were also MAI administrative changes. Mrs Pellew was unable to continue as part-time paid secretary and was replaced in late August by Mrs Olive Bodley, wife of the composer Seóirse Bodley. Mairtín McCullough, who still continued to edit the very valuable *Bulletin* of the MAI every month, was anxious to be relieved of the position of Joint Hon. Secretary, so at its meeting on 2 September the Council approved a new arrangement for the Honorary Officers, namely that my mother would serve on her own as Secretary with Fr O'Brien as Assistant, whilst Alan Cowle assumed sole responsibility for the role of Treasurer, their appointments being subject to approval at the next AGM. But at the next meeting on 8 October my mother alluded to 'hints' she had received that there were Council members who felt that the Hon. Officers had been: 'fixing things without the authority of the Council'. She felt that it was essential for the Officers to have the full trust and support of the Council in dealing with the heavy workload, and this opinion was shared by Leon Ó Dubhghaill. Edgar Deale's view was that he should apologise if Council members thought he had proceeded too swiftly with the new appointments and that criticisms should be voiced at meetings, or else brought directly to the Chairman. Brian Boydell thanked my mother: 'for the forthright way in which she had brought this matter up' and suggested a vote of confidence in the Officers. This was carried unanimously and there the matter rested.

During 1958, the Council continued to lobby RÉ concerning the employment of Irish musicians in the RÉSO, with particular emphasis on the cello section. These negotiations were confidential, even enlisting the assistance of Erskine Childers. There was considerable satisfaction at the Council meeting in December when Edgar Deale gave the news that a decision by RÉ to create an extra desk would give two cellists permanent positions, with some deputy work for a third player.

As already mentioned at the end of Chapter 14, from the end of 1957 planning was underway for a production of Britten's *Let's Make an Opera* to be performed by the Studio Opera Group from Belfast, conducted by Havelock Nelson. Brian Boydell was the prime mover in this venture. He and Havelock had much in common; both had science degrees, but both had found the call of music too strong and had built their careers as composers, conductors and administrators. Havelock was on the music staff of the BBC in Belfast and greatly in demand as an accompanist. For this production they were assisted by James (Jim) Wilson, an English composer who had settled in Ireland towards the end of 1952; Brian had conducted excerpts from Jim's ballet *Esther* in 1953. Jim was keen to be involved in the work of the MAI and was a member of the Composers' Group. Several venues were considered before the Dagg Hall of the RIAM was decided upon and a grant of £100 received from the Arts Council. This delightful child-focussed opera was a big undertaking, with a cast of three adult singers and seven children, plus an orchestra of seven players including two pianists, all of whom had to be given hospitality in Dublin for a week. The production was by Denis Smyth and Havelock Nelson, with the responsibility for wardrobe and stage management in the hands of Daphne Bell and Jim Wilson. My mother assumed the role of chief co-ordinator, as well as keeping a close eye on the finances! The decision to stage it immediately after Christmas was an inspired one, with six evening performances and two matinées between 29 December 1958 and 3 January 1959, most of which were sold out, due to the clever idea of marketing tickets as Christmas gifts in a special greetings folder, with reductions for parties of at least ten. The Dagg Hall also proved to be an ideal venue with a big enough stage, an adequate pit and the next door foyer where refreshments could be served at the interval. I believe that my father was involved as a lighting assistant to Jim, and I certainly had enormous fun as an unofficial dogsbody, running backstage errands for all and sundry!

The MAI produced some rather stern publicity material for such an attractive project: 'In an endeavour to create an interest in good modern music among young people, the MAI are presenting *Let's Make an Opera* . . . We hope to make children realise that music is written to be enjoyed, and that the music of classical composers can give as much pleasure as any other kind'. Fortunately the *Evening Press* columnist who attended the official launch on 15 December caught the right note, as it were, and high-lighted the fun element of audience participation: 'Though the news was launched most solemnly at the Gresham Hotel with tea and buns . . . the fact is that this piece of musical *jeu d'esprit* gives many of us the touch of a light heart. I predict that you are going to have difficulty in even getting seats . . . this is going to be great fun and I envy the daddies and mammies who can bring along their singing children. The MAI is to be congratulated on this most luminous star of the Christmas programme of music. Do please accept this enchantment and do not attempt to fight the spell of the magician's baton'.[2] In fact, the press reception was sponsored by Lady Mayer and she was present herself. Anything to do with music and children was always close to her heart. At the first Council meeting in 1959 my mother was able to report that the whole venture had made a small profit and that this would be distributed amongst the cast and orchestra. It was agreed that a record token should be sent to Jim Wilson as a mark of thanks and appreciation. Thanks were also conveyed to the hostesses who had provided hospitality and to those who had looked after the refreshments. Special thanks were sent to Mary, wife of Mairtín McCullough, who had organised the most enjoyable final night party for the cast, orchestra, conductor and backstage team. All in all, a triumph for the MAI !

1959

Let's Make an Opera was certainly a landmark, another indication of the MAI's growing confidence as a musical organisation, but actually it was quite a small venture in comparison with the scope and ambition of the plans to commemorate, later in 1959, the bicentenary of the death of Handel. The initial suggestion for this came from Victor Leeson, conductor of the St James's Gate Musical Society and, following the Council meeting of 12 February 1958, my mother and Mairtín McCullough were asked by the Council to discuss the idea with him. At the March meeting, it was decided to hold the Festival in the autumn of 1959, and to form a committee representative of each of the prominent musical societies in Dublin, with power to co-opt. From then on, the project was seldom absent from the Council agenda. Some ambitious ideas, such as engaging either the Stuttgart or Hamburg Chamber Orchestra, or a group directed by Thurston Dart, were discarded early on, and at the Council meeting in September 1958 it was agreed to engage the Douglas Cameron String Orchestra, with additional wind and brass players from the RÉSO as needed, plus two D trumpet specialists from London. In October a sub-committee of the Council, consisting of the three Hon. Officers, together with Victor Leeson and David Lee, was appointed to take matters forward; Jim Wilson was later co-opted.

It was apparent from the outset that there was great interest amongst choral societies, both in Dublin and the provinces, in giving performances as part of the Festival. The majority of these would be with orchestra and the sub-committee recommended that a highly experienced choral conductor, who could hold rehearsals in London with the orchestra and soloists beforehand, should be engaged for the week. Douglas Cameron suggested Frederic Jackson, chorus-master of the London Philharmonic

Choir, who was also the choral conductor at the RAM. He came to Ireland several times in the months before the Festival to take some rehearsals with each choir, and then conducted all the choral concerts with orchestra. In the case of the Culwick, whose conductor Joe Groocock had retired the previous year, Frederic Jackson came as guest conductor for their concert on 12 February 1959, with a programme of mostly *a capella* works. My mother was asked to be the chorus mistress for this concert and also trained the choir for the oratorio *Samson*.

The following list will give an idea of the scope of the celebration, which spread far beyond the confines of Dublin or Cork, and of the exacting schedule for the performers. Frederic Jackson was in charge of all the choral performances, whilst Douglas Cameron conducted the orchestral concerts and school concerts. The chorus master for each choir is in brackets.

30 SEPTEMBER – Carlow Town Hall: Orchestral concert – Purcell, Handel, Grieg & Dvořák.

1 OCTOBER – Kilkenny City: Orchestral concert – same programme.

2 OCTOBER (morning) – Waterford: Orchestral concert for schools.

2 OCTOBER (evening) – Waterford: Orchestral concert with David Galliver (tenor).

3 OCTOBER – Cork City Hall: *Samson* – Cork City Choral Society (Staf Gebruers).

4 OCTOBER – travel to Dublin and rehearse.

5 OCTOBER (morning) – Unveiling of the commemorative plaque at Fishamble Street, and the official opening of the Handel Exhibition at the Civic Museum.

5 OCTOBER (evening) – Dublin, St Francis Xavier Hall (SFX): *Samson* – Culwick Choral Society (Olive Smith).

6 OCTOBER – Birr, Marian Hall: Orchestral concert – programme as Carlow.

7 OCTOBER – Boyle, St Joseph's Hall: Orchestral concert – same programme.

8 OCTOBER – Galway: *Messiah* – Franciscan Choral Society (Fr Cassian O'Byrne OFM).

9 OCTOBER – Tralee: Orchestral concert with Veronica Dunne (soprano).

10 OCTOBER – Limerick: *Messiah* – Limerick Oratorio Society (Revd Dermot Carmody).

11 OCTOBER – travel to Dublin and rehearse.

12 OCTOBER – Dublin, SFX Hall: *Solomon* – St James's Gate Musical Society (Victor Leeson).

13 OCTOBER (morning) – Dublin, SFX Hall: Orchestral concert for schools.

13 OCTOBER (evening) – Dublin: *Jephtha* – Centenary Church Choir (with organist William Watson), conductor: Sylvia Fannin.

Perhaps the most notable event in the whole Festival was the first performance in Galway of *Messiah*. The four vocal soloists were Veronica Dunne (soprano), Helen Watts (alto), David Galliver (tenor) and Roger Stalman (bass). They were joined by Flora Vickers (soprano), George Dunlop (tenor) and William Young (bass) for *Samson*, and Flora Vickers also sang in *Solomon* and *Jephtha*. The continuo player for all the choral concerts was David Lee, using the first harpsichord built by Cathal Gannon, and he also acted as répétiteur and rehearsal assistant to Frederic Jackson. A pleasing unity between all these concerts was created by utilising the same programme cover, tastefully designed by the Dolmen Press, which incorporated an excerpt in Handel's handwriting of a recitative from *Messiah*. The whole celebration was preceded by an introductory lecture entitled 'Handel in Dublin and the Oratorios to be performed during the Festival' given by Brian Boydell who was, of course, an authority on the music of 18th century Dublin. By way of helpful advance publicity, he also contributed a five-page illustrated article on Handel's Dublin sojourn to the July/August issue of a magazine entitled *Ireland of the Welcomes*.

An exciting development was reported to the Council at their meeting in January 1959 – a letter had been received from Dr James Hall of the

Deal and Walmer Handelian Society, proposing that a suitable monument should be erected in Dublin to commemorate the first performance in 1742 of *Messiah* at Fishamble Street Musick Hall. This was not only a surprise – Deal and Walmer are seaside towns on the coast of Kent – but the suggestion added a whole new dimension to the planning of the Festival. It was decided to commission the Irish sculptor Michael Biggs to design a bronze plaque for casting by McLoughlin's Foundry, which would, with permission from Dublin Corporation, be mounted on the wall of the premises of Kennan and Sons, next to the original site of the Musick Hall. The total cost, including the wall-mounting, was £100 of which the Deal and Walmer Society had already collected £90. Bord Fáilte responded favourably to a request to make up the difference and Dr Hall was invited to perform the unveiling ceremony.

In addition to the almost daily programme of concerts, the organising committee made the innovative suggestion of organising an exhibition of Handel memorabilia, to run for three weeks at the Civic Museum in South William Street, courtesy of Dublin Corporation. Jim Wilson agreed to curate this and recounted to his biographer, Mark Fitzgerald, in later years that the exhibition: 'contained manuscripts from Mercer's Hospital and Marsh's Library, a double bassoon from the National Museum believed to have been used in Handel performances in London, word books for Handel operas and oratorios, reproductions and facsimiles of Handel manuscripts, portraits, engravings and other Handelian relics'.[3] During an interview in 2002,[4] Jim also mentioned a snuff box which he acquired from Mrs Putzel Hunt, wife of the founder of the Hunt Museum in Limerick. There is a picture of this delightful item, engraved '*George F. Handel, Dublin 1741*' in the brochure for the exhibition. A number of items were lent by Dr Hall, who contributed the foreword to the brochure. This also contained a diary of the chief events of Handel's time in Ireland. Another exhibit featured a special enlargement, made by my father, of a photograph of Handel's memorial in Westminster Abbey.

It is surely remarkable that the MAI was able to bring off such a venture over a period of about two weeks, involving so many choirs, so many venues, six or eight soloists, a touring orchestra and conductors, not to mention the exhibition and the commemorative plaque. But it is clear from the Minutes that this was a project embraced by all the Council. My mother was heavily involved but so were a great number of other people, and it could be said that the successful organisation of the Handel Festival marked a coming-of-age for the MAI.

There were problems, of course. The unveiling of the plaque was scheduled for 12 noon on 5 October, to be followed by the official opening of the exhibition and a luncheon for Dr Hall and other dignitaries. Correspondence, which commences on 18 September 1959,[5] between Michael Biggs and Edgar Deale, makes it clear that, for various technical reasons, completion of the plaque by the due date was very uncertain, and that for financial reasons there was a danger of serious deterioration in relations between the sculptor, the foundry and the MAI. However, the plaque was completed in time and was in place for the unveiling ceremony on Monday 5 October,[6] thanks to McLoughlin's being willing to install it over the preceding weekend. The dispute over money was eventually resolved.

Financially, the Festival was well supported. The Arts Council gave funding of £1,080 which comprised £600 towards the oratorio concerts and £80 for each of the orchestral concerts outside Dublin. They also agreed an additional sum of £50 after the Festival was over. A grant of £50 was received from Guinness, another from the Shaw Trust, and sixty names appear on the list of guarantors – this method of raising finance had worked well for the Bach Festival nine years earlier. The Orchestra's all-in fee was £200 and their transportation by Scraggs Coaches of Wicklow cost £142.10s. At least my father was relieved of his role as bus-driver, though he did drive the car to some venues, as did my mother. An overall deficit of £92 was reported to the MAI Council on 2 December, which involved the guarantors in a payment of 14s.6d in the pound. This was felt to be satisfactory.

The MAI Council's report for 1959, as well as covering the Handel Festival in great detail, contained the following tribute to my mother, written by Fr O'Brien as Hon. Assistant Secretary: 'Finally, the writer of this report feels that he is echoing the mind of the Council when he singles out for a special word of thanks the Hon. Secretary, Mrs Olive

Smith. It can be simply said that without her the Festival, if it existed at all, would have been incomparably poorer and less successful'.

While it is not surprising that the Handel Festival dominated the year's activities, it is important to record other events. The first Members' Meeting of the year, on 4 March 1959 at the Shelbourne Hotel, was given by the Wind Quintet of the Melos Ensemble from London. Their mostly 20th century programme attracted an audience of about 200. It should have included the first performance of a quintet by Arthur Benjamin, but their agent apologised afterwards because, in fact, the composer had only completed one movement! Charles Lynch gave a piano recital at the Royal College of Physicians on 27 May, as the second Members' Meeting of the year, with an interesting programme of Mozart, Chopin, John Ireland, Barber and Bartók, and the Benthien Quartet from Germany were engaged for a Country Tour.[7] They had already played in Ireland in 1952, the first German Quartet to do so after the Second World War, and had toured in 1953 and 1954. For this MAI tour, their repertoire included Brian Boydell's 2nd Quartet; their Cork concert was recorded by RÉ and they also played at the RDS.

Towards the end of the year, it became necessary to move from the office at 37 Molesworth Street, so from the beginning of November the MAI was to be found at 42 Dawson Street, with Miss P. O'Kelly employed as Assistant Secretary.

[1] NLI – ACC 6000 : both letters in box 46, beige file 1.

[2] *Evening Press*, 16 December 1958.

[3] See *The Life and Music of James Wilson* (Cork University Press, 2015).

[4] Interviewed by Pat O'Kelly, 18 November 2002.

[5] NLI – ACC 6000, box 42, beige folder 4. This folder and several others in Box 42 contain the archived material concerning the 1959 Handel Festival.

[6] The plaque was later taken down during renovations of Kennan's building at 19 Fishamble Street. This nowadays houses the Contemporary Music Centre. For a while the plaque's exact whereabouts was uncertain, but it was found in the care of the Office of Public Works and eventually replaced in its original position.

[7] Birr, Cork, Galway, Gorey, Nenagh, Portarlington and Waterford.

CHAPTER 18

The Concert Hall: Part 3
– 1957 to 1960 –
The fund-raising begins

1957

The start of 1957 brought something new. Hector Legge, editor of the *Sunday Independent*, wrote to my mother drawing her attention to the leading article in the previous Sunday's paper[1] and suggesting that she might like to comment. The Government had allocated £400,000 per annum towards the development of tourism in Ireland and the article proposed that £100,000 a year could be diverted instead to the erection of a Concert Hall: 'We believe that the reduction of the tourist grant by £100,000 for three or four years would not seriously hamper the bodies concerned. The money would go far towards giving Ireland at long last a building of art and culture worthy of the nation. It would for the most part be spent in wages and on materials of Irish manufacture. And it would be an investment that in good time would give a fair return in money and an incalculable return in prestige.' The following Sunday, the paper carried a 6-column spread entitled 'Dublin's Need for a Concert Hall' with statements by prominent people. It was a clever ploy, possibly even tongue-in-cheek, predictably drawing forth outrage that a quarter of the tourism budget might be reallocated in such a cavalier fashion during times of straitened finances; and equally predictably giving those who campaigned for a concert hall a new opportunity to state their case. It was thus very welcome, bringing the whole matter back into the public domain. The articles continued to appear on several Sundays – Ernest Blythe and John F. Larchet gave their views on 3 February, my mother and P. J. Little in the final article on 17th.

On 14 February, the Lord Mayor Councillor Robert Briscoe received a deputation from CAH in the persons of my mother and Michael Scott and afterwards released a statement, saying that agreement in principle with the Corporation had been reached 'some considerable time ago' and that he would arrange to have the matter considered by the Town Planning and Streets Committee the following Tuesday, at which: 'the views of the deputation will be heard'.[2] *The Irish Times* picked up on this with a leading article on 15 February, which referred to the frustration of CAH over the site and praised them for not giving up, remarking: 'the case for a concert hall is as familiar as it is persuasive'. As with the *Sunday Independent, The Irish Times* recognised that the building and maintenance costs could be set off against well-managed hiring charges. Furthermore, the paper deplored the fact that Cork and Belfast were better served with concert venues than Dublin! My mother's 'letter to the Editor' appeared on 18th, stressing that it was the view of CAH that the intended Hall could pay its way, and referring to the Lord Mayor's words at CAH's recent interview: 'from his many contacts with Bord Fáilte he clearly saw the urgent necessity for an assembly hall'. The CAH Board must have been delighted when another leading article, this time in the *Irish Press*, appeared on 23 February, also broadly in favour of the whole project. A letter dated 15 March from the City Manager's office informed CAH: 'that negotiations have been put in train for the necessary property acquisitions'.[3]

The Irish Times leader mentioned 'the present crisis', and indeed not without foundation, as the storm clouds gathered over the Inter-Party Government and an election was called for 5 March 1957, following the tabling of a motion of no confidence by Fianna Fáil. The crisis was precipitated by the Government's handling of the very poor economic situation. Fianna Fáil mounted a strong campaign, highlighting the inherent weakness of coalition and the need for stable government. It was de Valera's last time to serve as Taoiseach, and his majority of 9 seats owed much to the input of his heir-apparent, Seán Lemass. The CAH Board used the opportunity to canvas candidates for their support and received quite a number of positive replies, from all parties. When some normality returned after the election, each of the Board members undertook to try to find 10 people who would each subscribe £25 and also sought the support of Bord Fáilte through its director general, T. J. O'Driscoll. Unfortunately, this fund-raising move caused upset to one much-valued Board member, A. W. Bayne, who objected strongly, feeling that it was ill-timed and unwise. He wrote to my mother on 2 April 1957: 'The situation in the Republic, because of lack of funds to carry out planned capital investment, is very critical and we must face up to severe, even harsh measures for some years in order to avoid national bankruptcy. I would not like to be associated with an appeal for the support of the project at the present time'. He indicated that he intended to resign, but in fact did not do so until December 1957. Undoubtedly the Board was going to miss his clear-headed and committed presence. Mr Creede also indicated at that time that he did not wish to continue as a representative of Our Lady's Choral Society, so the decision was taken to invite Councillor Robert Briscoe and Sir Alfred Beit to join the Board.

1958

In January 1958 my mother wrote to a number of American-Irish business men, in the hopes of kindling some interest, but there was certainly a drop in activity within CAH itself, as is clear from the small number of Board meetings in 1958 and 1959. The fact that the MAI was so busy may have partly obscured CAH's lack of progress, though an optimistic article in the *The Irish Times* of 23 July 1958 hints that an opportune time for fund-raising may come in the autumn, having been put on hold due to the credit 'squeeze'. In November 1958, the *Irish*

Tatler and Sketch published a generally supportive piece, but commented: 'That Concert Hall is still a mirage. We now have an option on a site and the usual amiable, but hopelessly conditional, promises of help that keep the distinguished promoters moving in circles'.

1959
The CAH report for 1959, however, shows that valuable contacts were continuing out of the public eye. On 12 May 1959, my mother wrote to Seán Lemass as Minister for Industry and Commerce, referring to the correspondence in 1956 which had given some hope of further consideration, should the public finances improve. CAH wished to be able to indicate in their planned fund-raising appeal that Government support would be forthcoming in the shape of a financial guarantee. About a month later Lemass became Taoiseach, just before Éamon de Valera's inauguration as Uachtarán na hÉireann on 25 June 1959. A. P. Reynolds reported to the CAH Board on 22 October that: 'he had spoken to the Taoiseach, who said the Government would be willing to assist us, as they had Cork'. On 8 December, the new Minister for Industry and Commerce, Jack Lynch, received a deputation from CAH with Sir Alfred Beit, Edgar Deale and my mother representing the Board. They were encouraged to hear: 'that the Government was sympathetic to the project and with Cork as a precedent would be prepared to give a guaranteed loan for at least one third of the cost, possibly more'. Sketch plans and estimates of probable income and expenditure were requested. The reference to Cork concerned the funding given towards the rebuilding of the Opera House, which was destroyed by fire on 12 December 1955. These encouraging statements must have played a part in the decision by the CAH board, taken towards the end of 1959, to move towards a much more pro-active and public form of fund-raising. At this point, there was a timely intervention from an unexpected source.

The Hungarian conductor, Tibor Paul, first worked with the RÉSO in November 1958. He created a good impression and was invited back for a series of concerts in September/October 1959. At that time he held the position of conductor of the National Opera in Sydney and professor of conducting at New South Wales Conservatory. Towards the end of his autumn visit to Dublin, Mr Paul gave a press conference during which he deplored the lack of a suitable hall in Dublin. As a result, plans emerged for the RÉSO to be involved in the launch of a fund-raising drive for a concert hall. This exciting development was reported in a leader in the *Evening Herald* on 29 October 1959 entitled 'That Concert Hall'. A few days later, on 3 November, my mother informed the MAI Council and there was some discussion about the venue and soloist. By the next Council meeting on 2 December, all was in place. The venue was the Theatre Royal, the date 15 January 1960 and the distinguished Italian violinist, Gioconda de Vito, regarded as the foremost female violinist of her time, was engaged as soloist to play the Brahms concerto. The rest of the programme was the *Sicilian Vespers* overture by Verdi, a new ballet suite *Careless Love* by A. J. Potter, and Beethoven's 5th Symphony. As a fine gesture towards the significance of the event, the RÉSO offered to play without a fee.

1960

Conscious of the huge number of seats to be sold (3,400 – far more than the 2,000 envisaged as the optimum for Dublin by the CAH Board), a big publicity drive was launched in December with good co-operation from all the papers. But in early January my mother was still concerned that there might be a small audience and wrote to numerous firms, suggesting that they take a block booking of seats for their staff. The press coverage immediately before the concert, with articles in the *Sunday Review*, the *Irish Independent* and *Irish Times*, together with photographs and interviews with de Vito on her arrival at Dublin airport, seem to have done the trick. On the night, the audience numbered 3,200! I have rarely seen my mother more excited and apprehensive – so much was hanging on this opening move into the public domain, including her reputation as an organiser, given that her previous experience of the Theatre Royal had been the stress-ridden concert of the NYOGB two years earlier.

The reviews[4] reported on the full house and on the presence of President de Valera, Taoiseach Seán Lemass, Ministers MacEntee and

Childers, members of the Diplomatic Corps and of the Judiciary. In the *Irish Independent* Mary McGoris wrote: 'A definite mandate for a concert hall would seem to have been conveyed, not alone by the enthusiasm of the audience but by its size'. James Delany of the *Sunday Review* summed the concert up as: 'An evening of unalloyed pleasure' whilst Charles Acton (*Irish Times*) described de Vito's playing: 'This was Brahms at its greatest and best with a cadenza and its aftermath beautiful enough for tears'. In this context, it is worth noting that she suffered a broken string during the first movement, leaving the stage to replace it and then returning to play as if nothing had happened! The RÉSO and Tibor Paul also received plaudits all round: 'The performance of the symphony was masterly on all counts' (*Evening Mail*) and Mr Paul endeared himself to everyone by playing Berlioz's *Hungarian March* as an encore. Only the poor acoustics of the theatre were criticised, which of course served to emphasise the purpose for which the concert had been given. The amount raised was £1,000, a most encouraging start!

In February 1960, Dr John F. Larchet accepted an invitation to join the Board of CAH as the representative of the Dublin International Festival of Music and the Arts (DIFMA), of which he was President. This Festival ran for about a week in the summer of 1959, and again in 1960 and 1961. It was a high-profile event, well funded, with a very varied programme.[5] Apart from his eminent position as Professor of Music at UCD, Dr Larchet's role with the DIFMA meant that he had much useful experience to impart to CAH as it moved into a period of active concert promotion.

The MAI led the way by designating its long-awaited concert by Peter Pears and Benjamin Britten in aid of the Concert Hall Fund (CHF). This took place on 28 April 1960 at the SFX Hall. A recital by this charismatic partnership had initially been suggested to the MAI Council in October 1958, but this was their first availability. Their visit to Ireland included concerts in Cork and Waterford. My mother and I went to meet them at Dublin Airport on the evening of Sunday 24 April, both of us excited and a little nervous at the prospect of meeting such famous musicians! I remember that Britten sat in the front, but said very little, whilst Peter

Pears was a more out-going conversationalist from the rear seat beside me. They stayed at the Gresham and then went to Cork by train the next day, where their recital was a Bax Memorial concert. The Waterford concert on 27th was recorded by RÉ for future transmission. The British Ambassador and Lady MacLennan entertained them for lunch on the day of the Dublin concert, so they arrived to rehearse at the SFX Hall at 11.00 a.m. where my mother and the piano tuner were awaiting them. My mother told me that they rehearsed very little together but that Britten, who was a wonderful pianist, spent a long time playing the opening bars of the Schubert song '*Im Frühling*' until he was happy with his control of the piano. Their programme consisted of songs by Purcell and Schubert, with Britten's *Winter Words* cycle after the interval. Many people who attended considered their performance to be the musical highlight of the year and this was reflected in the uniformly enthusiastic reviews. Charles Acton, in the *The Irish Times* wrote of: 'the complete understanding between the performers, in combination with their individual musicianliness', whilst Brian Quinn (*Evening Herald*) commented: 'It is not often that we hear a voice of such beauty'.

In many ways, the most important result of this recital was that it unleashed a flood of small-scale fund-raising events in support of CAH's campaign. An MAI member raised £2.16s.8d by inviting friends to his house to listen to the recording of Britten's opera *Peter Grimes*, and indeed film shows and gramophone recitals became a popular means of raising money for the CHF. The MAI Chamber Music Group sent in £5.14s.6d from one such venture, another at Mrs Pringle's house made £8.10s.0d and a piano recital by Miss Alice Barklie made £7.0s.0d.

There were also notable initiatives amongst professional musicians, all giving their services without fee. János Fürst (violin) and Patricia Herbert (piano) played at the Shelbourne on 23 May in a programme of Corelli, Mozart, Brahms and Bartók, followed by a memorable recital by Veronica Dunne (soprano) and Kitty O'Callaghan at the same venue on 8 June. Her eclectic programme included song cycles by Ravel, Wolf and de Falla and a stunning performance of Annina's aria from *The Saint of Bleecker Street* by Menotti. The Dowland Consort, directed by Brian Boydell, sang at Malahide Castle on 22 June, and a scheme called the Vanishing Coffee Mornings, which operated on the principle of a chain letter, was initiated by the Vocal Group of the MAI. This brought in £80 in the first few months.

It is interesting too that my mother began to be recognised as a personality in her own right. Her photograph appeared quite frequently in the papers and she attracted some interviews and articles: 'Mrs Olive Smith is behaving with the confidence of one who sees the foundation stone already laid and the structure going up fast'.[6] Or: 'Mrs Smith, a charmer with a pair of keen grey-blue eyes . . . answered our questions'.[7] She had to deal with a couple of awkwardly critical letters to *The Irish Times* in June 1960, from two anonymous writers calling themselves 'C sharp' and 'B flat'. The tenor of these letters was that the affairs of CAH were very secretive, that there were rumours of big plans by Tibor Paul, but the writers feared that CAH's ideas were confined to: 'sales of work, coffee drives and raffles'. An officially run, nationally organised campaign was needed to give some hope of reaching a target and indeed, what precisely was the target? 'If ever the campaign gets properly started, will it stand any chance of success? If it fails through secrecy, lack of proper publicity, small-time ideas, we shall never get a chance to launch another in our generation because the Government will interpret that failure as a lack of public demand' (C sharp – 24 June 1960). The second letter (B flat – 30 June) pointed out that: 'Many people not particularly interested in music supported the concert (January 1960) because they felt that it was a disgrace for Ireland's capital city not to have a concert hall' but the writer feared that this public support might wane if the momentum were not maintained. My mother's reply (12 July 1960) gave an outline of the concerts planned for the coming season and suggested that 'C sharp' and 'B flat' might like to visit the CAH office where she would: 'welcome the help they seemed so anxious to give'.

The CAH programme of events for 1960/61 received good press coverage after its announcement by A. P. Reynolds at Jury's Hotel in early September. These included the preliminary details of the exciting Beethoven Festival planned for March 1961 – one hopes that 'C sharp' and 'B flat' were suitably impressed! However, the Board was keen to include events which would spread their fund-raising net more widely, so the opening entertainment was in fact a Fashion Show, sponsored by Newell's of Grafton Street, which was held at the Shelbourne on 20 September with an audience of 100. The *Irish Independent* carried an enthusiastic account the following day, including the information that the show was opened by the actor Micheál MacLiammóir: 'This was indeed a show with a difference. Two ramps allowed a pair of models to parade simultaneously, and the evening followed a young woman's life – teenage years, early twenties . . . wedding day . . . maternity wear . . . mother and child outfits'. An acquaintance of mine, Brendan Staveley, was 'at the piano', and happily the Show raised £142 for the CHF.

At the other end of the spectrum, as it were, was a Jumble Sale, held at 41 York Street on 29 September, which raised £140 in three hours! My mother had been tipped off that a number of charities regularly used this weekly sale as a handy means of fund-raising.

An orchestral concert, billed as a Viennese evening, was given by the RÉSO on Sunday 2 October 1960. Internationally-acclaimed Belfast soprano Heather Harper was the soloist with Tibor Paul on the conductor's rostrum. I think my mother was relieved at the decision to steer clear of the Theatre Royal and move instead to the Olympia Theatre on Dame Street. It was run by the theatrical impresarios Stanley Illsley and Leo McCabe, and it is worth mentioning that my mother forged a very good working relationship with them, leading to the use of this theatre for a great number of CHF events. The programme was a delightful one with arias by Mozart and Johann Strauss, the overtures to *Il Seraglio* and *Die Fledermaus*, the 'Unfinished' Symphony of Schubert and Mozart's *Eine Kleine Nachtmusik*. On 30 September *The Irish Times* carried a very good article about Heather Harper and her illustrious career, and the theatre was almost full. Strangely enough, the reviews were not entirely favourable either to Harper or to Tibor Paul, as well as being critical of the acoustics.

But my mother attracted more press coverage in an article in the *Evening Herald* on 30 September: 'Mrs Olive Smith is one woman who is not letting a single penny escape her that would go towards the erection of the proposed Concert and Assembly Hall, which this city badly needs'.

The evening following the Viennese concert a very different genre was given pride of place at the Shelbourne, also in aid of the CHF. This was a programme of Irish traditional music – Leo Rowsome, widely regarded at that time as the foremost exponent of the uilleann pipes took part, as did the tenor Liam Devally, Seán Maguire (fiddle), Michael Tubridy (flute), the dancer Gráinne Ní Chormaic and the Claisceadal choral group. The star of the evening was the harpist and singer Mary O'Hara. I recall her performance very well – aged just 25, and already a much-travelled musician – the sweet purity of her voice and the artistry of her presentation won everybody's heart. Of course her personal story was very sad, having been widowed in 1957 just months after her marriage to the American poet Richard Selig. She withdrew from public performance between 1962 and 1974, entering a Benedictine convent in England, but happily she eventually returned to the world of music.

There were two further Monday evening concerts at the Shelbourne in aid of the CHF – the London Harp Trio on October 10 and, a week later, the Trostan Singers in a programme of English part-songs conducted by Molly Dunlop. The Harp Trio played in Dublin as part of a tour organised by the MAI. Their leader was the brilliant and formidable Russian harpist, Maria Korchinska, with flautist John Francis and viola player Max Gilbert. Their interesting programme included music by J. C. Bach, Arne, Stephen Dodgson, Debussy and the Arnold Bax Trio. Madame Korchinska requested a page-turner and my mother volunteered me for the job. At the age of 17, I had some experience of turning pages for pianists, but this turned out to be a highly embarrassing situation, as the black notes and arabesques of the florid harp music flew by, with scarcely 5 or 6 bars per page. In the end I got totally lost and was glad to retreat to the back row of the balcony for the second half of the concert!

One of the most extraordinary, and most profitable, ventures in aid of the CHF took place towards the end of October 1960. In March, Mrs Mabel Kapp, who had a fine reputation as a fund-raiser for the Adelaide Hospital, had proposed to my mother that she could make a lot of money for the CHF by running what she called a Monster Bazaar, sponsored by the MAI. Amazingly, my mother persuaded the Council to agree to this, the Round Room of the Mansion House was booked for the entire day of 26 October, and with Mrs Kapp at the helm the plans for the 'Autumn Fair' began to take shape. It was a very memorable day! The hall was buzzing with industry and excitement from early morning as the stalls were laid out and stocked, and it seemed as if there were customers all day long – not just concert hall supporters, but citizens of Dublin looking for a bargain and a nice cup of tea and cake. The best account is in the MAI Council's report for 1960: 'The most concrete proof of the existence of a determination to do something about the Concert Hall was the success of the Autumn Fair . . . Under the sponsorship of the MAI, a very fully representative number of musical organisations in the city volunteered to staff the various stalls. Among these were the Feis Ceoil, the Culwick Choir, the Students' Union of the RIAM, the Municipal School of Music, the Olivian Singers, the St James's Gate Choir, the Clontarf Parish Musical Society, the Trostan Singers, the Dublin Orchestral Players, the Dublin Gramophone Society, the Old Guides and Trefoil Guild, together with individual members of the MAI who organised several stalls. To all of these, to the ladies who organised the refreshments, to Messrs McCullough who provided the transport, to the great number of members who gave goods for the stalls and helped to sell them, to the many business firms who contributed in various ways and especially to Mrs Kapp, are due genuine thanks'. My recollection is of an exhilarating and exhausting day. I was given brief instruction as to what was expected of a waitress and spent the day carrying trays! My mother and MAI Council members were here, there and everywhere, but as the proceedings drew to a close, a profit of over £1,200 had been made and a great feeling of common purpose had been born. The final cheque for £1,285 was presented by Alan Cowle (MAI Hon. Treasurer) to A. P. Reynolds at the AGM of the MAI on 25 January 1961.

Before the end of 1960, a number of other small events took place, in particular a concert given by Geraldine O'Grady with her sisters Eily, Moya and Sheila at the Ely Hall on 27 November, a recital on November 30 by the College Singers of TCD, conducted by Julian Dawson, and a larger-scale choral concert by the St James's Gate Choir, conductor Victor Leeson, at the SFX Hall on 1 December. But from the point of view of this narrative, perhaps the most interesting was the first performance in Ireland on 23 November 1960 of Britten's *Missa Brevis*, written in 1959. This was conducted by my mother with the Olivian Singers and William Watson (organ) and took place at Scots Church, Lower Abbey Street. I was proud to be one of the choristers in this notable event.

1 *Sunday Independent*, 13 January 1957.

2 NLI – ACC 6000, box 8, small brown packet.

3 Ibid. box 47.

4 Ibid. box 8, CAH Scrapbook.

5 The DIFMA engaged orchestras such as the Hallé, the National Orchestra of Monte Carlo, and the Virtuosi di Roma; also the Ballet of the Paris Opera, the Sistine Chapel Choir, the Aachen Cathedral Choir, the D'Oyly Carte Opera Company, and Antonio and his Spanish Dancers. Distinguished soloists included Isaac Stern and Gina Bachauer, as well as many Irish musicians and the RÉSO.

6 *Evening Herald*, 20 April 1960.

7 *Dublin Post*, 13 May 1960.

CHAPTER 19

The Concert Hall, part 4
– 1960 to 1963 –
Sites and more sites!

All this activity represented the new public persona of CAH, but it is important to document also the events behind the scenes.[1] In January 1960, CAH took out a two-year lease on a pair of offices at 3 Molesworth Street at £60 a year, and on 9 February Miss Marjorie Nicholson commenced work as an assistant secretary to my mother at £10 per month for a ten-hour week. Marjorie was a great friend of my mother's older sister Alice and had, presumably, just reached retirement in her previous employment. Her expertise must have been a great help to my mother. The CAH Board were aware that they needed to gather information on the practicalities of running a concert hall, and instructed my mother to embark on a series of consultations with the Ulster Hall in Belfast, the Free Trade Hall in Manchester, the Royal Festival Hall in London, and the Usher Hall in Edinburgh. She received helpful information from all four.

Regarding possible sites, there were some unexpected developments. In March 1960, the CAH board became aware that the developers of the Intercontinental Hotel in Ballsbridge, on the site of the former botanical gardens of TCD, were considering the inclusion of a conference or concert hall in their plans. Bord Fáilte and Aer Lingus were involved, so my mother wrote on 1 April to Thomas O'Gorman of Bord Fáilte, indicating that CAH might be interested. A week later she wrote to Jack Lynch, Minister for Industry and Commerce, as a follow-up to CAH's meeting with him in December 1959,[2] sending the more detailed information he had requested. A further letter on 17 August reminded the Minister of her April letter, but also informed him of CAH's interest in the Ballsbridge hotel site. This letter asked him to use his influence to set up a meeting with the developers as this was a very good site, building costs would be less, the projections for conference business were good, and there could be a shared car-park and gardens. Moreover: 'My Board understands that the Government has a direct interest in this hotel through Bord Fáilte and Aer Lingus'. A reply dated 9 September informs CAH that the Minister has asked Bord Fáilte to meet with CAH. Unfortunately, after due consideration, the hotel company wrote to A. P. Reynolds on 20 December to say that they could not proceed with CAH's proposal as the site was not adequate, but suggested that CAH might consider acquiring some additional land from TCD. This was not followed up.

Meanwhile, on 27 October 1960, Jack Lynch had written to CAH saying that he was prepared to recommend that the Government should seek approval from both Houses of the Oireachtas, for a guaranteed loan of £125,000 towards the building of the concert hall, subject to eight conditions which were set out in the letter. My mother replied on 7 November to say that the CAH Board were gratified at the Minister's offer and agreeable to the eight conditions, except that more detailed estimates of cost would have to wait for the conclusion of negotiations regarding the Ballsbridge site.

A further piece of the jigsaw concerned the Local Government Bill 1960 which the Dáil had passed on 20 July: 'An Act to enable the Corporation of any county borough to provide, or assist the provision of a concert hall, theatre or opera house'. This allowed for 'the making of a free grant, for making a loan, or guaranteeing the repayment of the whole or part of any loan received'. Having written to the Lord Mayor, Maurice Dockrell, on 30 December 1960 to inform him that negotiations over the Ballsbridge site had fallen through, and re-stating their interest in the High Street site, the CAH board applied in January 1961 under the terms of the new Act for a grant of one-third of the estimated cost of £450,000 – the letter of application stating that: 'The remaining capital will be raised by public subscription and guaranteed loan from the Government, in equal amounts. The Minister for Industry and Commerce has indicated his intention to recommend the guarantee to the Government'.

1961

Also in early 1961, the Board of CAH were made aware that the RDS were considering building a concert hall on their land and would like to explore whether CAH would be interested in collaborating. Negotiations commenced and a press statement was issued on 27 April 1961: 'The proposal to provide Dublin with a Concert Hall and Conference Centre has been discussed by the RDS and the Directors of CAH Ltd. It has been agreed that the problems involved will be most effectively approached if the RDS undertakes their examination and, in the event of a favourable decision, assumes responsibility for the building and administration of the hall'. This announcement was carried by all the principal newspapers. A letter from CAH to the RDS with the same date states that: 'the Company will invest its funds in the project and will continue organising entertainments to foster public interest and assist in raising the necessary capital'. Meanwhile Dublin Corporation offered CAH an interview with the Finance Committee to discuss their application for funding, and scheduled this for 28 March. Unfortunately the CAH board felt that they had to request a postponement of this meeting, due to the sensitive state of their talks with the RDS, and this confidential information was relayed in phone calls to the Lord Mayor and the City Manager by A. P. Reynolds. In spite of these precautions, *The Irish Times* published an article in July suggesting that CAH had been discourteous to the Corporation in not attending the meeting on 28 March. My mother sent a letter to the Editor on 7 July 1961, clarifying that the true cause of the postponement had been conveyed to the Lord Mayor and City Manager at the time, and that there had been no discourtesy.

Discussions with the RDS continued during 1961 without resolution, in spite of an optimistic article in the *Evening Herald* of 31 August 1961 which said that a decision: 'is expected within the next few days'. The Board of CAH, whilst busy with their concert season, continued with their own plan of approaching international concert halls for information and advice.[3] But in August 1961, CAH were: 'perturbed to learn that the RDS had been advised that a suitable building would cost £750,000. As this figure was very much in excess of our estimate we decided to ask Professor Robert Matthew, architect of the Royal Festival Hall, London, for his advice and opinion'. He advised that CAH should plan: 'on the basis of approximately £125 per place for the concert hall and the small hall, giving totals of £187,500 and £50,000 respectively'. An allowance of £150,000 would need to be added to cover foyers, bars and other ancillary facilities. Asked about the conversion of an existing hall, he said that: 'the acoustics of a converted building are unpredictable' and that: 'estimate of exact cost is said to be impossible'.

Then on 17 November 1961, CAH took a surprising course of action by sending a memorandum to RÉ, which set out a possible scheme to revive the project to build a concert hall at Montrose. This can only serve to reinforce the view that CAH had anxieties about the RDS decision. The approach regarding Montrose, in tandem with their interest in the High Street site, meant that they were hazardously attempting to ride three horses at once. In the event, misgivings concerning the RDS proved to be well-founded. On 2 February 1962, CAH was informed that the RDS were not prepared to go ahead with a new hall, diverging quite markedly from CAH in their costing, but would alter and extend their existing hall. This was not acceptable to CAH who were convinced that only a purpose-built hall could provide the fundamental amenities required for a National Concert Hall.

1962

There followed, in March 1962, a short-lived approach to the Rank Organisation in London who were known to be preparing to demolish the Theatre Royal and rebuild on the site. The suggestion had come from

179

the AGM of the MAI on 28 February 1962 that it might be feasible to include a concert hall and conference centre in the plans. My mother got as far as having a meeting in London with Sir Thomas Bennett, whose firm were architects to the Rank Organisation. Although she was courteously received, and Sir Thomas was very sympathetic to the aims of CAH, it was clear that Ranks would stick to their original intention of building an office block on the site.

From May 1962 onwards, matters moved forward quite swiftly. The Taoiseach, Seán Lemass, met A. P. Reynolds and my mother on 7 May and afterwards she wrote to thank him: 'for having once more so kindly given of your time to discuss our problems, and in particular for your appreciation and understanding of our responsibilities towards the musical community in Dublin'. On 6 July, my mother wrote to the City Manager, enquiring about the current position regarding the High Street site, and informing him that the negotiations with the RDS had broken down. She followed this with a letter on 18 July, which requested that the postponed meeting (28 March 1961) to discuss CAH's application for a Corporation grant with the Finance Committee, might be reinstated – nearly a year and a half later!

But within the privacy of the CAH Board a new scenario was beginning to unfold. A pair of interesting letters in the CAH files of the MAI archive can provide clarification. Both were written to my mother in June 1962. The first is from A. P. Reynolds, dated 7 June, asking her to circulate a document to the members of the Board and also to call a meeting so that it could be discussed. In this he expresses extreme reservations as to the suitability and capability of CAH to take the campaign forward, particularly regarding future financial liabilities and the management of the Hall, should it be built. He advocates employing a firm of accountants to prepare a blueprint and to then hand everything back to the MAI. The second letter, from Edgar Deale, dated 14 June, gives his outraged reaction to Mr Reynolds' proposal, stating that the prospect is unthinkable and that: 'boldness and vision and not timidity' are required. He continues: 'why wind up when we have at last, after nine years, actually put the Government in the position that they are forced to do something financially?' Edgar suggests that the

Board be strengthened and, in spite of the fact that he will be out of the country on the day of the meeting, hopes that they will think along these lines rather than: 'abandoning the fight when it is practically won'.

This was indeed the approach decided upon by the Board at their meeting on 20 June and it is greatly to A. P. Reynolds' credit that he did not resign but stayed as Chair to help implement the decisions reached. It was proposed that the links between the MAI, as the parent organisation, and CAH be strengthened by forming a defined legal affiliation as a safeguard for the future, thus ensuring the continuance of the MAI's influence regarding the Concert Hall project. Legal advice was sought on the necessary changes to the Memorandum and Articles, on changes to the company membership, and on provision for the distribution of any CAH assets to another body having similar objects, should CAH be wound up. There was another meeting on 4 July, and a further one on 15 August. The Minutes of that meeting record the satisfaction of the Board that a solution had been found to the complicated problem of continuity of membership. This would now be secured by an alteration of the Articles, and: 'it was felt that the control and stability thus established would create a feeling of confidence in the minds of the public and members of the Government, and render less difficult the task of preparing the appeal for funds'.

The Extraordinary General Meeting of CAH, needed to authorise all these legal changes, took place on 31 August 1962. From then on there were three classes of company members: twelve Permanent Members,[4] Music Association of Ireland Members, up to a maximum of twenty-one, and Associate Members. Regarding the MAI Members, I quote from the Minutes of a special MAI Council meeting, held on 23 August 1962: 'These members will take the place of the ordinary shareholders of a Company; they will have the right to attend all general meetings and ask for an extraordinary general meeting to be called, if so desired. Their only liability in the event of the winding up of the Company is a maximum of £1.' After lengthy discussion the Council agreed willingly to this proposal, and planned to put the matter before the next AGM, having made sure to obtain legal advice as to the wording of the required resolution.

On 26 June, the Council had received a confidential and detailed report from my mother on CAH's negotiations with the RDS and other bodies, so they were well briefed. At that meeting Sir George Mahon was requested, as MAI Chairman, to write to Mr James Meenan of the RDS Executive Committee to inform him that the MAI could not support the proposal to adapt their Members' Hall.[5] Sir George was also authorised to write to the Taoiseach (18 July) to express the hope of the MAI: 'that the Government will not regard the RDS's modified scheme as an alternative to a project for a full-scale National Concert Hall, and that if the Government decides to provide financial support for the scheme, it will not in any way detract from such financial support as the Government may ultimately make available for a National Concert Hall'. On 25 July, the private secretary to the Taoiseach replied to say that Mr Lemass had noted the MAI's views, and stated that the Government had not been asked to make any financial contribution towards the modified building scheme of the RDS.

Also in July, renewed contacts with RÉ took on some urgency as a 3-page proposal was sent by CAH on 10 July, which re-traced the previous negotiations in the 1950s and the reasons that these had been abandoned. It requested that negotiations might be reopened, whilst recognising that the original location on the site plan envisaged for the Concert Hall might now need to be revised. CAH's proposal was that the large hall would become the home of the RÉSO for rehearsals, public concerts and studio broadcasts, thereby saving the cost of the Phoenix Hall and the transportation costs of bringing the orchestra to other halls, which was understood to be about £3,000 per annum. The recital hall could be used for rehearsals and studio broadcasts by the RÉLO, making it easy for this group to move across to the TV studios if required. All this usage should be agreed in a contract between CAH and RÉ, and otherwise CAH would have the use of the building for its own promotions or hire to other promoters.

The Director General of RÉ, Edward J. Roth replied on 20 July 1962, saying that CAH's proposal had been discussed by the RÉ Authority at their meeting on 18 July. He indicated that the Authority was willing to consider seriously the use of one or two acres, but only if certain conditions were met. They would have to first seek assurance, under their terms of reference in the Broadcasting Act of 1960, that they could apportion land for a concert hall. Concern was also expressed about responsibility for the care and maintenance of such a hall and about the architectural design. Mr Roth mentioned that when he had spoken to my mother on the phone on 10 July, he had strongly urged CAH to submit a more formal proposal, complete with rough architectural sketches. Before the Authority could discuss the matter further it was essential that they receive: 'complete financial information, the aforementioned architectural drawings and a general policy statement concerning the use to which this proposed concert hall would be placed'. My mother responded on behalf of the Board on 27 July, saying that of course CAH would be responsible for the care and maintenance of the hall and would consult the RÉ Authority regarding design. She promised a formal proposal in due course, but explained that CAH wished to go ahead with their appeal to the public for funds, and were hoping that the Authority might say in principle that the hall could be built at Montrose.

It seems that the situation regarding sites had thrown the CAH board into some confusion as there is a letter, also dated 27 July, to the Taoiseach requesting that he would meet A. P. Reynolds and my mother as they would like to consult him about the Montrose and High Street sites. In this letter my mother writes: 'You will recollect that Montrose was our first love, and that in our memorandum sent to the Government in December 1954 we recommended this site as being the most suitable available at that time'. An appointment was arranged for 29 August but there is no record in the MAI archive of what transpired.

A meeting did take place between A. P. Reynolds and Mr Roth in early September 1962. Following this, in a long letter dated 11 September, Mr Reynolds set out the current CAH position, covering the fund-raising appeal and other financial matters. He also explained the changes which CAH had made to their Memorandum and Articles in order to make their financial situation legally secure. He pleaded again for certainty regarding a site at Montrose, so that the planned appeal could go ahead.

But it was all to no avail – Edward Roth wrote to Mr Reynolds on 18 October 1962 to say that the RÉ Authority had thoroughly considered the CAH proposal at their meeting on 17 October and had decided to reject it. It might not be unreasonable to deduce from Mr Roth's phrase: 'I very deeply regret' that he himself had been in favour of the idea, but had been unable to convince the members of the Authority.

I refer to my metaphor of riding three horses at once – two of the horses had fallen and the track of the third horse, namely the Corporation and the High Street site, must now be followed. An unexpected obstacle arose in the form of an article published in the *Sunday Press* on 23 September 1962, which reported on the breakdown of negotiations between CAH and the RDS. The timing is puzzling, as this had actually happened in the spring of 1962. The focus was chiefly on the wide gap (probably exaggerated by the paper) between the financial projection of the RDS (up to £1 million) and that of CAH (no more than £500,000). But such a journalistic intervention at this juncture was definitely not helpful. CAH had received no reply to their letter of 18 July which requested that the postponed meeting with the Corporation Finance Committee might be reinstated, and the response when it came, dated 2 October, merely informed CAH that consideration of their application had been deferred. But the next letter of 30 October stated that the Finance Committee, having noted press references, wanted to know the exact position regarding the RDS before discussing the matter further.

On 2 November 1962, my mother sent a lengthy reply on behalf of CAH, clarifying the large difference in projected expenditure between the CAH figure of £450,000 and the RDS estimate of £750,000. The letter also explained the CAH position that the conversion of an existing hall would not be suitable as a National Concert Hall and that a purpose-built building must remain the goal to strive for. Copies of this were sent to the Lord Mayor and the City Manager, followed by a short memorandum to all the City Councillors on 3 December. Finally, the Finance Committee offered to meet CAH on 14 January 1963, the deputation to comprise A. P. Reynolds, Michael Scott, Leon Ó Dubhghaill and my mother.

1963

Before that meeting could take place, a letter dated 9 January 1963 on behalf of the Minister for Finance, James Ryan, informed CAH that: 'the Minister is prepared, subject to the approval of Dáil Éireann, to make provision for a state grant not exceeding £100,000 towards the project sponsored by your organisation.' This welcome decision was subject to four conditions and the previous offer of a loan guarantee was withdrawn. A certain amount of favourable press coverage followed, notably in the *Evening Herald* and *Irish Times*, and my mother replied on behalf of the CAH board on 22 January, indicating that the decision was well received and much appreciated. The Board felt that this news would strengthen their hand at the meeting with the Finance Committee of the Corporation on 14 January. My mother kept pencilled notes of that meeting and of the points raised by the Councillors. She obviously felt that the CAH deputation had acquitted themselves well, particularly Leon Ó Dubhghaill who had pointed out that the city would acquire a building worth £450,000 for an input of £150,000 from the Corporation. Significantly, however, the Finance Committee made it clear that it had no remit as to the question of a site.

In her letter of 22 January, my mother informed the Minister that CAH would go ahead with their fund-raising appeal as soon as: 'the result of our request for a grant to the Corporation is known.' She wrote the same day to the City Manager, seeking clarification of a disquieting rumour that the High Street site would be affected by a road-widening project: 'We understand that the site originally set aside by the Corporation . . . has become too small, due to the necessity for providing for street widening under the Town Planning scheme.' She asked whether more space could be made available on the present site, or if another site could be provided. This was a very worrying situation, and to make matters worse the Finance Committee wrote on 2 February to say that it had deferred its decision: 'until the RDS had completed its scheme for the accommodation of concerts and conferences.' But the real body-blow was still to come! On 4 February 1963, a letter from the Town Planning Department stated: 'As you have been informed in previous correspondence, the City Council did not at any time agree, nor had it before it for consideration, any firm proposal to dispose of the site to your Board . . .The correspondence and discussions which have taken place with the Planning Office have at all times made it clear the amount of the High Street site which could be considered for your purpose. . . . As was pointed out to you in the Planning Officer's letter of 26 November last, your architect has conveyed the impression to the Planning Officer that he does not consider the High Street site to be the most attractive for your purpose.'

Unfortunately, the letter of 26 November 1962 does not appear to be in the MAI Archive, but the possibility that Michael Scott was the architect in question cannot be ruled out, as no other architect was involved with CAH at that time. That sentence feels like the sting of a scorpion's tail! But overall, one cannot help recalling a quotation from Oscar Wilde: 'To lose one parent may be regarded as a misfortune; to lose both looks like carelessness!'[6] Apply this to sites and one can only wonder how a Board with such combined experience, business acumen and political connections could have ended up dealing so ineffectively on so many fronts? Admittedly, they had been led to believe for a number of years that the High Street site was ear-marked for them. But why were they content to deal just with the Planning and Finance departments of the Corporation and not insist that matters were brought before the City Council at various stages for ratification?

Regarding the Montrose site, why did they not produce the financial information, architectural drawings and general policy statement so pointedly requested by Edward Roth, which might have facilitated him in persuading the RÉ Authority that CAH was a body with which they could do business? One can hardly accuse them of being amateurish; perhaps there was not sufficient participation by all the Board members all of the time? Whilst my mother's name appears at the end of almost every item of correspondence, on major matters she was surely carrying out the policy and decisions of the Board. Besides, a huge amount of her energies in the early 1960s must have been channelled into the concerts for the Fund.

At this point in early 1963, only two things had been achieved – a promise of £100,000 from the Government and a greatly heightened public awareness of the need for a National Concert Hall.

On 7 May Lord Moyne, who was rarely present at CAH board meetings, wrote to my mother asking her to put his suggestion to the Board of a site in the Phoenix Park, including a little sketch to make the location quite clear.[7] This idea would probably have been politically controversial, but Lord Moyne was anxious that the Board would consult with Donogh O'Malley, Parliamentary Secretary to the Minister for Finance, and indeed my mother had already arranged an interview with him on 14 May. The outcome of this was that Raymond McGrath, senior architect at the Board of Works, was asked to make a report on available sites. Ironically, he recommended Montrose, apparently unaware that this had been rejected by RÉ the previous October!

On 26 September my mother had another meeting with Mr O'Malley and this time a potential site at Haddington Road, part of the former Beggar's Bush barracks, was mentioned. There was further contact with Raymond McGrath, and Michael Scott was also consulted, though he feared that the site might not be large enough to include the recital hall. It seems that the CAH board were informed officially, as my mother wrote to Mr O'Malley on 21 November 1963, saying that there had been an enthusiastic response from the Board to the suggestion of Haddington Road and that: 'the Board members undertook to regard this matter as confidential until the decision of the Minister is received.'

[1] NLI – ACC 6000, boxes 11 and 18, are the source for most of the archived CAH material referred to in this chapter, including negotiations with the Intercontinental Hotel, Rank Organisation, the RDS, Dublin Corporation and the Irish Government. The report from Prof. Matthew is in box 18, green folder 2; documents relating to Montrose and RÉ in box 18, grey folder 7.

[2] See Chapter 18.

[3] In 1961 these included the Colston Hall, Bristol, the Eastbourne Theatre, Fairfield Hall in Croydon, the Liverpool Philharmonic Hall, the Sydney Opera House, and the Berlin State Academy of Music.

[4] Following the changes to the Memorandum and Articles in 1962, the twelve Permanent Members of CAH were:- Sir Alfred Beit, Edgar Deale, Laurence Kennedy, Dr John F. Larchet, Lord Moyne, A. P. Reynolds, Michael Scott and M. Olive Smith; A. W. Bayne, Sir George Mahon, Fr Cormac O'Daly and Leon Ó Dubhghaill. The first eight names were also the Directors. A. W. Bayne was a former Director who resigned in 1957, but was willing to become a Permanent Member.

[5] NLI – ACC 6000, box 26, beige folder 7.

[6] *The Importance of Being Earnest*, Act 1.

[7] NLI – ACC 6000, box 47, blue file 3.

CHAPTER 20

The MAI – 1960 to 1964, including the German Tours

1960

When CAH decided, with the encouragement of Tibor Paul, to launch their campaign actively before the concert-going public, an entirely new and exciting dynamic became evident in Irish musical life, and particularly so in the capital city. The MAI could not fail to be affected, especially as there were people involved in both organisations, notably my mother and Edgar Deale. MAI members were offered priority booking vouchers for the Gioconda de Vito concert on 15 January 1960, and the talk following the AGM on 27 January was given by Michael Scott on the subject of Concert Halls.

There were two new elections to the Council in 1960 – Sir George Mahon and Andrew Healy. Following the AGM, Edgar Deale retired as chairman and, having served in this capacity unofficially and officially for at least ten years, was warmly thanked for all he had done for the MAI. He was replaced by Leon Ó Dubhghaill, who had been attending Council meetings since 1953 as the representative of An tOireachtas, and was then co-opted in his own right in March 1958. Leon was the principal of St Finbar's Boys National School at Cabra West, Dublin, and had been secretary of An tOireachtas from 1938 to 1953, later serving as chairman. He was also one of the Permanent Members of CAH. To

189

the MAI Council he contributed wide administrative experience and a wonderfully calm temperament; I know that my mother often looked to him for advice.

Two Coming-Out recitals were planned for the year 1960. The first was given by Mary Gallagher (violin) on 17 February at the Hibernian Hotel. She was partnered by Rhona Marshall in a programme of Mozart, Bach, Debussy, de Falla and Wieniawski. The second, on 18 November, was given by Bernadette Greevy accompanied by Jeannie Reddin. The main works in her recital were the *Frauenliebe und Leben* cycle of Schumann, *Five Tonadillas* by Granados and some Britten songs.

Country Tours, with funding from the Shaw Trust, were undertaken in February by the Irish violinist, Hugh Maguire, then leader of the London Symphony Orchestra, with Joyce Rathbone (piano),[1] and by the newly-established Radio Éireann Quartet in March.[2] This quartet was, of course, domiciled in Cork, so there was no need for my mother to drive them around the country. But she did receive a very warm letter of appreciation and praise from Roger Raphael, the leader, on behalf of the group. The 2nd violin was Brendan O'Reilly, who had given his Coming-Out recital for the MAI in 1958. The other two members were Peter Sermon (viola) and Gwenda Milbourn (cello).

Two of the Members' Meetings were designated as being for the CHF – the recital by Peter Pears and Benjamin Britten on 28 April, and the October concert of the London Harp Trio (see Chapter 18). The Trio also undertook a Country Tour, visiting Cork, Nenagh, Birr, Wicklow and Portarlington. A third Members' Meeting on 26 September at the College of Physicians was given by the very fine Australian oboist, Ian Wilson, with Dorothy White (piano).

1961

At the AGM in 1961, Andrew Healy's appointment was confirmed as a second Hon. Assistant Secretary, to work alongside Fr Oliver O'Brien. It would be fair to say that, at this stage, my mother was so preoccupied with the organisation of concerts for the CHF that she had come to rely more and more on Fr Oliver to carry out the day-to-day administration of the MAI, and so he in turn was in need of an assistant.

The year 1961 was relatively quiet for the MAI, perhaps slightly overshadowed by the larger-scale promotions of CAH, but also suffering a financial setback due to the visit of the Hague Philharmonic Orchestra, conducted by Willem van Otterloo. The MAI was involved at the request of Aloys Fleischmann, who engaged the orchestra for a concert in Cork, but needed the promise of a Dublin performance to complete his negotiations. My mother had very little to do with the arrangements, most of them being handled by Victor Leeson, though I do remember attending the concert. It was in the Theatre Royal on 6 May, the Saturday afternoon of the Bank Holiday weekend, not a good time to attract an audience. The sad outcome was that the MAI lost £107, making a sizeable hole in their finances. During the autumn, a drive to bring in new members was successful, with an increase of 70 by the year's end, bringing the total membership up to 580. A new secretarial arrangement also brought some savings when the MAI moved into an office at 3 Molesworth Street on the same floor as CAH, at a rental of £30 per annum. Furnishings for the room were provided by Brendan Dunne, former Council member and at that time working in interior design, whilst a typewriter was given on permanent loan by Sir George Mahon. Incidentally, about this time Brendan Dunne designed and furnished a wonderfully contemporary dining-room for our home.

The Members' Meeting on 22 February 1961 upheld the MAI's reputation for unusual programming in a recital at the Overend Hall on Upper Leeson Street by the London Consort of Viols. There were five musicians, between them playing all the instruments of the Viol family (treble, alto, tenor and bass) and one player doubling on recorder. Their programme was mostly English 16th century, but included some French and Italian music. They were entertained to lunch at Guinness's Brewery (with the advance warning that four of them were vegetarians). This visit was arranged by Andrew Healy, as was the spring Country Tour given by Bernadette Greevy and Mary Gallagher, with accompanist Jeannie Reddin.[3] Funding for this

191

and for the November tour of Veronica Dunne and Patricia Herbert[4] came from the Shaw Trust.

On 15 May, the Members' Meeting was given by the young British violinist, Tessa Robbins, with her duo partner, the Canadian pianist Robin Wood, soon to become my professor at the RAM in London. Tessa was the winner of the prestigious Queen Elizabeth of Belgium competition, as well as two other international prizes, and had new works by three distinguished composers dedicated to her. My mother and I had met Robin at my audition for the RAM, so I was very proud to turn pages for him in Dublin (and a lot more successfully than for Madame Korchinska!). Their programme was very exciting with the Duo Concertante of Stravinsky and Beethoven's 'Kreutzer' Sonata. There were no Coming-Out recitals in 1961, but there was another Members' Meeting on 30 October in the Oak Room of the Mansion House, which took the form of a symposium organised by Brian Boydell on Joe Groocock's recently published *General Survey of Music in the Republic of Ireland*. Joe was the main speaker, as well as Havelock Nelson and Bernard Curtis (Cork) with Edgar Deale in the chair. On 8 November, P. J. Malone addressed the Council meeting on the concerns of the Irish Federation of Musicians regarding the future of the RÉSO and received assurances of support, should there be any real threat to its existence.

An image of the MAI at this period could be that of an ocean liner with nearly 600 passengers on board and a steady, long-term crew to guide the ship. These were two of the four founding members, Brian Boydell and Edgar Deale plus my mother, Mairtín McCullough, Madge Clotworthy (Bradbury), Rhona Marshall, Winifred Parkes, Mrs Mercedes Bolger (Gorey), Joe Groocock, Leon Ó Dubhghaill, Aloys Fleischmann, Archie Potter and Victor Leeson. Some of these Council members never held the position of an Honorary Officer, but their input, support and service on various sub-committees was constant and essential. News of the vessel's progress (and other events in the world of music) was posted monthly through the indispensible MAI *Bulletin*, edited and distributed by Mairtín McCullough. To continue with this image – from time to time other crew

Gilbert & Sullivan at Christ Church Rathgar and Handel at the Gaiety

43. *Edgar Deale as Pooh-Bah and Olive as Pitti-Sing in* The Mikado.
44. *'Three Little Maids from School', Olive as Pitti-Sing –* The Mikado.

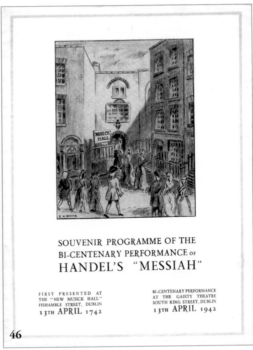

45. *Olive in her costume as Tessa in* The Gondoliers.
46. *Olive and her sister Alice sang in this Bicentenary (1942) performance of* Messiah.

47 and 48. Baby pictures of the author, early 1944.

49. Olive with her mother-in-law, Isabella Smith, and the author.

50. *Brian Lusk with Olive, c.1942.*
51. *Second World War photo of Lyall in the uniform*
of the Slua na Mara, which patrolled Dublin Bay.

52. *The Irish Girl Guides Choir, conductor Olive Smith,*
winners of the competition for Ladies' Choirs at the Dublin Feis Ceoil in 1949.
The choir members were drawn from the senior ranks of the organisation.

Three of the four original founders of the Music Association of Ireland 1948

53. Brian Boydell　　　　*54. Edgar Deale*　　　　*55. Frederick May*

It has not been possible to source a photo of Michael McMullin.

56. Olive with the vocal soloists for the bicentenary performance of
Bach's B Minor Mass, 29 September 1950.
LEFT TO RIGHT: *Margaret Field-Hyde (soprano), Owen Brannigan (bass),*
Olive Smith, Ronald Bristol (tenor), Anne Wood (alto).

57. *Assessing the Ferdinand Weber harpsichord in the National Museum, 1950.*
L TO R: *Olive Smith, Brian Boydell, John Beckett (seated at the instrument), Otto Matzerath (conductor) and Liam Gogan, keeper of the musical instrument collection.*

58. *Dedication page of presentation score of Bach's B Minor Mass.*
59. LEFT TO RIGHT: *Dr Thomas Armstrong, Edgar Deale and the author, Wicklow Mountains, August 1949.*

60. *New London String Quartet arrive at Dublin Airport, 28 March 1954.*
LEFT TO RIGHT: *Douglas Cameron, Lionel Bentley,*
Olive Smith, Keith Cummings, Erich Gruenberg.

61. *On the way to Cork for the Bax Memorial Concert, 31 March 1954.*
LEFT TO RIGHT: *Charles Lynch (pianist), Mairtín McCullough (MAI),*
François D'Albert (violinist), Lionel Bentley (violinist).

62. *New London String Quartet on tour, October 1954,*
lunch stop at Ashford Castle, Cong, Co. Mayo.
L TO R: *Olive, Erich Gruenberg, Lionel Bentley, Douglas Cameron.*
63. *Douglas Cameron plays unaccompanied Bach in a hotel bar after a concert.*

64. *The London String Quartet rehearses in the sitting-room at Rockview, October 1955.*
LEFT TO RIGHT: *Frederick Grinke, Keith Cummings, Douglas Cameron, Lionel Bentley.*

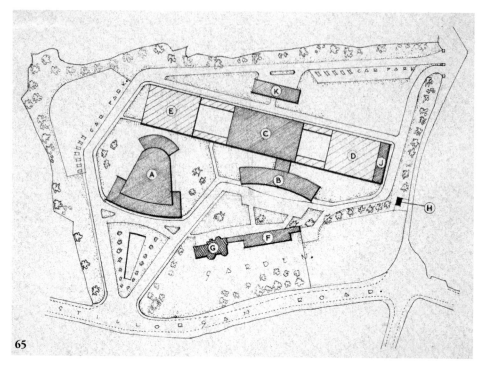

65

65. *Site plan for the proposed development by Radio Éireann of TV studios and ancillary buildings at Montrose, Donnybrook, including the Concert Hall proposed by Concert and Assembly Hall Ltd. The plan was drawn up by the Office of Public Works and dated 21 September 1953.*

A. Concert Hall

B. Administration Block

C. Studios and Rehearsal Rooms

D. Television Studios

E. Future Studio Extension

F. Staff Restaurant etc.

G. Montrose House

H. H.T. Sub-station

J. Engineering Services

K. Garage

66. *Flora Nielsen (mezzo-soprano) took part in a Schumann recital for the MAI on 7 July 1956 and a Country Tour in January 1957.*

The Music Association of Ireland

ROYAL HIBERNIAN HOTEL

Tuesday, January 15th, 1957

at 8 p.m.

MARY O'BRIEN
Violin

with **KITTY O'CALLAGHAN**
Piano

Programme will include works by

CORELLI, BRAHMS, YSAYE & RAVEL

Tickets   -   5/- & 2/6

From GILL'S, McCULLOUGH'S, MAY'S & PIGOTT'S

67. *Publicity leaflet for the inaugural MAI Coming-Out Recital.*

68. *Gerard Hüsch (baritone) gave a Lieder recital for the MAI on 22 February 1957.*

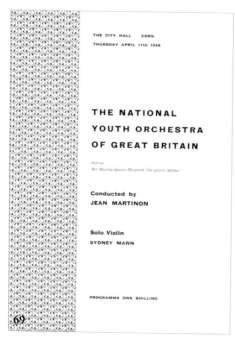

THE CITY HALL   CORK

THURSDAY APRIL 17th 1958

THE NATIONAL
YOUTH ORCHESTRA
OF GREAT BRITAIN

Patron
Her Majesty Queen Elizabeth The Queen Mother

Conducted by
JEAN MARTINON

Solo Violin
SYDNEY MANN

PROGRAMME ONE SHILLING

69

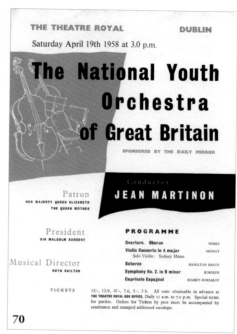

THE THEATRE ROYAL   DUBLIN

Saturday April 19th 1958 at 3.0 p.m.

The National Youth
Orchestra
of Great Britain

SPONSORED BY THE DAILY MIRROR

Conductor

Patron   JEAN MARTINON
HER MAJESTY QUEEN ELIZABETH
THE QUEEN MOTHER

President   PROGRAMME
SIR MALCOLM SARGENT
                   Overture. Oberon   WEBER
                   Violin Concerto in A major   MOZART
                     Solo Violin : Sydney Mann
Musical Director   Scherzo   HAMILTON HARTY
     RUTH RAILTON Symphony No. 2. in B minor   BORODIN
                   Capriccio Espagnol   RIMSKY-KORSAKOV

TICKETS   15/-, 12/6, 10/-, 7/6, 5/-, 3/6. All seats obtainable in advance at
           THE THEATRE ROYAL BOX OFFICE, Daily 11 a.m. to 7.0 p.m. Special terms
           for parties. Orders for Tickets by post must be accompanied by
           remittance and stamped addressed envelope.

70

69. *Programme for the Cork concert of the National
Youth Orchestra of Great Britain, 17 April 1958.*
70. *Publicity leaflet for the Dublin concert of the NYOGB, 19 April 1958.*

71

71. *The NYOGB in rehearsal in the Cork City Hall, conductor Jean Martinon.*

72. *Lyall Smith at the door of his chemist shop, John Smith & Son, Rathgar.*
73. *Official photo of Lyall and Olive for his presidency of the Photographic Dealers Association – dinner-dance at Grosvenor House, London, 8 October 1953.*

74. *The Olivian Singers, conductor Olive Smith, following their success in winning the International Competition for Ladies' Choirs at the Cork Choral Festival, May 1958.*

75. *Mairtín McCullough and Olive –*
post-concert administration!

76. *Irish violinist Hugh Maguire with*
pianist Joyce Rathbone, publicity
leaflet for their MAI Country Tour,
February 1960.

77. *Joseph Groocock playing*
Olive's Bechstein piano.

78. *Programme for the performances during*
the Christmas holiday period 1958/59.

THREE LOGOS FOR THE MAI BULLETIN

79. *Woodcut, used up to 1964.*
80. *Lyre design by Jim Wilson, 1964-68.*
81. *Harp design by Jim Harkin, 1969-1981.*

THE MUSIC ASSOCIATION OF IRELAND

GEORGE FRIDERIC
HANDEL
1685 — 1759

Commemoration in Ireland 1959

82. *Douglas Cameron, conductor of the orchestral concerts.*
83. *Frederic Jackson, conductor of the choral concerts.*
84. *Commemorative plaque at Fishamble Street.*
85. *The Festival programme cover, designed by Dolmen Press with a recitative from* Messiah, *and used for all the performances countrywide.*

86. *Olive welcomes President de Valera to the concert at the Theatre Royal,*
15 January 1960; Tibor Paul (LEFT) *and the Australian Ambassador* (RIGHT).

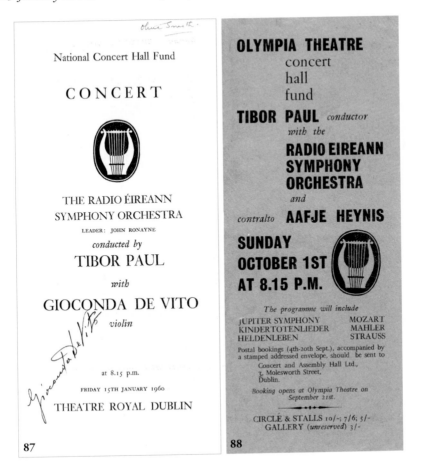

National Concert Hall Fund

CONCERT

THE RADIO ÉIREANN
SYMPHONY ORCHESTRA

LEADER: JOHN RONAYNE

conducted by

TIBOR PAUL

with

GIOCONDA DE VITO

violin

at 8.15 p.m.

FRIDAY 15TH JANUARY 1960

THEATRE ROYAL DUBLIN

87

OLYMPIA THEATRE
concert
hall
fund

TIBOR PAUL *conductor*

with the

RADIO EIREANN SYMPHONY ORCHESTRA

and

contralto **AAFJE HEYNIS**

SUNDAY OCTOBER 1ST AT 8.15 P.M.

The programme will include

JUPITER SYMPHONY	MOZART
KINDERTOTENLIEDER	MAHLER
HELDENLEBEN	STRAUSS

Postal bookings (4th-20th Sept.), accompanied by
a stamped addressed envelope, should be sent to
Concert and Assembly Hall Ltd.,
3, Molesworth Street,
Dublin.

Booking opens at Olympia Theatre on
September 21st.

CIRCLE & STALLS 10/-; 7/6; 5/-
GALLERY (*unreserved*) 3/-

88

89. Peter Pears and Benjamin Britten gave a recital at the St Francis Xavier Hall, Dublin, for the Concert Hall Fund (CHF), 28 April 1960.

90. LEFT: *Bernadette Greevy (contralto) and* RIGHT: *Mary Gallagher (violinist); publicity photo for their MAI Country Tour, spring 1961.*

members came on board, sailed with the ship for a period, perhaps even for five or six years, and then for some perfectly valid reason were called away to other duties. One of these was the banker Sir George Mahon, who took over as Chairman in February 1962. Another was a young Englishman, David Laing, who had come to Dublin to read geology at TCD in 1958. He was quickly drawn into musical activities, both at TCD and through friendships with some members of the RÉSO. Noting the energy emanating from the MAI and CAH as the fund-raising campaign got under-way, he introduced himself to my mother and offered to help. He was appointed to the salaried Assistant Secretary post for the MAI in January 1961 and shortly after that began working for CAH as well, due to the ill-health of Miss Nicholson. The two offices being in the same building ensured a steady clientèle of musicians for the quaint Turf Fire Café on the ground floor, run by the Misses Gavin Duffy.

1962

The 1962 AGM was held on 28 February and was followed by a Coming-Out recital by Brighid Mooney (cello) with Gerard Shanahan (piano). Two other Coming-Outs took place in 1962 – Carmel O'Byrne (soprano) and Patricia Dunkerley (flute), accompanied by Jeannie Reddin on 19 October, and Deirdre McNulty (piano) on 25 October. There was another Country Tour by the RÉ Quartet in March,[5] whilst the spring Members' Meeting on 21 March 1962 brought Julian Bream, that very celebrated exponent of the lute and guitar to the Exam Hall in TCD. As with the Britten and Pears recital in 1960, it was decided to promote Bream's concert as part of the MAI's contribution to the CHF. The Council's report for 1962 describes it as a recital of great distinction, playing to a very large and appreciative audience. The programme was certainly fascinating – a first half of Renaissance lute music from Spain, Italy, France and England, and then a change to guitar for the second half, which included music by Weiss, Bach, Villa Lobos and Turina. The concert was recorded by RÉ for future transmission and was attended by the British Ambassador and Mrs MacLennan. The next event, on 14 May 1962, was an illustrated lecture by the Hon. Gerald Lascelles on

'Jazz: some aspects of its evolution' which was held at the Ely Hall. He was an interesting personality, a first cousin of Queen Elizabeth and younger brother of the Earl of Harewood. His knowledge of jazz was encyclopaedic, his other great interest being racing cars!

Going back to March, there was a brief controversy in the letters' pages of *The Irish Times* over the MAI's perceived tendency to engage musicians from the UK when, arguably, there were just as good Irish performers available. This arose from comments by Charles Acton in his review of a recital by Jaroslav Vaneček and Rhona Marshall. My mother defended the MAI's record from 1954 to 1962, detailing the proportion of Irish artists who had been engaged (letter of 28 March) saying that his comments were: 'factually incorrect, misleading and possibly damaging to the Association'. Mr Acton however maintained that, in the previous three years, six recitals by British players had been arranged and only one Irish – Charles Lynch. He did not include Coming-Out recitals or Country Tours, which was perhaps an error, as my mother corrected him with very convincing statistics in both these areas (30 March). A contribution from Michael Yeats followed on 4 April, highlighting the aims of the MAI and concluding that: 'without in any way belittling the excellent record of the MAI in bringing good music to many centres throughout the country, an occasional prod by your Music Critic will be well worthwhile if it results in the provision of more frequent performance opportunities for Irish artists'.

A special meeting of the Council was called for 23 August 1962: 'to consider and approve a proposal from CAH Ltd which will ensure the continuance of the MAI's influence in the Concert Hall project'. This matter was dealt with in considerable detail in Chapter 19 but something can be added here from the MAI's perspective. Obviously my mother and Edgar Deale knew the whole situation extremely well, and could provide clarification of all the issues, but the Council needed plenty of time to deliberate. The following resolution was passed unanimously: 'That this Council agrees to become members of Concert and Assembly Hall Ltd, and recommends to the next Annual General Meeting of the Music Association of Ireland that all future Council members shall, by reason of their membership of the Council, become members of Concert and Assembly Hall Ltd, for the duration of their membership of the Council'. It was further agreed to take separate legal advice as to whether any alteration to the MAI Constitution would be needed.

The next Council meeting on 18 September heard with regret that Fr Oliver O'Brien had resigned because of his move to Limerick, and that Andrew Healy was also unable to continue as Joint Hon. Assistant Secretary. It was decided to allow these honorary positions to lapse, in view of there being a permanent and paid Assistant Secretary. From this time forward, my mother resumed overall control of the MAI Country Tours, deciding on the artists and dealing with the music societies who were all Corporate Members of the MAI. In the autumn of 1962 she organised three tours – Charles Lynch with János Fürst (violin) gave five recitals,[6] the Irish violinist John Ronayne, leader of the Royal Philharmonic Orchestra, with his wife Elgin Strub (piano) played in Galway and Limerick prior to their RDS recitals on 3 December, and the O'Grady Ensemble played in Nenagh and Tralee. In conjunction with the tours, my mother very often took a hand in the organisation of the three Members' Meetings each year, a Dublin recital being an important part of the package for visiting performers. She was not involved with the organisation of Coming-Out recitals; there was a separate committee for these, drawn from the Council.

In September the MAI co-operated again with Havelock Nelson, this time in a production of *Noye's Fludde* by Benjamin Britten. This was a big undertaking involving a cast of children and adults, a small orchestra, scenery, props and lighting, all to be transported from Belfast for two performances on Saturday 29 September. As the first performance in Ireland it was an exciting prospect. Permission was obtained from TCD to hold it in the Public Theatre (Exam Hall) at 5.00 p.m. and 7.30 p.m. and to have the use of the hall all day. With an Arts Council guarantee of £150, the way was clear to promote it as a Members' Meeting. It was David Laing's first big involvement on behalf of the MAI. According to the MAI archive[7] a special section of the early-morning Enterprise train from Belfast was allocated for the transportation of this large group. Unfortunately the Irish weather decided to provide a suitable backdrop: 'an all-too-realistic downpour accompanied by gale-force winds, which provided a veritable flood' (Council's report for 1962) and the reviews were mixed – very good from the *Irish Press*, but unenthusiastic from the *The Irish Times*.

Also in September 1962, my mother represented Ireland at a UNESCO Congress in Rome entitled 'Music and its Public'. It ran from 27–30 September and she received a travel grant of £52 from the CRC. Apart from the excitement of visiting Rome for the first time, this trip provided an opportunity for my mother to meet with her Canadian cousin, Joyce Meyer, granddaughter of her mother's sister Sara, who was working in Rome for the UN Food and Agriculture Organisation (FAO). The Irish singer Carmel O'Byrne also worked for FAO to support herself during her vocal studies in Rome, and was most helpful in arranging my mother's accommodation. My mother gave a paper on 'Music in Ireland' at the congress, speaking about the role of the FÉ Music Advisor and the funding available for music from the Mayer, Carnegie and Shaw Trusts. Following her return, she once again put pressure on the CRC to pay the annual dues so that Ireland could be represented on the UNESCO Music Council.

1963

The year 1963 began with a high-calibre recital by the Berlin Philharmonic Octet on 16 January at the SFX Hall. This was a Members' Meeting arranged in association with the German Cultural Institute. There had been a last-minute change of programme, occasioned by the tragic deaths of two members of the Octet in a car crash, in which a third was very seriously injured. Other players from the Berlin Philharmonic had replaced them and they performed a lovely group of chamber works – a Horn Sextet by Boccherini, the Mozart Clarinet Quintet and the Beethoven Septet.

The AGM on 20 February dealt with the Resolution required to set up the new relationship with CAH (see Chapter 19) which read as follows: 'That the right given to the Music Association of Ireland to nominate any person as a Music Association Member of Concert and Assembly Hall Ltd, and to remove any person so nominated under Article 4 of the Articles of Association of the said Company, shall be exercised by the Council who may nominate for membership of the said Company such persons as they shall in their absolute discretion think fit, and who may likewise in their absolute discretion remove such persons so nominated'. This was passed by a large majority. Immediately after the AGM, in compliance with the solicitor's advice, the Council met and passed a further resolution: 'That the members of this Council, save those who are already members of Concert and Assembly Hall Ltd, be nominated by the Music Association of Ireland as members of the said Company, pursuant to Article 4 of its Articles of Association'. At the March Council meeting, my mother reported that eight more members were needed to bring the MAI numbers up to the required twenty-one, and asked that a procedure for their nomination be agreed. By 10 May the list was complete and was sent to A. P. Reynolds. All had signed the necessary application forms.[8] As previously noted, they had the right to attend all general meetings and to ask for an extraordinary general meeting. In the event of the winding up of CAH, their liability would be limited to a maximum of £1.

The AGM was followed by a Coming-Out recital given by Eily Markey (soprano) with Gerard Shanahan (piano). In March, Victor Leeson was elected as chairman of the Council and a vote of thanks proposed to Sir George Mahon: 'who had steered the Council through some delicate negotiations with great tact and skill'. Also in March, on Monday 11th, there was a Members' Meeting given by the London Baroque Trio at the College of Physicians. This group – Michael Thomas (harpsichord), Graham Kinsman (flute) and Caroline Butcher (oboe) – also enjoyed a Country Tour.[9] For their programme of Trio Sonatas and some keyboard solos, they used a harpsichord and a clavichord, both made by Michael Thomas, for which they had their own transport. There was a lot of interest in the tour. Gorey, for instance, reported a capacity audience and were delighted with the technical explanations of all the instruments.[10] In February and March, the ever-popular O'Grady Ensemble gave recitals as a continuation of their tour begun in November 1962.[11]

In April, the Council learned that David Laing would be leaving his post of paid Assistant Secretary shortly and that his replacement would need to be found. His 2½ years working for the MAI and CAH had a significant influence upon his future career, leading to administrative positions at the Fairfield Halls in Croydon, the Newcastle Festival, the London Mozart Players, as curator of Russborough House and as founder of the Festival in Great Irish Houses. He continued to promote occasional celebrity concerts in Dublin, engaging artists such as Elizabeth Schwarzkopf, Gérard Souzay, Rita Streich, Paul Tortelier and Sviatoslav Richter. Endowed with a naturally charming manner, David undoubtedly learned a great deal about the music business from my mother, remarking in an interview in 2002[12] that she was invariably in the CAH office before him when he arrived at 9.30 a.m. Through her, he established contacts with major London agents such as Wilfred van Wyck, Harold Holt and Ibbs and Tillett, which benefitted him as his career developed. He reminisced that my mother had a very agreeable relationship with them all, particularly because she looked after artists very well. Apparently she was known in London as 'Dublin's Mrs Tillett' – a reference to the lady who ran Ibbs & Tillett and was 'a bit of a dragon'.

The question of David's replacement was resolved with the appointment of Mrs Nancy Glenn as paid Assistant Secretary and the adjustment of the office hours to a settled schedule of 10.00 a.m. – 12.30 p.m. and 2.00 – 4 p.m., Monday to Friday. Nancy was an ideal appointment; already a member of the MAI, she was an aunt of the Treasurer, Alan Cowle, and her sisters Helen Pasker and May Cowle were members of the Olivian Singers. She got on very well with my mother, who came to rely greatly on Nancy's efficiency and her calm and dependable personality.

The Autumn Members' Meeting was given by the New London Wind Ensemble in the newly-opened Irish Life Assurance Theatre on Mespil Road on 10 October 1963. This group was led by the oboist Ian Wilson, well known to Dublin audiences from his solo recital for the MAI in September 1960 and his oboe d'amore playing in the B Minor Mass in April 1962. The other members were David Sandeman (flute), Keith Puddy (clarinet), Timothy Brown (horn) and Cecil James (bassoon). The Quintet's availability for a Country Tour prompted a terrific response, resulting in nine concerts[13] in just ten days, and many enthusiastic letters afterwards from various centres. Another Country Tour in the autumn of 1963 was arranged for Carmel O'Byrne (soprano) with Veronica McSwiney and Mary Gallagher.[14]

1964

Meanwhile, another project very dear to my mother's heart had come to fruition. As far back as the Council meeting in January 1963, it had been noted that an increasing number of foreign musicians were getting a chance to play in Ireland through the work of the Cultural Institutes and Embassies, and it was felt that a way should be found for Irish performers to have similar opportunities to play abroad. Discussions were held between my mother and Mr Coffey of the CRC, with the assistance of CRC member Aloys Fleischmann, and also with Dr Eugen Vetter of the German Cultural Institute. My mother reported to the Council on 17 September 1963 that the CRC had granted £300 for three groups to tour in Germany in the spring of 1964. Some of the travel and subsistence expenses within Germany would be borne by local organisers, and there was invaluable assistance from the Irish Consuls in Bremen and Hanover, in particular from Dr E. J. Brennan in Hamburg.

Bernadette Greevy and Jeannie Reddin toured from 27 February to 4 March 1964, performing in Bremen where they gave a recital and recorded for radio, in Bad Godesberg near Bonn, where their concert was at the residence of the Irish ambassador and in Hanover – a recording for Norddeutsche Rundfunk (NDR). Mary Gallagher and Veronica McSwiney also recorded for NDR in Hanover, and gave concerts there and in Hamburg under the auspices of *Jeunesses Musicales*. Their third recital was in Bremen. The longest tour, 15 days in all, was undertaken by the duo for two Irish Harps of Gráinne Yeats and Mercedes Bolger. They flew into Amsterdam, played in Bückeburg, Kiel, Bremen, Hamburg, Bonn and Stuttgart and then flew home from Frankfurt. Like the other groups, they broadcast from NDR in Hanover, but their stay in Hamburg was much longer as they had two concerts, a TV appearance and a radio recording. They were in Bremen on St Patrick's Day where they were joined by Mary and Veronica for a performance under the auspices of the *Archiv für Deutsche Musikpflege*.[15] It seems that the whole venture was very successful, all were invited to return the following year, and my mother noted that Mary and Veronica had been in to see her and told her that they 'both felt the experience gained was of the greatest value to them'.

Perhaps best of all were the enthusiastic reviews. A selection of these, in translation, was printed in the *Bulletin* for April 1964. The *Landes-Zeitung* of Bückeburg wrote about Mary Gallagher: 'This young violinist is undoubtedly gifted in the highest degree. Her technique is already astonishingly advanced and her musicianship has reached a high level . . . in her ability to present fully, not only the form of the work, but also its emotional content'. Veronica McSwiney also received high praise: 'She showed musicianship, excellent technique and an intelligent grasp of her material, these qualities combined to create a sympathetic partnership with the violinist'. The *Hanoverische Presse* were at a recital by Gráinne Yeats and Mercedes Bolger and commented: 'The instrumentation has a charm of its own; Boydell's *Studies* show that the harp is fully adapted for major works and need not be regarded merely as an instrument for folk music or accompaniment' and the same critic praised Gráinne for singing folk-songs: 'in a simple and natural style and a voice of sweetness and charm'. All four musicians received equally good reviews from Hamburg. Bernadette's recitals in Bremen and Bonn received a number of excellent comments, but this quote from the *Weser-Kurier*, Bremen, must suffice: 'This charming artist possesses the pre-requisite for a great career; a perfectly trained, pleasing voice, great musicality, and a strong personal radiance. Her most beautiful accomplishment was her interpretation of Schumann's *Frauenliebe*.'

My mother was justifiably proud of the success of this venture and continued to take a great interest in the distinguished careers of all involved. It was sad, however, that such commendable official funding did not, at that time, become a regular element in facilitating Irish musicians to perform in Europe, although both Bernadette and Mary did receive a grant from the CRC towards the costs of their London debut recitals at the Wigmore Hall.[16]

1 Cork, Gorey, Tullamore and Waterford.

2 Ballina, Listowel, Nenagh, Portarlington, Tullamore, Waterford and Wicklow.

3 Athlone, Ballina, Gorey, Portarlington, Roscommon, Tralee and Wicklow.

4 Athlone, Ballina, Gorey and Tralee.

5 Athlone, Ballina, Birr, Carlow, Galway, Gorey, Tullamore and Wicklow.

6 Athlone, Carlow, Gorey, Sligo and Wicklow.

7 NLI – ACC 6000, box 19, beige file 13.

8 They were: Seóirse Bodley, Mercedes Bolger, Brian Boydell, Madge Clotworthy, Declan Costello, Alan Cowle, Alec Crichton, Maurice Dockrell, James Fagan, Aloys Fleischmann, Mark Hely Hutchinson, Felix Hughes, Victor Leeson, Mairtín McCullough, Patrick Malone, Rhona Marshall, Michael McNamara, John O'Sullivan, Archie Potter, Gerard Victory and Alice Yoakley.

9 Ballina, Cork, Gorey, Sligo and Tralee.

10 Letter from Mrs Mercedes Bolger, ACC 6000, box 46, beige file 5.

11 Athlone, Birr, Castlebar, Gorey and Wicklow.

12 Interviewed by the author and Pat O'Kelly, 7 December 2002.

13 Ballina, Castlebar, Cork, Galway, Gorey, Maynooth, Sligo, Tipperary and Tullamore.

14 Athlone, Castlebar, Limerick and Tipperary. Patricia Dunkerley replaced Mary Gallagher in Athlone.

15 Archive of German musical heritage, founded 1955.

16 Both these artists went on to enjoy eminent careers – see entry for Bernadette Greevy in *The Encyclopaedia of Music in Ireland*. Mary Gallagher's career as a soloist and chamber musician took her to Gstaad in Switzerland, to Italy where she played with Camerata Lysy, and on fellowship to Tanglewood, USA. She went on to play with the Cologne Chamber Orchestra and was leader of the New Irish Chamber Orchestra (NICO) from 1970 to 1980, undertaking a number of important foreign tours with this group. She was leader of the Orchestra of St Cecilia (OSC) from 1995 to 2004.

CHAPTER 21

Raising the Profile and the Money –
the Concert Hall Fund, 1961 to 1965

1961

By the beginning of January 1961 plans for the Beethoven Festival from 13–25 March were well advanced. Leo McCabe had persuaded my mother that the most economical way to promote such an event was to rent the Olympia for two weeks. This overcame any difficulties regarding rehearsals, and opened up the possibility for recitals by the soloists, in addition to the main core of five Beethoven concerts which featured all the symphonies, all the piano concertos and the violin concerto. The entire event was billed as the Concert Hall Fortnight and was indeed a *tour de force* in that the theatre was 'dark' for only one night in the two weeks! On 16 March the Irish Girl Guides presented their Jubilee Year Pageant and on 17th the RÉLO took over for their traditional St Patrick's Day Concert. On 23 March the world-famous Humphrey Lyttleton and his band played to a sell-out audience, fully justifying the decision to move outside the strictly classical repertoire. The Fortnight was really an extraordinary undertaking. Nothing quite like it had ever been attempted in Ireland, the over-riding motivation being, of course, to shout to the Government with the loudest possible voice that the Irish musical public were behind the campaign for a Concert Hall.

The success of the Fortnight was really driven by two people, my mother and Tibor Paul. My recollection is that the idea was Tibor's, always keen

202

to raise the profile of the RÉSO with Irish audiences and, it has to be said, ambitious for his own career. But in proposing the Beethoven series to my mother he rightly judged that she was probably the best person to carry it off. In spite of being both very strong characters, they were able to co-operate and had, I believe, great respect for each other. My mother also felt greatly supported by Val Keogh, orchestra manager of the RÉSO and by Leo McCabe. Ticket sales were strong, particularly the season-tickets, and there was helpful press coverage prior to the Fortnight, in particular an article by Charles Acton about Beethoven[1] in which he praised RÉ for the involvement of the RÉSO in the project and gave his opinion that: 'Tibor Paul is not only a versatile and dynamic conductor, but one who can be trusted with Beethoven'. The article continued: 'Concert and Assembly Hall are now well into the second year of their campaign to raise enough money to prove, not that we need a concert hall – even the tone-deaf know that by now – but that you and I, by our shillings or pounds, really do want one'. However, there can always be an unexpected gremlin, and in this case it was a bus strike during the first week of the Fortnight, which appeared to affect audiences to some extent. Another mishap concerned the agreed modifications to the stage ceiling, promised following complaints about the acoustics at the Heather Harper concert the previous October. Unfortunately, these were not in place until the third orchestral concert, and at that concert the house-lights were inadvertently extinguished! But the fine large portrait of Beethoven, suspended above the orchestra for each concert, looked very impressive.

The soloists in the five piano concertos were, in numerical order, Fou Ts'ong, Anthony Hughes, Charles Lynch and Shura Cherkassky (Nos. 4 & 5). Of these, the Chinese pianist Fou Ts'ong was particularly highly praised: 'His interpretation combined vigour and lyricism in proper measure which, expressed by particularly fluent technique, made this an exhilarating performance' (Mary McGoris, *Irish Independent*). And of his solo recital: 'Fou Ts'ong is a very vital player – he plays with every part of him, alert and alive to each note . . . using his command of dynamics to the full' (*Irish Times*). His recital programme included Mozart's Sonata in

B flat K.570, the Schubert B flat posthumous sonata, Prokofiev's *Visions Fugitives* and a Chopin group – he had been 3rd prize winner at the Warsaw Chopin competition in 1955. Cherkassky's recital in the second week began with Scarlatti and progressed to the monumental *Phantasie in C* by Schumann and Stravinsky's *Petrouchka*. Val Keogh told of going to the airport to meet Cherkassky at about 10.30 p.m. on 19 March, to bring him to his hotel. Cherkassky's first question was: 'Can I practise there?' Upon being told this would not be possible he became quite upset, insisting that he must practise right away, it could not wait until morning. So Val brought him to the RÉ studios at the GPO, explained matters to the attendant on duty and installed Cherkassky in a vacant studio with an upright piano. The story goes that he practised until 2.00 a.m. and then walked over to the Gresham to take up his room.

With the buses running again in the second week, audiences increased to capacity and there were supposedly 'hundreds' unable to get seats for the Choral Symphony on 25 March. There was interest too from politicians, the Taoiseach attending the opening concert and the President on the final night. On 24 March, the Theatre was filled with school-children to hear the final rehearsal of the Choral Symphony. Sadly, the advertised tenor soloist, James Johnston from Belfast developed laryngitis, giving the Dublin tenor Richard Cooper a valuable opportunity to take his place. The other soloists were Veronica Dunne and two singers from the UK, Helen Watts and Roger Stalman. The Hungarian, Tibor Varga, was the soloist in the violin concerto and also gave a recital with Kitty O'Callaghan at the Shelbourne on 24th, while the final rehearsal of the Choral Symphony was taking place in the Theatre. Only one element in the whole structure seems to have been a miscalculation – the inclusion of a 4-day Fashion Show at the Shelbourne, probably encouraged by the success of Newell's show the previous autumn. But it was not run by the same person and the supposed profits (£32 in cash) disappeared mysteriously. When one considers that the overall profit to CAH of the Fortnight was less than £400, the loss of even £32 was quite significant.

Indeed, this brings home the dilemma facing CAH – they had been successful in generating interest and support from the public, but how would this goodwill be harnessed and new projects devised in order to build up the CHF to the target sum of £50,000?

However, for the meantime the public seemed content, and the flow of small fund-raising efforts continued unabated over the following months, each generating its own sense of solidarity for a worthy cause and excitement that the actions of music-lovers were actually having an effect. For instance, on 1 February Anthony Hughes gave a piano recital at the Building Centre on Baggot Street, with a programme of Bach, Beethoven, Schubert and Fauré, and in the same month a series of Bach organ recitals, organised by F. C. J. Swanton at the RIAM, raised £10.0s.0d. The Prieur Ensemble played at Russborough House, Co. Wicklow, on 8 April at 4.00 p.m., the audience being invited by Sir Alfred Beit to view the picture collection at 3.00 p.m. The proceeds were £61.0s.0d, and the John McCormack Society held an evening of recordings on 3 May which brought in £12.0s.0d.

David Laing planned a delightful outing for the evening of the summer solstice, 21 June 1961, featuring the Dowland Consort singing on a barge moored at the 13th Lock of the Grand Canal at Straffan. I have noted that the programme for this event is a particularly lovely example of the work of Liam Miller's Dolmen Press, who did so much fine printing for CHF and MAI events. The only problem was, of course, the weather – performers and audience alike had to seek refuge in a nearby barn at Robertstown, but the concert went ahead and the outcome was £19.16s.0d. On Saturday 8 July, which I remember as being a much more clement evening, David Lillis (violin) and Maeve Cunningham (piano) played at the home of Sir George and Lady Mahon at Castleknock with a delicious supper to follow – £43.10s.0d was the result. On Wednesday 6 September the distinguished Irish violinist John Ronayne with his wife, the German pianist Elgin Strub, put on a fine recital at the College of Physicians, playing Bach, Handel, Reger, Mozart and Brahms, and on St Cecilia's Day (22 November) David Laing organised a concert of vocal and chamber music at the Pocket Theatre.

There were plans for two major CHF concerts in the autumn of

1961. Tibor Paul proposed another collaboration with the RÉSO at the Olympia on 1 October, bringing the Dutch mezzo-soprano Aafje Heynis to sing Mahler's *Kindertotenlieder* and highlighting the orchestra in *Ein Heldenleben* by Richard Strauss. This concert was particularly memorable for Heynis' singing – she was noted for her Mahler interpretations and that same year received the Harriet Cohen Medal for her 'outstanding artistry'. She also gave a recital in Wexford on 28 September. The other event was to have been a recital at the Theatre Royal on 4 November 1961 by the world-famous soprano Victoria de los Angeles, accompanied by Gerald Moore, and there was great disappointment when it was announced that she had cancelled. It turned out that she was expecting her first child.

1962

The American musician, Rosalyn Tureck, noted for her interpretation of Bach on both piano and harpsichord, had performed at the Gaiety on 3 September 1961. Her striking, characterful playing inspired my mother to devise a Tureck Bach Festival Weekend in February 1962 in the SFX Hall, in association with the German Cultural Institute. It was a veritable feast of Bach, beginning on Friday 16 February at 8 p.m. with a piano recital which included four Preludes and Fugues, the Sixth Partita, the C minor Fantasia and the Toccata in D major. On the Saturday at 3 p.m., pieces were performed on the clavichord, harpsichord (*Chromatic Fantasy and Fugue*) and piano (3rd English Suite). The clavichord belonged to Desmond Guinness and the harpsichord to RÉ, who recorded the concert. On Sunday 18th at 8 p.m. the soloist was joined by the Tureck Bach Players led by Robert Masters in a marathon of concerti – three of the piano concertos (in F minor, D minor and G minor) and the 5th *Brandenburg* Concerto in which Tureck and Masters were joined by William Bennett (flute). It was a very successful weekend, attracting large audiences, and I was sorry to miss it as by that time I was studying in London. I had heard Madame Tureck play in the Gaiety Theatre at a previous concert back in 1958 and was blown away by her dynamic interpretation and incredible rhythm. Edgar Deale marked the success of the festival with a note of congratulation to my mother: 'I was pleased beyond measure and proud too of our Tureck recitals. It is many a day since such quality has been offered to Dublin. The credit must go to you again for having the necessary vision and ability to organise it all'.[2]

I was back in Dublin, however, to sing in a performance of Bach's B Minor Mass, which formed part of CAH's second Concert Hall Fortnight in 1962. This ran from 3–14 April in the Olympia and, as with the 1961 Fortnight, the planning was very much in the hands of Tibor Paul and my mother. The RÉSO were involved in four concerts, each focussing on a different composer. The opening night was a Tchaikovsky programme with the 1st Piano Concerto (soloist: Abbey Simon), the 6th Symphony and the *1812 Overture* in which the St George's Brass Band joined the orchestra. 7 April was a Wagner evening with soprano soloist Elsa Cavelti – the Overture and Venusberg music from *Tannhäuser*, *Siegfried Idyll* and the Prelude and Liebestod from *Tristan und Isolde*. On 10 April, Julius Katchen joined the orchestra as soloist in the monumental 2nd Piano Concerto of Brahms, which was paired with his 4th Symphony, and the final concert with the RÉSO was the Bach B Minor Mass on 14 April. As in the 1961 Fortnight, the concerto soloists also gave solo recitals. Both pianists were American and had previously played at the RDS. Abbey Simon enjoyed a long career, still active into his nineties, whilst Julius Katchen sadly died in 1969 at the age of 43 from lymphatic cancer. They both chose fine programmes for their recitals – Bach-Busoni Organ Toccata in C, Beethoven Op. 109, Prokofiev's 3rd Sonata and the B flat minor sonata of Chopin for Abbey Simon, and Beethoven's 'Appassionata', the Brahms-Handel Variations and the Liszt Sonata for Julius Katchen. To this rich musical tapestry of orchestral and piano music were added two evenings of films on 5 and 6 April, the first presented by the Italian Institute and the second a showing of *Le Bourgeois Gentilhomme* under the auspices of Gael Linn.

The second week opened with a Jazz concert on 9 April featuring five Irish groups – the Eblana Jazz Band, the Ian Henry Quartet, the Jazz Heralds, Jack Flahive and his Orchestra and Bryan Hopper's Chicagoans.

On 12 April, the night after Katchen's solo recital, the RÉLO presented an evening of popular music, conducted by Robert Murphy, leaving the theatre available on 13th for the rehearsals of the big choral work. This used the combined choral forces of the RÉ Choral Society, the Culwick and the Olivian Singers, with soloists Lucilla Indrigo, Bernadette Greevy, Dermot Troy and James Shaw. The performance had a number of memorable moments, particularly the wonderful singing of the *Benedictus* by Dermot Troy (his last appearance in Ireland) and the stylish oboe d'amore playing by the Australian Ian Wilson, and indeed both these artists were singled out for special praise in the reviews. Otherwise, these were rather mixed, Tibor Paul being criticised in one paper for his boring and sanctimonious approach and in another for tempi that were too extreme. For me, it was the amazing experience of singing the choral part of this Bach masterpiece for the first time, though I was somewhat taken aback when Tibor Paul expressed his displeasure at the trumpets by sticking his tongue out at them!

During the summer two small fund-raising events took place. The first, on 12 June 1962, was a concert of Vaughan Williams, Delius and madrigals by the College Singers of TCD, conducted by David Laing, at the home of Sir George and Lady Mahon. The second (30 June) was hosted by the Olivian Singers at the Enniskerry home of my mother's friend, Pat McKnight. This was a fun event on a beautiful summer's afternoon, a 'Bring and Buy' sale with pony rides and other entertainments.

In early July the German soprano, Elizabeth Grummer, gave a recital in Dublin and after the concert a chance meeting in the bar of the Shelbourne Hotel produced an unexpected windfall. David Laing was engaged in conversation by an Irish-American visitor who expressed great interest in the work of CAH, then took out his cheque-book and wrote a cheque for £1,000 on the spot, saying that it was to be used for publicity or expenses, whatever would be most helpful! He asked for anonymity at first, but it did transpire later that his name was John Galvin; my mother wrote to thank him most warmly for his opportune assistance.

On 30 May 1962, there was a major musical event in England, in the newly rebuilt Coventry Cathedral – the first performance of Benjamin Britten's *War Requiem*. Always a great lover of Britten's music, my mother listened to the transmission on BBC radio and recorded it on her reel-to-reel machine. I still have this tape, but have also had it transferred to CD. It is of course a remarkable work, and makes a huge impact on listener and performer alike. My mother resolved then and there to bring the work to Dublin and set about convincing Tibor Paul and RÉ that it could be done. From this point on, it became a major element in her planning of CHF concerts for 1963. It was decided that the venue should be St Patrick's Cathedral and the date was set for 27 March, with the Culwick Choral Society (augmented by the Olivian Singers) and the boys of the Cathedral Choir. Tibor Paul was of course the chief conductor, but a director is also needed for the chamber orchestra and Seóirse Bodley, conductor of the Culwick at that time, was asked to take this on. The sheer size of the forces involved and the rather awkwardly cramped performance area in the cathedral were certainly a headache for Val Keogh and for those involved in recording the performance. Jim McHale, as RÉ balance engineer and producer, felt that it would be very helpful if he could attend the performance scheduled for Westminster Abbey on 6 December 1962, so he and my mother decided to travel to London to attend some rehearsals and the performance. Unfortunately this was the period of one of the worst 'smogs' ever experienced in London, temperatures were close to freezing all the time and visibility down to a few feet. They were able to travel by train and tube, but when they came out of the tube station they couldn't see the cathedral and had to be helped across the road! There was fog even inside the building. Nonetheless, it was a most useful visit, Jim received a lot of helpful tips from the BBC engineers and my mother was made aware of potential organisational pitfalls. Also, the experience of hearing the work 'live' was a wonderful inspiration to carry forward to the Dublin performance.

Meanwhile, there was excitement in Dublin in anticipation of the rescheduled recital by Victoria de los Angeles on 9 December at the Olympia. She was accompanied by Gerald Moore in a programme of lieder by Schubert and Brahms, French song by Fauré and Ravel and a Spanish group including Nin, de Falla and Rodrigo. The recital began with a short group of 18th century arias. My mother's programme, signed with warmest good wishes from both singer and accompanist, is in the MAI archive.[3] There was an unprecedented demand for tickets, and with a 'sold-out' house and the previous year's cancellation, my mother took the unprecedented step of procuring 'non-appearance' insurance. The reviews were ecstatic – in *The Irish Times*, Charles Acton described: 'as lovely an occasion as we had hoped. . . a presence that charms one's heart before she sings a note. . .the quality of her artistry is nearly beyond comment. . . every word was audible in Italian, English, German, French and Spanish'. Mary McGoris in the *Irish Independent* wrote: 'it was the expressiveness, vitality and musical intelligence of Victoria de los Angeles' singing which enchanted an overflow audience. Mr Moore was throughout a brilliant partner; memorable among many felicities was the opening of the Brahms *'Mainacht'* where for a few bars his playing made moonlight visible'. Edgar Deale wrote to my mother the next day: 'Last night was a triumph and has done our cause nothing but good. Congratulations again.' This was another concert that I missed, but when I came home for Christmas I think my mother was still walking on air: it had been a truly wonderful musical experience.

1963

The first CHF event of 1963 was on 9 March, a Saturday afternoon recital at the Olympia given by the young Russian pianist Vladimir Ashkenazy. With the benefit of hindsight, knowing the long and prestigious career of this musician as both pianist and conductor, it is fascinating to read the press comments on his first appearance in Dublin. Just the previous year, at the age of 25, he had been the joint winner, with the British pianist John Ogdon, of the Tchaikovsky competition in Moscow. His programme for Dublin was a Mozart Sonata (K. 311), Prokofiev's 6th Sonata, and the second book of Chopin *Études* – it appears that his reputation preceded him, as the concert was completely sold out. My mother was, of course, very proud of this success, and spoke most warmly, not just of Ashkenazy's playing but also of his modest, almost self-effacing demeanour. The reviews were fulsome in praise of his technique, pedalling, lyrical feeling and romantic expression. Charles Acton wrote: 'As soon as he started playing, one sensed the presence of a master' and went on to describe the 'succession of perfectly and exquisitely presented details of playing, and the sensuous and emotional experience of the sound.'[4]

This memorable concert was followed on 27 March by Britten's *War Requiem.* It was actually the eighth performance, the one in Westminster Abbey having been the fifth. To my great regret, I was not present, being detained in London for exams, but I know that for my mother it lived up to all her expectations. By this stage she knew the work very well, having prepared the Olivian Singers for their participation and, like many people who had lived through both world wars, she was deeply moved by Britten's masterful setting of the Wilfred Owen poems. It was a great honour to have Heather Harper as the soprano soloist. The Belfast singer had famously stepped in to give the first performance when the Russian soprano, Galina Vishnevskaya, was refused permission to travel. Singing from the pulpit, Miss Harper's voice soared over choir and orchestra. The other two soloists were David Galliver (tenor) and Donald Bell (baritone). The cathedral was, of course, the appropriate setting for such a work, but Charles Acton thought that the tonal quality of the choir had been affected by the acoustics. He praised the orchestra highly and stressed the demands that the work placed upon the conductor, stating that: 'It would be hard to find an interpreter better qualified to direct it than Tibor Paul.' The review concluded: '. . . and pray that all the old men with their hands on the trigger may absorb the *Offertorium* into their hearts. Hearing the work, one feels it must be more powerful than hundreds of CND marches.'[5]

It is indeed a tribute to my mother's planning that CAH were able to follow two remarkable concerts with another of the same calibre. This was the recital by the legendary pianist, Artur Rubinstein, at the Olympia on 26 May. Fifty years older than Ashkenazy, he brought the experience of his years of music-making and his exceptional pianism to a programme of Beethoven (Op. 2, No. 3), Schumann's *Carnaval,* and groups of pieces by Debussy and Chopin. My mother found him very friendly and completely without 'airs and graces'. He invited her and my father to join him after the concert for a meal, was the most delightful of hosts, and talked animatedly on all manner of topics until late into the night. He was also happy to join Edgar Deale the next day for a drive along the coast, followed by lunch at the hotel near Bray owned by Count Cyril McCormack, son of the famous tenor.

There were no further collaborations with the RÉSO during 1963, but two visiting chamber orchestras gave performances for the CHF during the autumn, both at the SFX. On 8 November, I Solisti Veneti, in co-operation with the Italian Institute, presented popular string repertoire by Rossini, Geminiani and Vivaldi with Schoenberg's *Verklärte Nacht* in the second half. The Los Angeles Chamber Orchestra played on 10 December in a richly varied programme of Purcell's Suite from *The Faerie Queen*, Cantata 199 by Bach 'Mein Herz schwimmt im Blut', a song cycle *Silent Boughs* by the American composer William Kraft, and the Bartók Divertimento. The soloist was the mezzo-soprano, Marilyn Horne, then not quite 30 years old, whose husband Henry Lewis was the orchestra's conductor. The *Evening Herald* of 11 December wrote: 'The winner of all hearts in this superb concert was Marilyn Horne, who has the type of voice that would have had the Dubliners of the last century drawing her carriage through the streets.' The reviewer (PMcG) refers to the 'astonishing virtuosity' of her performance of the Bach, and such was the impact of the song cycle that she gave an encore, an 18th century aria. The orchestra was well entertained with a lunch at Guinness's, and the American Ambassador and Mrs McKinney were at the concert. My mother wrote to Mr McKinney afterwards: 'This was one of the musical highlights of the year, and those who were privileged to hear this very fine orchestra and their very distinguished soloist will long remember it.'

1964

The main CHF project for 1964 was another Beethoven Festival with the RÉSO, to be held in the late spring, this time presenting all the piano concertos paired with three of the nine symphonies. Two CHF recitals took place in January – János Fürst and Charles Lynch played sonatas for violin and piano by Bach, Brahms, Bartók and Franck at the Dagg Hall of the RIAM on 14th, and another Hungarian, the pianist Tamás Vásáry gave a programme of Mozart, Schumann, Bartók, Chopin and Liszt at the SFX on 21st. Like János Fürst, Vásáry had left his homeland following the 1956 rising. He was just 30 at the time of this first visit, and over the years became a very popular recitalist in Ireland. On this occasion, his recital was almost overshadowed by the Government announcement on 17 January that the National Concert Hall would be built as a memorial to President Kennedy. On 23 January, CAH issued a statement welcoming the decision and making it clear that they would continue with fund-raising concerts for the moment.

Accordingly, the Beethoven concerts, conducted by Tibor Paul with Julius Katchen as soloist in all five piano concertos, went ahead from 29 April to 2 May.[6] The venue of the National Stadium only served to emphasise the need for a proper hall. My mother had formed a very high opinion of Katchen's playing during his previous visit for the 1962 Concert Hall Fortnight, and rightly felt that such a series would be very popular with the public. Several people have told me the story of an altercation that arose between conductor and soloist at one of the rehearsals, following a complaint about the tuning of the piano. The tuner worked on the instrument at lunch-time and Katchen expressed himself satisfied. However, Tibor Paul insisted that it was still out of tune and when the pianist would not agree, the conductor stormed off the platform. My mother took matters in hand, went to his dressing-room, and is reputed to have told him not to be acting in such a ridiculous fashion! Tibor Paul returned to the podium and the rehearsal continued.

Victoria de los Angeles was, of course, one of the most popular artists, and from the time of her recital in December 1962, which could have been sold twice over, my mother had been hoping for an opportunity to bring her back to Dublin. Having been offered Monday 4 May 1964, and in spite of the problems of a venue, my mother decided to go ahead, solving all the logistical difficulties with one bold stroke by holding the recital at 11.30 p.m. in the Gaiety! Although unusual, the public embraced the idea wholeheartedly. Her programme included 18th century arias and lieder, accompanied by Gerald Moore. To everyone's delight, she sang some of her Spanish repertoire to her own guitar, and included the Irish air 'I once loved a boy' as one of her encores.

It appears that there was only one more CHF recital in 1964, given by the pianist Thomas Rajna, on 27 October at the Metropolitan Hall. Born in Hungary in 1928, he had moved to London in 1947 where he built a reputation as an interpreter of Liszt, Bartók and Stravinsky. At the time of his Dublin recital he was professor at the Guildhall School of Music. He later moved to South Africa where he built a significant career as a composer. His interesting Dublin programme included the *Wanderer* Fantasy of Schubert, works by Brahms, Bartók and Liszt and Stravinsky's *Circus Polka*.

1965

The same hall was used for two CHF celebrity recitals in early 1965, the first on 15 January by the wonderful Swedish tenor, Nicolai Gedda accompanied by Geoffrey Parsons, and the second by Igor Oistrakh (violin) and Vsevolod Petrushansky (piano) on 18 February. Gedda's programme had quite a Russian focus with songs by Tchaikovsky, Mussorgsky and Rachmaninov, as well as Schumann's *Dichterliebe* and some Swedish songs. Jim Wilson's verdict in the *Bulletin* was 'a singularly beautiful recital.' Oistrakh played sonatas by Schumann and Beethoven, the Bach Chaconne, Prokofiev's *Five Melodies* and *Italian Suite* by Stravinsky.

There is very little information in the MAI archive on these last mentioned concerts, from which I infer that, for my mother, the inspiration to campaign and raise funds for the Concert Hall had almost completely evaporated. Just two more concerts took place, in the autumn of 1965, and I was involved in both of them. The continuing search for a good concert venue led my mother to book the auditorium at the new Liberty Hall building on Eden Quay, for a concert on 27 September by the Irish Chamber Orchestra (ICO), conductor János Fürst, and exactly a month later, the Dublin debut of the Argentinian pianist, Martha Argerich. The ICO presented a programme of Handel, Geminiani, Mozart and Webern with Hugh Maguire as soloist in violin concertos by Marcello and Francis Baines. My involvement was as harpsichordist, my first professional engagement in Ireland as a continuo player.

Throughout the years of her work for music in Ireland my mother encouraged so many young musicians. I think in retrospect, therefore, that it was fitting that her final concert for the CHF was given by one of the most stunningly talented pianists of the 20th century, then aged just 24. Martha Argerich had been the winner of the Geneva and Bolzano Competitions at the age of 16, and of the Warsaw Chopin Competition in 1965. In Dublin she played the 2nd Partita of J. S. Bach, Schumann's *Phantasie in C*, Prokofiev's 3rd Sonata and the B minor Sonata of Chopin. She had one main request of my mother: that she would not be left alone backstage before the concert or between the items. She seemed very happy when it was suggested that I might fill this role – after all, she was only two years older than me – and I was fascinated to see her unroll her simple non-crush concert dress from a small bag, along with her hair-brush which she used vigorously every time she came off the stage! It was an encounter that I have never forgotten, though sadly I heard only a rather muffled version of her performance through the back-stage door.

Thus ended five rather extraordinary years in which Irish audiences were treated to some wonderfully memorable concerts and were able to demonstrate, by their enthusiastic support, that a Concert Hall was needed. But it had also become clear that the profits from concert promotion would not be sufficient to build up a large fund. For instance, the CAH accounts for 1962 show £2,038 on deposit, plus £625 in Prize Bonds and £262 in the current account, assets of just under £3,000. The income that year was £516.19s 4d – this included the proceeds of concerts, subscriptions, income from other functions and deposit income – whilst expenditure for running the concerts plus rent, salary, light and heat, and the expenses of the office, came to £494.11s 4d. An excess of income over expenditure of £22.8s 0d! It is worth recording, however, that CAH never ran at a loss, and that when its financial assets were handed over to the MAI at the end of 1967 they amounted to £2,478.3s7d.

[1] *The Irish Times*, 15 March 1961.

[2] NLI – ACC 6000, box 11, beige file 6.

[3] Ibid. beige file 5.

[4] *The Irish Times*, 11 March 1963.

[5] *The Irish Times*, 28 March 1963. CND was the Campaign for Nuclear Disarmament – the Cuban Missile Crisis had occurred just the previous October.

[6] 29 April: Symphony No. 8, Piano Concertos Nos. 1 and 4;
1 May: Symphony No. 4, Piano Concertos Nos. 2 and 3;
2 May: Piano Concerto No. 5 'Emperor' and Symphony No. 3 'Eroica'.

CHAPTER 22

The Concert Hall: Part 5
– 1964 to 1967 –
The John F. Kennedy Memorial Hall

1963

On 22 November 1963, John F. Kennedy, President of the United States of America, was assassinated at Dallas, Texas. In the aftermath of this momentous event, and with memories still fresh of his visit to Ireland in June 1963, the Government was under considerable pressure to make an announcement of a suitable memorial. Many official bodies were asked for their opinion, including the Arts Council, and it was they who made the suggestion of building the National Concert Hall in the President's memory. Not a whisper of this was conveyed to CAH in a letter of 3 January 1964, in which Donogh O'Malley tells the Board of the need for patience due to the slowness of land acquisitions at Haddington Road. But on 17 January came the official announcement from the Government Information Bureau,[1] that the memorials would be the John F. Kennedy Memorial Hall in Dublin and the Arboretum in Co. Wexford.

1964

To say that there was general acclamation in musical circles would be an understatement. A constant stream of congratulation reached the CAH and MAI offices, and the press were no less generous. The news

217

dominated the front pages of the *Irish Independent, Irish Times* and *Irish Press*, giving due credit to the Arts Council for its recommendation and stating that the Government would bear the entire cost, estimated at about £750,000. It was even mooted that the site might be in the Phoenix Park. Writing in *The Irish Times*, Brian Boydell: 'praised the activities of Concert and Assembly Hall who had been working on the idea for nearly 11 years. Their efforts now have been crowned with success'. And indeed this was true. The dogged persistence of CAH, the high-profile concerts, the involvement of so many musicians and the music-loving public, even the reported failures over sites, had all contributed to this crucial moment. The groundwork had been done and the Concert Hall was the project which came to the forefront of the Arts Council's mind. A. P. Reynolds announced that CAH Ltd would stay in existence until the completion of the Kennedy Memorial building, adding that there was much they could do in the way of giving advice on the project. He also said that they would be anxious to see that everything was properly carried out from the point of view of music lovers, and that any money they had in hand would be disposed of in the interests of music. My mother was utterly delighted and, I think, relieved that the burden of fund-raising was lifted and that, because of its memorial nature, there would be a momentum to propel the project forward. What could possibly go wrong?

On 23 January, CAH issued a press release welcoming the decision regarding the Kennedy Hall (JFK) and announcing that they would continue with their planned concerts in 1964. On the same date my mother added a personal note to the end of an official letter to Tibor Paul: 'May I say that the fact that we are now going to get a Concert Hall is due to a great extent to the help and encouragement you have given the project over the years . . . Your enthusiasm and determination to have a hall helped to revive mine when the many frustrations I had to contend with got me down. I hope we shall give many concerts together in the intervening years before the concert hall is an accomplished fact'.[2] She also wrote to the Director of the Arts Council, Fr Donal

O'Sullivan, expressing appreciation of the Council's role. Then, on 5 February, the CAH Board wrote to the Minister for Finance, offering to be of assistance, and began to plan a competition for a new work by an Irish composer, to be performed at the opening concert in the Hall. Meanwhile, the Government had set up an Inter-Party Committee under the chairmanship of James Ryan as Minister for Finance to bring the project forward. Its members included P. J. Hillery (Minister for Education), Donogh O'Malley, Noel Browne, Brendan Corish, Liam Cosgrave, Sean Dunne and Gerard Sweetman. On 24 March my mother, Edgar Deale and Brian Boydell, representing CAH, were invited to meet the Committee to discuss the design and scope of the Hall. In March it was announced that Raymond McGrath had been appointed as the architect for the project and was congratulated by the CAH board. Raymond had a long-standing interest in concert-hall design, having made a study trip to Denmark, Sweden, Holland and Belgium in 1946 during the time that he was preparing designs for the Rotunda site (see Chapter 6). In March 1948 he had delivered an address to the Architectural Association on 'Building for Music and Broadcasting'.[3]

On 16 September 1964, my mother spoke with Raymond McGrath, who told her that he thought the plans would not be ready to go to tender for another 12 months, and that building would not commence until 1967 and might take three years. At a chance meeting on 29 September at the US Embassy however, he was able to tell her that the Department of Finance had approved the expenditure. But a month later she had two disquieting phone calls, one from Raymond McGrath and the other from Maurice Dockrell, both of whom told her that the Town Planning Office had said that no site was currently allocated to the JFK Hall! It seems that this may have been a smoke-screen as, in fact, the Inter-Party Committee had decided that the Haddington Road site was the best option and there were plans to build a new National Library there as well. On 4 November, CAH wrote to the secretary of the Inter-Party Committee, offering to assist by submitting a memorandum on the management of the Hall, and at the same time expressing misgivings concerning a site. There was a swift reply on 9 November, taking up the offer of the memorandum, which was sent on 2 December 1964, but there is nothing further in the MAI archive which refers to this. In truth, CAH were beginning to find themselves side-lined, which was really only to be expected as they had, in effect, handed everything over to the Government. At this point the MAI archive almost ceases to be a detailed source of information.

1965 – 1966

The Board and all the MAI Members of CAH were invited to the reception, hosted by the Government, on the evening of 9 March 1965 at Iveagh House, at which Raymond McGrath's design and models for the JFK Hall on the Haddington Road site were unveiled. The Taoiseach referred to the role of CAH and the MAI and the long years of work which had led up to that moment. But alarm bells surely rang when Mr Lemass gave the current estimated cost as having increased to £1.75 million. The next evening Raymond McGrath came to address a Members' Meeting of the MAI, held at 16 St Stephens Green, bringing with him his models and copies of the plans. There is a finely bound set of the drawings in the MAI Archive, which Raymond presented to my mother at that time.[4] Chapter 37 of *God's Architect*, the biography of Raymond McGrath by Donal O'Donovan, also highlights these designs. McGrath's vision for the JFK Hall was truly a notable concept, incorporating so many of the aspects considered indispensible by CAH, an elegant and thoroughly contemporary building that would have greatly enhanced the locality for which it was conceived.

On 5 August 1965, CAH had a meeting with the Inter-Party Committee to discuss the proposed composition competition, and in September attempted to consult with the Director General of RTÉ, Kevin McCourt, as the chosen piece would presumably be played by the RTÉSO. Mr McCourt, however, indicated that he felt it premature to enter into a discussion as the completion of the Hall could still be far into the future. Between January and July 1966, CAH tried to get a response from the Inter-Party Committee to the idea of the proposed competition. It seems that the Committee met in late February but did not discuss the CAH letters of 24 January and 2 February, which set out the draft rules of the competition and gave suggestions of international names who might act as adjudicators. Finally a letter dated 28 July from a civil servant, acting as secretary to the Committee, informed CAH that no meeting of the Inter-Party Committee had been held since February and that none was planned.

The account written by Pat O'Kelly in pages 116 – 121 of *The National Concert Hall*[5] gives an overview of the vicissitudes, both practical and political, endured by the project in the nine-year period from March 1965 up to May 1974. It is extraordinary that, in spite of having the support of the Government and the Office of Public Works, the location of a suitable site continued to be a major stumbling-block, a situation which must have had a certain bitter-sweet element of *déjà vu* for the CAH Board. Ironically, as costs escalated for Haddington Road, a number of sites previously considered by CAH were re-investigated, including the RDS and the Phoenix Park. *God's Architect* refers to this period as a 'cat and mouse' game, which caused Raymond McGrath great anguish. Chapter 37 of his biography contains a wealth of background information as it deals with architectural points, as well as giving insights into the political stone-walling which was very similar to CAH's experience, but on a grander scale. According to an anecdote in *God's Architect*[6] it seems that McGrath also did not have the whole-hearted support of some major figures in the world of architecture and the arts, notably Michael Scott and Fr O'Sullivan, chair of the Arts Council. But ultimately it was financial pressures, combined with the political uncertainty engendered by the deteriorating situation in Northern Ireland, which tolled the death-knell of the Kennedy Hall. Raymond McGrath's original estimate for the JFK Hall was £1.75 million, but in mid-1970 £3,540,000 was the figure which the then Minister for Finance, George Colley, put before the Dáil. In late 1973 he gave his opinion that 'the cost of the JFK Hall was out of the question in the present financial situation'.[7]

1967

During 1967, the Directors of CAH Ltd came to the conclusion that the Company had no further function. As to the need to limit the liabilities of the members of the MAI, in the almost certain event of CAH being wound up, an ingenious solution was arrived at. The legal advice was that the obvious, and least expensive, course of action would be to merge the two bodies. CAH would take into membership all the members of the MAI and then change its name to The Music Association of Ireland Ltd. This course of action had the important result of giving the MAI the protection of becoming a company limited by guarantee, not having a share capital. The Council members would become Directors, there would have to be some amendments to the Articles, and of course the whole proposal would have to be agreed at the AGMs of both bodies.

The MAI AGM took place 14 February 1968 and all necessary legal Resolutions were agreed.[8] The fifteenth and final AGM of CAH was held on 21 March 1968 at 5.30 p.m. and was followed immediately by an Extraordinary General Meeting at which more Resolutions were passed, namely: i) that the name of the Company be changed to the Music Association of Ireland Ltd; ii) that the provisions of the Memorandum of Association of the Company be amended by the deletion of Clause 3 thereof.

There followed a re-working and re-wording of the original objects of the MAI, now adopted as the main objects of the new Company with an amended schedule of sub-sections. There is a final paragraph which states: 'The revised Clause 3 in the Memorandum of Association of the Company and the revised Articles of Association of the Company have been approved on behalf of the Music Association of Ireland, and are in the form required to enable the Music Association of Ireland to take over control of the Company and to continue in existence through the Company.' The document was signed by my mother as Secretary, and thus ended an extraordinary fifteen-year journey.

[1] NLI – ACC 6000, box 18, beige folder 1.

[2] Ibid. box 18, beige folder 1 – this and beige folder 3 are the sources of much information in this chapter.

3 Ibid. box 18, pink folder.

4 Ibid. box 18.

5 See *The National Concert Hall* by Patricia Butler and Pat O'Kelly (Wolfhound Press, 2000).

6 See *God's Architect* (Kilbride Books, 1995 – page 250).

7 See *The National Concert Hall*, pages 120 and 121.

8 See Chapter 26 'The MAI – 1968 to 1971'.

CHAPTER 23

The MAI – 1964 to 1967, including the Mayer Piano

1964

As already described in Chapter 22, the major excitement at the start of 1964 was the announcement, on 17 January, that the Government proposed to build the National Concert Hall in memory of President Kennedy. A special meeting of the MAI Council was convened for 24 January, attended by the MAI Members of CAH, and also by A. P. Reynolds who addressed the meeting as chairman of CAH. To quote from the Minutes: 'The meeting decided to send a letter of thanks to the Taoiseach and the Arts Council, and to make a statement to the press welcoming the announcement. The meeting expressed the hope that the specialised information gained by CAH Ltd over the years should be used by whatever body is set up now to complete the project, and it was hoped that the company and the MAI would be able to exert some influence on the course of events, to ensure that Dublin got the building particularly related to its needs.'

The *Bulletin* for February 1964 carried the following statement: 'The recent sensational announcement by the Government regarding the proposed Kennedy Concert Hall overshadows all else on the musical scene. That one of this nation's memorials to an outstanding statesman and friend should take the form of the long-awaited concert hall will be a matter of pride and gratitude for many generations to come.' The Council's report to the AGM on 13 February expressed similar sentiments, combined with a certain amount of self-congratulation on the significance of the roles played by the MAI and CAH.

The recital following the AGM was given by David Lillis (violin), Coral Bognuda (cello) and Maeve Cunningham (piano) playing trios by Haydn, Brahms and Shostakovich. On 20 February, pianist Emily Wilson gave her Coming-Out recital at the Irish Life Theatre with a programme of Bach, Mozart, Schubert, Ravel and Bartók, and the same venue was used for the Members' Meeting on 5 March for a welcome return to Dublin by Hugh Maguire and his duo partner, Joyce Rathbone. Their programme included the first performance of Seóirse Bodley's Violin and Piano Sonata as well as sonatas by Mozart, Beethoven and Debussy. This was followed by a Country Tour of nine recitals.[1] The Council meeting on 3 March elected Edgar Deale as chairman for the coming year, Victor Leeson having indicated that pressure of work prevented him from serving for a second term. This meeting also discussed a very important project, namely that the MAI should produce a *Catalogue of Contemporary Irish Composers* which would be printed and distributed by the CRC of the Department of External Affairs. A sub-committee of the Composers' Group was established to bring the matter forward, led by Seóirse Bodley and Edgar Deale.

The Council meeting on 14 April 1964 heard with much regret that Mairtín McCullough had indicated that, due to additional business commitments, he could no longer continue as editor of the MAI *Bulletin*. Dating from the first few months of the MAI's existence (the first issue was November 1948), the significance of the *Bulletin* to Irish musical life cannot be overstated. In his tribute to Mairtín (June 1964 issue), the chairman Edgar Deale wrote that: 'This *Bulletin* has in the opinion of many members been responsible for placing the Association in a very special position. As far as I know, it is the first bulletin of its kind which gives advance information on musical events, and thanks to the efficiency with which Mairtín McCullough handled it, we all found our copy in our possession by the first of each month . . . thanks are due for the unselfish and devoted way he took on a task which was often a thankless one'.

It is worth noting that each issue also carried all the RÉ music broadcasts for the month, as well as occasional special articles and opinion pieces. Nowadays its archived issues form a rich and irreplaceable resource for research.[2] Mairtín had served as editor for 11 years, preceded by Madge Clotworthy, Dorothy Stokes and Anthony Hughes. His successor was the composer, Jim Wilson, who indicated to both me and his biographer[3] that he took on the role of editor in gratitude to my mother for her support of his children's opera *The Hunting of the Snark*. Jim introduced a new format, replacing the large Xeroxed sheets which had a cute wood-cut of a medieval organ-player at the top, with a brightly-coloured booklet of several pages carrying advertisements and the logo of a lyre.

The Members' Meeting on 25 May 1964 featured the return of John Beckett, already enjoying a growing career in London with the group Musica Reservata, who gave a harpsichord recital of the 4th, 5th and 6th Partitas of J. S. Bach. This was held at the College of Physicians. Also in May, Alan Cowle arranged a recital by the highly-regarded British organist, Melville Cooke, under the auspices of the MAI. The Members' Meeting on 19 October in the TCD Exam Hall marked a return visit by the LSQ, although with two new members, violinists John Tunnell and Carl Pini. Always very popular, they received a tremendous welcome during their tour following the Dublin concert[4] – 12 concerts in as many days! In Dublin they played quartets by Haydn, Shostakovich and Brahms. Other Country Tours offered performance opportunities to Patricia Herbert (piano) who visited five centres with the financial assistance of the Shaw Trust, and the newly-formed ICO (leader David Lillis, conductor János Fürst) which gave two concerts with a grant from the Arts Council. There were also two Coming-Out recitals in the autumn of 1964. The violinist Máire Ní Chuilleanáin, daughter of the writer Eilís Dillon, played at the Hibernian Hotel on 8 October, accompanied by Veronica McSwiney, and Gerard Gillen gave the first organ recital of the series on 5 November at Leeson Park Church. He played a programme of Buxtehude, Bach, Franck, Tournemire and Flor Peeters.

Another resignation from a key position was announced at the October council meeting when Alan Cowle gave notice that he would not be able to continue as Hon. Treasurer after the AGM in February 1965. The Chairman expressed the sincere thanks of the Council to Alan for his work over the past five years, and regretted that he found it impossible to continue. About 18 months later Alan moved to Toronto where he took up a new career in Canadian TV and radio. The search for a new Treasurer began and also for a Concerts Secretary, to take over some of my mother's work. These positions were filled at the December meeting when Mrs Ronnie Perrem took the latter position, and Brían Howlett agreed to become Treasurer from 1 January 1965. A chartered accountant who was a member of the St James's Gate Choir, Brían was an ideal appointment.

1965

At the start of 1965, the production of a new opera for children, *The Hunting of the Snark* by James Wilson, occupied everyone's mind. It had first been proposed at the Council meeting on 17 September 1963, and it was agreed that the MAI would sponsor a week of performances. Jim Wilson was very involved in *Let's Make an Opera* at New Year 1958, and upon attending another performance of this in 1963 in the company of the noted philanthropist Lady Mayer, he was encouraged by her to write something similar. The background to this work is covered in some detail in *The Life and Music of James Wilson* by Mark Fitzgerald, and it seems that up to that time Jim felt unaccepted and unacknowledged as a composer in Ireland. He wrote the libretto himself, drawing on the Lewis Carroll poem, and having shown this to Lady Mayer, accepted her commission of £50 to compose the music. Interviewed in 2002,[5] Jim recalled inviting my mother to dinner, together with Sir Robert and Lady Mayer, and playing through the completed score. He described the Mayers as 'a little perplexed by it' but my mother was enthusiastic and indicated that she would ask the MAI to support the venture. The January 1964 issue of the *Bulletin* announced the project, with the première planned for January 5th 1965 at the Dagg Hall of the RIAM. All sorts of helpers were sought from amongst the membership – dressmakers, carpenters, scene painters, electricians and makers of props out of papier mâché – in effect, Jim wanted the MAI to feel it was '*Making an Opera*'.

The performances ran from 5 to 9 January with matinées on the Thursday and Saturday. Even my father was involved as 'Chief Electrician' and, according to Jim: 'did all the electronics, which required animal sounds relayed through a speaker at the back of the auditorium'. The two main roles were taken by Herbert (Herb) Moulton as the Bellman and Victor Leeson as the Baker. Herb was an American-born baritone who had come to live in Ireland and was studying under Hans W. Rosen. Victor Leeson, in contrast to the seriousness of his choral conducting, had a remarkable gift for the comic singing roles of Gilbert and Sullivan, and was an ideal choice as the Baker. Audrey Park led the orchestra and the animals' parts were taken by seven boys from Sandford Park School, whose music master Brian Grimson was the conductor, tasked with holding all the disparate groups together. These included the Olivian Singers as an off-stage chorus, the dancer Nadia Stiven, and three mimed parts. *The Snark* is a very unusual work (an Agony in Eight Fits) which takes up Britten's idea that a group of amateurs, with the assistance of one or two professionals, can present their own original opera.[6] Lady Mayer was very supportive and hosted the press launch at the Gresham on 1 December 1964, whilst my mother's organisational skills can be seen in every aspect of this successful production. Perhaps it brought back happy memories of her own participation in Gilbert and Sullivan during the war years. The MAI was proud of its involvement, mentioning in the Council's report for 1964 that there had been full houses and offering thanks and congratulations to all who had taken part. I should mention that both my parents got on well with Jim and his partner, John Campbell, a retired naval commander, and we were all invited to dinner quite frequently at their beautiful and artistic home in Monkstown – Jim was an excellent cook. My father enjoyed exchanging sea-faring stories with John and I would get a chance to play their grand piano. In fact Jim wrote a number of works for me including *Anna Livia* (a piece for piano and orchestra which was a wedding present) and a harpsichord concerto.

Spring of 1965 continued as a busy time for the MAI with a Coming-Out recital on 4 February at the Hibernian Hotel by the soprano Anne

228

Cant, accompanied by Dorothy Stokes. Her programme included some Purcell (in realisations by Britten), lieder by Brahms and Wolf, and the *Seven Popular Songs* of de Falla. The AGM on 24 February was followed by a talk by Brian Boydell on *The Versatility of Lassus*, with vocal illustrations by the Dowland Consort. Edgar Deale was re-elected Chairman, to serve for a second term. A special event was the address on 10 March to MAI members by architect Raymond McGrath, on the day after the Government's official launch of Raymond's plans for the JFK Hall. The Spring Members' Meeting followed on 20 March in the TCD Exam Hall, given by the ICO in a lively and interesting programme of music for strings by Vivaldi, Geminiani and Roussel, a trumpet concerto by Richard Addison played by the American principal trumpet from the RTÉSO, Thomas Lissenbee, and the first performance of *Two Pieces for Strings* by John Kinsella.

Another Members' Meeting was held on 18 May at the Ely Hall as a joint venture with the German Institute. Following tours in Germany by young Irish musicians in 1964, it had been suggested by the organisers that a visit by a young German group might be in order. *Der Spielkreis Espitalier*, a folk-music group from the Bremen region, playing flute, cello, accordion, guitar, double bass and percussion and directed by Georg Espitalier were *en route* to the Cork Choral Festival, so a stop-off for a concert in Dublin worked out very well.

During 1965, my mother also organised a number of Country Tours. The most extensive was for Herb Moulton (the Bellman in *The Snark*) with Gerard Shanahan (piano).[7] There were concerts outside Dublin by the ICO and the David Lillis Trio, and then two shorter tours in the Autumn featuring performers who had recently given Coming-Out recitals. Those involved were Emily Wilson (piano) and Anne Cant (soprano)[8] and Deirdre McNulty (piano)and Patricia Dunkerley (flute).[9] The author was the piano accompanist for both these tours. My mother was involved in the Members' Meeting on 11 October at the Hibernian Hotel, when the Prieur Ensemble stood in at very short notice for the Dublin String Quartet. The final MAI concert for the year was the Coming-Out recital of Brian McNamara (violin) accompanied by Veronica McSwiney on 3 November at the Hibernian. This was preceded by a short Country Tour from 21 to 26 October in which Brian and Veronica were joined by the clarinettist Brian O'Rourke.[10]

At this point, the MAI had been involved in organising concerts in Dublin for 15 years, and for a little over 10 years nationally, so it is interesting to note the increase in concert promotion amongst other bodies. For instance, in December 1964, the St James's Gate Musical Society announced a monthly chamber music series featuring Irish musicians at the Rupert Guinness Hall. This initial experiment was followed by a group of concerts by the Aeolian Quartet in April 1965 and a mini Bach Festival involving the ICO and other musicians in June. All these were organised by Victor Leeson. During the summer the ICO, conducted by János Fürst, in tandem with another newly-formed body, the Irish Opera Group, presented Pergolesi's *La Serva Padrona* and *Dido and Aeneas* by Purcell at the Dagg Hall. The Dowland Consort, one of Ireland's most eminent ensembles, promoted a series of three recitals on 5 April, 17 May and 21 June at the Royal College of Physicians, in which they sang from their extensive English, French and Italian repertoire and invited Irish instrumentalists to play contrasting 20th century works. The UCD Music Society celebrated its move to the Belfield campus with a set of nine concerts, and in June and July there was a series of lunchtime concerts at the Crawford Art Gallery in Cork. It would seem that there was a growing confidence amongst classical musicians that the public would support good programmes, well performed. Undoubtedly the vision and encouragement of the MAI and its Council, combined with the organisational abilities of many of its members had contributed to this.

With the campaign for a Concert Hall somewhat in abeyance, the MAI needed to develop new activities, and these were not long in appearing. As 1965 drew to a close, the Council prepared to support a memorandum of the Irish Federation of Musicians concerning the employment of non-nationals in the RTÉ Orchestras, and regarding the separation of the posts of Director of Music and Principal Conductor. Recommendations for an incremental salary scale for orchestral musicians were also agreed. Work continued, under the guidance of Edgar Deale and Dr Seóirse Bodley on the preparation of the first *Catalogue of Contemporary Irish Composers*. It is important to acknowledge that Seóirse Bodley[11], whilst never acting as chairman or an officer of the MAI Council, served for many years as one of its most influential members, particularly in the cause of Irish composers.

1966

Much the same pattern of work continued in 1966. The Dublin String Quartet gave their postponed recital following the AGM on 24 February with a programme of Haydn, Schubert and Bartók. My own Coming-Out recital was at the Hibernian on 9 March, a programme of Haydn, Bach, Schubert, Hindemith and Chopin, and Eileen Donlon (soprano) accompanied by Havelock Nelson, gave her Coming-Out recital on 17 November, presenting songs by Mozart, Schubert, Schumann, Wolf, Strauss and Rodrigo. The German Cultural Institute was another organisation which frequently promoted musical events, quite often in association with the MAI. The Members' Meeting on 21 March at the Hibernian was one of these occasions. The musicians were the Ulrich Gebel Ensemble – flute, violin, cello and harpsichord – who played a programme of Telemann, Bach and Handel. My mother also organised a Country Tour for them – nine concerts with Arts Council funding.[12] This was possible because the Ensemble were able to transport their own harpsichord. Another Country Tour, by the violinist Margaret Hayes with pianist Joyce Riddle, took place in April.[13]

My mother had not found it easy in 1965 to arrange a follow-up tour of Germany for the Irish performers who had played there in 1964. However she did receive encouragement from Aedán O'Beirne, the Consul General in Hamburg, when she proposed a tour by the organist Gerard Gillen, who had given his Coming-Out recital in 1964 and was a prizewinner at the 1965 Bruges International Organ Competition. Gerard wrote to me in 2017: 'Your mother was indeed vital to arranging those first concerts for me in Germany which took place in March 1966, though the planning certainly took place in 1965. By the time of my recitals, Aedán O'Beirne had been replaced by Aidan Mulloy, who invited me to stay with him in the consulate residence for the Hamburg recitals – I had also played in Bremen, arranged by the honorary consul Herr Veschoff. Through the prestige of his office, Aidan initiated contacts for me with influential organists and Kantors from Lüneburg to Lübeck. These contacts were most productive and endured for several decades. I have much to thank him, and primarily your mother, for setting them up.'[14]

The performers at the Members' Meeting on 2 May brought a wonderful array of colour, even a touch of the exotic, to the Exam Hall in TCD. They were the highly-acclaimed Paranjoti Chorus from Bombay under their conductor Victor Paranjoti. The choir was performing at the Cork Choral Festival and their Dublin concert was part of a European tour, visiting Italy, Switzerland, France and Germany. My mother was very excited about their visit, pulling out all the stops and arranging some 20 host families from amongst MAI members, most of whom welcomed two choir members. Notes in my mother's hand record that they were given hospitality in the evenings by the University of Dublin Choral Society and by St Patrick's Training College, where they also gave a short recital. They were guests of the Indian Tea Centre on Suffolk Street on the day of their concert and had lunch at Guinness's Brewery the following day. Their performance of music by Bach, Tallis, Hassler and Orff, as well as some traditional Indian arrangements, fully lived up to their reputation for exciting dynamics and choral colour, not to mention the vivid hues of the ladies' saris.

Another significant MAI event during 1966 involved a further collaboration with Havelock Nelson's Studio Opera Group from Belfast, in a production of Britten's *Albert Herring* on 23 and 24 September. This venture turned out to be somewhat problematical, both financially and organisationally, involving a large MAI team of backstage helpers as well as members who were willing to give hospitality to the cast and players. Many of the usual venues were unavailable, so my mother was greatly relieved when Muckross School in Donnybrook were willing to make their hall available and even arranged additional electric power for the stage lighting. There was disappointment that the Arts Council guarantee was only £200, and though an additional £100 sponsorship was given by Lyons Tea the MAI incurred a loss of about £140. The large cast included

such well-known Northern Irish singers as Irene Sandford and Uel
Deane, but attendances were somewhat disappointing, perhaps due to
the unfamiliarity of the venue. Havelock wrote to my mother afterwards:
'Hope we haven't left the MAI destitute for the rest of the year and are
only sorry that box office receipts weren't higher'. In the same letter he
complemented her: 'There is no-one I find more pleasant or efficient . . .
I only hope Dublin really appreciates all you do. Believe me, you'd get the
CBE if I had anything to do with it.'[15]

In October 1966 my mother was pleased to arrange a Country Tour[16]
for the Amici Quartet, led by her old friend Lionel Bentley. They were in
Ireland to take part in a BBC Invitation Concert at the TCD Exam Hall on
25 October, in company with the Dowland Consort who had recently been
honoured with the Harriet Cohen Medal. Also in October two pianists were
on tour – Deirdre McNulty[17] and Audrey Chisholm[18].

The autumn of 1966 witnessed a game of musical chairs arising from
the establishment of the Ulster Orchestra, which attracted a number of
RTÉSO players to move north of the Border, notably János Fürst and other
members of the ICO. The consequent demise of the ICO was a blow to
audiences in the south; almost four years would elapse before another group
of comparable size and standard emerged in Dublin. As it turned out, my
mother's Olivian Singers had the honour of performing in one of their
final concerts – Pergolesi's *Stabat Mater* on 24 April 1966, with Bernadette
Greevy and Violet Twomey as soloists and Gerard Gillen playing an organ
concerto by Handel. There were also notable developments in provincial
opera: Courtney Kenny promoted three performances each of *La traviata*,
Don Pasquale and *Don Giovanni* in Castlebar in September, and directed the
new Irish National Opera in *The Marriage of Figaro* and *La Bohème* in Cork,
Longford, Mullingar, Naas and Castleknock College in December. These
performances were all given with piano accompaniment.

The Mayer Piano

The Council minutes of 9 November 1966 record the receipt of a letter
from Sir Robert Mayer: 'which indicates that it is possible that the Dorothy

Mayer Foundation may consider undertaking the provision of a piano and trailer.' Some explanation is called for here. Lady Mayer, formerly the singer Dorothy Moulton, was the wife of Sir Robert Mayer, the wealthy philanthropist who ran the Mayer Concerts for Children in London. Although English-born, she had connections with Cork and owned a beautiful house on the Vico Road at Killiney and another in Ticknock at the foot of the Dublin mountains. Through her Foundation she liked to support Irish musicians and musical bodies – her name has already appeared in various contexts in this narrative. In 1952 she provided the finance needed by James Blanc to set up Ceol Chumann na nÓg, which organised the school concerts given by the RÉSO. Lady Mayer gave some funding towards the studies of the pianist Veronica McSwiney, having first heard her as the soloist at a Ceol Chumann na nÓg concert in March 1958, and supported other young performers by means of Moulton-Mayer awards. In 1956 the Mayer Foundation was one of the instigators, together with the Carnegie Trust, of the position of National Music Organiser to which Joe Groocock was appointed. She also supported the MAI's production of *Let's Make an Opera* in 1958 and commissioned Jim Wilson to write *The Hunting of the Snark*.

The Dorothy Mayer Foundation was established in September 1958 with an initial capital of £20,000 to be spent over 10 years. Its aims were: i) To assist music in the 26 counties; ii) To aid groups as opposed to individuals; iii) To work outside the main centres. There were four Trustees – Charles J. Brennan (chairman), Erskine Childers, Lord Glenavy and Terence de Vere White – and three music advisors, Brian Boydell, Aloys Fleischmann and Joe Groocock. A note from the Foundation's secretary, James Blanc, dated 8 September 1962, records that since its inception 286 applications had been received and 158 grants disbursed to all but one of the 26 counties.[19] The breakdown for the 4-year period (1958-1962) was: £3,598 to schools, £743 to orchestras, £990 to choirs, and £1,130 to music courses, a total of £6,461.

Sir Robert's letter to the MAI in late 1966 was written in anticipation of the winding-up of the Foundation in 1968, and was followed by one from Lady Mayer to my mother, dated 30 January 1967, in which she expresses the desire of the Foundation: 'to alleviate the almost complete dearth of playable pianos throughout the country by providing a Steinway piano and specially adapted Rice trailer which can be taken easily from place to place.' She hoped that this might 'be considered as a memorial to the aims and achievements of the Foundation.'[20] The letter further set out the understanding that the MAI, as well as using the piano for its Country Tours, would facilitate the use of the piano and trailer by organisations and promoters other than the MAI, subject to the approval of the Council, would keep it fully insured and arrange to have the piano housed at McCullough's premises when not in use. Remarkably, the Rice trailer in question was a horsebox – to be accurate, a New Forest Double Pony Trailer Mk 3! Even though Rice said that they had already done a similar job for the popular pianist, Russ Conway, a lot of planning was required regarding the best method for moving the piano in and out of the trailer. My father became involved and produced three drawings which show clearly how the piano should be mounted on a bogie with castors which ran down parallel rails fixed to the tailboard, the whole thing being operated by means of an exterior winch.[21] This was the system which was adopted. The purchase of the piano took longer - Sir Robert was dealing with the firm of Jaques Samuels Pianos in London and was very anxious to find the best possible instrument. Eventually a reconditioned Steinway upright with a very nice brown case, made in 1926, was chosen and it was arranged to send it up to Rice's in Leicester to be united with its horsebox, in preparation for the journey to Dublin.

Meanwhile my mother was dealing with all sorts of red-tape regarding import duty and various taxes, whilst Edgar Deale arranged the insurance. She was able to obtain 'duty-free' status from the Minister for Industry and Commerce for the piano, for which Sir Robert paid £292.19s.0d in London. He then sent her a cheque for £400 to cover the cost of the trailer (£279) and the expenses and taxes. Her total expenditure amounted to £390.16s.2d. A brilliant solution was arrived at regarding the journey from Leicester – David Laing was at that time Director of the Chester

Festival and was agreeable to take a few days off. He and the horse-box crossed on the MV *Adriatic Coast* on 3 August and apparently the shipping company didn't even notice the strange occupant of the horse-box! The first celebration of this generous gift was a lunch in honour of Lady Mayer, hosted by the MAI Officers, at Bernardo's Restaurant in Lincoln Place on 21 August. Then the official launch followed on 21 September 1967 at 12 noon outside the National Gallery where Lady Mayer, a sprightly octogenarian, stepped daintily into the horse-box and formally handed it and the piano over to Mairtín McCullough as Chairman of the MAI. The whole event attracted very good press coverage the following day, and it was announced that Charles Lynch would inaugurate the piano in a Country Tour of eight recitals between 6 and 22 November. This would be followed by recitals in February 1968 by Mary Gallagher and Veronica McSwiney. It is probable that Veronica played this Steinway more frequently than any other pianist. She recounted that during her time as Music Director of Irish National Opera she towed it behind her Vauxhall Viva all over Ireland and blamed it for causing the necessary replacement of three gear-boxes![22] Nonetheless, the piano and trailer did fulfil all of Lady Mayer's hopes and proved a most valuable asset to performers and promoters alike. The piano remained in service until 1983 when it was sold to Newpark Music School.

1967

At the Council meeting on 8 March 1967, Sir Robert and Lady Mayer were elected Life Members of the MAI, Mairtín McCullough was elected Chairman, and the organist David McConnell was co-opted as Hon. Records Secretary, to be responsible for Council and AGM minutes, and generally to assist my mother. The meeting also drafted a letter to the Arts Council, expressing concern at the proposed cuts in grants to music, and to the Taoiseach, suggesting that Mrs Jacqueline Kennedy should be asked to lay the foundation stone of the JFK Hall during her expected visit to Ireland in 1968. The Members' Meeting on 14 March 1967 was given by Bernadette Greevy and Jeannie Reddin at the TCD Exam Hall in a programme which included the first performance of Jim Wilson's *Three Birds*, as well as Bach, Purcell, Brahms, Mahler's *Lieder eines fahrenden Gesellen* and *Colección de Tonadillas* by Granados. There was a Country Tour early in 1967 for the Cremona Quartet, led by Hugh Maguire, who were in Ireland for RDS recitals in January.[23] Other performers for whom my mother arranged Country Tours during the spring of 1967 included singer Violet Twomey (with the author),[24] Patricia Dunkerley (flute) and Una O'Donovan (harp),[25] and the Lund University Choir.[26] This Swedish male voice choir, the oldest in Scandinavia, was also due to sing at the Cork Choral Festival, and gave an MAI Members' Recital on 17 May at the RDS, with interesting 20th century repertoire including some Swedish composers.

News broke on 30 June 1967 of the sudden death of Leon Ó Dubhghaill. This was a great shock to everyone, as he died in his office at the school in Cabra where he was principal. At the start of the Council meeting on 17 August, Mairtín McCullough spoke of Leon's death as a grievous loss, of his service to the Council since 1953 and his two years as Chairman. He paid tribute to his quiet and balanced approach to problems, and how often it was Leon who found a solution favourable to all when a controversial point was under discussion. I know that he contributed a great deal of wisdom to the deliberations of CAH and was also, of course, a very prominent figure in the Gaelic League and An tOireachtas. I have come across a tribute to him by Joe Deegan in the August 1967 issue of *Feasta*, an Irish language publication: 'Más mó a shaothraigh aon fhear eile ná é riamh ar son na teanga agus an chultúir dhúchais, ní heol dom é.'[27] He was perhaps unique in his ability to encompass so many aspects of Irish life and culture. About a year after Leon's death his widow, Peig Bean Uí Dhubhghaill, took his place on the MAI Council as the representative of An tOireachtas.

There was a busy season for the MAI in the autumn of 1967 and my mother continued to organise Country Tours. Firstly, in early October, the baritone Peter McBrien, accompanied by Courtney Kenny[28]; then on 12 October the New London Wind Ensemble arrived to begin a seven-concert tour.[29] They rounded off their visit with a recording for RTÉ and the MAI Members' Meeting recital in Dublin at the College of Physicians on 23 October. It was a return visit for this very popular group who had toured for the MAI in 1963, though their oboist at that time, Ian Wilson, had been replaced by Neil Black, who had been my husband's oboe professor in London.

In November, as already mentioned, Charles Lynch gave the inaugural tour of the Mayer Piano[30] with a programme of Scarlatti, Beethoven, Chopin, Liszt, Rachmaninov and Albéniz. The final Members' Meeting of the year, a high-profile event on 15 November at the RDS, in co-operation with the German Institute, introduced the world-famous soprano Rita Streich for the first time in Ireland. She was accompanied by Geoffrey Parsons in a fascinating programme which featured *The Ugly Duckling* by Prokofiev, as well as Mozart arias and lieder by Schubert, Schumann, Mendelssohn and Mahler.

All these concerts and music-making were a source of joy and satisfaction to my mother, but hanging over her was the shadow of my father's illness, first diagnosed in the autumn of 1967.

[1] Athlone, Castlebar, Galway, Limerick, Sligo, Tipperary, Tralee, Tullamore and Wicklow.

[2] NLI – ACC 6000, box 34.

[3] See *The Life and Music of James Wilson* (Cork University Press, 2015, p.28).

[4] Athlone, Birr, Castlebar, Cork, Galway, Gorey, Limerick, Sligo, Thurles, Tipperary, Tralee and Wicklow.

[5] Interviewed by Pat O'Kelly, 18 November 2002.

[6] NLI – ACC 6000, box 3 – press release for *The Hunting of the Snark*.

[7] Gorey, Kilkenny, Limerick, Sligo, Tipperary and Waterford.

[8] Athlone, Carlow, Castlebar and Wicklow.

[9] Galway, Gorey and Sligo.

[10] Ballina, Galway, Sligo and Waterford.

[11] Dr Seóirse Bodley, a prolific and ground-breaking composer, also a conductor, was on the staff of the UCD Music Department for almost 40 years. See *Seóirse Bodley* (Field Day Publications, 2010).

[12] Birr, Cork, Galway, Gorey, Limerick, Rockwell College, Sligo, Tullamore and Wicklow.

[13] Kilkenny, Rockwell and Tipperary.

[14] Email – 20 October 2017. Gerard Gillen is one of the most notable Irish musicians of his generation – as performer, university professor, church musician, teacher and tireless promoter of the organ – see entry in *The Encyclopaedia of Music in Ireland*. Also *A Musical Offering: Essays in Honour of Gerard Gillen* (Four Courts Press 2017).

[15] NLI – ACC 6000, box 3, file 12, letter of 26 September 1966.

[16] Cork, Limerick, Rockwell, Waterford and Wicklow.

[17] Gorey and Sligo.

[18] Carlow, Gorey, Rockwell and Sligo.

[19] NLI – ACC 6000, box 26, beige folder 7.

[20] Ibid. box 48.

[21] Ibid. box 42, beige folder 5.

[22] Interviewed by the author and Pat O'Kelly, 19 September 2016.

[23] Athlone, Birr, Cork and Gorey.

[24] Athlone, Carlow, Cork, Galway, Gorey, Rockwell, Sligo and Tullamore.

[25] Birr and Limerick.

[26] Galway, Kilkenny, Waterford and Wexford.

[27] 'I do not know of any man who worked harder for the cause of the language and national culture.'

[28] Castlebar, Galway, Gorey, Navan, Rockwell and Tullamore.

[29] Athlone, Birr, Galway, Gorey, Limerick, Tipperary and Waterford.

[30] Ballina, Birr, Castlebar, Galway, Limerick, Monaghan, Rockwell and Wicklow.

CHAPTER 24

Family Life in the 1960s

My departure for London in September 1961, to commence study at the
Royal Academy of Music, meant that I was no longer a daily observer of
my mother's organisational and musical activities, so for news of interesting
concerts and her latest plans I had to rely on letters and the occasional
visit. The success of my father's photographic business brought with it
a problem of lack of space, which was solved towards the end of 1963
by the purchase of Islington, a very large detached house at 47 Terenure
Road East, Rathgar, just up the road from the chemist shop. This had a
huge basement which could accommodate most of the heavy processing
machines, plus storage for photographic chemicals. There was ample space
in the back garden to extend the building as needed, and a useful mews
which opened onto a back lane. At the front, a flight of granite steps led to
the main entrance where rooms on the hall floor accommodated the offices
of the administration department. The whole top floor was designated as
a most spacious apartment for my parents, and a smaller flat on the hall
floor was available for visitors or tenants. Garryknock was sold and by
the spring of 1964 my parents had returned to their roots, in the part of
Dublin where they had both grown up.

The business was now known as Lyall Smith Laboratories Ltd (LSL)
and continued to be very strongly linked to Agfa in Germany. It occupied
much of my father's time, though he was of course still running the chemist
shop with the help of Christy Morrissey. My father had a great aptitude

for building long-term relationships with his staff: Vincent Trotman continued as his right-hand man at LSL and Annie Gregan, who had lived with us when I was very young, was the most senior of the female staff. Garret Sunderland, who had married Nellie, our home-help in Rockview in the 1950s, held a responsible position as one of the van drivers who covered hundreds of miles every week, collecting films and delivering wallets of completed prints. Two new faces came into the picture – Tommy McManus and his wife Patricia, always known as Mrs Mac. She was my mother's home-help at Islington from 1964 and became a firm friend, right to the end of my mother's life. Tommy worked in the parks department of Dublin Corporation, but came to LSL several evenings a week as gardener and handyman. LSL always had a trade stand at the RDS Spring Show and Horse Show and David Laing recounted augmenting his MAI and CAH salaries by helping my father at these exhibitions.

I imagine that, for my mother, it must have been very convenient to live closer to the centre of Dublin, but I wonder whether she missed the garden at Garryknock. Possibly my parents' holidays in the West in 1958 and 1959 had planted the germ of an idea because, very shortly after they had settled into Islington, they began to look for a plot of land in Connemara with the intention of building a holiday home. For my father, an essential requirement was proximity to a safe anchorage, as he had dreams of owning a cruising yacht and exploring the islands off the west coast. By great good fortune, they found an ideal location on the shore of Fahy Bay, a sheltered inlet off Ballinakill Harbour, which lies between Letterfrack and Moyard in the north-western corner of Co. Galway. Two elderly brothers, Tom and Pat Coyne, had an acre of land beside their cottage that they were willing to sell, a deal was done and my parents lost no time in commissioning architect's plans. The house was called Derrylahan after the townland, and enjoyed a most beautiful view of the Twelve Bens with the bay in the foreground. The builder, Neil O'Donoghue, was from Dublin, but was happy to stay through the spring of 1965 in the caravan which my parents placed on the site, and by the time I came home from London that summer the house was virtually complete. It was situated almost at the highest point of the sloping ground which was laid out in a large expanse of grass. Over time the garden developed to include many varieties of flowering shrubs and roses. For both my parents, it provided a much-needed escape from their busy and often stressful working lives, though my father would occasionally grumble at the extent of the grass-cutting and the frustrations of a wet weekend visit. They enjoyed entertaining visitors there – particularly my mother's sister Kay and her husband David, Pat McKnight, and Lily Butler, who had come back to Ireland following her retirement and settled in Co. Cork.

Through talking to people in the course of researching this book, I have been told many stories of my mother's generosity and kindness. The pianist Veronica McSwiney recounted to me[1] that when she married Michael O'Dea in August 1964 their new-build house was not yet completed, so my mother offered them the flat on the ground floor of Islington and included the facility for Veronica to practise as much as she wished on the Bechstein piano upstairs. They stayed until March 1965. I was still studying in London during this period, but I do recall Veronica working intensely at the *Burlesque* for piano and orchestra by Richard Strauss, which she had to learn in just 3 weeks in early September 1964. She had been engaged to perform it by Tibor Paul, notwithstanding that her wedding was in August!

Writing in 1998, in the concert programme for the 50th anniversary celebrations of the MAI, the singer Bernadette Greevy paid tribute to my mother: 'At the beginning of every successful life in the performing arts, you will find that there is a special person with the foresight and organisational ability to advance the career of a young professional musician. I owe a great debt of gratitude to the Music Association of Ireland in the person of Olive Smith, who organised my Coming-Out recital in Dublin, and later had a huge input into my London debut at the Wigmore Hall. This meant that I was launched as a fully professional singer on the international stage at a very early age, and I have never looked back'. This was certainly true. It was my mother who personally invited the London agent, Wilfred van Wyck, to attend the Wigmore

Hall concert on 20 March 1964. Bernadette's performance impressed him most favourably, thereby securing the future of her international career.

The soprano, Violet Twomey, who was originally from Waterford, told me that she felt very grateful for my mother's help when she first came to Dublin.[2] My mother heard that there was a delay in moving Violet's piano and immediately invited her to call in to Islington each evening on her way home from work, making sure that the room with the piano was free so that she could have an hour or so to practise. Violet also credited my mother with contacting musicians in Northern Ireland who recommended that she should have lessons with Miss Carys Denton, the well-known singing teacher. A performance by the Olivian Singers with the ICO of Pergolesi's *Stabat Mater* (24 April 1966) included both Violet and Bernadette as the soloists.

I know that my mother lent money to Garret and Nellie Sunderland to help them buy a cottage in Co. Kildare, after the stud farm where he had worked was put into receivership. And Mrs Mac told me that my mother lent her £500 in 1972 towards the deposit on her house in Tallaght, as well as helping to arrange a bridging loan. I suspect that these stories may just be the tip of the iceberg, and that there could be many more 'behind-the-scenes' examples of people my mother assisted.

In the summer of 1963 my mother and I spent about 10 days at the Edinburgh Festival. This was a memorable experience for me as an enthusiastic music student and, I think, highly enjoyable for her also. We certainly had opportunities to hear wonderful performances by some of the greatest interpreters of the day. Three concerts in particular made a huge impression: Yehudi Menuhin playing the Bartók Sonata for Unaccompanied Violin; a performance of all the Britten *Canticles* by Pears and Britten, with other musicians; and the ballet *The Miraculous Mandarin* by Bartók. We also heard the London Symphony Orchestra, led at that time by our old friend, Erich Gruenberg, with the added interest of seeing John Beckett on stage as the orchestral keyboard player.

In 1966, my father purchased a small cruising yacht, *Carregwen*, in Oranmore, Co. Galway. With the help of Maurice Brooks and Jan Jefferiss he sailed her first to Roundstone and then on around the coast to Fahy Bay.[3] Photos record her lying peacefully at anchor within view of Derrylahan. At the end of the summer he set off again, sailing southwards past the Aran Islands and the Clare coast, then up the Shannon estuary to Limerick docks, where the mast was unstepped in preparation for a transit to Dublin via the Grand Canal. This turned out to be a fascinating journey for crew and skipper alike as they experienced a side of Irish life rarely seen by the average traveller, passing delightful villages and negotiating some 40 canal locks. The main impediment was the detritus from decades of dumping in the canal as the boat's progress was constantly halted by submerged prams, bicycles and bedsteads, not to mention the occasional dead dog! But my father was in his element, never happier than dealing with practical challenges, and all the time assembling a new collection of yarns about this latest adventure.

The major family event in 1966 was the wedding of Lindsay and myself. It was a family celebration, with my relatives from England and Ireland, Lindsay's numerous relations from Northern Ireland, and one or two close friends including my bridesmaid, Lizzie Richardson (my flat-mate in London). We all returned to Islington following the church service to dine on a magnificent meal, prepared for us with loving expertise by Pat McKnight. On returning from honeymoon, Lindsay and I set up home in the same flat over the chemist shop in Rathgar where my parents and my father's parents had begun their married lives.

So 1966 ended on a joyous note, but in 1967 a dark shadow came over the family. In early June, my father undertook an exciting but strenuous 2-week cruise in Scottish waters, reaching Oban and Tobermory in spite of some difficult weather conditions. On his return he drew my mother's attention to a lump on his neck. The diagnosis was not good, this was Hodgkin's disease, cancer of the lymph glands, and effective treatments were still in their infancy. He underwent radiotherapy and chemotherapy at St Luke's Hospital in Rathgar where, ironically enough, he held the position of pharmaceutical chemist. By the year's end he appeared to be considerably better. But I have discovered that he had no illusions about the seriousness of his condition, as during the late autumn of 1967 he conducted negotiations for the sale of the shop, John Smith & Son. He chose to approach Canice Flynn, who had done his apprenticeship at Smith's in the 1950s, retaining a connection with my father. He told Canice that he had a terminal illness and set out the conditions under which he hoped Canice might take over the business. Canice became the owner of John Smith & Son from early 1968, so the deal was done quite quickly and he felt that my father was 'glad to have the business off his hands.'[4] The building was sold to Canice by my mother in April 1973.

The photographic business of LSL was quite another matter with its extensive premises and large number of employees. There were periods during 1967 and 1968 when my father was quite weakened by his illness and its debilitating treatment, so my mother began to take a more active role in the organisation. Around this time she was also dealing with the winding up of CAH and the early stages of the establishment of the MAI Schools' Recital Scheme. Fortunately there were two family members amongst the Board of Directors of LSL, my cousin Brian Lusk and his father David. My mother relied particularly on Brian, who had set up the accounting system of the company and oversaw the finances on a quarterly basis, even when he was working in Venezuela for Shell. It must also have been very helpful that she had known Vincent Trotman and Annie Gregan for so many years, and it was undoubtedly fortuitous that the business and my parents' apartment were in the same building.

The year 1968 began optimistically for my parents with a springtime holiday on the island of Crete, well recorded in their collection of photographs of the wild flowers and archaeological sites. In August, my father had sufficient energy and enthusiasm to sail *Carregwen* southwards and westwards around the Irish coast, navigating waters where he had sailed as a young man and coping with the usual Atlantic mixture of fair and foul weather, eventually reaching his safe anchorage at Fahy Bay. An account of this voyage, written by Maurice Brooks, is included in the 1968 *Irish Cruising Club Annual*. My father's final goal of bringing *Carregwen* up on to the beach, to rest during the winter in a special wooden cradle he had made, was achieved in the following days with some willing local assistance. This effort may have sapped his strength, however, and as autumn progressed his health continued to deteriorate, necessitating blood transfusions and longer spells in hospital.

It was at one of these times that my mother enjoyed a most unusual musical experience. David Laing engaged the great Russian pianist, Sviatoslav Richter, to play at the RDS on the evening of Saturday 16 November 1968. Upon meeting Richter and an entourage of 'minders' at Dublin airport, David was amazed to learn that Richter did not want to practise on the piano in the RDS. He wished to practise, but not on the concert piano! David phoned my mother in a panic to ask if Richter could come to Islington for the afternoon and of course she was thrilled. It was arranged that I would go to sit at my father's bedside in St Luke's, leaving my mother free to welcome the great man. He came to the house in the embassy car with David and an interpreter, who then departed. My mother made him a cup of black tea and he settled down with the Bechstein. My mother sat outside the door, anxious not to miss a note, and reported that he did not rehearse any of the music for that night's concert, but rather the *Études Symphoniques* of Schumann, which he was due to play at his Belfast recital the following night. The most extraordinary element of his visit was his insistence that he would be able to walk back from Rathgar to the Shelbourne Hotel, finding his way from having observed the route taken by the embassy car! My mother could vouch that he left Islington on his own and he certainly appeared safely at the RDS that evening, but how he came to be allowed to do that un-chaperoned walk, in those days of KGB vigilance, remains a mystery. But one thing that Lindsay and I knew, sitting in the audience, was that when he strode out onto the stage, to give one of the most memorable piano recitals Dublin audiences have ever heard, he was approaching that particular Steinway completely afresh, without rehearsal, a fascinating insight into the workings of a great master. Charles Acton's review[5] is worth reading, as it conveys with great immediacy the extraordinary effect of Richter's performance.

As the year drew to a close, my father's condition continued to worsen. He was able to be at home on Christmas Day but returned to hospital soon after, and died in St Luke's on 21 January 1969. My mother was with him. There was a huge attendance at his funeral in Christ Church Rathgar, and I know that he was comforted in the days before his death by the Minister, Revd T. A. B. Smyth. He had hoped that there would be 'lots of flowers', and indeed there were. He was laid to rest in the same graveyard as his parents, brother and sister at St Patrick's Church, Enniskerry.

I know little of my mother's frame of mind following my father's death. She left Dublin within a couple of days and went to the West, to their beloved holiday home at Derrylahan. I imagine that she must have kept in touch with LSL by telephone, and with the MAI also. But it seems that solitude was what she sought to help her cope with her bereavement.

[1] Interviewed by the author and Pat O'Kelly, 19 September 2016.

[2] An informal conversation with the author on 17 June 2017.

[3] Maurice Brooks was interviewed by the author, 14 September 2017.

[4] Interviewed by the author, 6 September 2017.

[5] *The Irish Times*, 18 November 1968, also reproduced in *Acton's Music*, page 112.

CHAPTER 25

The Schools' Recital Scheme, Ógra Ceoil and the Irish Youth Orchestra – 1967 to 1971

A development which was to have a long-lasting significance for the MAI was mentioned for the first time at the Council meeting on 8 March 1967. For some time Sir Robert Mayer had been trying to convince my mother to start a music organisation for young people under the auspices of the MAI, something on the lines of the work he was doing in London. The minutes of 8 March record that: 'The Hon. Secretary outlined her ideas for starting a "Youth and Music" (*Jeunesses Musicales*) movement in Ireland, and for making a renewed effort to get the scheme for Recitals to Schools going.'

Not surprisingly, given the MAI's stated aim: 'to further musical education and to awaken a musical consciousness in the nation', there had been two earlier attempts at establishing a Schools' Recital Scheme (SRS). The idea first emerged in the Council minutes of January 1959, following a letter to the MAI from Mr Peter Killian, Inspector of Music in Secondary Schools, suggesting something similar to the Country Tours concerts. My mother was much preoccupied with the organisation of the Handel Festival at the time and felt that she could not give the commitment required, but put forward the name of Andrew Healy as a possible organiser. Andrew was an oboist, son of Arthur Healy, and the eldest of the talented Healy family from Galway, many of whom became professional musicians, though in fact Andrew made his career in the Guinness Brewery. A committee was formed with Andrew, Peter Killian of the Department of Education, and Fr O'Brien (MAI Hon. Assistant Sec.), who acted as a link to the Council. Their brief was to engage the David Martin Trio from London for a pilot project of concerts in three Killarney schools on 21 April 1959, followed by three Dublin schools a couple of days later. The Arts Council agreed a grant of five guineas per recital and each school was asked to contribute seven guineas. Recitals of fifty minutes were planned, the schools being provided with written programme notes. But there is no report in the Council minutes as to the success, or otherwise, of the experiment, and the only follow-up was a half-hearted effort in the autumn of 1960 that came to nothing.

In October 1964 Victor Leeson suggested to the Council that another attempt should be made. There was support for this and Victor undertook, in the following months, to come up with a definite proposal. He wrote to secondary schools in Wicklow, Kildare and Westmeath but it seems that responses were disappointingly slow. However in June 1965 it was decided to request a grant from the Arts Council to enable 10 concerts to go ahead in September. In the event, just five recitals took place and Victor reported that it was very difficult to get three schools in a district to take a recital on the same day. He felt that a tremendous amount of organisation would be required before the SRS could work as he envisaged, and that it would require personal visits to kindle interest in many of the schools.

1967

It may have been a case of 'third time lucky' but it is much more likely that it was my mother's decision in 1967 to take this ailing project under her wing that ensured its transformation from lame duck into one of the MAI's flagship successes. I also like to think that she was encouraged by the series of schools' concerts which Lindsay Armstrong and I, newly-married at the time, arranged on our free weekends from the RTÉSO. An oboe and piano duo seemed to appeal to the hard-pressed principals of boarding schools, anxious to provide some Saturday or Sunday evening entertainment for their pupils, and assisted by the kindly loan of my mother's small Fiat, we were able to travel like troubadours to the Midlands, South and West. I think my mother was genuinely surprised at the ease with which we arranged these trips, underlining Victor Leeson's view that personal visits would be one of the keys to unlock the door.

It was almost certainly Sir Robert who suggested to my mother that the Gulbenkian Foundation could be a possible source of funding. This charitable body, based in Portugal but operating internationally, was founded under the terms of the will of Calouste Sarkis Gulbenkian who died in 1955. He was a British oil magnate and philanthropist, born in Turkey of Armenian parentage; his Foundation's main interests were in social, cultural and educational projects. Following her usual practice, my mother wasted no time in seeking a meeting with Christopher Rye, the Foundation's representative in the UK and Ireland. Brian Boydell reported to the MAI Council on 3 May 1967 that he and my mother, together with Seóirse Bodley and Mercedes Garvey, had formed a delegation: 'to discuss with Mr Rye possible schemes for submission to the Trust. A suggested scheme for recitals to schools and for the formation of the Irish equivalent of "Youth and Music" appeared to him most likely to receive a favourable response from his trustees.' The four members of the delegation, in consultation with the MAI chairman and treasurer, had drawn up a fully documented application for submission by 14 April and a response was awaited. In the meantime, my mother had discussed the projects with the Minister for Education, Donogh O'Malley, who promised his support.

There is no record as to who created the name Ógra Ceoil (ÓC) for the new 'Youth and Music' organisation, but my guess is that it was either Seóirse Bodley or Leon Ó Dubhghaill. Its name was certainly established by the next Council meeting on 7 June when my mother reported that ÓC was ready to be launched. Its committee would consist of members nominated by the MAI Council and some young musicians, drawn from the Student's Union committees of the College of Music and the RIAM.

It would have its own constitution and not be a financial burden on the MAI – the initial funds coming from twenty-five Vice-Presidents, each contributing a minimum of £5. The position of Patron or President would be filled at a later date.

Confirmation of the Gulbenkian Foundation's willingness to support the MAI's proposals was received at the end of July 1967 in a letter to my mother from James Thornton, director of the UK branch of the Foundation.[1] He wrote that the MAI's request for £6,000 over three years would be granted: 'To help launch the schemes to provide recitals in secondary schools and to establish the proposed Ógra Ceoil organisation. The grant is intended to provide a sum of £1,250 a year to meet the salary and expenses of an organiser appointed by the Association to administer the two schemes; the balance of £2,250, allocated over the three year period, is to be used to subsidise the recitals given in schools.' He continued: 'The Ógra Ceoil scheme is expected to provide opportunities for young people between the ages of 15 and 25 to attend concerts . . . support will be sought from local industrial and commercial firms. Arrangements will be made for groups to attend concerts at reduced rates, and special concerts will be arranged from time to time.'

From the MAI's point of view, the most important stipulation was that the grant was offered on the understanding that the Department of Education would be willing to take over the schemes when the Foundation's support came to an end. My mother already had a verbal commitment from Minister O'Malley, but had to wait until October to receive it in writing. A special meeting was convened on 17 August 1967, at which the Council agreed to accept the grant offered by Gulbenkian, subject to the condition concerning the Department. The meeting was informed that my mother had updated Mr Thornton on the progress in setting up ÓC, that twenty-one people had subscribed a total of £200, and that she planned to have young members attend their first concert in November, followed by opera in December. Mr Thornton had initially not been in favour of proceeding so quickly with the establishment of ÓC, but in a letter of 11 August he seems to bow to my mother's enthusiasm, agreeing also that the MAI should start to draw up advertisements for the position of Organiser, but defer an appointment until the Minister's decision was known. At the meeting on 17 August, the Council also discussed the practicalities of advertising the post and nominated an appointments committee, who would interview the candidates and make the final selection. They were: Sir George Mahon, Mr James Fagan, Mrs Alice Quirk and my mother.

A press conference to launch ÓC was planned for 25 October 1967 and my mother wrote to Mr Thornton shortly beforehand to say that she was pressing the Minister for his assurances in writing, so that the SRS might be announced on the same day. This must have been effective as the important letter from Donogh O'Malley, stating that the Department would take over the funding with a grant of £2,000 from the fourth year onwards, is dated 31 October 1967.[2]

The SRS which had won Gulbenkian's approval was very much on the lines proposed by Victor Leeson to the Council in early 1965, namely that a group of three musicians would give recitals in three secondary schools in the same area on the same day, possibly staying overnight and travelling on to another set of three schools the next day. Each recital had to be carefully timed to fit into a 40-minute school period, to include about 10 minutes of introduction to the music and demonstration of the instruments, and just over 25 minutes of music. The performers were advised to choose fairly short pieces in a range of styles from different periods, and encouraged to give thought to making their spoken introductions imaginative and teenager-friendly. Each school was expected to give a contribution, whilst the performers were paid a fee for the day. As the scheme developed, it became possible to pay the car driver something extra for petrol expenses, and subsistence was paid if an overnight stay was involved.

On 17 August, the MAI had also appointed a small team to assist with the considerable fieldwork that would be needed to get the project off the ground. Their remit was to visit the schools, to select the groups of artists, to advise about their choice of music and presentation if needed, and to have overall responsibility for the Organiser. In addition to my mother, these were the harpist Mercedes Garvey (née Bolger) and Alice

Quirk, formerly Yoakley, well known throughout the country as a choral conductor and examiner for the Department of Education. They co-opted the singer and harpist, Gráinne Yeats, who was bilingual in Irish and English. In the autumn of 1967 they visited schools in many parts of the country, explaining the nature of the Scheme and preparing the ground for the Organiser.

1968

Mary Elizabeth Minihan took up the dual position of SRS and ÓC organiser in January 1968. A native of New Ross, she came to Dublin to work and, being interested in music, had become a member of the Guinness Choir where she was friendly with Victor Leeson and Brían Howlett, the MAI Treasurer. An immediate plan of work was in place for Mary Elizabeth, which was to re-establish contact with all the schools visited the previous autumn. I think it would be fair to say that the SRS was an instant success. The report for 1968 states that 121 recitals were given in 70 different schools, with 40 performers taking part. Some of the schools took two or three concerts and fifteen counties in all were represented: Carlow (3), Dublin (2), Galway (16), Kildare (4), Laois (4), Leitrim (1), Longford (2), Louth (6), Mayo (10), Meath (6), Offaly (3), Roscommon (2), Sligo (2), Tipperary (2) and Westmeath (7). The financial contribution from each school was set at a minimum of £5, but the SRS ledger[3] shows that the amounts varied considerably, some schools paying £6 or £7 and others up to £10 or £12 per concert. It was a definite policy that a school should not be barred from the Scheme on financial grounds, but it was also recognised that a better-off school could contribute according to its resources. It was very encouraging that by the end of the year there was a waiting list of schools who wanted to be included. There were no visits to Munster because there was a very active branch of the Music Teachers' Association in that region, which had already been organising Schools' Concerts for some years.

The calibre of the performers can be judged from this list: Sheila and Moya O'Grady, Veronica McSwiney, Betty Sullivan, Seán Lynch, Patricia

Dunkerley, Lindsay Armstrong, Gillian Smith, the RTÉ String Quartet (David Lillis, Audrey Park, Archie Collins, Coral Bognuda), John O'Conor, Thérèse Timoney, Patrick McElwee, Anne Woodworth, Hilary O'Donovan, Gearóid Grant, Sunniva Fitzpatrick, Sydney Egan, Mercedes Garvey, Gráinne Yeats, Doris Keogh, Ann Kinsella, Kathleen Behan, Mary Gallagher, Seamus O'Grady, Brian O'Rourke, Philip Martin, Charlie Maguire, Geraldine O'Grady, Aisling Drury-Byrne, Jenny Robinson, Lynda Byrne, Herb Moulton, Pádraig O'Connor, Loretta McGrath and Carole Block. The singer, Anne Woodworth recollects[4] that, in the early stages, my mother kept a close eye on the results of each trip and would telephone her to enquire how the children had enjoyed the music, and whether the performers had encountered any problems. There was also regular feedback from each school.

The fees paid were modest: £12 for a day with three concerts, £8 if there were only two. Pianists were paid £14 for three concerts because they played accompaniments as well as their own solos. For the first two terms there were no two-day trips, but a limited number are recorded from October 1968 onwards. For these, the fees were pro-rata at £24 and £28 for pianists. An overnight subsistence rate of £1.10s was paid to each musician, plus a travel allowance of £1.15s to the car-driver to cover petrol costs. Some of these musicians were right at the beginning of their careers, whilst others were more experienced professionals, so it may seem that this was not princely pay. However, for all the performers, this was a very welcome source of additional income, and for the younger players in particular a wonderful training in the skill of communication, both through the instrument and the spoken word, and in being able to cope with all manner of audiences. I can say, as one of those involved from the outset, it was also a lot of fun!

Jenny Robinson, whose father Joe Groocock has figured in earlier chapters, was a frequent performer, playing both flute and recorder. In chatting to me about her recollections, she said that she felt my mother had done a wonderful service in setting up the SRS as it benefitted the schools, the pupils and the performers.[5] 'So many musicians got a chance to participate. The fact that you played the programme a number of times meant that you could improve on your presentation, and gain experience in learning to judge your audience. I gave my choice of pieces a lot of thought. Plus it was an amazing opportunity to travel to parts of Ireland that were completely unknown to me.'

ÓC was also established relatively smoothly, its work being mostly concentrated on obtaining concert tickets at reduced prices and then making these available to members. The students on the committee[6] were John O'Conor, Thérèse Timoney, Honor Ó Brolcháin, Jenny Robinson and Antony Lewis-Crosby, and the older members were Mrs Phyllis O'Donovan, Lady Suzanne Mahon and Mrs Nuala Hughes (wife of Professor Tony Hughes). The first concert which ÓC members attended was given by the Bamberg Symphony Orchestra on 3 November 1967 under the auspices of the German Embassy. This was followed by some of the DGOS productions in their winter season and also subsidised admission to chamber music recitals. Occasional concerts specifically for ÓC members, such as that on 8 February 1968 at TCD by the Iowa String Quartet, were also arranged, and it became the norm for reduced price tickets to be offered to 'ÓC and students'. Membership was open to those aged between 14 and 25 and grew quickly. The subscription was 2s.6d, young people were encouraged to form groups amongst their friends with a minimum of 6 members, and all received membership cards with particulars of forthcoming performances at ticket prices from 2s.6d to 5s.0d. The *Bulletin* for July 1968 reported 800 members and detailed that tickets had been supplied for the Bolshoi Ballet, the RTÉSO Subscription Concerts, RDS recitals, and productions by the Rathmines and Rathgar Musical Society. Another special recital for ÓC, featuring the Wind Quintet of the BBC Training Orchestra in Bristol, took place on 26 October 1968 at Loreto College, St Stephen's Green, Dublin.

The intention of the SRS was that participating schools should have a concert each term by a different group, thus ensuring that the students would see and hear most instruments of the orchestra during their time at secondary school, as well as broadening their knowledge of composers other than those on the curriculum. Enthusiastic letters often accompanied a school's cheque payment: 'The whole school was present in the Assembly Hall and the attention and interest shown by the children agreeably surprised me. They loved the piano pieces and especially the Mozart. Most of them had not seen a clarinet, except of course on TV. It was really good to see it so near and to listen to the beautiful sounds drawn from it by Mr Egan. I could not say enough in praise of the group – they were so friendly and helpful as well as being excellent.'(Our Lady's, Greenhills, Drogheda). Another example: 'Some of the children commented that it was not long enough. Some spoke in favour of the Fauré, some of the Mozart, while others were attracted to an instrument for its own sake rather than the composer.'(Drogheda Grammar School). By the end of 1968 it was clear that the blueprint for the Scheme was a good one.

1969

But in the early months of 1969 a difficulty arose which was completely outside the MAI's control. This was a school strike which went on for several weeks, making forward planning of recitals almost impossible, and leaving an aftermath of uncertainty amongst teachers. It was a very challenging situation for Mary Elizabeth Minihan, with just a year's experience in the position of SRS Organiser. The period of most acute difficulty was just after my father's death, when my mother was away in the West and not in daily contact. However she was definitely back in Dublin on 12 February as she attended a Council meeting on that date, as well as the AGM and an EGM on 20 March. But at some point it appears that the hitherto good relations between my mother and Mary Elizabeth were soured. Brían Howlett[7] described Mary Elizabeth to me as lively, intelligent, great fun and with a flair for PR, and he knew that she admired my mother very much, but found her intimidating. Perhaps she found it hard to come up to my mother's high standards, but I also suspect that there had been a lack of guidance during my mother's absences from the MAI office before and after my father's death. On 25 June the Council heard that Mary Elizabeth's resignation would take effect from 4 July 1969 and two new Organisers were announced. A brief paragraph in September's *Counterpoint* wished Mary Elizabeth many years of happiness following her recent marriage.

In deciding to separate the positions of SRS Organiser and ÓC Secretary into two part-time jobs, sharing the salary that had been paid formerly, my mother's mind had turned to her old friend Helen Watson (mentioned in Chapter 3) who had recently retired after a long career on the administrative staff of TCD. Another good choice was made in the appointment of Mary Timoney, Thérèse's younger sister, as secretary for ÓC. Under Helen Watson's care, there was a period of consolidation for the SRS, following the initial excitement of establishing such a worthwhile project. Helen brought her years of administrative experience to the office regime, though she did introduce one quaintly academic innovation in denoting the autumn and spring sessions as the Michaelmas and Trinity Terms. In spite of the restrictions of the strike in 1969, schools in four additional counties – Clare, Donegal, Kilkenny and Monaghan – joined the Scheme and more performers became involved. There were encouraging comments: 'The girls appreciated the performers very much ... especially since they were so youthful' (Brigidine Convent, Goresbridge, Co. Kilkenny) and 'It was a delightful treat. Both music and musicians made a tremendous impression' (Loreto Convent, Kilkenny).

1970

During 1970, my mother's main concern was to ensure that the Department of Education would abide by the commitment given by Minister O'Malley in his letter of 31 October 1967. It will be remembered that Donogh O'Malley had died in 1968 at the young age of 47. In the intervening period, my mother was in touch with the succeeding Ministers, Brian Lenihan and Pádraig Faulkner, and was greatly relieved when the Department paid the first instalment of its grant of £2,000 in May 1971.

1970 was also the year of the foundation of the Irish Youth Orchestra (IYO), and I do not think it is too great an exaggeration to say that this was the project which revitalised my mother's spirits and revived her energy following my father's death. It was the realisation of a dream and an ambition nurtured ever since the visit of the NYOGB in 1958, and her plan was to establish it initially under the aegis of ÓC. She always maintained that her most brilliant idea was to ask Hugh Maguire to direct it.

When she phoned me from Derrylahan, sometime in February 1969, and announced that she had decided to found a youth orchestra with Hugh as conductor, I assumed that she had only just thought of the project. In fact she had broached the idea to Hugh the previous year. Hugh wrote to her on 27 February 1969, from a train travelling between Switzerland and Germany: 'I'm still enormously interested in the Youth Orchestra idea and am keeping the period – 29 June for about a week – free. What is the latest on this project? Maybe you have been trying to contact me and now find it even more impossible. Let me know whenever you have anything fixed. I'll be back in London on 22 or 23 March.'[8] Hugh's inaccessibility would seem to have been due to the very busy touring schedule of the Allegri Quartet, and he had not heard of my father's death. In the next letter, dated 25 March, he writes: 'I am so sorry to hear about Lyall, I hadn't heard and I send you and all the family my deepest sympathy.' He goes on to discuss dates for a possible course in the summer of 1969, but a third letter dated 19 April reads: 'It's a pity about the Youth Orchestra for this year, but next year I shall look forward to it.'

Honor Ó Brolcháin[9] formed the view that my mother, right from the outset, had intended using ÓC as the vehicle for the establishment of a Youth Orchestra. In so doing, she was assured of the help of Mary Timoney as secretary, and also of the support of the twenty-one original subscribers, some of whom became members of the IYO committee. The initial announcement appeared in the March issue of *Counterpoint*: 'The ÓGRA CEOIL Summer Orchestral Course will take place at Our Lady's School, Rathnew, Co. Wicklow, from 17 July to 24 July. Hugh Maguire will be the Director and the Course will be open to pupils between the ages of 14 and 21. Participants will reside at the school and take part in sectional and full orchestral rehearsals. The object is to give secondary pupils from all over the country a chance to play with other musicians of their own age and to receive first class orchestral tuition. Social and other events are being arranged for course members, Details from the Secretary, Ógra Ceoil, 11 Suffolk Street, Dublin 2.'

Mirette Dowling, who had long been the MAI's contact for Country Tour recitals in Wicklow, was the music mistress at Our Lady's School, and it was through her that permission was obtained to hold the course at this girl's boarding school. Set in secluded grounds, with ample dormitory accommodation and a large hall, it was an ideal location for the first course. Also it was just down the road from the famous Hunter's Hotel where rooms were available for the musicians who were coaching the young players. The strings were looked after by Hugh Maguire and Thérèse Timoney, Hugh's brother Charlie (viola) and Bruno Schrecker (cellist with the Allegri Quartet). From the RTÉSO came the bassoonist Gilbert Berg (woodwind) and the principal horn, Victor Malirsh (brass). The planned repertoire was Schubert's 'Unfinished' Symphony, two movements from Symphony No.39 by Mozart, and excerpts from *Soirées Musicales* by Britten, challenging music for approximately 65 young players, most of whom had never played in anything but their school orchestra. I was there myself as a member of staff, with our baby daughter Deirdre, and remember well the rather excruciating intonation of the lower strings as they searched for the opening low-B of the 'Unfinished' at the first full rehearsal. But the patient work of the coaches at the sectional rehearsals paid off and Hugh was able to create some shape and sense of ensemble playing at the final concert, given before an audience of parents.

Ian Fox, as editor of *Counterpoint*, visited the course and contributed a lively article to the September (1969) issue, illustrated with a fine sketch in profile of Hugh by Ian's partner Jim Harkin. Hugh is quoted as saying: 'Everyone is working very hard and yet enjoying themselves, it's marvellous!' My mother made good use of my father's old ciné camera and, with the help of Hugh's friend James Plunkett, produced a short colour film which is very entertaining and caught much of the atmosphere of the whole proceedings. There is also a tape-recording of the concert, which undoubtedly conveys that musically there was plenty of room for improvement! Apart from my mother and Hugh, the most important member of staff was Mary, the ÓC secretary, who looked after the day-to-day organisation and had great rapport with all the players. She was helped by committee members John O'Conor (orchestra manager), Anthony Lewis-Crosby, Mrs O'Donovan, Mrs Hughes and Lady Mahon. My mother had also asked Helen Watson to be involved.

Gerry Kelly and Evelyn Grant met for the first time at the course. Gerry, who led the cellos, was there with three of his brothers – his twin Chris who played in the first desk of first violins, and John and Paul, both viola players. Their father, the composer T.C.Kelly, who taught at Clongowes Wood College, insisted that they should take part, rather than attend a course organised by Havelock Nelson – he could see that this new venture had the possibility of becoming a national orchestra. Gerry has told me that, as it turned out, his father was somewhat disappointed at the standard of the concert! Evelyn came with her sister Bríd (violin) and played first flute, even though she had been learning just a few months and had to be shown fingerings for some of the high notes. Their recollections of the course[10] were the excitement of the music-making, meeting Hugh for the first time – Bruno was also a great favourite – and of the lasting friendships formed. There were certainly high spirits, only to be expected amongst such a crowd of teenagers, many of them taking part in a residential music course for the first time, and the staff found it hard to enforce bed-time regulations. Card-playing kept some people awake, and there was even a dawn escape down to the near-by beach, possibly only noticed by one observant nun! My mother's nickname 'Granny Smith' had emerged by the second day, partly because the young people thought she looked like a Granny, 'severe but with a twinkle in her eye', and anyway the connection with apples was irresistible.

Another viola player, Susan Carolan, remembered vividly the start of the very first rehearsal and: 'the extraordinary effect of Hugh Maguire's personality.'[11] For her, it was the quality of the music which made the biggest impact, and she referred to the spine-tingling sensation produced by the Schubert 'Unfinished', something she also experienced in the Brahms 4th Symphony in 1972. Her recollection is that Hugh's rehearsals were very concentrated, but that he held everyone's attention. Susan is quite convinced that, had she not attended that course, she would not have been motivated to continue playing the viola.

1971

The first course was such a success that it was decided to run another from 31 December 1970 to 4 January 1971, I was intrigued to learn from Gerry and Evelyn that, following the first course, my mother invited some of the players to her house for tea and a chat. It seems that discipline at future courses was on her mind and how best to proceed with the running of the orchestra. Evelyn said that this approach of 'treating me like an adult' was something she never forgot and that it shaped her own thinking in years to come. To me, there are echoes here of my mother's Girl Guide training with its emphasis on giving early responsibility to a group of leaders. It was decided that the one recreational element missing at Rathnew was a swimming-pool, and for that reason the Christmas course was transferred to Gormanston boy's school, Co. Meath. This time at least 80 applications were received and auditions were held in late November. The same instrumental coaches were happy to give their time, the main work being Bizet's *L'Arlésienne* Suite No. 1, and of course Hugh Maguire directed.

The charge to the participants was £10 for the week, so one of the major concerns during 1971 was the establishment of a secure source of funding. My mother wrote to the Gulbenkian Foundation on 19 May 1971[12] to enquire whether a further grant for the orchestra might be considered, but their reply of 26 May did not hold out much hope. However, the Department of Education grant, the first instalment of which was paid in May 1971, covered the work of the secretary of ÓC, in addition to funding the SRS. My mother was successful in obtaining a grant for each course from the Carnegie Trust, Lady Mayer gave some financial assistance, and there was commercial sponsorship from Cement Ltd, from Guinness's and P. J. Carroll & Co.

In 1971, due to another threatened teachers' strike and its effect upon exam preparation, there was an unspent sum of £150 – £200 remaining from the SRS portion of the grant. My mother sought the permission of Department officials to transfer this money to ÓC, to assist with the costs of the orchestra course held that summer, and this was agreed.[13] The overall Department grant for 1972/73 was increased to £2,500, with £500 of this being allocated to the IYO (20%). Each year there was an incremental increase in the grant, and from 1973 onwards the percentages allocated were approximately 62% to the SRS and 38% to the IYO. In addition, the schools were encouraged to increase their contributions, which greatly assisted the SRS income. By the time Helen Watson retired, at the end of June 1975, most schools were contributing between £8 and £12 per concert and performance fees had risen to £15 for three concerts, £12 for two, and a pianist's fee of £18. But whilst the IYO was able to attract additional commercial sponsorship, the dependence of the SRS on government funding meant that it was slower to blossom and reach its full potential.

However, in spite of financial restrictions its work was hugely important. Gerry Kelly was a frequent participant and recalled touring on different occasions with Cormac Ó Cuilleanáin (violin) or David Carmody (horn). A week's work in the West and Donegal would involve three concerts a day for five days which, when subsistence money was added, was actually good pay for musicians at that time, and there was always the hope of being in a convent school at lunchtime, which would mean a really good meal in 'the parlour'. Gerry recalled one nun who advised him that he needed to speak more to the children – a lesson he took to heart! Chatting to me in February 2018, Cormac,[14] said that the SRS trips: 'opened a window on Ireland, which I would not have experienced in any other way.' To him, certain schools were memorable for all the right reasons – Our Lady's Bower, Athlone, the St Louis Convent at Balla and Gortnor Abbey in Crossmolina, both in Co. Mayo, Sligo Grammar School and Wilson's Hospital at Multyfarnham in Co. Westmeath – whereas he also recollected a school where there was no music desk on the upright piano and John O'Conor played the concert with the music balanced on the lid!

I remember a school where the poor state of the piano was blamed upon a family of mice who had made it their home for the winter and nibbled the felt heads off the hammers! In fact, the unpredictability of pianos was a perennial problem. The horn player Colin Block recounted[15] his experience of arriving at a school about noon, with just enough time to check the tuning of the piano before lunch. It was a semi-tone flat. The anxious school principal enquired whether it was satisfactory, to which Colin replied that it was 'a bit low.' When he and the other players returned to the hall to give the concert they found that the piano had been raised well off the floor by means of pallets. Not only did Colin still have to transpose all his music by a semitone, but the pianist must have been pretty uncomfortable too!

In September 1975 Helen Watson was replaced by Mrs Eilís MacGabhann. She responded to a newspaper advertisement for the job of Organiser and was interviewed by my mother and Mairtín McCullough. Eilís was an Irish speaker, a friend of Peig Bean Uí Dhubhgaill and also an amateur cellist.[16] The part-time hours suited her, as her daughters were still at school, and, by her own account, she found the MAI office a congenial place to work, forming a particular friendship with Nancy Glenn, the MAI's assistant secretary. In November 1975 my mother announced that she would be retiring from all her MAI commitments, with the exception of her chairmanship of the SRS committee. So Eilís benefitted from working with her throughout 1976. A new feature was the number of established groups who had become regular performers, such as the RTÉ String Quartet, the Georgian Brass Ensemble and the Douglas Gunn Ensemble. In 1976 the total number of recitals was 153 in 94 schools, and it was estimated that 61,000 young people had attended the concerts! But by the end of the year my mother felt that the time had come to retire from that committee as well, chairing her last meeting on 10 January 1977. A serendipitous inspiration led my mother to suggest that Helen Watson might take over the chair, which Helen accepted, with Brian Grimson, Anne Woodworth and Patrick McElwee forming the rest of the committee.

Regarding the original ÓC scheme for the provision of free or reduced price concert and opera tickets, the MAI Council minutes of 20 March 1974 record an increasing lack of interest and a decline in membership numbers. The decision was taken to allow this aspect of ÓC's work to lapse, with the option to revive the scheme at a future date if needed.

[1] NLI – ACC 6000, box 20, beige folder 8, for this and following correspondence with the Gulbenkian Foundation.

[2] Ibid. box 20, beige folder 8.

[3] Ibid. box 6.

[4] Interviewed by the author, 27 December 2017.

[5] Interviewed by the author, 15 February 2018.

[6] John O'Conor – one of the most distinguished Irish musicians of his generation, founder of the Dublin International Piano Competition (1988), Director of the RIAM (1994-2010), and a noted professor of piano at the highest international level. His performance career has had a particular focus on the works of Beethoven, Mozart, Schubert and John Field, and his discography is extensive (see article in *The Encyclopaedia of Music in Ireland*).

Thérèse Timoney – violinist with an illustrious career as an orchestral leader: RTÉCO, NICO and the OSC; also a member of the Cologne Chamber Orchestra. Founder, artistic director and leader of Christ Church Baroque, Ireland's first professional period instrument orchestra (1996), she plays baroque violin with the English Concert. She was appointed Adjunct Professor in the UCD Music Department in 2017.

Honor Ó Brolcháin – author and musician, an authority on her ancestors, the Plunkett family. Her books include *All in the Blood* (A&A Farmar 2006) and *Joseph Plunkett* (O'Brien Press 2012). She also writes poetry and played the viol with the Consort of St Sepulchre. Honor was the first editor of *SoundPost* magazine.

Jenny Robinson – one of Ireland's finest recorder players, a founder-member of the Consort of St Sepulchre and a much-loved teacher of flute and recorder.

Antony Lewis-Crosby – has been Arts Director of the Barbican Centre, London (1979-1994), Chief Executive of the Royal Liverpool Philharmonic Society (1994-2000), Managing Director of the London Mozart Players (2004-2009) and currently runs the concert series at St Luke's Church, Battersea.

[7] Interviewed by the author, 30 January 2017.

[8] NLI – ACC 6000, box 3, file 9.

[9] Interviewed by the author, 19 February 2018.

[10] Interviewed by the author, 20 January 2018. Evelyn Grant is a presenter and producer for RTÉ Lyric FM; Gerry Kelly has retired as teacher of cello at the Cork School of Music, and together with Evelyn runs the Cork Pops Orchestra. All of their children have been members of the IYO.

[11] Interviewed by the author, 23 January 2018. Susan Carolan later married the harpsichordist Malcolm Proud, and since 1982 has organised numerous musical events and concerts for the Kilkenny Arts Week and 'Music in Kilkenny'.

[12] NLI – ACC 6000, box 20, beige folder 8.

[13] Ibid. box 20, beige folder 8, letter of 24 November 1971.

[14] Cormac Ó Cuilleanáin is an author and former Professor in Italian at TCD.

[15] Informal conversation with the author, 15 February 2018. Colin Block is a well-known conductor and was a member of the horn section of RTÉSO for many years.

[16] Interviewed by Pat O'Kelly, 26 November 2002.

CHAPTER 26

The MAI – 1968 to 1971

1968

The year 1968 was a significant one for the MAI as it marked the 20th anniversary of its foundation and also the inauguration and development of a number of important projects. These included the SRS and ÓC, the publication of the *Catalogue of Contemporary Irish Composers* and the initial planning of the first Dublin Festival of 20th Century Music. The work of the SRS and ÓC is described at length in Chapter 25. Regarding the *Catalogue*, the preparation of which had begun in 1964, Edgar Deale (as editor) informed the Council on 6 December 1967 that he had obtained a grant of £595 from the CRC towards the printing and publication costs of 1,000 copies. Six months later he brought the good news that the *Catalogue* would be ready at the end of June, that the MAI would be getting 200 free copies to distribute in Ireland, and the CRC would look after distribution abroad.

This was, of course, most encouraging news for composers, as were the plans for the inaugural Dublin Festival of 20th Century Music. These were first relayed to the Council by my mother on 6 March 1968 when she reported: 'that she had heard from Professor Boydell concerning the Contemporary Music Festival, and that it was now proposed to hold it in Trinity College during the week commencing 5 January 1969. She outlined the provisional programme – the net cost, after deducting RTÉ fees, would be approximately £1,000 – it was likely that the Arts Council would guarantee this amount.' The minute records that: 'Council agreed in principle that the Association should run the Festival.' It is interesting that this idea, which originated with the Composers' Group of the MAI, should have followed so swiftly upon its counterpart in the contemporary visual arts, the ROSC Exhibition, established in 1967 by Michael Scott, which ran at four-yearly intervals until 1988. Of course, as a painter himself, Brian Boydell was very well aware of the excitement in artistic circles generated by ROSC.[1]

The MAI was deeply involved in the whole process of the winding up of CAH (see Chapter 22). The all-important AGM of the MAI was scheduled for 14 February 1968 and in preparation the chairman, Mairtín McCullough, sent a circular to all members on 1 February, explaining the rationale and the necessary legal steps. He assured members that: 'For our part, the other members of the Council and I have no hesitation in recommending to our members that they wholeheartedly support the Resolution to be put to our AGM.' There were three parts to the resolution: ' i) to transfer and make over to Concert and Assembly Hall Ltd all the assets of the Association; ii) to merge the Association and its affairs in Concert and Assembly Hall Ltd; iii) to execute all documents and do all things necessary to give effect to such a merger and the directive of the Resolution, provided that Concert and Assembly Hall shall have first changed its name to "The Music Association of Ireland Ltd" and altered its Memorandum and Articles of Association to accord with the terms of the draft Memorandum and Articles of Association submitted to this Meeting, and which for the purpose of identification have been signed by the Chairman.' In layman's language, the MAI reaped the advantage of becoming a company limited by guarantee, taking over all the assets of CAH, with the Council members becoming Directors. The Resolution passed without difficulty.

The MAI took on the rental of both offices at 3 Molesworth Street, telephone and electricity accounts were altered accordingly and the financial assets were also transferred. The final audited CAH accounts for the year ended 31 December 1967 show a balance of £2,478.3s.7d of which £1,700 was held in 6% Exchequer Stock 1980/85 and £625 in

Prize Bonds. These investments were transferred into the name of the MAI and continued to appear in their accounts. In 1971 the prize bonds finally produced a return and the resulting £1,000 was invested in 9¼ % Exchequer Loan.

Other MAI activities continued on accustomed lines. On 24 January 1968, Anne Woodworth (mezzo-soprano) gave her Coming-Out recital, accompanied by Dorothy Stokes. The main work in her programme was Schumann's *Frauenliebe und Leben*. Songs from another Schumann cycle, the *Liederkreis*, were performed by Violet Twomey and the author in a recital following the AGM. Country Tours in the spring of 1968 featured a series of recitals by the RTÉ String Quartet – David Lillis, Audrey Park, Archie Collins and Coral Bognuda – in February,[2] whilst Mary Gallagher and Veronica McSwiney's tour spanned February and March.[3]

The MAI's 20th Anniversary was celebrated with a special concert on 8 March 1968 at TCD Exam Hall. This was given by the Cremona Quartet, who had already toured for the MAI in January 1967. Its distinguished members were Hugh Maguire and Iona Brown (violins), Cecil Aronowitz (viola) and Terence Weil (cello). They played a complete Beethoven recital: Op. 59 No. 2, Op. 95 and Op. 135. I detect my mother's hand in this programme – she loved Beethoven Quartets above any other music, especially as she grew older – and I think that it is also appropriate to comment at this juncture that my mother had become very friendly with Hugh Maguire. I feel that his musical influence had superseded that of Douglas Cameron, who was no longer active in the string quartet field.

The Members' Meeting on 11 June was given by the Los Angeles Brass Quintet, a highly polished and virtuoso ensemble, all members of the Los Angeles Philharmonic Orchestra, who visited Ireland as part of a European tour. They played at Castletown House, their programme built around 17th/18th century repertoire plus 20th century pieces by Bartók and Horowitz. Prior to this, my mother arranged a short Country Tour.[4] They travelled with a total of nine instruments, often switching during a concert as the music required, and requested that my mother hire a mini-bus for the tour to accommodate themselves and their valuable cargo. She also had to apply for their work-permits. They turned out to be a very entertaining group and there was considerable interest in a possible return visit in 1970.

The autumn of 1968 was also a busy time. The final Members' Meeting of the year on 22 October was given by Herb Moulton and his Swedish wife Gun Kronzell, who was the leading mezzo-soprano at Graz Opera House in Austria. With their accompanist Karl Bergemann, they presented a most attractive programme of duets and solos, including Jim Wilson's *3 Songs of Innocence*. The concert was in the TCD Exam Hall, in association with the German Institute, and was attended by the Swedish Ambassador. They undertook an extensive Country Tour,[5] and there is a very informative file on their visit[6] – Herb was a prolific letter-writer. They were mostly very popular; for instance, Mona Curry of Ballina wrote: 'Everyone enjoyed it immensely, for the Moultons are wonderful singers and with lovely personalities. It was one of the most enjoyable nights we have had.' But it is intriguing to note that the duo's appearance on the 'Late Late Show' on RTE TV produced mixed reactions amongst some promoters who thought that the publicity had not helped, and that some members of their regular audience had stayed away because of it!

On 12 November, John O'Conor gave his Coming-Out recital at the Hibernian Hotel with a programme of Mozart, Beethoven, Chopin and Prokofiev. John was on the MAI Council at that time – there was a definite trend to involve younger members including Lindsay Armstrong, Ian Fox, David McConnell and Thérèse Timoney. A Country Tour by the mother-and-daughter duo of Gráinne Yeats (Irish harp) and Caitríona Yeats (concert harp) commenced in December 1968 and extended into the spring of 1969.[7] Meanwhile, the Council was preoccupied with the arrangements for the 20th Century Festival, a major venture for the Association and one that would continue well into the 1980s. In its first year (January 1969) it was organised by Victor Leeson with a supporting committee. My mother had little involvement, mostly because my father's illness meant that she was spending an increasing amount of time in overseeing the running of his business.

As 1968 drew to a close, there were concerns about the MAI office and about the *Bulletin*. It was known that the premises at 3 Molesworth St were due for demolition, the MAI had only a short-term lease and the rent was quite high because CAH were no longer using the second office.[8] The search began for alternative accommodation. Regarding the *Bulletin*, back in June 1968 Jim Wilson had given almost a year's notice that he would like to be replaced as editor, having served in this capacity from mid-1964. Jim had been successful in attracting some advertisements when he initiated the coloured cover format in September 1964, but nonetheless the *Bulletin* was losing money and the MAI was running a bank overdraft. It was decided to appoint Council member Ian Fox, who worked in the field of advertising, as the new editor and to employ Gladys McNevin as advertising manager. The *Bulletin* would, in effect, become a magazine from the first issue of 1969 under the new name of *Counterpoint*. It carried an impressive selection of full-page advertisements and had a new cover featuring Jim Harkin's iconic harp design, somehow conveying a vision of the past, present and future of Irish music. This harp remained the MAI's logo for many years to come.

The year 1968 had been a good one for the MAI and my mother must have been gratified that the efforts of all those involved were bearing such welcome fruit. But at the same time there was, for her and the rest of the family, the ever-present spectre of my father's illness. He died on 21 January 1969. At its meeting on 30 January, the Council passed a vote of sympathy to my mother and stood in silence in my father's memory.

1969

The first Dublin Festival of 20th Century Music took place from 5 to 10 January 1969. All the concerts were at the TCD Exam Hall, except for the RTÉSO concert at the SFX Hall. It offered a wonderful showcase for Irish composers and performers and, in turn, brought a selection of the best of international contemporary music directly to Irish audiences. There were lunchtime and evening concerts each day – attendances averaging at 180 – with an eclectic mixture of local and visiting performers, amongst them the Gabrieli Ensemble, the pianist John McCabe, James Blades (percussionist) and the conductor Gerard Schürmann. An initial Arts Council guarantee of £1,000 was increased to £1,182, and the overall loss was less than £50. The Festival was particularly well-received by celebrated music critics from the UK, Felix Aprahamian (*Sunday Times*) and Ronald Crichton (*Financial Times*). Kenneth Loveland, writing in *Music and Musicians* thought that it: 'succeeded to an extent which, one imagined, even the organisers had not thought possible.' By way of contrast, Edgar Deale contributed a humorous, but rather tongue-in-cheek and intolerant article in the April issue of *Counterpoint* (pp. 5&6). Victor Leeson and his committee received warm congratulations from the Council and it was resolved to forge ahead with plans for another Festival in 1970.

At this point I feel tribute should be paid to Victor Leeson's extraordinary contribution to Irish musical life. His good friend, Brían Howlett,[9] described him as: 'charismatic in a good way, an influential member of the MAI Council both musically and personally'. He worked in the personnel department of Guinness's and founded the St James's Gate Musical Society in 1951. A fine choral conductor, he gave the first complete performance in Ireland of Bach's *St Matthew Passion* in 1958, and conducted the choir in Italy and Sicily in five performances of the *St John Passion* in 1977, with the New Irish Chamber Orchestra. Another side of his musical character emerged in his much-loved performances of the comic roles in the Rathmines & Rathgar Musical Society's productions of Gilbert & Sullivan operas. As recorded elsewhere in this book, he served on the MAI Council for many years and in many ways.

The AGM in 1969 was on 20 March and was followed by a talk by Sheila Larchet-Cuthbert on her newly-published book *The New Tutor for Irish Harp*. Sheila, principal harpist with the RTÉSO and a most distinguished performer and teacher, was for many years a member of the MAI Council. An EGM was held on the same evening, to tidy up one or two legal matters outstanding from the merger of the MAI and CAH. A new chairman was elected at the Council meeting on 26 March – he was James Fagan, the solicitor who had advised on the merger. My mother continued as Hon. Secretary, Brían Howlett as Treasurer and

David McConnell was re-elected Hon. Record Secretary. Nancy Glenn's office hours were increased to 15 per week at a salary of £300 a year. Nancy had been the greatest possible help to my mother during the last months of my father's illness, dealing with her correspondence and keeping in touch by telephone.

There was a memorable spring Members' Meeting at the RDS on 20 April when the MAI co-operated with David Laing to bring Victoria de los Angeles back to Dublin with accompanist Geoffrey Parsons. Thérèse Timoney (violin) and John O'Conor (piano)[10] took up the opportunity of a Country Tour in March, as did Lindsay Armstrong (oboe) and the author[11]. A new committee was appointed to plan the programme for the 1970 20th Century Festival[12] but there were financial concerns when the Arts Council inexplicably turned down the MAI's request for funding. This decision was eventually reversed. Victor Leeson indicated that he did not wish to continue as organiser, however the October meeting of Council[13] was informed that David Laing was willing to take this on.

At the meeting on 10 September 1969, my mother informed the Council that negotiations were successfully concluded with McCullough Pigott's regarding office space on the 3rd floor of their new premises, and that the MAI would be moving to 11/13 Suffolk Street, at a rent of £265 per annum. Fortunately there was a lift!

The autumn of 1969 was very busy. In early October my mother had taken on quite an ambitious Country Tour by an English dance company called Ballets Minerva[14]. With funding from the Arts Council, they performed on six consecutive nights in Ballina, Birr, Cavan, Tullamore, Wicklow and at St Patrick's College, Drumcondra in Dublin. Founded by Edward Gaillard and Kathleen Gray, their aim was to bring live ballet of a high standard to provincial venues, using a small company and their own choreographers. As a travelling company they had their own transport, scenery, costumes, stage staff and recorded music. They required a stage at least 24' x 16' – unpolished and with no holes or splinters – and just two dressing rooms. Their programme was the same each night – firstly *Les Sylphides*, then a ballet called *Wedding Song* to the music of Schumann's

Frauenliebe und Leben, and as a finale a more modern work entitled *Radio Music*. My mother was understandably apprehensive that all would go well, but she need not have worried as they delighted their audiences everywhere and several centres were very keen to have a return visit. I can quote an enthusiastic letter from Wicklow: 'A very good attendance . . . what a pleasure to encounter such a courteous and highly-organised group – they were no trouble whatsoever, and they gave a most enjoyable performance too!' A producer from RTÉ was at one of their shows and invited them to do an interview and a short performance at the Montrose studios before returning to England.

Also in October, Eileen Donlon (soprano), Hilary O'Donovan (cello) and Mary Ellison (piano) gave five country concerts.[15] The final Country Tour of 1969, commencing on 30 November, brought the Allegri String Quartet to nine centres.[16] This was an ensemble of long-standing which had made its debut in 1954. Originally led by Erich Gruenberg's brother, Eli Goren, this role had passed to Hugh Maguire who had written to my mother on 27 February 1969 to say that he had been with the Allegri for about 6 months – 'having the time of my life' – following a triumphant 8-week tour of the USA. The other members of the Quartet were David Roth, Patrick Ireland and Bruno Schrecker. Hugh was keen for them to tour in Ireland, following two appearances at the Belfast Festival at the end of November, and so the first concert was in Sligo. They offered five programme options with works by Haydn, Mozart, Beethoven, Schubert, Ravel, Bartók and Stravinsky, and a sixth possibility which was a lecture-recital on either Beethoven's Op.131 or Bartók's 4th Quartet. Margaret Lynch of Rockwell College chose this option and wrote an appreciative letter to say what a memorable evening it had been: 'entertaining and yet instructive.'

The Members' Meeting on 23 October in the RDS was given by Italian pianist, Maria Tipo, who had built a considerable international career, having been hailed by Artur Rubinstein as 'the most exceptional talent of our time.' Even though the recital was in co-operation with the Italian Institute, it proved to be a troublesome event for my mother, especially as Miss Tipo changed her programme after all the advance publicity had been done.[17] At this time, my mother must have been very stretched by all that was required of her, principally the responsibility of LSL with its many employees, large premises and competitive business environment. I think that the complications of Miss Tipo's recital brought it home to my mother that she would need to prioritise her activities. The minutes of the Council meeting on 12 November record that the chairman had received a letter from my mother in which she stated that: 'because of pressure of business, she could no longer be responsible for the arrangement and conduct of Members' Meetings, and that she wished to be relieved of all her duties as Hon. Secretary, except the task of organising Country Tours which she would prefer to continue, and she would like suitable arrangements made as soon as the Council could conveniently do so.' The remainder of the minute indicates that the Council was aware of the Hon. Secretary's difficulties and regretfully acceded to her request, placing on record: 'its sincere appreciation of the invaluable services of the Hon. Secretary to the Association since its foundation.' This resignation must have been unwelcome news to the Council, but fortunately it was decided to discuss the implications at the next meeting, which did not take place until January 1970.

1970 – 1971

When the Council reconvened on 14 January 1970, there was more bad news concerning the Officers – Brían Howlett had tendered his resignation as from the AGM in March, due to pressure of work. At the same meeting, my mother made it clear that while she wished to be relieved of the Members' Meetings, she wanted to remain as Chair of the SRS and ÓC, as well as organising the Country Tours. She retained the title of Hon. Secretary. When the Council appointed a sub-committee to consider the future administration of the Association, my mother was one of its members, along with James Fagan (chairman), Brían Howlett, David McConnell, Ian Fox and John O'Conor. Some progress was achieved at the meeting of 3 February in that David McConnell agreed to be treasurer, Ian Fox was the new records secretary, and Enid Chaloner (daughter of

274

Alice Yoakley) the new concerts secretary, although she was not on the Council. It was agreed that a Standing Committee of the officers would administer the day-to-day affairs of the MAI, reporting to the Council.

These decisions were ratified on 23 March, at the Council meeting following the AGM. But matters were still very unsettled and the meeting heard objections to the concept of the Standing Committee from Lindsay Armstrong. On 22 April 1970, he presented a document with seven points which had as its main proposal: 'That the Council reaffirm its right to decide policy and to take musical, financial and administrative decisions in pursuit of that policy.' It further proposed that the Standing Committee be abolished and that all administrative matters be carried out by the responsible officers or relevant sub-committees. Matters of extreme urgency could be dealt with by the officers after consultation with other Council members, all correspondence should be brought to the attention of the Council, and Minutes circulated as soon as possible after each meeting. His proposals were seconded by Mrs Mercedes Bolger and passed unanimously. It seemed that, for the moment, the crisis had passed, but in fact some turbulence continued until the end of 1971.

On 27 May 1970, the Council heard that David McConnell had resigned both from the Council and as treasurer – he had served in this role for just four months – due to his appointment as Executive Officer to the Arts Council. He was replaced by David Wilkes, who made a good start, surveying the MAI's financial position and producing a budget for 1971. It appears, however, that he was unable to continue following the AGM in May 1971. The Association's financial year was altered to end on 31 July, and this in turn meant an extra AGM in 1971, which was held on 25 October. At the Council meeting on 15 September 1971, Brian Grimson was elected as Hon. Secretary and my mother as Hon. Treasurer! This was actually a surprise to me, I had not realised that she returned to her old role during the last few years of her work for the MAI. There were other officers elected following the October AGM – Mairtín McCullough began another term as chairman, Brian Grimson agreed to also become concerts secretary, Ian Fox was records secretary and Enid

Chaloner continued in the role of organiser of the 20th Century Festival – she had done this most successfully in January 1971.[18] There were also two newly elected Council members – Pat O'Kelly and David Carmody. The outgoing chairman, James Fagan, was thanked by my mother: 'for the wisdom and patience with which he guided the MAI through a difficult transition period.'

Regarding the day-to-day running of the MAI office, the Association was very fortunate to have the commitment and efficiency of the paid staff, Nancy Glenn, Helen Watson and Mary Timoney. Members recitals during this period were given by Colin Tilney (harpsichord) on 24 April 1970, and by Edward Beckett (flute) accompanied by Veronica McSwiney on 9 October. Both were at the College of Physicians. Pianist Lynda Byrne gave her Coming-Out recital on 19 November 1970 at the Hibernian Hotel. My mother arranged an extensive programme of Country Tours, as usual supported by funding from the Shaw Trust – Doris Keogh (flute) and Mercedes Garvey (harp) in April and May,[19] Anne Woodworth and Veronica McSwiney (voice and piano) in October,[20] and the newly-formed Jupiter Ensemble, directed by Colin Block, in November.[21] The Ensemble's members were Mary Gallagher (violin), Seamus O'Grady (viola), Moya O'Grady (cello), Herbert Nowak (bass), Brian O'Rourke (clarinet), Colin Block (horn) and Gilbert Berg (bassoon).

Another new group which made its debut in May 1970 was the New Irish Chamber Orchestra (NICO), conductor André Prieur. My mother was able to procure an Arts Council grant for their performances in Cavan, Rockwell, Galway and Birr in the autumn of 1970, and in Carlow, Killaloe, Tullamore and Ballina in the spring of 1971, making the case strongly that: 'towns such as these never get the chance of hearing a first class professional orchestra.'[22] My husband, as the manager of NICO, availed of an introduction from my mother to the Gulbenkian Foundation, which resulted in three years of funding that enabled this orchestra to establish its reputation.

MAI Members' Meetings in 1971 were a lecture-recital on Beethoven's *Sketchbooks* by the distinguished British pianist Denis Matthews on 28 April, and a recital by Frank Patterson (tenor) with Eily O'Grady (piano) on 13 October. The Coming-Out recital by Moninne Vaneček (violin), daughter of Jaroslav Vaneček, took place on 23 November, with pianist Veronica McSwiney.

On 24 January 1972, a delegation consisting of my mother, Brian Grimson and Ian Fox was invited to attend a meeting of the Broadcasting Review Board, which had received a submission from the MAI the previous October. This was based on an earlier document written by Brian Grimson in 1970 – A Report on the Treatment given to Serious Music by Radio Éireann.[23] The text of the submission is reproduced in the January issue of *Counterpoint* (pp. 10 & 11). It was a golden opportunity for the Association to press for a significant increase in performances of classical music on both television and radio.

[1] The ROSC Exhibition was drawn to my attention by Dinah Molloy during her interview with me on 7 January 2018. Translated from Irish, ROSC means 'poetry of vision'.

[2] Athlone, Ballina, Galway, Rockwell College, Tullamore and Waterford.

[3] Ballina, Castlebar, Cork, Gorey, Limerick, Rockwell and Wicklow, and schools' concerts in Crossmolina and Ballina.

[4] Ballina, Castlebar, Cork, Gorey and Limerick.

[5] Ballina, Birr, Cork, Galway, Gorey, Rockwell, Tullamore, Waterford and Wicklow.

[6] NLI – ACC 6000, box 44, beige file 1.

[7] Athlone, Ballina, Birr, Cork, Limerick, Rockwell, Waterford and Wicklow.

[8] NLI – ACC 6000, box 18, blue folder 3.

[9] Interviewed by the author, 30 January 2017. See also the entry about Victor Leeson in *The Encyclopaedia of Music in Ireland*.

[10] Athlone, Ballina, Limerick and Tullamore.

[11] Athlone, Galway, Gorey and Wicklow.

[12] Victor Leeson, Seóirse Bodley, Brian Boydell and Lindsay Armstrong.

[13] Council Minutes for 1969 -1976 are in NLI – ACC 6000, box 2 of 2.

[14] NLI – ACC 6000, box 3.

[15] Carlow, Donegal, Gorey, Rockwell and Tullow.

[16] Ibid. box 3 – Athlone, Ballina, Birr, Carlow, Cork, Galway, Gorey, Rockwell and Sligo.

[17] Ibid. box 3.

[18] Interviewed by the author and Pat O'Kelly in October 2001, and again by the author on 20 July 2015. Enid Chaloner's connection with the author's family goes back to the 1930s. Enid is a pianist, teacher and examiner, a keen choral singer and was a member of Brian Boydell's Dowland Consort. She is also a skilled administrator, having organised several 20th Century Festivals for the MAI, served as President of the Feis Ceoil, and many years as a member of the Music Committee of the RDS.

[19] Athlone and Gorey.

[20] Birr, Carlow, Cavan, Gorey, Killaloe, Nenagh and Rockwell.

[21] Athlone, Carlow, Gorey, Maynooth and Rockwell.

[22] NLI – ACC 6000, box 20, green folder 1.

[23] Ibid. box 5 and another copy in box 8.

CHAPTER 27

The Irish Youth Orchestra takes off – 1971 to 1974

1971–72

The third ÓC course was also at Gormanston from 25 June to 2 July 1971, by which time the orchestra had grown to full symphony size of 75 players. Some aspects of this course were also captured by my mother's ciné camera. The musical focus was on Beethoven's 5th Symphony and Weber's *Oberon* overture, but the concluding concert was still a private event for parents and family members. However, it was felt that the orchestra was now ready to be launched with a public concert under the official name of The Irish Youth Orchestra (IYO) and that this should follow the 1971 Christmas course. The Exam Hall in TCD was booked for 3 January 1972, the major work on the programme being the Beethoven symphony. The first half opened with *Oberon*, followed by two *Canzonas* for woodwind and brass by Giovanni Gabrieli and the Vivaldi Concerto for 4 Violins. This was clever planning, as it gave different sections of the orchestra the opportunity to shine in their own right, and yet save energy for the all-important symphony in the second half. There was a capacity audience, the Taoiseach Jack Lynch and Mrs Lynch were present and led a standing ovation at the end, and there were good press reviews. John Honohan (*Sunday Independent*) wrote: 'It was most heartening to hear this 80-strong orchestra . . . to have attained such a high standard augurs well for the future of music in Ireland.' The symphony, a notoriously difficult work, was particularly praised – to quote from *The Irish Times* (Carol Acton): 'Beethoven's Fifth was the surprise. A difficult work for any orchestra, one's hopes for this performance were not high and one wondered if the choice was wise. But a most devoted attention to good tuning, so that one's ears were never assaulted, and an equal care for dynamic markings brought it off.'

Joan Mooney led the orchestra from 1970 until 1973. She described Hugh Maguire as: 'authoritative but calm' and commented that he could make the players feel at ease, but yet keep his distance.[1] He would often take her violin and demonstrate how he wanted something played. Joan felt that the courses were very well organised and the atmosphere fantastic – 'all the players thought they were great!' The experience of the IYO confirmed for her that she wanted to become a professional musician, as it did for so many others. At one course, all the members of the Allegri Quartet were present and arranged some rehearsals in the afternoons. Being allowed to sit in on these sessions, and witness how a professional group worked together, made a lasting impression on Joan. She made her career in Holland, playing for many years in the Hilversum Radio Chamber Orchestra.

Flautist Madeleine Berkeley joined the IYO following the auditions in November 1970.[2] Her most vivid memories were of Beethoven's 5th and Brahms' 4th Symphonies, both of which she played in 1972. To her the whole experience: 'was amazing, I would love to have had the opportunity even younger – the training was so beneficial, opening up the orchestral world in such an exciting way.' Looking at the names of those who played in that January concert, I have noted how many became professional musicians, both teachers and performers. My mother's inspiration in asking Hugh to direct the orchestra meant that these talented young people, at a very important stage in their musical development, came under the influence of one of the most remarkable musicians Ireland has produced. Hugh's orchestral experience and knowledge of the repertoire was enormous. Having been leader at different periods of the Bournemouth Symphony, the London Symphony and BBC Symphony Orchestras, he had played under the most inspirational conductors of the time, and understood the inner workings of an orchestra. He possessed an acute ear for tone and intonation, but the most notable aspect of his performances with the IYO was the sheer musicality of the shaping and balance. Even when there were technical blemishes, as one might expect from a group of relatively inexperienced players, these never took away from Hugh's ability to present the essence of the composer's intentions. In rehearsal he could be quite tough, but leavened his demands with an impish sense of humour and explanations which appealed to the players' imaginations. A week's course was an intense time for young players and Hugh understood very well the need for recreation, relaxation and 'letting off steam'.

He and my mother made a rather remarkable team. She greatly admired his musicianship and eminent career, but she also was bringing a lifetime of experience as a motivator and administrator to her new project. In particular, I feel that her early years as a Guide leader enabled her to meet the challenges of organising such a large group of young people with great confidence. Making travel plans, arranging timetables and rehearsal schedules, compiling lists and anticipating logistical problems were all really second nature to her, and in addition she rejoiced to see the players enjoying the music-making, realising their individual potential and rising to the challenges of the music. She also encouraged players who were interested to form into chamber-music groups and explore some new repertoire. Madeleine commented: 'you felt that her influence was behind everything.' Indeed, several players said that, in spite of her 'Granny' nickname, she was really the authority figure, and someone to be scared of if you were caught out in a misdemeanour.

From the outset, my mother and Hugh were very anxious to extend the membership of the IYO to Northern Ireland, and there was an incentive in that the standard of wind and brass playing was higher there, because of the system of peripatetic teaching. At least three players from the North – Erwin Shaw (oboe), David McKee (bassoon) and Lorraine Fox (horn) – played in the launching concert, the first step in some very important cross-border co-operation, encouraged initially by clarinet teacher John Johnston from Belfast. In later years Fr Kevin McMullan, who taught at

St Malachy's College in Belfast, was the IYO's most important link with Northern Ireland and encouraged many Ulster-based players to join the orchestra, as did Daphne Bell of the Ulster College of Music.

Another player who joined the orchestra after the 1970 auditions was the cellist, Justin Pearson.[3] His interesting comment was that Hugh ran the IYO almost as if it was a professional group, and that there was always great competition to be amongst the players in the front desks of strings. Justin remained in the orchestra until January 1976 and described the experience as life-changing, saying: 'I still think of what Hugh taught us when I play.' He felt that socially one of the strengths of the IYO was that, with the exception of my mother and Hugh, there was not a great age gap between the staff and the players. There were always great Irish music sessions in the late evenings, and the many coach journeys, rather than being tiresome, were occasions for joyful and enthusiastic singing!

The mezzo-soprano Alison Browner, acknowledged internationally as one of Ireland's most distinguished singers, was a violinist in the IYO from 1971 to 1976. Her impression was that: 'most of the players were a little in awe of Mrs Smith. Though her manner was quiet and she never raised her voice, there would be "no messing" when she walked into a room.'[4] Alison recognised that whilst Hugh's musical personality was charismatic, much of the success of the IYO was due to my mother's unobtrusive organisation behind the scenes, and that the many Irish musicians playing now in European orchestras owe a great deal to her. Alison also mentioned that my mother wrote her a lovely letter of congratulation, having heard her sing in the RTÉ television programme *For Your Pleasure*.

For the residential and administrative staff also, the two weeks of the courses were eagerly-awaited high points of the year. John O'Conor remained as orchestra manager for the 2nd and 3rd courses, before going away to study in Vienna, and then from 1972 onwards this role passed to Anton Timoney, brother of Thérèse and Mary, and a sound engineer with RTÉ. He had played trumpet in the first two or three courses, but explained to me that by the fourth course a number of other trumpeters had joined and someone was needed to deal with all the logistical problems of moving the orchestra to the TCD Exam Hall for the concert.[5] He sensed that my mother was happy to let him get on with matters such as staging, risers and stands whilst she dealt with the front-of-house and the welcoming of dignitaries. In the early years, members of staff included David and Brenda Wilkes, Jenny Robinson, David Carmody and Honor Ó Brolcháin (librarian), Carl Corcoran,[6] Paul Dorgan, Brian Grimson and Fr Pat McCarr from the Salesian Boys College at Ballinakill, Co. Laois. Thérèse also occasionally acted as staff, as well as coaching the 2nd violins for about twenty years! Apart from those dedicated people, there were all the invaluable supporters – parents, siblings, aunts and uncles, hosts and hostesses who provided overnight accommodation, volunteers who helped provide snacks, meals or transport, and of course the enthusiastic and encouraging audiences. The IYO, from its earliest days, assumed an important position in Irish musical life which it has never lost.

The finances needed for such a venture were never far from my mother's mind. The programme for 3 January acknowledged the commercial sponsors and included particular mention of IBM Ireland Ltd who had: 'undertaken to provide a grant of £200 a year for three years . . . this kind of financial support is very valuable as it provides security and enables us to plan ahead.' A most generous gift was received from Lady Mayer, following the January concert. She wrote to my mother: 'As you know, I had hoped to launch a National Youth Orchestra of Ireland as a closing act of my Foundation which was able, during its 10 years of existence, to work constructively for the remarkable expansion of the country's musical life which we are now witnessing. Unfortunately it proved impossible to ratify this idea. I am therefore very happy that the Irish Youth Orchestra has now been created and gave its first public concert in Dublin in January, thanks to your tremendous enthusiasm, persistency and efficiency. I am confident that this is only the beginning of the movement which will benefit alike the cause of music and the youth of Ireland. To facilitate the expansion of the Youth Orchestra and for its express use, I have pleasure in enclosing a cheque for £1,000 with my congratulations to you and my very best wishes for the success of the enterprise.'[7]

There was also some positive news on funding in a letter to my mother, dated 19 May 1972, from the Secretary of the Department of Education. He confirmed that £500 of the grant to the Schools' Scheme and Ógra Ceoil for the year 1972/73 could be allocated to the IYO (see Chapter 25). From 1973 onwards the IYO received approximately 38% of the Department grant to the SRS and ÓC.

The next concert was in Cork City Hall, sponsored by the Cork Orchestral Society. This formed the climax of the summer course which ran from 30 June – 7 July 1972 at Gormanston. There were 82 players in the orchestra, and they presented the *Egmont* overture by Beethoven, the *Canzonas* for wind and brass by Gabrieli, the Mozart Bassoon Concerto (soloist David McKee) and the 4th Symphony of Brahms. A special train was organised for the IYO and friends, which left Connolly Station at midday on Friday 7th, returning again immediately after the concert and arriving back in Dublin at 2.00 a.m. There was an amazingly good deal, an all-in price of £4.50, which included lunch and supper on the train and a reserved seat for the concert. MAI members were advised to apply in good time to avail of this bargain. Once again there were good reviews, this time from Geraldine Neeson who wrote for both the *Cork Examiner* and *The Irish Times*. She summed up her overall impression as: 'Playing with confidence and a youthful verve that was very refreshing, but never distracted from the serious consideration that has to be given to the music. It is a splendid group of performers, ably led by Joan Mooney and excellently conducted by Hugh Maguire, who coaxes and encourages them in order to gain his effects, but does not lower his standards in any patronising manner because of the limited experience of the forces under his command. He expects a great deal and he gets it.' The reviewer picked out good points in each work, and gave particular praise to the stylish playing of both soloist and orchestra in the bassoon concerto.

It was the first course for clarinettist John Finucane[8] who described to me how, but for the kindly and sympathetic intervention of Hugh Maguire, he would have gone home on the second day! He had very little orchestral experience at that time and was coping with the difficulty of playing the Brahms 4th Symphony on a B flat clarinet. This work is written for clarinet in A, an instrument rarely in the possession of a student player, and although the part had been written out in transposition for him by Brian O'Rourke,[9] John was still struggling. Hugh took him aside, 'talked to me about how wonderful music is' and John agreed to stay – 'Once I settled, I fell in love with the whole thing!'

A recording was made at the concert of the Mozart and Brahms works, undertaken by the New Irish Recording Company and a vinyl disc produced for purchase by the players. This record confirms the reviewer's good impression of the bassoon concerto, particularly the playing of the slow movement. At times the Brahms seems a mountain almost too high to climb, but both the second and last movements have passages of great beauty and there is a sense of passionate commitment to the music throughout. It has been noticeable, in speaking to players about the early years of the IYO, that without exception they have mentioned playing this Brahms symphony as their most memorable experience. The orchestra was barely two years in existence, but Hugh understood that, by throwing down the gauntlet of this mighty work, it would inspire the young musicians in a very special way.

The bassoon soloist, David McKee, was from Northern Ireland where the year 1972 was marked by terrible sectarian violence. Stephen Parker, a 14-year-old horn player from Belfast was at the IYO summer course until 7 July, but just two weeks later the IRA carried out a series of twenty-two separate bombings in Belfast within the space of just over an hour – the 21 July became known as 'Bloody Friday'. Stephen spotted the bomb at the shops on the Cavehill Road, but was killed as he tried to warn passers-by. He was posthumously awarded the Queen's Commendation for his bravery, and a Trust fund in his memory was set up by the City of Belfast Youth Orchestra in which he also played. This tragedy had a huge effect on those who had got to know him at the IYO course, and brought them into a deeper understanding of the situation in Northern Ireland.

1973

The Brahms symphony and the bassoon concerto were repeated at the Christmas concert on 4 January 1973, which was held at the RDS Concert

Hall in Dublin, the remainder of that programme being Rossini's overture *The Thieving Magpie* and Britten's *Soirées Musicales*. Cellist Niall O'Loughlin[10] had joined the IYO at Christmas 1970/71, so this was his fifth course. He reminisced about the fine cellists who coached his section during this period – Betty Sullivan, Coral Bognuda and Bruno Schrecker – and the memorable highlight of a performance by the Allegri Quartet when all four members were there as coaches. He especially enjoyed Hugh's rehearsals as he chatted to the players about music in general, and about the works that they were preparing. He described my mother as: 'a strong dynamic character – very much in charge'. Niall particularly relished his recollection of the RDS audience struggling to their feet, thinking mistakenly that the side-drum rolls at the start of the Rossini overture heralded the National Anthem!

It was the first course for oboist Patricia Harrison from Cork.[11] She wrote to me in February 2018: 'Being a member of the IYO changed my life forever, this was when I realised that I really wanted to make music my career. The in-depth coaching and rehearsals that we received were exhilarating and the music still remains some of my favourite orchestral repertoire.' A potentially tricky element was added to the RDS concert in that it was recorded for television, and there were concerns that the warmth from the powerful lighting would create intonation problems. John Finucane confirmed that it was very uncomfortable, particularly for the wind and brass. However, all the reviews reported that the players coped well with the situation. Once again there was generous praise for the remarkable accomplishments of the orchestra, but some unanimity that the Brahms symphony was perhaps too demanding.

King's Hospital School at Palmerstown, Co. Dublin, was the venue for the summer course in 1973, running from 29 June to 5 July. Hugh's colleagues from the Allegri Quartet were the string tutors. The concert took place at the Emerald Ballroom in Ballinasloe, Co Galway, a last-minute change when the planned Galway concert was unable to proceed. One of the IYO committee members, Lady Suzanne Mahon and her husband Sir George, owned a stately house called Castlegar at nearby Ahascragh, and invited the whole orchestra there for a meal before the evening concert.

The only problem was that the orchestra's bus was unable to negotiate the turn into the driveway up to the house! *Counterpoint* reported that the concert audience was most enthusiastic and that my mother had said that this was the IYO's best concert to date. The programme combined the Rossini overture from the Christmas course with Bizet's *L'Arlésienne* Suite No.1 and the 8th Symphony of Dvořák. There was also a children's concert the same afternoon. An account in the *Connacht Tribune* referred to the standing ovation and described how the players: 'swept the audience along with them into the world they had created.' Both this report and another that appeared in the *Evening Herald* [12] were impressed that the members came from all parts of Ireland, including the North. Almost immediately after the concert, three of the players left for Brussels to take part in the summer *Jeunesses Musicales* orchestra course. This was an innovation for young Irish musicians and all three were awarded bursaries to attend. They were Cian O'Mahoney (bassoon), David Daly (double-bass) and Rosemary Moss (clarinet).

Lady Mayer's generous donation enabled the IYO to buy a double-bass, and a bassoon was very kindly presented by McCullough Pigott – both instruments to be the property of ÓC. There was an urgent need to encourage young people to take up these instruments – there had been only one double-bass player in January 1972. The MAI magazine *Counterpoint* carried an announcement in the April 1972 issue: 'The Irish Youth Orchestra needs bassoon and double-bass players and offers scholarships in both these instruments for 2 years. Auditions will be held at a future date. Applicants should be between 12 and 15 and do not need to be able to play these instruments already.' The scope of this project was broadened in 1973 with the acquisition of an oboe, so that *Counterpoint* was able to report in June 1973 that eight young musicians were currently studying under the auspices of ÓC – two oboists, two bassoonists, a double-bass and three french horn players.

Two of these horn players were Fergus and Kevin O'Carroll, sons of the well-known teacher and composer from Waterford, Fintan O'Carroll. Fergus later became Principal Horn in the RTÉ NSO.[13] He wrote to me in

November 2017: 'I was 15 and playing horn for only a few months when I auditioned for the IYO. I was awarded a place on the course and a scholarship to Victor Malirsh.' The first course Fergus attended was at King's Hospital in July 1973. He reminisced about how the IYO changed his life: 'I was to be a national school teacher, always wanted that. But a scholarship from the IYO started me on a whole new whirlwind path, a path that I am still travelling nearly 45 years later. It was never work, though, just something I loved, something that the IYO and Hugh Maguire instilled in me.'

In the autumn of 1973, the Mönchengladbach Youth Orchestra came from Germany for a series of concerts sponsored by ÓC and the IYO. They arrived on 6 October and were given hospitality by MAI members, playing concerts at Muckross Park in Dublin, in Kilkenny and Wicklow, and at the Loreto Convent in Rathfarnham. This venture involved a huge workload for Mary and Anton Timoney, and for my mother. The *Wicklow People* of 19 October reported that she accompanied the group on their travels and that the visit to Wicklow included: 'a sightseeing tour… about which the boys and girls of the orchestra were enthusiastic in their praise of the natural beauty of the countryside and sea coast.' The trip also included lunch at Greystones. Anton was involved with the logistics of transport and staging, and also the orchestra's visit to the Guinness Brewery. The players were very much the same age-range as the IYO, and the intention was for the IYO to make a return visit to Mönchengladbach in 1974. In anticipation of this, the IYO Christmas course (29 December 1973 – 4 January 1974) concentrated on the proposed repertoire for Germany but, significantly, also included some preliminary study of movements from Bartók's *Concerto for Orchestra*. A final concert for friends and relations was held at Wesley College, the course venue.

1974

The planning and organisation for the IYO's first foreign tour, assisted by funding towards the air fares from the CRC, soon reached fever pitch. Anton told me that the preparations for this trip were something of a nightmare. Each instrument's identifying details had to be recorded on triplicate forms, for Customs clearance when leaving the country and, even more importantly, for identification upon return. In addition, every instrument had to be weighed in its case and this information supplied to Aer Lingus in preparation for the charter flights. All this work was done by Mary and himself. The orchestra flew to Düsseldorf on 13 July, accompanied by my mother, Mary and Anton and were met at the airport by Herr Sprothen, director of the Mönchengladbach Orchestra. Hugh Maguire travelled separately. The 75 Irish players were given hospitality by German host families and reported that: 'despite the language problem, we had very little difficulty in communicating. We were treated as members of the family, and many of us received gifts at the end of our stay.' These comments come from a report of the trip by an IYO member, unfortunately anonymous, which appeared in *Counterpoint* in the August/September issue 1974.

The orchestra played at a teacher-training college in Neuss, in the concert hall at Viersen-Boisheim, and in the hall of the Stadt Gymnasium at Mönchengladbach, in programmes which included Rossini's overture *The Thieving Magpie* and Dvořák's 8th Symphony. There was a special focus on the brass section in Gabrieli's Sonate Pian e Forte, and on the strings in the Concerto for 4 Violins by Vivaldi (soloists: Paddy Fitzgerald, Dermot Crehan, Catherine and Helen Briscoe). The leader of the IYO at that time was Chris Kelly, and his twin brother Gerry was still leading the cello section, so it was particularly appropriate that the Irish piece on the programme was *Fantasia on Two Irish Airs* by their father, T. C. Kelly. There is a fine recording of the final concert in which the playing of the Dvořák, in particular, is of an extraordinarily high standard. It was received with sustained applause and cheering for about 2½ minutes, following which the final section of the last movement was played as an encore. The 'thank-you' speeches are included in the recording, given by Dermot Crehan in English and in German by Gerry Kelly (who had been studying with Paul Tortelier in Essen for the previous two years). This was Gerry's last concert with the IYO as he and Evelyn married in 1975 – the first 'IYO couple' to do so.

It is worth quoting again from the article in *Counterpoint*: 'We found the system of applauding very different from that in Ireland – after the initial applause the audience clapped in unison when they wanted an encore. Apart from our three concerts, we had a very enjoyable sightseeing tour of Mönchengladbach, ending with a reception in the City Hall where we were received by the Lord Mayor, who presented us with souvenir booklets of the city and a plaque of the famous Münster, commemorating the 1000th anniversary of its foundation. On the Wednesday we went on a day trip to Aachen by bus, with time for sightseeing and shopping, and an exciting forest walk (for some!), ending with an excellent lunch at a restaurant on the edge of the forest. An evening of Irish Folk Music, given by some of the orchestra in one of the city's oldest cafés *St Vith*, attracted an overflowing audience and this most enjoyable and successful evening was reported in the local newspaper. Our tour of Germany was, in the opinion of the members of the orchestra, our most enjoyable and successful course to date. This was due to the wonderful hospitality of our German hosts who made us very welcome, and seemed to enjoy our stay as much as we did, and also to the smoothness and efficiency with which the entire tour was organised. As always, Hugh Maguire made our rehearsals and concerts most enjoyable. He was an inspiration to the orchestra and also found time to join with us in our Irish music session.' The article omits mention of another highlight, a visit to the football stadium – Mönchengladbach were an internationally famous team at that time – and also fails to credit Dermot Crehan as the originator of several 'trad' sessions.

The *Counterpoint* article ends with warm expressions of thanks to my mother and to Mary and Anton. The local German press were also enthusiastic. The *Rheinische Post* of Neuss wrote on 17 July that the IYO displayed: 'competence in dynamics and shading, with a natural charm in solo passages and an almost blooming string melody, which made it clear that this orchestra found in Hugh Maguire an excellent string player and guide.' Just the 3rd and 4th movements of the Dvořák were played in Neuss: 'Both movements offering a surprisingly solid musical and plastic (*sic*) interpretation for such a young orchestra.'[14] The whole trip had been a notable triumph and a source of great pride to my mother, rewarding her dedication and her conviction of the potential of Irish musicians. There was an opportunity for the audience at the inaugural Kilkenny Arts Week to hear the IYO repeat the Vivaldi, Gabrieli and Dvořák at St Canice's Cathedral on 28 August. The most notable feature of this programme was, however, the playing of movements 1, 2 and 4 of Bartók's Concerto for Orchestra. This is a notoriously difficult work for orchestra and conductor alike, and its inclusion clearly signposted Hugh's intention that he would continue to open doors and create new experiences for the young orchestral players in his charge. A complete list of the IYO's repertoire from 1970 to 1982 can be found in Appendix 3.

By this time, Anton Timoney was an experienced orchestra manager, and gave me some insights into the pitfalls which might crop up in venues unused to staging such a large group of musicians. His approach was to supply detailed plans and measurements beforehand, but in practice these were very often altered or ignored, with the result that players' chairs were in danger of tilting off the platform (large gaps having been left at pillars), that the risers for the wind players failed to accommodate music stands, or that the timpanist might find himself many feet up in the air above the rest of the orchestra! On one occasion, Dean Harvey of Kilkenny actually set to and helped Anton rebuild the staging in St Canice's, having first requisitioned a supply of pallets from the nearby market! Another logistical problem concerned the insurance of school premises during the summer holidays. Anton and my mother learned to make detailed inquiries well in advance of booking a new venue. He told me that he got on well with my mother, though she was a 'tough lady'. He always called her 'Granny' and could not recall that they ever exchanged a cross word, even in fraught circumstances. In practice, he found Hugh more difficult and they had arguments about the number of string players that could be accommodated on a particular stage, or about rehearsal schedules when moving the orchestra from one venue to another.

John Finucane's recollection of the IYO at this time, apart from the inspirational music-making, was that: 'it was a very nice place to be.' He spoke about the friendly mixing of the more senior players with the tutors at the local pub, and the fairly relaxed attitude to discipline even though: 'there was quite a lot of going in and out of toilet windows after "lights-out"!' Apparently my mother's method for dealing with this was to patrol the grounds with a torch! John's view was that, whilst she had a really commanding presence, she was actually quite benevolent and the nickname 'Granny' conveyed the orchestra's affection for her: 'She seemed very much on top of the situation, quite unflappable, and it was clear that she and Hugh had a very good relationship.' John took on the role of tutor from 1976 and became friendly with Rachael, Anna and Philip, the children of Hugh and his first wife Suzie, all of whom played in the orchestra. John and his wife Siobhán (another IYO couple) were welcome to stay at Hugh's house in London, and Hugh was godfather to their daughter Caitríona.

[1] Interviewed by the author, 30 January 2018.

[2] Madeleine Staunton (née Berkeley) – sub-principal flute, RTÉ NSO 1974-2017, founder member of the contemporary music ensemble Concorde, principal flute in NICO and the OSC. Interviewed by the author, 8 January 2018.

[3] Artistic Director and General Manager of the National Symphony Orchestra UK, and Artistic Director of the Locrian Ensemble, London. Interviewed by the author, 2 February 2018.

[4] Interviewed by the author, 14 January 2018.

[5] Interviewed by the author, 5 February 2018.

[6] Also known as the singer, Jamie Stone, and for many years a much-loved late-night broadcaster on RTÉ Lyric FM.

[7] Quoted from *Counterpoint*, July 1972, p.7.

[8] Principal clarinet RTÉCO, 1976-1995, and principal clarinet RTÉ NSO from 1995 to the present, also conductor of the Hibernian Orchestra since 1986. Interviewed by the author, 2 February 2018.

[9] Principal clarinet of the RTÉSO from 1966 to 1994 and a noted soloist and chamber musician, Brian O'Rourke, coached the clarinet section of the IYO frequently from 1970 until about 1996. Interviewed by the author (14 April 2018), he recalled some uncomfortably cold conditions at the Christmas courses in Gormanston! From 1995 onwards, Brian held a number of positions in the Personnel Department of RTÉ, and was General Manager of the RTÉ NSO from 2003 to 2009. He also served for a number of years, from 1976 onwards, on the Council of the MAI.

[10] A member of the RTÉ NSO since 1980, and principal cellist with the OSC. Interviewed by the author, 25 March 2018.

[11] Patricia Corcoran (née Harrison), a member of the RTÉ NSO, RTÉCO and NICO, and principal oboist with the OSC.

[12] *Evening Herald*, 7 July 1973.

[13] Currently head of the Wind, Brass and Percussion faculty at the RIAM.

[14] Review is quoted in a translation from the German (translator unknown).

CHAPTER 28

The Concert Hall again:
1969 to 1974 –
JFK out and NCH in

Significantly, the MAI in its new incarnation as a Limited Company had retained one of its originally stated aims: 'To work for the establishment of a National Concert Hall' although now expressed differently as: 'To promote, build or acquire a public Concert Hall and Assembly Rooms and to conduct and carry on the same for the use and enjoyment of the public.' CAH having been wound up in 1968, the MAI moved into the resulting vacuum, ensuring that the topic was kept alive through the pages of its magazine *Counterpoint* by means of editorial comment and an occasional letter or article, such as the 3-page contribution, illustrated with some of Raymond McGrath's sketches for the JFK Hall, which appeared in November 1969. There was also spasmodic coverage in the daily press, including an article in the *Evening Herald* of 23 December 1971 which reported that the All-Party committee had not met since June 1967, and that the Government seemed to be putting the project 'on the long finger'. The situation was aired at the AGM of the MAI on 24 November 1972, and a decision taken to set up a Concert Hall Action Committee (CHAC) to bring the matter before the general public. Its members were Sean Rowsome, Anne-Marie Stynes, Yvonne Copeland, John Hughes, Brian Grimson and Ian Fox.[1] A press release resulted in coverage in the *Evening Press* and *Evening Herald* (28 November), *Irish Independent* (2 December) and a thoughtful article in *The Irish Times* (13 December) by Fr John Brady SJ in which he argued that the building of the Kennedy Hall could only be beneficial to the country's economic situation and future development.

1973

Also in December 1972, *Counterpoint* published a trenchant 2-page article by Brian Grimson, Hon. Secretary of the MAI, in which he berated the musical public for not caring enough to keep the Government to their word and asked MAI members to write in with expressions of support for the JFK Hall. My mother was not directly involved, but she did have a meeting with another campaigner, Gerard AE Watson. He initially made contact with the CHAC, and was invited to attend an MAI Council meeting, but favoured a more professional campaign headed by influential public figures. He was preparing a memorandum entitled 'A National Concert Hall' and wrote to my mother on 6 April 1973, thanking her for her time and the information she had been able to give him.[2] In March 1973, the CHAC reported a steadily growing number of helpers, many from provincial centres. Signed petitions had been arriving in the MAI office at the rate of 1,000 per week from mid-January, and the CHAC appealed to MAI members and their families and friends to write individually to the Minister for Finance and to newly-elected TD's, demanding that the JFK Hall go ahead. There had been a general election in February 1973, resulting in a Fine Gael – Labour coalition led by Liam Cosgrave, so it was a good time to canvas support.

The April issue of *Counterpoint* reported that 10,000 signatures had been collected and that there had been good press coverage.[3] A slogan sticker was enclosed with each copy of the magazine and people were asked to display these. *Counterpoint* covered the CHAC campaign each month, noting expressions of support from TDs, even from the presidential candidate Erskine Childers, and a promise of a meeting from the new Minister for Finance, Richie Ryan. In September, Minister Ryan announced that he intended to convene a meeting of the Inter-Party committee which had not met for several years! On hearing this, the CHAC felt it was an opportune moment to hand in their petition, amounting to approximately 10,500 signatures, and requested that this be put before the meeting.

Another statement to the press was released by the MAI following the AGM on 17 October 1973, resulting in further coverage on 18th and 19th. On 16 November in *Hibernia* there was a rather negative article by Fanny Feehan, giving her view that the MAI would not succeed in its campaign because it did not represent all musicians. On 23 November *The Irish Times* in its 'Arts and Studies' section, carried a 3-column piece by Brian Grimson, and on 12 December the *Dublin Post* reported on the AGM of the MAI and the petition.

1974

Charles Acton offered a major contribution in a three-part series in *The Irish Times* which appeared on 2, 3 and 4 January 1974. In this he revealed that a quarter of a million pounds had already been spent on plans and consultants, and gave his opinion that if the JFK Hall had been called a Congress Centre it would have attracted commercial interest and would already have been built. Critical of the CAH campaign, he described it as 'inefficient and parochial' and stated that a concert promoted by Noel Pearson, featuring Henry Mancini and Elmer Bernstein (who gave their services free) raised as much in a single night. The 3rd article points out that the current estimate for the JFK Hall was about one third of the cost of a jumbo-jet and that the Government had bought at least one of those. Mr Acton goes on to query why there appears to have been no attempt to engage wealthy (and living) Irish Americans in the project, who could avail of the enlightened US tax laws on donations. It is worth noting that he seemed to be aware of a proposed plan to convert the Aula Maxima of UCD on Earlsfort Terrace into a home for the RTÉSO and, interestingly, does not give this his support.

The Irish Times 'Arts and Studies' offered a balancing opinion on 9 January from John Slemon, manager of the Abbey Theatre, who advised that it would be unwise to proceed with the JFK Hall at that time, there would not be sufficient use to justify it, and it would be better to wait until the state had established an integrated arts policy. He thought that musicians should make do with existing halls and feared that subventions for provincial venues would suffer if all resources were given to a concert hall in Dublin. Not surprisingly, a storm of 'Letters to the Editor' followed! For the next two weeks, one or two appeared every second day, some supporting Mr Acton and some the views of Mr Slemon – the cause of the JFK Hall was certainly in the public eye. The *Sunday Independent* also entered the fray on 19 January, picking up on the suggestion under discussion in some circles that the JFK Hall might be located in the Phoenix Park.

Of course this was not the only activity during 1973 and early 1974 regarding a possible Concert Hall. Details of developments and manoeuvres behind the scenes can be found on pages 123–124 of *The National Concert Hall*,[4] with some complementary material in *God's Architect*.[5] The Inter-Party committee were called to a meeting on 17 April 1974 at which Richie Ryan, Minister for Finance, outlined the Government's proposal that the conversion of the UCD Aula Maxima should go ahead and become the future National Concert Hall, at a cost of £70,000. *The Irish Times* reported next day that the meeting had taken place and that Minister Ryan would bring the views of the committee back to the Government. This bland sentence, however, camouflaged the huge rumpus at the meeting, with threats even of resignation. The journalist, James Downey, wrote in *The Irish Times* on 29 April 1974 that the Minister was 'shaken' at the nature of the 'turbulent' meeting. He also reported that the news had: 'caused anger, but little surprise, in musical circles in Dublin . . . the Earlsfort Terrace project has been in the air for months.' Asked by James Downey to give an opinion, Brian Boydell said: 'A concert hall is a musical instrument. You have to build it from the start. This will be a makeshift.' On 3 May, James Downey had another piece headed 'Concert Hall architect raps new project', based on Raymond McGrath's letter to Richie Ryan of 26 April in which he refuted the whole idea on the grounds of the small seating capacity of 900, the apparent disregard for the recommendations of CAH, even though these represented the fruits of ten years' research, the lack of architectural merit in the building, and as: 'a make-shift project, difficult to plan and difficult to cost.'

Always anxious to maintain balance, *The Irish Times* published (also on 3 May) an article by Anthony Cronin under the heading 'Viewpoint'. He favoured the refurbishment of Earlsfort Terrace, rather than a costly new building, in the hopes that the balance of the money might be spent on developing the arts and Irish culture nationwide. Predictably, there were more contributions to the 'Letters' columns on 6 May, but in reality very little time was allowed to elapse before the Government's official announcement at a press conference on 9 May 1974. In an interview with Pat O'Kelly some thirty years after the event, Richie Ryan recollected the event as: 'the most hostile and vicious press conference I ever experienced . . . I will never forget it. The previous forty years of promises made no impression. The know-alls were not interested in my contention that, as the "Kennedy Hall Dream" could not be achieved for a long time, it was better to accept a compromise which would give Dublin a good hall in Earlsfort Terrace within reasonable time. The funny thing is, had I done nothing I would not have attracted so much abuse.'[6]

Newspaper coverage the following day reflected the various shades of opinion faithfully. Predictably, the MAI was very unhappy – headlines in the *Irish Independent* pick up on this: 'New concert hall plan "ridiculous" says music society' and 'Music patrons scorn plan to use UCD Great Hall' in *The Irish Times.* My mother was furious and is reported by Geraldine Kennedy (*IT*) as making 'constant interjections after the formal conference.' 'The lack of vision is incredible,' Mrs Smith told the Minister and (typically reverting to a Biblical phrase at a moment of great stress): 'The Government has sold the nation's birthright for a mess of potage.'[7] The *Irish Press* also carried front-page headlines, whilst the leader in the *Irish Independent*, having first discussed the pros-and-cons, came to the conclusion that: 'Dublin is being awarded a second-rate concert hall.' The Arts Council were also very annoyed, particularly because they had not been consulted.

In its official statement, the MAI criticised the basic concept which carried the possibility that RTÉ would be in constant use of the Hall, leaving little opportunity for other concert promotions. The seating capacity was also judged to be too small for modern audiences, classical or pop, with the result that promoters would not be motivated to bring international soloists and orchestras to Dublin. The same points were made by my mother, speaking as chairman of the MAI, in a radio interview on the day following the launch. She reiterated that what the Government was offering was not a public concert hall, but a new home for the RTÉSO and that it was too small for even their public concerts. In fairness, this criticism was addressed early on in the reconstruction stage by the architect Michael O'Doherty and the team from the OPW, as they sought to increase the capacity from 900 to 1,200, chiefly through the addition of balconies.

I think that my mother's way of dealing with her huge disappointment over Earlsfort Terrace was, in effect, to 'wash her hands' of the whole thing and turn her attention and energies to her other projects, principally the development of the IYO.

[1] NLI – ACC 6000, box 2 of 2, MAI Minutes 1972.

[2] Ibid. box 47, pink file.

[3] Ibid. box 47, blue files 1 and 2 – much of the information in this chapter is drawn from these files.

[4] *The National Concert Hall* by Patricia Butler and Pat O'Kelly.

[5] *God's Architect*, towards the end of Chapter 38.

[6] *The National Concert Hall*, page 125.

[7] Genesis 25: 29-34

CHAPTER 29

Final years with the MAI
– 1972 to 1976

1972

The first concert of the year was the public launch of the Irish Youth Orchestra on 3 January at TCD Exam Hall. This was followed by a recital on 4 March by the Chinese pianist Fou Ts'ong, replacing the New London Wind Ensemble. The 20th Century Festival took place in June, an experiment which was not wholly successful – it was decided that the next one in 1974 should revert to January – and the autumn Members' Meeting was given by the Indian musicians Nikhil Banerjee (sitar) and Faiyaz Khan (tabla) on 16 November. In the May issue of *Counterpoint* Ian Fox informed readers that he would be handing over the editorship to Pat O'Kelly from July onwards. Ian went on to enjoy a highly successful career in music journalism and broadcasting.[1] There was unexpected but welcome news that one of the Prize Bonds which the MAI had inherited from CAH had produced a windfall of £1,000 and it was decided to put the money on deposit, towards a future MAI project. Also, as the year progressed there was considerable discussion at Council about the celebration of the Association's 25th Anniversary in March 1973, resulting in plans for a dinner at TCD. At the AGM on 24 November 1972, members expressed great concern over the Government's failure to progress the JFK Hall, and a sub-committee was appointed to act as a pressure group, with Brian Grimson as convenor. His article in the December *Counterpoint* and the ensuing campaign have been covered in Chapter 28 'The Concert Hall again'.

At the Council meeting on 6 December 1972, my mother was elected chairman. This appointment confirmed her move away from the executive roles of secretary and treasurer, and was also significant in that she was the last of the founding members to hold this office. With Brian Grimson as secretary, Pat O'Kelly as record secretary and editor of *Counterpoint*, Enid Chaloner as 20th Century Festival organiser, and a new treasurer in Doreen Bradbury, the administration of the MAI transferred to the next generation. Doreen was greatly involved with the Irish Girl Guides and had been a member of my mother's Girl Guides' Choir. Her working life was with the Dublin office of a British insurance company and she had just recently retired when my mother approached her about the position of treasurer of the MAI.

1973

The 25th Anniversary dinner was at TCD on the evening of 31 March, at which members and guests enjoyed a menu of smoked mackerel, spiced tomato soup, roast lamb and pavlova, accompanied by three wines chosen by Brian Boydell. The meal was preceded by a sung grace, a canon in 3 parts by Byrd 'Non nobis Domine'. Edgar Deale took the role of master of ceremonies, there were speeches and a programme of piano duets and Haydn *Canzonettas* performed by John O'Sullivan, John Beckett and Frank Patterson. I remember it as a very convivial and celebratory evening. To mark the anniversary, there was a major article in *The Irish Times* the previous day 'Twenty-five years of the Music Association of Ireland: Charles Acton looks back on the achievements of the MAI.'[2] He praised many of the Association's activities and wrote the following about the Country Tours: 'These only happened through the tireless energy, idealism and enthusiasm of Olive Smith, the original treasurer, the present chairman, who has been an officer throughout the Association's quarter century. Her vigorous and controversial personality has moulded the persona of the MAI, to a large extent pointed

the directions of its activities, and ensured its successes and its few failures.'
RTÉ Radio also played a role in the anniversary commemoration with a
special programme about the MAI on the evening of 30 March. My mother
took part in this, as did Brian Grimson, Seóirse Bodley, Enid Chaloner,
Helen Watson, Mary Timoney, Eric Sweeney and Anne Woodworth. The
programme included musical excerpts from the Irish Youth Orchestra. To
round off the celebrations, at its meeting on 11 April 1973, the Council
presented gifts of record tokens to my mother, Edgar Deale and Brian
Boydell, as a mark of appreciation for their 25 years of service.

Edgar stayed on the Council for just a few more months, giving notice
of his resignation to the meeting on 12 September 1973. He had just
completed the huge task, on behalf of the MAI, of revision of the *Catalogue
of Contemporary Irish Composers*, first published in 1968. This 2nd Edition
set out the work of thirty composers, including some who had not featured
in the first Edition, and thereby brought details of compositions and
performances up to date. The *Catalogue* was widely distributed abroad,
through its sponsor the CRC, and contributed greatly in continuing to
raise awareness of the scope and status of Irish classical composition. The
Council expressed regret at Edgar's decision to retire and appreciation for
his dedication to the MAI for so many years. His role as a founder member
and chairman was, of course, especially significant, as was also his important
position as a director of CAH during the 1950s and 1960s.

Members' Meetings during the year began with a concert by the New
Irish Wind Ensemble (NIWE) on 14 February. In June, a series of five
recitals was given by the Allegri Quartet[3] in programmes which explored
the last five great quartets of Beethoven and five quartets by Shostakovich.
The Consort of St Sepulchre, Ireland's leading exponents of medieval music
at that time, performed following the AGM on 17 October, and Peter
Sweeney (organ) gave his Coming-Out recital at the Pro-Cathedral on 8
November playing works by Bach, Clérambault, César Franck, Duruflé,
Hindemith and Messiaen. The autumn Members' Meeting marked
Benjamin Britten's 60th birthday on 22 November with a programme of
his music at St Andrew's Church, Dublin, including the *Three Canticles, A*

Charm of Lullabies and *Rejoice in the Lamb*. The performers were Bernadette Greevy, Frank Patterson, Victor Malirsh, Veronica McSwiney, and the Trostan Singers (conductor Molly Dunlop), with organist Alison Young.

From autumn 1971 until mid-1974, my mother organised between 85 and 90 concerts in about twenty different towns throughout Ireland.[4] Appropriately, the autumn of 1974 marked the twentieth anniversary of the first Country Tour by the NLSQ. I have made an inventory of all the centres which took Country Tour recitals between 1954 and 1974, and find that they total almost 40.[5] At least two-thirds of these promoted several concerts each year, whereas in 1954 there were probably just five centres outside Dublin which organised classical music recitals on a regular basis. They were Cork, Waterford, Galway, Sligo and Limerick. In most instances, as activity developed in smaller centres, the key factor was the presence of one or two committed and enthusiastic music-lovers or professional musicians who could motivate a small committee and generate interest, not just in their own town, but in the surrounding area as well. The success of the Country Tours and the Corporate Membership of the MAI had two essential ingredients – the response of the music-loving public and the dedication of my mother to the MAI's stated aim to encourage music throughout the country.

The groups who toured in this three-year period included the Gaudeamus Duo (flute and piano) from Holland, Anne Cant and the author (voice and piano), Aisling Drury-Byrne and John Gibson (cello and piano), the New London Wind Ensemble (wind quintet), the RTÉ String Quartet, Charles Lynch (piano), Elizabeth Tait and Jane Tovey (piano duets), the Douglas Gunn Ensemble (recorders, voice, cello and harpsichord), the Georgian Brass Ensemble (brass quintet of principal players from the RTÉSO), Frank Patterson (tenor), Geraldine O'Grady (violin) and Eily O'Grady (piano and Irish harp), the Jupiter Ensemble (strings and wind), Thérèse Timoney and John O'Conor (violin and piano), Padraig O'Rourke, Peter McBrien and Veronica McSwiney (songs and piano solos), the Intimate Opera Company, directed by Courtney Kenny, who performed a double bill of *Il Maestro di Capella* by Pergolesi and *Three's Company* by Anthony Hopkins, and the Hesketh Piano Quartet (strings and piano). This well-balanced list offered the centres plenty of options and also very welcome performance opportunities for Irish musicians. All the tours were made possible by grants from the Shaw Trust, with the exception of Intimate Opera for which the MAI had obtained Arts Council funding. I have been intrigued to note, however, that there are rarely any references in the MAI minutes to the planning or funding of the Country Tours. However it is impossible to deduce whether this was due to my mother's independent cast of mind or to a general acceptance by Council members that this was her special area and that there was no need for their involvement.

I think that my mother may have been taken aback, therefore, to receive a letter of criticism in early April 1973 from FÉ, the body which administered the Shaw Trust. It was from Donal McGahon, who had taken over from Nancy O'Neill, the administrator for many years.[6] He wrote to complain that the MAI had not been complying with the working arrangements whereby prior approval of projects was required, and that there had been no consultation concerning the year's programme, for which grant aid was being sought. He continued: 'The sub-committee has also noted that the venues for recitals are being repeated each year and that there appears to be no initiative in organising recitals at venues which do not have MAI centres.' My mother sought the Council's opinion and replied on 12 April, pointing out that: 'Our scheme for Country Tours exists for our Corporate Members and has done since it began in 1955. If we hear through the Shaw Trust (as we used to from Miss O'Neill) of a Society likely to be interested, we follow it up and arrange a recital without requiring immediate membership of the MAI, but would expect the Society to join eventually.' Her letter refutes the criticism of repeat venues, pointing out that three new venues – Clonakilty, Shannon and Letterkenny – had recently been added to the list, whilst others – Wicklow, Nenagh and Donegal – had dropped out through lack of local support. A number of centres were also availing of the performances of NICO and Irish National Opera, which had alternative sources of funding. She appears to be surprised that FÉ had not received the information leaflet which she had sent in, outlining the plans for the coming season. But I suspect that the new administrator might have felt that was not really a consultation document, but more the presentation of a fait-accompli! My mother ends her response: 'I should also like to inform you that I shall not be organising these recitals next season. I have informed the MAI Council . . . and we are trying to find someone to take it on.'

My mother was fond of the biblical quotation: 'To everything there is a season, and a time to every purpose under the heaven.'[7] I do not believe that she was regretful as she prepared to hand over a major part of her work to a successor. After all, she had the new interest and challenge of the IYO, she needed to be involved in the continuing development of the SRS, and she was still very preoccupied with LSL. Undoubtedly the nature of music promotion in Ireland was changing, and for the better. The Festival in Great Irish Houses, brain-child of David Laing who had his early training under my mother's guidance, was established in 1970, the Killarney Bach Festival in 1971. There were also the Belfast Festival, Kilkenny Arts Week and the Dublin Arts Festival. John Ruddock, that most extraordinary advocate for classical music, founded the Limerick Music Association in 1967, and continued to bring the finest international recitalists, chamber music groups and orchestras to Ireland over a period of very many years.

Just before the end of 1973 the MAI agreed to administer, on behalf of the Arts Council, a pilot scheme of music scholarships aimed at assisting 3rd level students who wished to study abroad. Auditions were held in January 1974 and the recipients were Réidín Stevens (violin), Maureen Elliman (piano), Gerard Kelly (cello), Nora Gilleece (cello) and Naomi Gaffney (violin). Just £2,000 was allocated for 1974, but this was considerably increased in subsequent years.[8]

1974

The year began with the Festival of 20th Century Music from 5 – 11 January. The spring Members' Meeting on 26 March was given by the Georgian Brass Ensemble, and harpsichordist Emer Buckley gave her Coming-Out recital on 28 February in St Ann's Church, Dawson Street. For many people, the major talking-point of the year was the Government's announcement, on 9 May, of their decision to renovate the former UCD Aula Maxima at Earlsfort Terrace as the new National Concert Hall. This has been well documented in Chapter 28.

The May issue of *Counterpoint* carried a lovely obituary for Lady Mayer who died in England on 2 April at the age of 87. Áine Nic Gabhann (contralto) gave her Coming-Out recital on 17 October, accompanied by Darina Gibson. For this the MAI tried a new venue, the recently-renovated St Catherine's Church on Thomas Street. Whilst it was used again for the Members' Meeting on 14 November, a song recital by Patricia McCarry (soprano) with Courtney Kenny at the piano, it was felt that the venue attracted a poor attendance and the acoustics were not satisfactory. The recital following the AGM on 23 October, was given by Veronica McSwiney, who had recently released her recording of John Field's *Nocturnes*. She presented a number of his short piano pieces and his first sonata. This was held at the Goethe Institut.

At its meeting on 18 September, the Council heard that Brian Grimson wished to resign as Hon. Secretary, though he hoped to remain on the Council. This was for health reasons and there was much sympathy for Brian, who had served in several capacities for the MAI. In 1965 he had conducted the première of *The Hunting of the Snark*, and though his main subjects as a teacher at Mount Temple School were English and French, he also taught music at Sandford Park and enjoyed orchestral conducting. He was a gifted writer, producing important memoranda on music in broadcasting which the MAI submitted to the Broadcasting Review Board, and took a leading role in the CHAC in the 1970s. He deputised as editor of *Counterpoint* from April to August 1975, during Pat O'Kelly's absence, and later served on the SRS committee.

In the latter part of 1974, my mother had some assistance with the organisation of Country Tours from Yvonne Copeland, and from Nancy Glenn in the office. In October, Aisling Drury-Byrne, this time with Lynda Byrne as accompanist, played in Sligo and Clonakilty, and in November Patricia McCarry, with Courtney Kenny, gave recitals in Gorey, Kilkenny and Newport. The Purcell Consort, an Irish baroque group, directed from the harpsichord by John Beckett, played in Ballina, Galway and Kilkenny in December. My mother was spending more time at her Connemara home but she did deal with an application to the Arts Council for a £700 grant to assist the NIWE give seven recitals in 1975. This popular group were all members of NICO – Helmut Seeber and Lindsay Armstrong (oboes), Brian O'Rourke and Sydney Egan (clarinets), Gilbert Berg and Dieter Prodöhl (bassoons) and Victor Malirsh and Tom Briggs (horns) – playing repertoire for wind octet by Beethoven, Mozart and Schubert.[9]

By the end of 1974, my mother was satisfied that in Anne Woodworth she had found someone to whom she could hand over the Country Tours with complete confidence. Anne enjoyed a flourishing career as a singer, and was well acquainted with the work of the MAI from her participation in the SRS. She later moved to Waterford as Lecturer in Vocal Studies at the Waterford Institute of Technology (WIT), where she also founded the WIT Music School. Anne has told me that, had my mother not set out her blueprint for the running of this project with such clarity, taking it over could have been an onerous burden.[10] But, having explained how it all worked, she left Anne to develop her own ideas without checking up on her or 'looking over her shoulder'. It has to be said that my mother was 'a hard act to follow', not only because of her organisational skills and her encyclopaedic knowledge of Irish country towns, but because of the personal friendships she had built up over the years and the warm affection with which she was widely regarded. It is also remarkable to realise that her vision created a great deal of employment for musicians, and many performance opportunities for young players who realised that, whilst a Country Tour helped greatly in launching their career, the practicalities of organising it were certainly a daunting task. Eventually, in 1986, the Arts Council set up Music Network which, in many respects, conferred an accolade on the work of the MAI Country Tours, by developing and re-defining my mother's original concept.

1975

Joan Cowle was welcomed as the new Hon. Secretary at the Council meeting on 4 December 1974, and co-opted as a Council member on 19

February 1975. A niece of Nancy Glenn and a keen choral singer with the Trostan Singers and later the Guinness Choir, Joan worked for Standard Life Asssurance. She has also served on the Feis Ceoil Executive Committee from 1969 until the present day. Joan responded to an invitation to become MAI Hon. Secretary, remaining in this position for the next ten years. My mother and Mairtín McCullough agreed to become Joint Chairmen, but in the hopes of finding someone new to take this position. Dinah Molloy, who was appointed Music Officer of the Arts Council towards the end of 1975, was confirmed as the organiser of the 1976 20th Century Festival. A chamber-music enthusiast, Dinah had been involved in music management on a free-lance basis from about 1965, on behalf of János Fürst, Courtney Kenny, and also the Testore String Quartet.[11] There was no 20th Century Festival in 1975, however the Members' Meeting at TCD on 25 January marked the centenary of Schoenberg (b. 1874) with a performance of his *Serenade* Op. 24, as part of a mini-festival organised by RTÉ.

Unfortunately, the Association was heading into financial difficulties. On 5 July 1974, the Treasurer warned that the MAI was running an overdraft of £1,000, due to increased production costs for *Counterpoint* and the outlay on Members' Meetings. The Council's efforts to deal with this problem became a recurring theme in 1975 and for several years to come. The situation was reported to the membership in the magazine's issues of March and April 1975, stressing the Council's determination to return *Counterpoint* to a solvent position. A 'Ways and Means' sub-committee was set up, the Arts Council gave a grant of £500 and a raffle was organised. One of the prizes was an Agfa Super-8 camera and projector, donated by my mother. The Members' Meetings that autumn were given by the Allegri Quartet on 6, 7 and 9 October at TCD Exam Hall, in programmes devoted to Bartók and Schubert – members were entitled to one free ticket to a concert of their choice. Towards the end of the year there was better news of the MAI's financial position, although Pat O'Kelly wrote in his November editorial that *Counterpoint* was still a worry.

The AGM was held on 5 November 1975 and in one particular way marked the end of an era, as my mother had let it be known that she would not stand again for membership of the Council. In her letter of resignation she encouraged the members to: 'Think very deeply about getting new young members on to the Council and not to allow a generation gap to develop, as had happened in the past.' Mairtín McCullough was in the chair, and in his tribute to my mother said that she had been the chief architect of the MAI and expressed the Association's gratitude for all she had done over the years. He also spoke of the affection and respect in which she was held, and on behalf of all members wished her peace and happiness in her retirement.

In a tribute to her, published in the December issue of *Counterpoint*, Edgar Deale wrote: 'We all did our share, but always with the comforting knowledge that we could be certain that ideas – many of them hers – would be made to work, that Olive with her driving force, would supervise organisation and would control, inspire, cajole, wheedle, and sometimes blow up – and get things done. The fact that, as she says, she had more time to spare than others does not detract from her achievements. Most of us prefer time on our hands to unpaid work for others. No respecter of persons, her integrity and selflessness did persuade key people to co-operate. During most of these years Olive has been our Hon. Secretary and General Dynamo. Looking back on it all she says that she has an especially warm memory of Douglas Cameron who, then cellist in the LSQ, made such a personal impression in provincial centres that, to this day, it is string quartets that are most in demand in these towns; he died in 1974. She says that her greatest inspiration during her time in the MAI was "in thinking of Hugh Maguire as the conductor and Music Director of the IYO." She believes that now is the time for her to step down, when the Association has such excellent honorary officers and such a lively Council. She will continue, however, as chairman of the SRS and as director of the IYO. She has our best wishes and gratitude.'

1976

Pat O'Kelly was elected chairman on 12 November at the Council meeting following the AGM, Joan Cowle was hon. secretary, the hon. treasurer was Doreen Bradbury and Enid Chaloner was concerts secretary. The other Council members were Seóirse Bodley, Brian Boydell, Cáit Cooper, Sheila Larchet-Cuthbert, Brian Grimson, Dinah Molloy, Gladys Milne, Mairtín McCullough, Brian O'Rourke, Gillian Smith, Mary Timoney, Thérèse Timoney and Anne Woodworth. It is worth noting that Brian Boydell was the only original member still remaining – he had served for 28 years, many of them as chairman – and that Mairtín McCullough was the second-longest serving member, having been editor of the *Bulletin*, joint hon. secretary and chairman. At this same meeting, the Council elected my mother as a Life-Member of the Association.

Since my mother was no longer attending Council meetings, confidential plans could go ahead to organise a surprise presentation. A notification was sent to all members in February, setting out the plan and seeking subscriptions: 'Mrs Smith has given so much of herself to music in Ireland that the Council feels assured MAI members would wish to mark her retirement with a tangible appreciation of her services. After careful consideration it has been decided to establish a fund in Mrs Smith's name. This fund will be used to purchase an instrument for the IYO, something near and dear to Mrs Smith's heart. Subscriptions may be sent to Mrs Glenn and will be received up to 30 April when the fund will be closed. It is Council's wish that Mrs Smith does not have prior knowledge of this effort on her behalf. Please help in keeping our secret.'

The generosity of the contributions far exceeded expectations, sufficient to buy a pair of pedal tympani for the Orchestra and even have some money left over! Council decided to make the presentation after the IYO concert in Athlone on 9 July, having learnt that the tympani could be delivered to Rockwell College in time for the summer course. A great deal of connivance with Mary Timoney and other members of the IYO staff was needed, as my mother was still unaware of what was afoot. In the end, Pat O'Kelly decided to phone her the day before the course and it appears that the secret had been well kept because, in Pat's words: 'She was astounded and delighted.' Preparations went ahead for the big night in Athlone – Pat's editorial in the September *Counterpoint* describes the scene: 'The occasion went particularly well with a delighted Mrs Smith the centre-point of the evening. It being difficult to hand over percussion instruments, Mrs Smith was presented with a token illuminated scroll. This was beautifully inscribed by the Carmelite Sisters at Firhouse, with an expertise many thought had long passed. As well as the names of well-wishers, the scroll included the notation of the main theme from the Finale of Beethoven's Symphony No. 9, and was much admired by all who saw it.' The hall in Athlone was filled to capacity as many members of the Council and of the Association wished to be present, in addition to the family and friends of the orchestra members. Pat made the presentation as Chairman with an eloquent speech, reported in full in the September *Counterpoint*. I will quote an excerpt here: 'If I single out one aspect of her services to music it is her obvious devotion to youth and the promotion of music in its various forms for young people. Her efforts for them have had many happy results, even though these have been obtained by no small effort on Mrs Smith's own part. The culmination of her services – and here I am sure she will agree with me – has been the founding of the IYO. It can be said that the Orchestra has become, apart from the wonderful instrument we have just heard, Mrs Smith's adopted family, and I know I can include Hugh Maguire and Mary and Anton Timoney in this too.'

There was one more presentation to come. A sum of money remained after the purchase of the tympani and there was further discussion at Council. Some of us were aware that, a couple of years earlier, my mother had suffered a serious burglary of her apartment over the business in Rathgar. One of her favourite brooches, a large oval topaz surrounded by pearls, had been taken and I suggested that it might be possible to have a craftsman jeweller make a copy. The Council was in favour and the brooch was commissioned. It was presented to my mother following the AGM on 24 November 1976, as a small additional token of Members' appreciation for her many years of devoted service to the Association. My mother was totally delighted at this further expression of esteem, not least because of the personal nature of the gift.

Of course, my mother had celebrated her 70th birthday during 1976. She was still very active in running the IYO, but she could see that by relinquishing the chairmanship of the SRS she would undoubtedly be able to spend longer periods in Connemara. Her decision came just before the end of 1976 and her last meeting was on 10 January 1977; thus ended her official connections with the MAI. The new editor of *Counterpoint*, Eoin Garrett, who took over from Pat O'Kelly in early 1978, persuaded my mother to write a series of articles on the early history of the Association, the first three of which appeared in March, April and May 1978. These covered the initial foundation in 1948, the Bach Bicentenary in 1950, and the formation of the Composers' Group. Two further articles concerned the Coming-Out recitals and the tours of Irish musicians to Germany in 1964. The final two appeared in May and June 1979, in which my mother wrote about the Bax Commemoration of 1954 and the establishment of the Country Tours. Her reminiscences are well worth reading.[12]

---

[1] Ian Fox has been music critic for *Hibernia* and the *Sunday Tribune*, as well as writing for *The Irish Times*. He devised the quiz show 'Top Score' for RTÉ Radio, and has compiled and broadcast hundreds of programmes on many topics. Ian has written programme notes for the RTÉ NSO since 1989, and is greatly in demand as a lecturer on music, specialising in opera.

[2] *The Irish Times*, 30 March 1973, p 12.

[3] 18, 20, 21, 24 and 25 June 1973 at TCD Exam Hall.

[4] NLI – ACC 6000, box 44, several files.

[5] Athlone, Ballina, Birr, Boyle, Carlow, Carrick-on-Shannon, Castlebar, Cavan, Clonakilty, Clongowes College, Clonmel, Cork, Donegal, Drogheda, Galway, Gorey, Kilkenny, Killaloe, Letterkenny, Limerick, Listowel, Maynooth, Mullingar, Navan, Nenagh, Newport, Portarlington, Rockwell College, Roscommon, Shannon, Sligo, Thurles, Tipperary, Tralee, Tullamore, Tullow, Waterford, Wexford and Wicklow.

[6] NLI – ACC 6000, box 47, dark brown file.

[7] Ecclesiastes 3, v. 1.

[8] Later awards went to: Gerald Barry (organ), Kevin Brady (violin), Mary Brady (cello), Dermot Crehan (violin), Rosemary Flanagan (cello), Patricia Harrison (oboe), Val Keogh (flute), Geraldine Malone (oboe), Derek Moore (flute), Aubrey Murphy (violin), Niall O'Loughlin (cello), Frank Schaeffer (cello), Ursula Willis (cello) and Sara Bryans (piano).

9 Athlone, Ballina, Clonakilty, Gorey, Kilkenny, Port Laoise, Tullamore.

10 Interviewed by the author, 27 December 2017.

11 In 1974 Dinah Molloy published *Find Your Music*, a handy directory of music societies, bands, choirs, orchestras and many other musical organisations.

12 Copies of *Counterpoint* may be consulted at the National Library of Ireland – NLI H253.

CHAPTER 30

Family Life in the 1970s

From 1969 onwards, I feel that my mother regarded Derrylahan as her home, and her upstairs apartment in the LSL building as a useful place to stay whenever she was in Dublin. Three of the rooms were taken over by the business for a board room and additional office space, leaving my mother with a very manageable one-bedroom flat. Undoubtedly, at this time the responsibility of LSL weighed very heavily upon her as, even before my father's death, she was considering how the business might be sold as a going concern. She sought the assistance of Sir George Mahon, of the bankers Guinness & Mahon, whom she knew through his past involvement in the work of the MAI and CAH. Negotiations were opened in early 1969 with a subsidiary of the Rank Organisation but unfortunately this approach came to nothing, due to fears of competition from Kodak. My mother assumed the role of Managing Director of LSL and Dick Fletcher joined the company as General Manager. He took up his position from 1 October 1969.

On a happier note, my mother became a grandmother on 10 October 1969 when Lindsay and I celebrated the birth of our elder daughter Deirdre Margaret Olive. She was a much photographed baby as my mother enthusiastically took her camera out of hibernation! Christmas of 1969 was a sad time in the family, but little Deirdre was a source of new joy and interest for us all.

During 1970, I suspect that her musical interests – the MAI Country Tours, the development of the SRS, ÓC and the excitement of the first

IYO courses – helped to balance my mother's life and ameliorate some of her worries over LSL. In addition, she had to find a solution to the problem of the yacht *Carregwen* which had already spent two winters high and dry on the beach at Fahy Bay. Her generous gesture was to donate the boat to my father's yacht club, the Royal St George in Dún Laoghaire, as a sail-training vessel for young people. This gift was warmly welcomed by the Club, however there was still the problem of sailing her back half-way around Ireland. The 'George' sent two very experienced yachtsmen for the voyage, but the biggest challenge lay in getting *Carregwen* off the beach! A particularly high tide was selected in the hopes that she would float and Lindsay recalls that, even so, a neighbour's tractor had to be pressed into service in order to complete the final push. Our hearts were in our mouths as her hull scraped on the stones, but all was well. Her sails were raised and she sailed out of Fahy Bay for the last time.

By early 1971 my mother was feeling the strain of LSL again and initiated contact with some of the executives of the Agfa Company in Germany. In a letter of 23 March she wrote: 'In fact, to date, I have not found anybody I could hand over to. My problem is that very soon (in June) I will be 65 and I am finding the business a very heavy burden – too heavy, and it has become imperative for me to give it up.' She felt that she was looking at two options: either to slim the business down, or else to close it completely. Surprisingly, she wrote again to Germany three days later to say that a young man had been recommended to her as Administrative and Accounts Manager, and that his appointment: 'should ease my burden considerably, although I might not be able to retire until after this season.' So Desmond Simmonds joined the company and remained with LSL for more than a decade, during which time my mother retained her interest as Chairman of the Board.

During the summer of 1972, my mother had a family visit from her niece Helen with Dan, her husband, and their four children. Their eldest son John has told me that his family all loved Derrylahan and reminisced about the fun of skimming stones over the calm waters of Fahy Bay. He thinks that they visited at least twice over the following years. My mother's sister Kay and brother-in-law David also spent their holidays at Derrylahan that summer. It was during this time that their older sister Alice became very unwell, a return of the cancer for which she had treatment in the 1960s. The remaining months of 1972 were darkened by her illness and she died in February 1973, just a few days after our younger daughter Caitriona Kathleen Alice was born. Once again, the birth of a grand-daughter brought joy to my mother at a time of sadness.

In 1974 my cousin Brian, together with his wife Rosemary and children David and Bridget, all recently returned from Venezuela, enjoyed a memorable summer holiday at Derrylahan. As another example of my mother's generosity, Anne Woodworth has told me that, around this time, my mother offered Derrylahan to her and her family for a very welcome break. 1974 was also the year when the Government decision about the NCH was announced and the IYO played in Germany. During the following winter there was a burglary at my mother's apartment, upstairs over the LSL premises. Apparently it was the work of a cat burglar, who was able to gain access through a very high window, and fortunately she was away in Connemara. But she lost a great number of treasured possessions, particularly silver items that had come down through the family, and all her valuable jewellery save her engagement ring and the pearl necklace which my father had given her the Christmas before he died. I felt that this event was a big factor in her decision to move a couple of years later to a ground-floor apartment at Oaklands Crescent, just off Highfield Road in Rathgar, which suited her very well as a city-pad whenever she was in Dublin.

On 19 June 1976 my mother celebrated her 70th birthday, and 9 July was the occasion of her retirement presentation from the MAI.[1] Some weeks later, on 5 August, my mother wrote from Derrylahan to Pat O'Kelly as MAI Chairman, saying that she still felt:

a bit overwhelmed by it all. I find it very difficult to convey adequately, in a letter, my thanks to the Members for the wonderfully generous way in which they have expressed their recognition of my work for the Association. The munificence of the gift, I may say, quite took my breath away. It was a particularly happy inspiration of Council to decide that the presentation should take the form of a gift to the

IYO of very valuable instruments for the percussion section (long desired but hitherto unattainable). I have been studying again the beautifully illuminated scroll which you have given me with so many names inscribed on it. It is very heart-warming for me to read there the names of so many members, right from early days to the present time, including some of our Corporate members. I find the names of almost all, if not all, our former Chairmen, Officers and, I think, all our former Editors of the *Bulletin* and *Counterpoint*. I count it a privilege to have worked with all these people over the years towards the realisation of the aims of the Association and looking back, I realise it has brought much enrichment to my life. I am happy that so many members should have wished to remember my share in the development of the MAI in this way.

In November there was also the presentation from the Council of a brooch to replace one of those stolen in the burglary. And in 1976 the Richardson-Smith Trust was set up, of which more can be read in Chapter 31.

In some ways 1978 was even more memorable. In mid-January my mother received a letter from TCD signed by Mr Gerald Giltrap, Secretary to the College. She was informed that the Board wished to submit her name to the Senate of the University, proposing that the honorary degree of Doctor of Laws (LL.D.) should be conferred upon her. The letter asked whether she was willing to have her name submitted. It also informed her that the ceremony, known as Commencements, would be on the afternoon of Thursday 6 July and asked her to reply by 13 February. I believe that she had no hesitation in accepting. In a country which has no public honours system, the conferring of an honorary doctorate – in my mother's case, for her services to music – is one of the few ways in which the achievements of an ordinary citizen can be recognised. That the honour should come from her *Alma Mater* was of huge significance to her and, though she probably would not have admitted it, a source of great pride. It was also appropriate because 1978 marked the thirtieth anniversary of the founding of the MAI.

At the impressive ceremony in the Exam Hall, her citation was read in Latin by the Public Orator, Dr John Luce, whilst my mother stood before him and all the dignitaries in the hall, resplendent in her crimson-and-pink gown and mortar-board. Fortunately Lindsay and I, observing the proceedings intently from the front row, had a translation of Dr Luce's words:

Be not afeard; the isle is full of noises,
Sounds and sweet airs that give delight and hurt not.
Sometimes a thousand twangling instruments
Will hum about mine ears; and sometimes voices.

Marvellous sounds were to be heard, if we may believe the poet, in Prospero's kingdom. But what of our own island? If some noble piece of classical music now delights the hearts of our young people, if more pupils in our schools play musical instruments, if recitalists pay more frequent visits to our provincial towns, all this in large measure we owe to the sedulous and successful fostering of musical appreciation undertaken by MABEL OLIVE SMITH. For thirty years she has given devoted service to the Music Association of Ireland, first as Treasurer, then as Secretary, and finally as Chairman. Like another Ariel, she waved her wand, and the Irish Youth Orchestra appeared. She has performed all her tasks with such diligence and foresight that a renaissance of musical interest has spread splendidly through our land. We have it on the authority of Plato that people are sadly deficient in education if they are ignorant of the rudiments of music. The charming Irishwoman who now stands before you has left no stone unturned to protect our people, and especially the young, from suffering this deprivation. I present to you a tireless and much-loved servant of the Muses, who deserves the best thanks of all music-lovers in the country. For your part, members of the University, welcome her to our midst with a veritable Dublin symphony of applause.

By happy coincidence, those being conferred on 6 July included three people whom my mother knew – the harpsichord-maker, Cathal Gannon, who received an honorary MA, Muriel Gahan of the Irish Countrywomen's Association, and the politician Seán MacBride, already the recipient of the Nobel and Lenin Peace prizes. The others were scientist Sir Charles Frank, business man Michael Dargan, and the Scottish poet Hugh MacDiarmid. Following a reception at the College and all the customary photographs and congratulations, my mother was invited to dinner by the officers of the MAI. Her attendance at the Commencements Dinner was deferred until 7 December 1978, when I was honoured to be her guest. She sat at the top table with the Chancellor, Frederick Boland, on one side and the Provost, Professor Lyons, on the other, chatting animatedly and looking confident and proud amongst all the distinguished guests on that occasion.

There was another joyful event in 1978, the celebration of the Golden Wedding anniversary of her sister and brother-in-law, Kay and David. It was held on a beautiful summer's day, with all the family present, at my cousin Brian's house near Guildford in Surrey. My mother's gift was a framed photograph of the much-admired view from Derrylahan, looking across the bay to the Twelve Bens. Unfortunately, Derrylahan was also where my mother became quite ill in the late autumn of 1978, having unexpectedly contracted mumps from our daughter Deirdre. I was able to go down to look after her and then drive her back to Dublin to recuperate but, given her age, she was only just well again in time for the IYO Christmas course. By then, negotiations had started between the IYO and the car company Toyota,[2] and the announcement in the spring of 1979 of their major sponsorship was, for my mother, a matter of great satisfaction.

My mother retired as Chairman of LSL on 15 September 1980, whilst remaining on the Board; she had sold the Islington premises to the company in December 1979. Her retirement present from LSL was a wonderful Swan Hellenic cruise, visiting the Greek islands of Rhodes, Crete and Mykonos, as well as Troy and Istanbul in Turkey in April 1981. I was very fortunate to be given the chance to accompany her and enjoyed every minute. I had not spent such an extended period in her company for many years, and whilst this made the trip very special, I also returned home with the disquieting impression that she had become somewhat disorientated at times and experienced difficulty in retaining new information. I think she may have been unaware of this, and continued to be involved with the IYO upon her return, though she also retired from that at the end of 1981.

At this point my mother decided that it would be simpler to stay in a hotel whenever she came to Dublin, and that she would sell the apartment at Oaklands Crescent. In February 1982 she found a purchaser in John Forde, the nephew of Lily Butler, and looked forward to settling into a tranquil period at Derrylahan.

[1] See Chapter 29.

[2] See Chapter 32.

Music Association of Ireland

WILL
YOU
JOIN US

in working for a

CONCERT HALL
FOR DUBLIN?

Meanwhile securing (free) the "MONTHLY MUSIC BULLETIN." The only publication that gives all forthcoming Music, as well as furthering other Music objects.

Members of the Association are also entitled to attend (free) quarterly recitals of unusual music.

THE MUSIC ASSOCIATION OF IRELAND INVITES YOU TO FILL UP, TEAR OFF, AND POST :—

To MRS. LYALL SMITH (Hon. Treas.) "ROCKVIEW," TORQUAY RD,, FOXROCK, CO. DUBLIN.

FROM (Block Letters).......................................

ADDRESS...... ....

Please enrol me as a member of the Music Association of Ireland. I enclose Cheque/P.O. for 10/- made out to the Association, being my Annual Subscription.

91

THE NATIONAL CONCERT & ASSEMBLY HALL

DO YOU KNOW THAT DUBLIN IS THE ONLY capital city in Europe without a CONCERT HALL.

¶ WE HAVE A SYMPHONY ORCHESTRA which is a very good instrument, but the Dublin public have never had the opportunity of *hearing* it.

¶ A CONFERENCE HALL properly equipped is necessary also for International and other Conferences, which could be attracted here with tremendous benefit to the city and Tourist Trade generally.

¶ THIS IS A CHALLENGE to all who love music and who love their Dublin and are ashamed that their city has not the amenities available to the citizens of every other European capital.

¶ CONCERT & ASSEMBLY HALL LTD., was formed to meet this challenge. At their concert in January, 1960, to launch the Concert Hall Fund, 3,200 people were present and £1,000 was raised. This and other functions held since has enabled us to set in motion the machinery necessary to achieve our objective.

¶ SUPPORT all functions in aid of the CONCERT HALL FUND and BE VOCAL about the need for a CONCERT AND CONFERENCE HALL.

CONCERT & ASSEMBLY HALL, LTD.
3 MOLESWORTH STREET,
DUBLIN, IRELAND.
PHONE 70976.

DIRECTORS: SIR ALFRED BEIT · EDGAR M. DEALE LAURENCE P. KENNEDY · DR. JOHN F. LARCHET LORD MOYNE · A. P. REYNOLDS (*Chairman*) 92 MICHAEL SCOTT · M. OLIVE SMITH (*Secretary*).

91. MAI publicity leaflet, c.1951.
92. Concert and Assembly Hall leaflet, 1961.
Note the lyre design for CAH by architect Michael Scott.

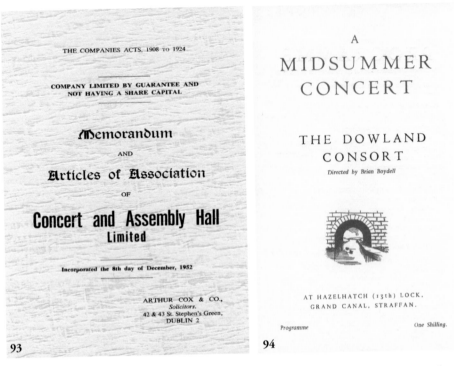

THE COMPANIES ACTS, 1908 to 1924

COMPANY LIMITED BY GUARANTEE AND
NOT HAVING A SHARE CAPITAL

𝕸emorandum

AND

𝕬rticles of 𝕬ssociation

OF

Concert and Assembly Hall
Limited

Incorporated the 8th day of December, 1952

ARTHUR COX & CO.,
Solicitors.
42 & 43 St. Stephen's Green,
DUBLIN 2

93

A
MIDSUMMER
CONCERT

THE DOWLAND
CONSORT
Directed by Brian Boydell

AT HAZELHATCH (13th) LOCK,
GRAND CANAL, STRAFFAN.

Programme   One Shilling.

94

94. Programme design by Dolmen Press, recital in aid of the CHF, 21 June 1961.

95

*95. The Dowland Consort. L TO R: Eilís O'Sullivan, Cáit Lanigan, Gráinne Yeats,
Mary Boydell, Enid Chaloner, Hazel Morris, Tomás Ó Suillebháin, Brian Boydell.
Not visible on left – Richard Cooper, George Bannister.*

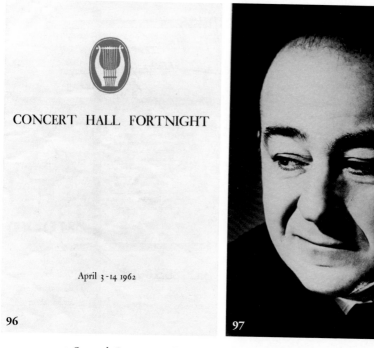

96. Second Concert Hall Fund Series at the Olympia Theatre, 1962.
97. Shura Cherkassky played two piano concertos and a solo recital
in the Beethoven Festival, March 1961.

98. Pianist Fou Ts'ong played Beethoven's 1st concerto and a recital, March 1961.
99. Vladimir Ashkenazy gave a piano recital on 9 March 1963.

100. Cover of the Tureck Bach Festival programme, February 1962.

101. Soprano Victoria de los Angeles gave recitals on 9 December 1962 and 4 May 1964.
102. Pianist Artur Rubinstein gave a recital on 26 May 1963.

BENJAMIN BRITTEN

WAR REQUIEM

104. *Rehearsal in St Patrick's Cathedral, Dublin, for the Britten* War Requiem
performance on 27 March 1963 – RTÉSO, Cór Radio Éireann, Culwick
Choral Society, Olivian Singers, Heather Harper (soprano – in the pulpit),
David Galliver (tenor), Donald Bell (bass), Tibor Paul (conductor).

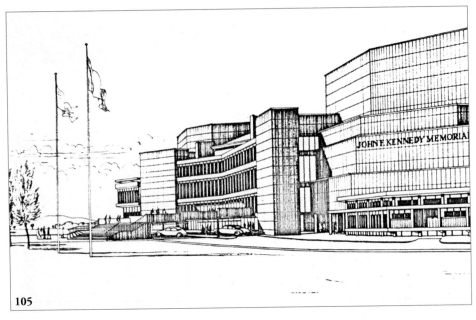

105. *John F. Kennedy Memorial Hall, sketch of the exterior of Raymond McGrath's design, 1965.*

The Minister for Finance
and the
Members of the All Party Committee
on the John F. Kennedy Memorial
have pleasure in inviting

Mrs. Olive Smith.

to an Informal Reception
in the Ballroom at Iveagh House, St. Stephen's Green
on Tuesday 9th March, 1965, 6.30 - 8 p.m.
on the occasion of the presentation of the architect's designs for
THE KENNEDY MEMORIAL CONCERT HALL

R.S.V.P. T. Ó Laidhin, Dept. of Finance

106. *Invitation to the official presentation of the architect's designs.*

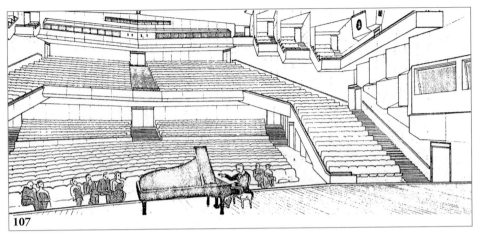

107. Kennedy Hall, sketch of the interior of the large auditorium.

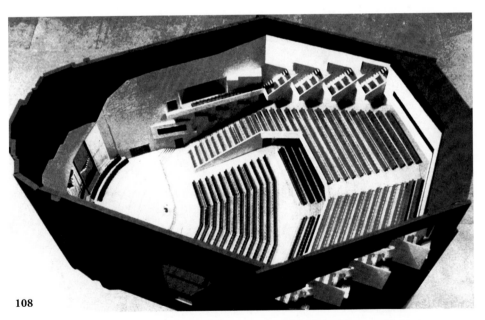

108. Raymond McGrath's 3-dimensional model of the large auditorium.

109. The author and Olive on holiday in the Engadin region of Switzerland, 1958.
110. Garryknock, Stillorgan Road, Co.Dublin, the family home from 1957 to 1964.

111. Lyall Smith on board Echo, c.1957.
112. Lilly Cameron, the author, Jan the Labrador,
Olive and Douglas Cameron, Connemara 1960.

113. The caravan on the site, 1965.
114. The house nears completion.

115. Fahy Bay and the Twelve Bens from the gate.
116. Olive at breakfast with her sister Kay and brother-in-law David.

117. Olive on the beach at Ballinakill Harbour.
118. Lyall's yacht Carregwen in Fahy Bay, 1966.

119. Veronica McSwiney, a frequent performer in MAI Country Tours, Coming-Out Recitals and Schools' Recitals.
120. Pianist Martha Argerich gave the final recital for the Concert Hall Fund, 27 October 1965.

121. The Paranjoti Chorus of Bombay – MAI recital 2 May 1966, pictured with Dr Stan Corran (Guinness director) and conductor Victor Paranjoti.

122. Presentation of the Mayer Piano to the MAI outside the National Gallery of Ireland, 21 September 1967. LEFT: *Lady Mayer steps into the horsebox, assisted by Olive Smith and Mairtín McCullough.* RIGHT: *John O'Conor, the author, Madge Clotworthy, Mary Gallagher, Charles Lynch.*

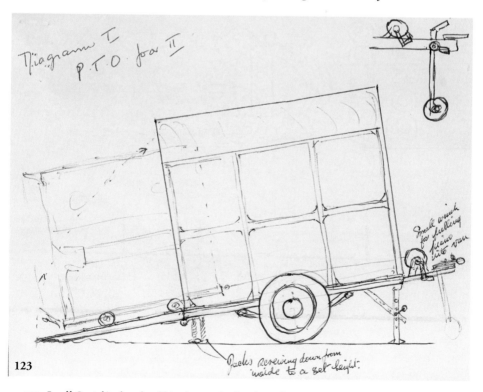

123. Lyall Smith's sketch of his design for loading the piano into the horsebox, 1967.

124. Hugh Maguire directs the first course of the Ógra Ceoil Irish Youth Orchestra at Our Lady's School, Rathnew, Co. Wicklow, July 1970.

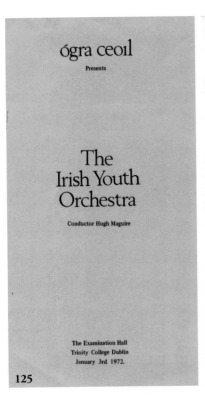

ógra ceoil

Presents

The
Irish Youth
Orchestra

Conductor Hugh Maguire

The Examination Hall
Trinity College Dublin
January 3rd 1972.

125

g. Harkin

126

*125. Programme for the first public concert of the
Irish Youth Orchestra (IYO), 3 January 1972.
126. Sketch of Hugh Maguire by Jim Harkin, Rathnew 1970.*

127. *Hugh Maguire with Mary Timoney, Ógra Ceoil and IYO secretary, 1969-1980.*
128. *Gearóid Grant conducts the Junior Irish Youth Orchestra, c.1981.*

129. *The IYO in St Canice's Cathedral, Kilkenny, 29 August 1975, with trumpet soloists Patrick Scarlett and James Cavanagh, and conductor Hugh Maguire.*

130. *The IYO in the National Concert Hall (NCH), Dublin, c.1983.*

AN CEOLÁRAS NÁISIÚNTA
THE NATIONAL CONCERT HALL

State Opening

WEDNESDAY, SEPTEMBER 9th 1981

Gala Concert

THURSDAY, SEPTEMBER 10th 1981

131

PROGRAMME £1.00

iRish youth oRchestra

Sponsored by **Toyota** (Ireland) Ltd.
Conductor: Hugh Maguire

Concert

THE NATIONAL CONCERT HALL,
Dublin
Saturday 2nd January, 1982
at 8 p.m.
PROGRAMME

RUMANIAN DANCES	BARTOK
NUTCRACKER SUITE	TCHAIKOVSKY
CELLO CONCERTO No. 1 IN A Minor	ST. SAENS
SOLOIST	DAIRE FITZGERALD
SYMPHONY No. 8 IN G Major	DVORAK

TICKETS: £3.00; £2.00
£1.00 CHILDREN & STUDENTS
Available from December 2nd, 1981.
at the Booking Office, National Concert Hall
from 12 noon — 7 p.m.
Postal Booking: Remittance and S.A.E. enclosed
Credit Card facilities by phone (01) 71153 — 10 a.m. to 6 p.m.

132 *Access, American Express and Visa Cards accepted.*

131. *Programme for the State Opening of the National Concert Hall, 9 September 1981.*
132. *Publicity leaflet for the IYO debut at the NCH, 2 January 1982.*
This was Olive Smith's last concert in Dublin.

133. *Olive is conferred with the honorary degree of Doctor of Laws (LL.D.) at TCD on 6 July 1978.*

134. L TO R: *Olive Smith, Muriel Gahan, Cathal Gannon, Sir Charles Frank, Hugh MacDiarmid, Michael Dargan, Seán MacBride.*

135. *Olive with David and Kay, her brother-in-law and sister, on the day of their Golden Wedding, 21 August 1978.*

136. Dr Smith

CHAPTER 31

The Irish Youth Orchestra flourishes – 1975 to 1978

1975

In contrast to the excitements of the visit to Germany, activities during 1975 and 1976 returned to the customary pattern of courses in the summer and during the Christmas holidays. The winter course from 28 December 1974 to 3 January 1975 was held at Wesley College, with a concert for family and friends on the final afternoon. Scholarships were offered in oboe and double-bass and the IYO also sought students who might be interested in playing percussion instruments.

Following the concert, the members of the Allegri Quartet who had been coaching at the course remained in Dublin and, under the auspices of ÓC, embarked on a set of three Beethoven recitals at the TCD Exam Hall on 6, 8 and 9 January 1975. Hugh and my mother planned to focus on the six early quartets of Op. 18 and the three Razumovsky quartets, Op. 59. She was very pleased at the success of the venture, another opportunity to bring string quartet repertoire before the Dublin public.

The summer course of 1975 was at Rockwell College from 22 – 29 August and included concerts in Waterford on 28th and in St Canice's Cathedral on 29th, which was a return visit to Kilkenny Arts Week. The programme was Weber's overture *Der Freischütz*, the Concerto for 2 Trumpets by Vivaldi (soloists: Patrick Scarlett and James Cavanagh), and

Tchaikovsky's 5th Symphony. Jimmy Cavanagh told me that he joined the IYO in 1972 and felt, as did so many other players, that this was a life-changing event. 'Playing Brahms 4th Symphony at the age of 16, meeting a musician of the calibre of Hugh Maguire . . . none of us had a chance of that type of experience elsewhere.'[1] He learnt a great deal from his days in the IYO, both as a player and a member of staff: 'Hugh was not intimidating, he dealt with the orchestra in quite an intellectual way, didn't drill but nurtured, and allowed the shape of the music to come through.' To Jimmy, my mother was an iconic figure who had a profound effect on the development of classical music in Ireland, and he felt that: 'she and Hugh complemented each other in their areas of expertise and in their vision.' Jimmy also spoke of the lifelong friendships that were formed in the IYO, of the camaraderie and of the marriages, including his own to violinist Pauline Carolan.

Another violinist, Rita Manning from Dundalk, joined the orchestra in 1975.[2] Her teacher was the renowned Fr Brendan McNally of Ravensdale, but apart from his small string group Rita had very little orchestral experience. Hugh asked her to play in the first violins, placing her in the inner row so that she was quite near him but not exposed, and telling her to watch him and the leader, Paddy Fitzgerald. His chief advice was not to try to play every note on the first day, but to keep with the rest of the section. As the week went on she played more and more notes and: 'went from being scared stiff to being so excited.' From then on, music became the biggest thing in her life, and she remembered some amazing concerts at which Hugh 'wove a magical spell'.

Christmas 1975 found the orchestra back at Wesley College, rehearsing a programme of the *Karelia* Suite by Sibelius, Malcolm Arnold's overture *Peterloo*, and the 7th Symphony of Beethoven. The concert was at the RDS on 4 January 1976, in the presence of President Ó Dálaigh and several government ministers. Hugh Maguire was friendly with Malcolm Arnold, which probably led to the inclusion of *Peterloo*. It was written in 1968, so this could have been its first Irish performance. Trumpeter Gerry Keenan told me[3] that Hugh talked to the orchestra about the piece, and how it depicts the panic and tragedy of the scene on 16 August 1819 at St Peter's Square in Manchester, when a cavalry charge was ordered upon a crowd of 80,000 who were demonstrating peacefully for parliamentary reform. It is recorded that 18 people were killed and thousands injured. A dramatic and rather noisy piece, which provides great scope for the percussion section, it was given unanimous praise in all four press reviews. Indeed, from this writer's perspective, commenting some 40 years later, it is a very sad aspect of the present-day Dublin concert scene that there is so little opportunity in the daily press for serious and invaluable music journalism. In 1976 it was not at all unusual that a concert would attract reviews from four or five music critics.

1976

The IYO had the honour of being invited to give the final concert of the Dublin Arts Festival on 14 March 1976, also at the RDS. As this occurred during term-time, there were logistical problems in collecting together enough players for two days of intensive rehearsals. Very wisely, the chosen programme featured works which had all been performed fairly recently – the *Karelia* Suite, the overture to *Der Freischütz*, and Tchaikovsky's 5th Symphony. Once again, the event drew critical approval with particular praise for the wood-wind principals, for the brass section as a whole, and for 'the warmth and weight of the violin tone'.[4] The IYO was now so well established that the Festival promoters recognised its general accomplishment and audience appeal.

The summer course in 1976 was again held at Rockwell, with concerts planned for Cork on Thursday 8 July and Athlone on Friday 9th. The programme was completely new: Glinka's overture *Ruslan and Ludmilla*, Tchaikovsky's *Romeo and Juliet*, and the 2nd Symphony in D by Sibelius. The Cork concert did not attract a large audience, but according to Geraldine Neeson's review it was a musical triumph.[5] She wrote of the 'brilliance and brio' of the Glinka, of the feeling of 'love and personal involvement' in the Tchaikovsky, and 'the grandeur, massive structure and great torrents of sound' of the Sibelius. She concluded: 'Mr Maguire must exercise a personal magic to extract so much beauty from the playing of these young people, and the orchestra is fortunate in its leader, Patrick Fitzgerald. String tone such as this might be the envy of many professionals, brass and wind played excellently, and the percussion section called for favourable comment. This concert will remain in the memory for a long, long time.' In fact, the only criticism I have heard of Hugh's conducting from the players themselves concerned his beat. A number of former members have mentioned that, while the strings seemed to keep with him almost instinctively, there were occasions when the wind and brass found his beat very hard to follow.

The events which took place at the Athlone concert the following night, when my mother received her retirement presentation from the MAI, are covered in some detail in Chapter 29. In his speech, the MAI Chairman, Pat O'Kelly, referred to my mother's foundation of the IYO as the culmination and crowning glory of her services to music in Ireland. It was particularly appropriate that the orchestra members, at the conclusion of their concert, formed the back-drop to the presentation, and that the gift itself was a pair of pedal tympani for the IYO. It was a night to remember!

The Richardson-Smith Trust

Another important event during 1976, in connection with the IYO, was the foundation by my mother of the Richardson-Smith Trust (R-S T). This body held its first Trustees' meeting on 5 November of that year. As already noted, the IYO had first offered tuition scholarships in 1972, to encourage young musicians to take up the lesser-played instruments such as bassoon and double-bass, and these had been financed through money donated by Lady Mayer. From 1973 onwards my mother had actually funded these scholarships herself, but was advised that, going forward, it would be better in every way if she were to set aside a capital sum and have the investment income administered by a legally established Trust with charitable status. This she agreed to, and as benefactor of the Trust invited Hugh Maguire, Brían Howlett, Kenneth Armstrong and myself to join her as Trustees. I know that she used the two names, Richardson and Smith, because she felt that any funds she had for this purpose were 'family money' and should be put to good use.

Just a word about the Trustees – it was no surprise that Hugh Maguire was involved; Brían Howlett had been MAI Treasurer from 1965 to 1970, working closely with my mother during the period of my father's illness. She held Brían in very warm regard. In 1976 he was company secretary and finance director at Irish Pensions Trust, and kindly made his office on Adelaide Road available to us for meetings of the R-S T. My mother also had a very friendly connection with Kenneth Armstrong who was her solicitor and, like Brían, a keen concert-goer. In an interview in 2001,[6] Kenneth related that he met my mother in the early 1960s whilst having lunch at the Turf Fire Café on Molesworth Street, which was in the same building as the offices of the MAI and CAH. My mother was very helpful to him when he lost his tickets for the Victoria de los Angeles late-night concert on Monday 4 May 1964. Some years later he moved to another firm and found that my parents were clients of the senior solicitor, their old friend 'Tubby' Lett. Upon Mr Lett's retirement, Kenneth became my mother's solicitor. The financial and legal advice of both Brían and Kenneth was of the utmost importance in the running of the R-S T. Brían has told me[7] that he was pleased and surprised at being asked to be a Trustee and that, as with his involvement with the MAI, he felt very honoured to be part of something close to his heart.

The aims of the Trust were:

i)   to pay all or any part of the tuition fees in respect of children of Irish parentage, or children resident in the Republic of Ireland, who are receiving or wish to receive musical education;

ii) to pay all or part of the travelling and other expenses incidental to the musical education of such children;

iii) to purchase musical instruments to be made available on loan to such children;

iv) to carry out such other legally charitable purposes for the advancement of musical education as the Trustees, being not less than five in number, shall from time to time by deed executed with their unanimous consent declare.

The sum of £8,300 was invested in three Government stocks and in those days, when an interest rate of 8½% was normal, there was an annual income of just over £700. It was agreed that the Trust would take over the funding of the existing scholars, and announce auditions for oboe, bassoon and viola in May 1977. As a result, nine more scholarships were awarded, three for each instrument. The successful candidates commenced study, some with private teachers, others at the RIAM or the College of Music in Dublin. Travel costs were reimbursed for two students. A pattern was established whereby auditions were held annually in May or June and the successful students took up their scholarships in September for the full academic year. The IYO was pleased that the Trust looked after the loan of instruments to certain scholars, and the Trustees were happy to offer scholarships in other instruments as needed – double-bass, harp, percussion, trombone, trumpet and tuba. The students were encouraged to join the IYO, and a considerable number became professional musicians.

One of these is the principal double-bass in the RTÉCO, Seamus Doyle. Originally from Waterford, he used his Trust scholarship both as a travel grant and for lessons at the RIAM with Helmut Engemann. 'I owe so much to the Trust and really appreciate what it did for me. The lessons with Helmut were really essential to my becoming a professional. He concentrated a great deal on orchestral excerpts and I specially remember him working on the rhythm of Beethoven's 7th Symphony.'[8] Seamus joined the IYO in 1979 and left in 1983 to take up a position in the RTÉSO, aged 19. He has been principal in the RTÉCO since 1995.

Peter Whelan, who has built an international reputation on both modern and baroque bassoon, and more recently as a conductor, is currently director of the Irish Baroque Orchestra. He teaches at the Guildhall School of Music, London. He told me[9] that he has the Trust to thank: 'for pointing me in the direction of the bassoon. I enjoyed playing the piano, but by my mid-teens I was craving more interaction with other musicians. Having left it a bit late to start a string instrument, it was decided that the bassoon might best suit my personality (and height!). This matchmaking proved successful and from that point to the present day the bassoon has remained a constant companion. I perform all over the world these days, but it is always a joy to teach the next generation, giving me the opportunity to pass on the care that was shown to me by the Trust.'

1977

The year 1977 began with a course at Wesley, culminating in a concert on 3 January. The soloist was Fergus O'Carroll in the first Horn Concerto of Richard Strauss, followed by Nielsen's 1st Symphony, and the opening work was the Handel/Harty *Water Music* Suite. This programme was repeated at the RDS on Sunday afternoon 13 March as part of the Dublin Arts Festival. Unfortunately there was a poor audience, unlike the previous year's concert, but the reviews were good, especially for Fergus whose performance was described by Carol Acton as: 'nothing less than a triumph'.[10] The summer course in 1977 was held at Wesley College from 25–30 June and concluded with two concerts, the first on 29 June as part of the Dún Laoghaire Summer Festival and the second, on the following evening, at the Church of the Holy Redeemer in Dundalk. The works chosen were *Finlandia* by Sibelius, the Mozart Bassoon Concerto (soloist John Lyons) and Schumann's 3rd Symphony in E flat. The Festival venue was the ballroom of the Royal Marine Hotel which turned out to be unsuitable as regards the acoustics, and also in terms of the accommodation of the orchestra. However, there were two music critics present who concurred that the concerto was the most enjoyable piece, praising John Lyons for his tone, phrasing and technical agility, and the orchestra for their sensitive accompaniment.

1978

There was good news and bad news at the start of 1978, the good news being that ten members of the IYO had been successful at the auditions for the prestigious European Community Youth Orchestra (ECYO) and would be taking part in their Easter tour,[11] playing under the baton of Claudio Abbado. The Irish members were Seán Bradley, Dara de Cogan,

Rita Manning, Brian Sherry, Mary O'Hanlon, Paul O'Hanlon, Patricia Gault, Donal Byrne, Mark Beddy and Féarghal O Ceallacháin. The same players participated in the ECYO summer tour of 1978, visiting the RDS on August 8th with a performance of Berlioz' *Symphonie Fantastique*, conducted by Lorin Maazel. This was the beginning of a long connection which has lasted up to the present day – a wonderful opportunity for young Irish orchestral musicians to meet players from all the European countries, to realise that their own playing measured up to international standards, and to perform in fine concert halls under some of the greatest conductors of the day. Rita Manning told me that conditions for the players were quite luxurious, staying in the best hotels and having top couturiers to design their concert dress. They had an audience with Pope John Paul II and met the Queen of Denmark. Amongst the conductors – Herbert von Karajan, Claudio Abbado, Georg Solti and Zubin Mehta – Karajan made the biggest impression with his sheer power and control: 'You couldn't take your eyes off him', whereas Abbado was more human, played table-tennis with the orchestra and took it in good part when they played pranks on him. Rita felt that, thanks to the training they already had with Hugh Maguire, the Irish were able to cope with this new and demanding environment, and to hold their own on the international scene.

Another violinist for whom membership of the ECYO was an important stepping-stone in her career is Maighréad McCrann, leader of the Vienna Radio Symphony Orchestra since 1993, and the first-ever woman leader of an Austrian orchestra. She joined the IYO at the age of eleven and remembers initially finding it difficult to keep up with the other players. She spoke of my mother as being very sympathetic and nurturing, describing her as: 'a visionary, and a very courageous woman.'[12] These were formative years for Maighréad, and the IYO courses were the high points, inspiring her to aim for a career in music and shaping her love of orchestral music. She succeeded Rita Manning as leader, and this experience confirmed her ambition to be an orchestral leader. Membership of the IYO opened the door for her to join the ECYO from 1978, which 'broadened her horizons' as she encountered young people from all over Europe who 'spoke the language of music'. The bad news in 1978 was that the Department of Education had, for the second year running, cut the grant to the IYO, which was, of course, paid through the MAI. In her review of the IYO's concert on 4 January 1978, Fanny Feehan (*Evening Herald*) took up the cudgels on behalf of the Orchestra: 'The Department of Education have made a holy show of themselves again by reducing the grant to the IYO. It is entirely absurd that a department purporting to act in the best interests of the youth of the country should behave in such a fashion.'[13] There was a particularly large orchestra, well over a hundred players, and it is interesting that Ms Feehan also commented: 'Very soon this orchestra will have to be divided into two . . . like Topsy it grows and grows.' The course had taken place at Wesley, preparing two new works, Mendelssohn's overture *The Hebrides*, and the 1st Symphony of Sibelius. The concert programme at the RDS on 4 January was completed by a revival of Tchaikovsky's *Romeo and Juliet*, first played by the IYO in 1976. This time all the critics were in danger of running out of superlatives, in particular regarding the symphony, as in Charles Acton's comments: '. . . so very much exposed and very tricky writing throughout, the wind were excellent individually and as a section, and there is no room in that symphony for anything but really accomplished and musical work. It also makes heavy demands upon the violin sections. These were fully met with strong luscious tone in the great sweeping melodies which so lift up the heart.'[14]

The 1978 summer course was at a new venue, Glenstal Abbey, Co. Limerick, from 1–8 July. My mother was absent on 6 July to go to Dublin for the conferring of her honorary doctorate at TCD. Upon her return, she was presented with an engraved silver dish from all the players and staff, to congratulate her and commemorate the event. Both the concerts were in the locality, making use of the hall at Shannon Comprehensive School on 6 July, and then moving to the Crescent Comprehensive at Dooradoyle on 7 July. The repertoire included *Le Carnaval Romain* overture by Berlioz, the *Karelia* Suite of Sibelius, and Dvořák's 'New World' Symphony; the important cor anglais solos in the Berlioz and Dvořák were played by oboist David Agnew, who had joined the orchestra at the previous course. The orchestra also had the completely new experience of taking part in a BBC TV *Songs of Praise* programme, which was recorded whilst they were at Glenstal. This involved several Limerick choirs and was conducted by Dr Havelock Nelson. It was transmitted on 26 November.[15] Eoin Garrett was a member of staff at this course[16] and spoke to me about the tremendous impact of the brass playing in the Sibelius, and also the lovely atmosphere at the Abbey. About this time a number of former players were welcomed back as residential staff, a practice that continued for many years. Among them were Jimmy Cavanagh, Fergus O'Carroll, his sister Deirdre and her husband Greg Scanlon.

The printed concert programme mentioned with regret the cut in the Department of Education's grant, and recorded grateful acknowledgement of financial assistance from nine firms – Allied Irish Banks, Bank of Ireland, Burmah-Castrol (Ireland), Cement Roadstone, Geimuplast (Ireland), Irish Distillers, Syntex (Ireland), System Cable and Wellworthy Ireland. Special appreciation was expressed to IBM, which had undertaken to repeat its three-year grant for the period 1977 – 1979. As it turned out, the IYO's precarious financial position would be greatly improved during 1979 from a new and unexpected source.

---

[1] Interviewed by the author, 21 October 2016. Initially Jimmy Cavanagh's career was as a trumpeter, also teaching at the RIAM. He founded the Irish Youth Wind Ensemble in 1985 and was appointed full-time conductor of the RIAM orchestras in 1988.

[2] Rita Manning settled in London, where she was co-leader of the Academy of St Martin-in-the-Fields from 1988 to 1994, and is currently the leader of the Locrian Ensemble. Interviewed by the author, 1 March 2018.

[3] Interviewed by the author, 5 February 2018. Gerry Keenan has worked in music management for many years, and is currently CEO of the Irish Chamber Orchestra.

[4] *The Irish Times*, 16 March 1976.

[5] *Cork Examiner*, 10 July 1976.

[6] Interviewed by the author and Pat O'Kelly, 23 October 2001.

[7] Interviewed by the author, 30 January 2017.

[8] Interviewed by the author, 6 February 2018.

[9] Email, 11 December 2017.

[10] *The Irish Times*, 14 March 1977.

[11] Copenhagen, Amsterdam, Rome, Milan, Brussels, Paris, Luxembourg and Bonn.

[12] Interviewed by the author, 25 March 2018. Maighréad McCrann played in the Chamber Orchestra of Europe for eight years from 1985, and also played baroque violin with Concentus Musicus Wien under Nikolaus Harnoncourt. She was appointed professor of violin at the Kunstuniversität Graz in 1997 – see article in *The Encyclopaedia of Music in Ireland*.

[13] *Evening Herald*, 5 January 1978.

[14] *The Irish Times*, 5 January 1978.

[15] Reported in *Counterpoint*, November 1978, page 3.

[16] Interviewed by the author, 26 February 2018.

CHAPTER 32

The Irish Youth Orchestra
– the future is secure

1979

The winter course from 28 December 1978 to 4 January 1979 was at Wesley. There were concerts in the SFX Hall in Dublin on 3rd and in the Church of the Holy Redeemer in Dundalk on 4th. The works were Weber's overture *Oberon*, *Vltava* by Smetana and the 1st Symphony of Shostakovich, replaced by Dvořák's 'New World' in Dundalk. In his review, Pat O'Kelly praised the Shostakovich in particular, writing that: 'the IYO sounded right inside the music. It blazed with excitement in its robust sections, yet took on a gentler expressive character in the music's more ruminative moments. The symphony abounds in solo passages for several instruments, many of them daunting for even the most experienced players, yet the young people of the IYO reached a very high standard of playing in these exposed and awkward interludes.'[1]

On 7 March 1979 came the announcement of the momentous decision by the Toyota car company to become sponsors of the IYO. The sum agreed was £6,200 for the first year, renewable for two more years. This welcome news came as the result of several months of patient negotiation. Dinah Molloy recollected[2] being at a meeting where Tim Mahony, Chairman and Managing Director of Toyota, Hugh Maguire (at that time a member of the Arts Council) and Colm Ó Briain, Arts

Council Director, were present. The possibility of sponsorship of the IYO was under discussion and it was clear that not only were Toyota open to involvement with an artistic venture, but that a connection with the IYO appealed to them. The press conference at which Tim Mahony presented the cheque to my mother was widely covered in the daily papers, together with some delightful photos of orchestra members and their instruments. In his speech, Mr Mahony explained the thinking of his Board: 'We hope that, in providing this sponsorship, Ireland's youthful musicians will be able to gain the necessary experience and education that they would have not otherwise been able to afford.'[3] In expressing her delighted acceptance, my mother said that: 'This major sponsorship is going to open up vast new horizons for the orchestra . . . and should guarantee, for at least a few years, an exciting future', whilst Mary Timoney commented: 'With this financial boost we now hope we can get together for at least one extra concert this year. This should also mean that the cost of the twice-yearly course for the members will not be as much.' The money also meant that the IYO could acquire proper rostrums, stands and lighting equipment and Toyota proved to be very willing to lend vans whenever orchestral transport was needed. The other welcome spin-off was that the IYO could afford to move out of the MAI office at Suffolk Street and move to the 'back office' of the Feis Ceoil at 37 Molesworth Street.

The celebratory extra course, held during the Easter holidays of 1979, ran from 17 to 20 April at Wesley College, with a final concert at the SFX in which the Orchestra played the Berlioz *Le Carnaval Romain*, Sibelius' *Karelia* Suite and a repeat of the Shostakovich 1st Symphony, which they had played on 3 January. One hopes that the new sponsors were encouraged by Charles Acton's assessment of the orchestra and its conductor: 'The whole performance and its details reflect very clearly the personal stamp that Hugh Maguire has imposed by his conducting and his staff of coaches. One aspect of this is meticulous intonation and, obviously, a willingness to spend as much time on tuning as would a Henry Wood. The result is an extremely high standard from the wind and a freshness of unanimity among the strings that is a joy to hear.'[4]

In the summer of 1979 the orchestra returned to Glenstal on 7 July to prepare a new programme – Chabrier's rhapsody *España*, the *Dances of Galánta* by Kodály and Tchaikovsky's 4th Symphony – for a concert at the hall of the Crescent Comprehensive in Dooradoyle on 12 July. There is a review from *The Irish Times* over the initials G.P.B. which reports an orchestra of more than 130 players and comments very favourably on the excellence of the eight young french horn players, the bowing of the strings and the fine woodwind tone, likening the orchestra in general to 'David taming a musical Goliath.'

1980

The winter course was at Wesley, starting on 29 December and travelling to Cork on 5 January 1980 for a concert in the City Hall. The ambitious programme consisted of Rachmaninov's 2nd Piano Concerto, with the young Cork pianist Nicholas O'Halloran, and the tone-poem *Ein Heldenleben* by Richard Strauss. Geraldine Neeson's review praised Nicholas very warmly: 'an impressive performance – fresh, ingenuous and controlled – very gifted and responsive, he established an immediate rapport with the conductor, with the happiest results.'[5] Ms Neeson described the Strauss as: 'an astonishing performance. . . the majestic horns, the magnificent trumpets, the piquancy of the flutes, the rumble of the bassoon, and of course the sweep of the strings – all these ingredients blended in a manner which some adult orchestras might envy. Leader of the orchestra, Dara de Cogan, had the mark of virtuosity in his solo work.' For harpist Andreja Malič, this was her first course and she described to me how she was: 'overwhelmed at the sheer scale of the sound and the whole experience of being involved in a work like *Heldenleben*.'[6] She played with the IYO until 1987, taking up the appointment of principal harp with the RTÉSO in 1988. She expressed huge admiration for Hugh Maguire and remarked that, in all those years, she never saw him lose his temper. For her, as for so many others, the IYO was where 'you made friends for life'.

Following the visit to Cork, however, came the sad news that Mary Timoney had resigned as Secretary to the IYO. This was noted in the

MAI Council minutes of 23 January 1980. Mary's level of commitment to the IYO was quite extraordinary, far beyond the hours which her job officially entailed. She continued to organise the ECYO auditions, under the auspices of the MAI, and in this role she travelled to Brussels each year for the annual meeting of representatives of each participating country. Given her pivotal role in the organisation of the Orchestra, right back to its inception under the umbrella of ÓC, it must have been a matter of regret that Mary was not involved in the next major development of the IYO.

During 1978 and 1979 the size of the IYO, now grown almost beyond manageable proportions, was a matter of frequent comment, and there was a waiting-list of about 150. Toyota's financial support allowed for the consideration of a solution and in 1980 the Junior Irish Youth Orchestra (JIYO) was formed under the baton of Gearóid Grant. A dedicated school teacher, but also making a mark as conductor of the Rathmines & Rathgar Musical Society, Gearóid was an inspired choice, given his musicality, enthusiasm and exceptional rapport with the young players. The age-range was set at 12 – 16 years, thus making a clear distinction between the JIYO and the IYO, which was redefined as 18 – 22. Of course the intention was that the JIYO players would ultimately progress into the IYO, having benefitted from starting their orchestral training at a younger age. Loretta Keating, who had been a member of the IYO committee for some time, and whose daughter Eilís was a cellist in the orchestra, was asked to be the Director. The staff included Gerry Keenan and David Agnew, the JIYO's first orchestra manager.

David organised the auditions in Cork and Dublin and reminisced to me[7] about the emerging talent of 10 and 11-year-olds, many of whom are still in the profession today. He recognised that the Toyota money had made a welcome difference, but also that it altered the dynamic of the IYO as an organisation, making it something larger than my mother and Hugh could manage on their own. My mother was in favour of the development of the JIYO, but it meant that she had to relinquish some control, and this was difficult as she had such a deep emotional attachment to the IYO.

In describing her as the source of the IYO's stability, David reckoned that almost every professional musician in Ireland, who is aged 65 or less, owes more to her than they may ever realise.

The initial JIYO course was held at Glenstal in July 1980, followed by a second at Wesley College during the 1981 Easter holidays, which attracted ninety-six participants. Each was followed by an informal concert for relatives and friends. The official launch was at Clongowes Wood College on 24 July 1981, conducted by Gearóid with Bróna Fitzgerald as leader, in a programme of Rossini's overture *The Italian Girl in Algiers*, Arthur Duff's *Irish Suite for Strings*, the second *Peer Gynt* Suite by Grieg, and the 'Unfinished' Symphony of Schubert. An informative article by Mary Milne about the early days of the JIYO was published in *SoundPost* in February 1981. From 1982, Gerry Keenan replaced David Agnew as orchestra manager.

Gearóid has stressed that Toyota's support was of enormous importance.[8] Tim Mahony had a great love of music, especially opera, and became very friendly with Hugh Maguire following Hugh's appointment in 1983 as leader of the Covent Garden orchestra. Tim was 'a very generous person', he sought no particular publicity in return for the sponsorship, and had to be pressed to bring corporate guests to the IYO's Christmas concerts. Gearóid's assessment is that the IYO opened doors to music for young people from all over Ireland, and that no-one was ever turned away for financial reasons – the money was always found. He described my mother as 'a musical visionary'.

Towards the end of the summer of 1980, a slightly smaller IYO met for rehearsals at the Loreto Convent, North Great George's Street, Dublin, in preparation for their second trip outside Ireland. The orchestra had been invited to participate in the International Festival of Youth Orchestras in the city of Aberdeen in August, an appropriate way to mark the 10 years of the IYO's existence! Some newspaper coverage was organised in Dublin prior to departure, resulting in a fine spread of photographs on 5 August of the players at rehearsal. Evidence of considerable support and interest can be deduced from the announcement by Olive Bodley, wife of the composer Seóirse Bodley, of a special coach excursion for

MAI members and friends, to attend the concert on 13 August. The orchestra's programme was wisely chosen from works already performed during 1979 – *Le Carnaval Romain* overture by Berlioz, the *Dances of Galánta* by Kodály, and Shostakovich 1st Symphony. Two Irish pieces were also included – *The Dirge of Ossian* and *MacAnanty's Reel* by John F. Larchet. The IYO gave two concerts, on 8 and 13 August. This was, of course, the first time an Irish orchestra had taken part in the Festival, and their high standard impressed critic Andrew Clarke who wrote that: 'Their sense of orchestral discipline and balance. . . . was matched by a glittering array of individual contributions in the *Dances of Galánta*. They are fortunate to have an able team of wind principals, and the *Dirge* and *Reel* by their countryman Larchet highlighted an ample range of tone and colour, notably in the cellos.'[9] The orchestra also responded well to the guest conductor, Rudolf Schwarz, formerly of the Birmingham and BBC Symphony Orchestras, who directed them in the Berlioz. It was a huge operation for my mother and the IYO staff, and although she was exhausted when she returned, she was enthusiastic about the whole experience, in particular the opportunities to hear orchestras from several different countries, the publicity which the IYO received, and the first-class organisation of all events. There was even a 'cabaret spot' which the Irish players quickly turned into a *seisiún*, giving players of all nationalities the chance to try some Irish dancing!

1981

The Documentary

Towards the end of 1980 the post of paid part-time secretary for the orchestras was advertised and Mrs Dorothy (Dot) Mills was appointed. The IYO winter course was at Wesley from 29 December to 3 January and concentrated on an exciting project to mark the first 10 years of the orchestra's existence. The noted writer James (Jimmy) Plunkett, author of *Strumpet City*, was at that time a producer in RTÉ. He was also a keen amateur viola player and a very old friend of Hugh Maguire. Jimmy proposed making an hour-long TV documentary about the orchestra, to be recorded at the winter course and transmitted sometime during 1981. It turned out to be a very fine film with the music of Rimsky-Korsakov's *Sheherazade* serving as a unifying theme throughout. It begins with some footage from my mother's ciné film of the first course in 1970, and then shows the players arriving at Wesley for the winter course of 1980/81 by train and coach from all parts of Ireland. It focuses on the sectional rehearsals under the direction of Sheila Larchet (harps), Helmut Seeber (oboes), Charlie Maguire (violas), Madeleine Berkeley (flutes) and Aisling Drury-Byrne (cellos). There are two narrators – Hugh Maguire and my mother. She concentrates on administrative detail whilst Hugh expands on musical matters, commenting on the paramount importance of choosing music that involves all the players and the appeal of the big romantic or 20th century works. On the significance of the IYO's role, Hugh says: 'There has been a tremendous upsurge of interest as a result of our activities during the last 10 years. I think it is the single most important thing that has happened in Irish musical life.' The film includes 'off-duty' scenes at the tuck-shop, playing table-tennis, Irish music sessions and chamber music, showing the players in a very relaxed and natural environment. Rita Manning, who played the important violin solo in *Scheherazade*, recollected that the camera men were there for a few days, but everyone just went on with normal life and rehearsals as usual. For me, it is fascinating to observe Hugh at work, to appreciate the qualities which endeared him to the players and confirmed him as a significant musical influence in their lives. At one point he says that making music has to be fun, and that he wants the young people: 'to feel the satisfaction you get from it, what a wonderful life a musician can have if they are devoted to their art.' The documentary was screened by RTÉ for the first time on 23 December 1981.

It has always been regarded as an accolade to a musical group to be invited to provide the music 'spots' on RTÉ's 'Late-Late Show'. The IYO was accorded this honour on 14 March 1981. Unfortunately the number of players was limited to fifty, so some hard decisions had to be taken, but the invitation was certainly another example of the IYO's growing reputation.

Sheherazade was the major work in the concert on 14 July 1981 at the RDS, together with the *Hungarian March* by Berlioz and a memorable performance of Prokofiev's *Peter and the Wolf* with Niall Tóibín as the Narrator. This was a particularly prestigious engagement, as it formed part of the 250th Anniversary celebrations of the RDS. The whole programme was repeated in St Canice's Cathedral at Kilkenny Arts Week on 22 August. By this time my mother had decided that the next winter course would be her last. Planning was already underway for another trip outside Ireland, this time to Rome for the International Festival of Youth Orchestras in the summer of 1982. My mother asked Enid Chaloner if she would be willing to take over as Director of the IYO, and when Enid agreed my mother felt that she could relax and enjoy her final course at Wesley.

There were two concerts, the first of which marked the IYO's debut at the National Concert Hall on 2 January 1982, with a programme of the *Romanian Dances* by Bartók, the Tchaikovsky *Nutcracker* Suite, the Cello Concerto No. 1 by Saint-Saëns with 14-year-old Dáire Fitzgerald as the youthful soloist, and Dvořák's 8th Symphony. The second concert on 3 January was also important as it was the IYO's first visit to Belfast, where they played the same programme at the Whitla Hall to great critical acclaim. The *Belfast Telegraph* critic 'Rathcol' wrote that: 'The glory of this very impressive orchestra is clearly the string section, boasting something like 50 violins. The sound from this group is rich, colourful and finely disciplined. Woodwind too have character, and the brass show fine precision and a telling presence.'[10] The *Irish News* review – over the initials G.O'R – described the Bartók pieces, referring to: 'Beautiful balanced playing all through with a good feeling for the rhythmic subtleties of this music and displaying an artistic use of rubato.'[11] Of the orchestra in general the comment was: 'Their obvious dedication and discipline spoke volumes for their tutors, and their sheer enthusiasm shone through every note they played.'

The Dublin reviews were also uniformly good, especially for the symphony, but only Pat O'Kelly mentioned that it was my mother's last Dublin concert. He wrote: 'Since its inception in 1970, the IYO has been guided (and ruled?) by the indefatigable Dr Olive Smith as just part of her voluntary services to music in the country. Saturday evening's concert… was in a way a tribute to Dr Smith, who now hands over her shepherding staff to Enid Chaloner, to lead the IYO into another decade of continuing success. A momentous occasion.'[12]

I am glad to say that the young players of the orchestra were fully aware of the significance of my mother's retirement. I found their enormous card, completely covered in their signatures and dated Christmas 1981, amongst her treasured possessions at the end of her life.

[1] *Evening Press*, 4 January 1979.

[2] Interviewed by the author, 7 January 2018.

[3] *Irish Independent*, 8 March 1979.

[4] *The Irish Times*, 21 April 1979.

[5] *Cork Examiner*, 7 January 1980.

[6] Interviewed by the author, 7 January 2018.

[7] Interviewed by the author, 14 April 2018. David Agnew has been oboist with the RTÉCO since 1982. He has established a separate solo international career as a recording artist of popular music.

[8] Interviewed by the author, 26 March 2018. Gearóid Grant remains the conductor of the NYOI, and has been a board member since 1983. He devised the highly popular 'Music in the Classroom' concerts, conducting these from 1989 to 2016, in collaboration with both RTÉ orchestras. In 2018, Gearóid celebrated 40 years as the musical director of the Rathmines and Rathgar Musical Society. See article in *The Encyclopaedia of Music in Ireland*.

[9] *Aberdeen Evening Express*, 14 August 1980.

[10] *Belfast Telegraph*, 4 January 1982.

[11] *Irish News*, 6 January 1982.

[12] *Evening Press*, 4 January 1982.

CHAPTER 33

Postlude – the Legacy

The MAI moves ahead
1977 – 1978

My mother's active connection with the MAI ended on 10 January 1977 when she chaired her final meeting of the SRS committee. The Scheme was seriously underfunded in the following two years, in spite of pleas to the Department of Education for an increase in the grant. However, a successful application by Eilís MacGabhann, the SRS Organiser, to the Ireland Fund[1] brought in additional income of £1,500 in 1979, with a resulting expansion in the number of recitals.

During the same period, 1977 and 1978, the MAI itself was in financial difficulties, largely due to the rising costs of producing *Counterpoint* and a number of measures were implemented to try to improve matters. In the Council minutes of 7 September 1977 there is the first mention, by Brian Boydell, of the Arts Council's interest in providing funds to the MAI for a full-time Music Organiser: 'to develop the framework already existing for schools' recitals, country tours and individual concerts.'

The report by J. M. Richards 'Provision for the Arts', which was published in January 1976, was a significant document. Funded by the Gulbenkian Foundation, and researched during 1974 and 1975 by Millicent Bowerman, it aimed to provide an in-depth study of the Arts in Ireland, as a means of defining the future role and funding of the Arts Council. As a result of its recommendations, there was a seismic shift in official policy. The responsibility for grants to important bodies such as the Abbey and Gate Theatres, and the Dublin Theatre Festival, was taken from the Department of Finance and added to the remit of the Arts Council, with greatly increased funding. Three Officers with specific areas of responsibility – Literature and Film, Music, Visual Arts – were appointed before the end of 1975, the Music Officer being Dinah Molloy. Ms Bowerman wrote of the MAI: 'The Association has very small funds and needs financial help in extending its activities into a nationwide service which would bring great benefits to Irish Music. Its activities should be widened to include jazz, pop and traditional music.'[2]

This was undoubtedly the impetus for the Arts Council's proposal to provide funding for an MAI Music Organiser. A sub-committee of Enid Chaloner, Anne Woodworth and Eilís MacGabhann was set up in September 1977 to investigate matters further, and by early 1978 agreement was reached. The Council minutes of 22 March record an initial funding offer of £5,000 for 1978 plus an additional £2,500 for the Country Tours. A further £4,000 was agreed in April, to ensure financial security up to June 1979. As Arts Council Music Officer, Dinah Molloy had a key role in the negotiations, having worked for the MAI as organiser of the 20th Century Festivals in 1976 and 1978. In preparation for the 1978 Festival, she was seconded by the Arts Council for 4 weeks.

At this point, I feel it is very appropriate to refer to the significance of Brian Boydell's contribution to music in Ireland – as Professor of Music at TCD, as a member of the Arts Council, as a renowned broadcaster and lecturer, as a conductor and as a highly-esteemed composer. All of these roles were reflected in his service to the MAI, and he continued as a member of the Council of the Association long after my mother had retired. His position with the Arts Council was certainly helpful during these moves to establish the MAI on a more professional footing.

The MAI membership were informed of the new development in a piece by the chairman, Pat O'Kelly, in the May 1978 issue of *Counterpoint*: 'Within the next few months the MAI hopes to be in a position to make a public announcement regarding a new and exciting appointment in music in Ireland . . . the MAI has decided to appoint a full-time Music Organiser. The funding of this new, important and developing position will be made through the Arts Council . . . their positive and continuing support is most heartening and their faith in the MAI's capabilities of making the project a success have been very reassuring.'

But in July, all associated with the MAI administration were very shaken by the sudden death of Nancy Glenn. The tributes to her from my mother and Pat O'Kelly in the September issue of *Counterpoint* demonstrate clearly how much she was appreciated for her personal qualities and her unfailing service to the MAI. Her loss must have been particularly felt by Eilís.

P. J. Power, who had previously been the director of Limerick Civic Week, took up the position of Music Organiser in September 1978 and by October was ready to outline his plans. His remit included the organisation of the Country Tours, Members' Meetings and the 1980 20th Century Festival, as well as generally seeking sponsorship. He was also asked to produce a comprehensive report on all the MAI's activities, and it was clear that he would need his own secretary. Anne Cant was appointed to this position in January 1979. Eoin Garrett became part-time Assistant Secretary following Nancy Glenn's death, and Eilís looked after the book-keeping as well as the SRS. There were also some changes amongst Council officers – Doreen Bradbury retired as treasurer and was replaced by Mary Leonard, and Anne Woodworth was appointed vice-chairman, in view of Pat O'Kelly's expectation that he might serve for only one more year. Anne Cant wrote of my mother: 'If I had one word to describe Olive Smith it would be – indefatigable! I first got to know her when the MAI shared an office with the IYO in Suffolk Street. Olive was astute, imaginative and had a good sense of humour – often with a twinkle in her eye. She was also kind and far-seeing, and contributed hugely to music performance and presentation all over the country at a time when other aspects of life in Ireland were quite stagnant.'[3]

1979 – 1980

A new project for 1979 was the organisation of the auditions for the ECYO, undertaken initially by Mary Timoney (see Chapters 31/32), and these auditions continued under the auspices of the MAI for many years. There was also the exciting news of Toyota's three-year sponsorship of the IYO, although in the Minutes of 6 February 1979 Pat O'Kelly reported: 'that he had written to the Chairman of the IYO, regretting the apparent separation developing between the MAI and the IYO and the lack of consultation in the appointment of the new IYO committee.'

In April 1979, there was considerable surprise when P. J. Power asked to be released from his Music Organiser's contract in order to take up another position outside Dublin. His successor was Eoin Garrett, who had taken over the editorship of *Counterpoint* from Pat O'Kelly in March 1978. A pianist and teacher,[4] Eoin had been co-opted to the MAI Council in 1977, was involved with the 1978 20th Century Festival and succeeded Nancy Glenn in the part-time post of Assistant Secretary. He took up the position of Music Organiser on 1 July 1979, Anne Cant remained as his secretary and Eilís reaped the benefit of a full-time job by combining the Assistant Secretary's hours with those of the SRS. Eoin's workload encompassed the organisation of the 20th Century Festival, administrative work for the Festival in Great Irish Houses and the Dublin Organ Festival, as well as editorship of *Counterpoint*. He also organised the Country Tours, though Anne Woodworth retained an oversight for planning these, which were renamed 'MAI Concerts' from 1981 onwards. Initially Thérèse Timoney agreed to take on the organising of Coming-Out recitals. After a somewhat fallow period, there was a revival of interest in these and Malcolm Proud (harpsichord), Una Hunt (piano) and Denise Kelly (harp) gave recitals during 1979 - 80.[5]

In September 1979, Eoin and Eilís met with Arts Council representatives to discuss the SRS funding. In light of the IYO's generous three-year sponsorship from Toyota, the suggestion was made that the MAI should arrange with the IYO that the entire Department grant would go to the SRS in 1980. This solution had, in fact, already come from a meeting with Department officials in 1978. The MAI Council was in agreement and accordingly Pat O'Kelly wrote to my mother on 12 October 1979.[6] His letter was not well received. Her reply, dated 22 October from Derrylahan, gave her opinion that a representative of the IYO should have been involved in any such discussion, and that she considered the MAI had acted in a high-handed and unethical manner. She said that she had great sympathy with the SRS, particularly as it was largely her brain-child, and she had been instrumental in securing the Department grant in the first place. But she would have preferred the option of negotiating a reduction in the IYO's portion. She was also concerned that the IYO might not be able to re-establish access to the grant, should Toyota not continue their support, and made the wise observation that: 'once a Government department is allowed to extricate itself from a commitment to give a grant to a specific group, it is very doubtful if it would be restored.'

The remainder of her letter consisted of a brief resumé of the complexities of the inter-dependence of ÓC, the SRS and the IYO, all financed from the same funding source. This, of course, was the root of the problem – these arrangements had been relatively straightforward when my mother was involved in the administration of all three, but now she felt that those dealing with the situation were ill-informed. If truth were told, her letter shows that she herself was slightly confused. In a second document, dated 24 October, she set out the procedures whereby the Department informed the IYO each year that it would receive a certain portion (an average of 38%) of the grant to the MAI.

In an attempt to ameliorate the situation, Pat wrote again on 8 November, in anticipation of an IYO committee meeting on 12 November, to be followed by an MAI Council on 14th. He clarified the sequence of meetings during 1978 and 1979 and asked her to note: 'that the proposal concerns only 1980 and that it is not the intention of the MAI to leave the IYO without funds thereafter, merely to tide the SRS over a bad patch.'

Fortunately, the crisis had a favourable outcome. The Department's overall grant for 1980 was increased to £5,000, with the IYO's portion pegged at £1,500 (30%), and for the first time the Arts Council made a grant (£2,000) to the SRS. Eilís wrote to the Education Officer, Adrian Munnelly, on 10 December 1980 to inform him that she had organised 186 recitals that year, in contrast with just 105 in 1979, and commented:

'I would venture to say that there are not many other state aided enterprises which stretch out to so many children and show such value for the cash received.' The problems associated with the shared funding from the Department of Education were not resolved until September 1985 when a complete separation was agreed.[7]

At the Council meeting on 10 October 1979, Eoin reported that there might be a resolution to the on-going problems of the ailing *Counterpoint* magazine, in that the Arts Council were proposing to fund a new, commercially produced, music magazine. Honor Ó Brolcháin took over from Eoin as editor of *Counterpoint* in early 1980 and reported to Council on 8 July that it was proposed to publish the new magazine *SoundPost* under the auspices of the MAI, including a section of MAI News in each issue. *Counterpoint* would cease publication. The Council, despite some misgivings, agreed that the *SoundPost* grant should be paid as part of the general Arts Council funding to the MAI and that editorial responsibility would rest with the MAI. Honor was appointed as editor and the first bi-monthly issue appeared in April 1981. From late 1981 Michael Dervan and Bernard Harris, took over as co-editors. The significantly larger format of *SoundPost* allowed for the type of in-depth journalism which had not been possible in *Counterpoint*, and one very good example was the article 'Olive Smith: Woman of Action' by Patricia Quinn which appeared in the August/September issue of 1983.[8] In writing this well-researched and perceptive biographical piece, Patricia had clearly benefitted from a personal interview with my mother.

The early 1980s were a very busy and successful period for the MAI, and since my mother had by this time completely withdrawn from all active participation in its organisation, it seems a good point at which to conclude my account of the Association's history.

I would just like to mention the retirement, in December 1982, of two people who had contributed hugely to the work of the MAI. Mairtín McCullough was a Council member from 1953, serving even longer than my mother. He was helpful from the outset by allowing the MAI's 'Diary of Musical Events' to be kept at his shop, and by his willingness to act, on more than one occasion, as chauffeur for touring musicians. He was editor of the *Bulletin* from 1953 to 1964, he also acted for a short period as joint hon. secretary with my mother, and fulfilled several terms as chairman. His business acumen was of great assistance to the Council, as was his calm and wise demeanour. Pat O'Kelly was editor of *Counterpoint* from 1972 to 1978, and chairman from 1976 to 1982 during a period of great change and expansion. Also, as music critic with the *Evening Press*, his wide knowledge of music and his journalistic skills were invaluable assets to the Council. He was music critic for the *Irish Independent* from 1998 until 2017, and currently contributes a fortnightly column on music to the *Irish Catholic*. Both men were honoured with a presentation to mark their retirement at the 'MAI Showcase' at the NCH on 4 September 1982, and were elected Life Members. Mairtín was appointed Chairman of the Arts Council in 1984. Pat is the author of *The National Symphony Orchestra of Ireland*, published by RTÉ in 1998, and jointly with Patricia Butler *The National Concert Hall*, published in 2000.

In reflecting upon all that she had achieved, my impression is that my mother was pleased and satisfied that three of her main interests – the Coming-Out recitals, the Country Tours and the SRS – were in good hands, and I know that she welcomed in principle the appointment of the Music Organiser. But she was disappointed that the MAI's campaigning and pioneering role of earlier years had become greatly diminished.

The Schools' Recital Scheme
The SRS, in particular, survived until the MAI itself went out of business. During the 1980s it enjoyed generous financial support from both the Department of Education and the Arts Council, as well as another grant from the Ireland Fund in 1983. For example, 313 concerts were organised by Eilís in 1982 – the result of additional funding and her organisational skills. I remember her as a softly-spoken, gentle lady, endowed with dogged determination in the face of any adversity, very supportive of all the performers who participated in the Scheme, and dedicated to the vision of what it could achieve. Her opinion of my mother was summed up

in the Irish phrase *Bean Stuama* – a sensible, level-headed, self-possessed and prudent woman.[9] With the encouragement of her committee, Eilís implemented an innovative programme of workshops, suggested by the Arts Council, each featuring a specially commissioned work for schools by an Irish composer. Apart from a short period of ill-health, Eilís continued to organise the SRS up to her retirement in 1998.

In its final years, the Scheme was organised by the MAI Education Officers, firstly Caroline Wynne who launched a new programme of events for schools called 'Music in Time', and later the harpist and musicologist, Teresa O'Donnell. By this time the SRS and the MAI itself were poorly funded and the decision was taken in 2003 to wind both up. It was Teresa who assembled the MAI's files of historical material prior to presentation to the National Library of Ireland. Regarding the SRS, it is a matter of enormous regret that it has never been revived or replaced – its live music programme reached out in a very special way to countless young people all over the country.

The National Concert Hall

With reference to my mother's intense participation in the campaign for a National Concert Hall from 1951 until 1967, and her disparaging remarks about the proposed Hall at Earlsfort Terrace in 1974, I should record that she attended the NCH opening night on 9 September 1981. The passage of time had softened her critical view of the project, perhaps helped by being involved peripherally through my husband Lindsay, the Hall's first general manager.[10] At any rate, she enjoyed the concert and approved of the acoustics of the auditorium and the general ambience of the building. It has, of course, proved to be a wonderful asset for the city of Dublin and for the musical life of the nation.

The Cultural Relations Committee

In early 1982 my mother was appointed to this voluntary body,[11] which advised the Minister for Foreign Affairs on the administration of the annual grant-in-aid from his Department towards the development of cultural relations with other countries. She had, of course, worked closely over the years with this committee on various projects. It was established in 1949, just one year after the MAI.

Lyall Smith Laboratories (LSL)

Regarding my father's business, a perusal of the Minutes of the Company from 1981 onwards does not make happy reading. It appears that a peak of productivity was reached in 1979 and the early months of 1980, with a huge increase in the number of films processed – it has been suggested that this could have been a spin-off from the visit of Pope John Paul II in September 1979! Considerable borrowings for new machinery and equipment were then contracted, so that by July 1981 the Minutes record concern that some payments would have to be deferred if the Company was to keep within its overdraft limits. The chief underlying cause for LSL's weak financial position was an unexpected shortfall in the quantity of films to be processed. Sadly, the downward trend continued, so that LSL went from being an employer of several hundred, with a country-wide business, to a much diminished operation. By May 1983, it was clear that the situation was irretrievable. The final Board meeting took place on 19 September and a Receiver was appointed on 23 September 1983.

My mother showed continuing concern for members of staff who had been with LSL for a considerable time, particularly Vincent Trotman and the five most experienced technical and administrative staff who formed a new company, LSL Photolabs Ltd, at Lennox Street in Dublin 8. In March 1984, they sent my mother a report of their work and a further letter in October of that year, from which it is clear that she had lent them £25,000 to get the business started, but now wished to make that a gift. Their letter expresses: 'sincere gratitude for your thoughtfulness and kindness' and informs her that the business is fully operational and that, thanks to her gift, they have no other borrowings. Vincent and his wife Anne remained true friends to my mother, visiting her regularly and faithfully in her old age, thus maintaining a connection with her and my father that began in 1942.

The Richardson-Smith Trust

My mother continued as a Trustee of the R-ST until her death in September 1993, and happily the Trust was able to continue its work until 2014. Hugh Maguire resigned as a Trustee in 1994, becoming Honorary Patron, and James Cavanagh and Lindsay Armstrong were appointed to replace Hugh and my mother. Kenneth Armstrong died in December 2009 and was replaced by our younger daughter Caitriona. From 1996 onwards, the Trustees sought to spread the benefits of their funding more widely by inviting applications from regional school and youth orchestras for specific music projects. In the next six years, fourteen orchestras received grants, the majority for the purchase of instruments. In 2004 it was decided to offer funds for workshops to orchestras in need of tuition and coaching, so during 2006 and 2007 grants of €500 each were given to school or youth orchestras in Carlow, Mayo, Cavan, Waterford, Tipperary and Dublin. The Trustees' attention was then drawn to a new venture in primary schools in disadvantaged areas, where violin lessons and orchestral playing were being offered to all pupils. There had been some accumulation of income and, as a result, grants totalling more than €4,000 were paid to five schools in 2010, mostly for instrument purchase. Further grants were given over the next three years, but there was no possibility of an increase in capital, and concern grew that low interest rates in the foreseeable future would result in a steady decrease in the Trust's income.

The Trust's minutes of 23 January 2014 state: 'There was a proposal before the meeting that, in view of the small annual income and uncertainties as to the practicalities of running the Trust in the future, consideration should be given to gradually winding up the Trust. This would involve the cashing-in of the capital presently invested in Government stock. Using the increased monies at the Trustee's disposal, it would be possible to make some quite substantial grants for a short period.'[12]

This was indeed the course of action which was followed. The NYOI received funding for two years for their 'Touch Bass' courses, which encouraged players of oboe, bassoon, viola, double-bass and trombone; a grant was made to the Irish Association of Youth Orchestras for the purchase of four oboes and four violas; and a further grant went to the St Agnes' School Violin and Orchestra Project (renamed in 2016 as Scoil Úna Naofa) in Dublin for instruments and equipment, as well as assistance with tuition for beginners and high achievers. In addition, a silver trophy named the Richardson-Smith Cup in memory of my mother was presented to the Scoil Úna Naofa Project, to be awarded annually to an outstanding student.

It is a matter of great satisfaction to me that, over a period of almost forty years, the Trust was able to assist orchestral playing amongst a great number of young people, probably quite out of proportion to the amount of funds at its disposal. My mother might have been surprised that the Trustees managed to follow her vision for so long, but I think she would have been pleased that this was another of her creations that stood the test of time.

The Irish Youth Orchestra

The National Youth Orchestra of Ireland (the title NYOI dates from 1989) is nowadays, of course, the body with which my mother's name is most closely associated. Following her retirement in January 1982, the senior orchestra was managed by Enid Chaloner for the remainder of the year, including the trip to Rome that summer, where a chamber group from the orchestra (led by Rita Manning) had the distinction of winning the International Chamber Music Prize for their performance of the Mendelssohn Octet. On 10 July 1982, the JIYO made its debut at the NCH. From early 1983, Mrs Loretta Keating, director of the JIYO, took over responsibility for the IYO as well, and during the year major changes to the governance of the orchestras were achieved.

A limited company, known as 'Irish Youth Orchestra Ltd', was incorporated on 22 September 1983 and held its first directors' meeting on 21 October. The first directors were Loretta Keating (Director), Anton Timoney and Gerry Keenan (the orchestral managers respectively of the IYO and JIYO), Hugh Maguire and Gearóid Grant (conductors of the IYO and JIYO). The company secretary was Mrs Marion Scott. Seven names are listed as Members of the Company on that date: Mr Justice Declan Costello, Fr Kevin McMullan, Dr Olive Smith, Mrs Loretta Keating, Lindsay Armstrong, David Agnew and Anton Timoney. At the first AGM of the new company, on 27 November 1983, Gerry Kelly, Jane Carty, Fr Kevin McMullan, Thérèse Timoney and David Agnew were elected as Directors and as many as twenty Members were listed. Tim Mahony, Chairman of the IYO's sponsors Toyota, declined an invitation to join the Board, but a representative of Toyota, Mr Denis Fitzgibbon, was admitted as a member. Fr Kevin McMullan was elected as chairman, a position which he retained until 1997, and indeed Hugh Maguire remained on the Board until the autumn of 1998. Fr McMullan proposed that there should be some long-term recognition of my mother's role and it was agreed that her name should appear on programmes and on the letterhead as Founder.

The continued and extremely generous sponsorship of Toyota enabled both the IYO and the JIYO to undertake tours outside Ireland, and there was also significant Government funding through the Department of Education and the CRC. The IYO travelled to the USA in 1983 and the JIYO to Cyprus in 1986. In the summer of 1987 the IYO toured to Strasbourg, Luxembourg, Brussels, Louvain and Metz, conducted by Robert Houlihan, former bassoonist with the orchestra. Hugh Maguire conducted his last concert in the summer of 1991 and was replaced by guest conductors including Bryden Thompson, Albert Rosen and En Shao. Towards the end of 1994, Loretta Keating indicated that she wished to plan her retirement and the Board's decision was, once again, to seek a Director for both orchestras. The Board minutes of 26 May 1995 record that Joanna Crooks, administrator of the Dublin Youth Orchestras (DYO) was their first choice. Joanna recalls[13] that she was telephoned by Hugh Maguire in the summer of 1995 to ask if she might consider the position, and it was agreed that she would take over from January 1996. Joanna guided the NYOI for the next ten years with the ongoing financial assistance of Toyota. This sadly came to an end in 2008 – after almost thirty years of the most enlightened support. There have been two Directors of the NYOI since 2007, firstly Zoë Keers and latterly Carol-Ann McKenna. The Irish auditions for membership of the ECYO, formerly arranged under the auspices of the MAI, are nowadays organised by the staff of the NYOI.

In 2018, Joanna Crooks wrote: 'One of the lasting effects of the NYOI is that the players are now so widespread and embedded in the music life of Ireland, at all kinds of levels. Its impact has been really profound in creating a pool of musicians, some professional players, some teachers, who have been able to network easily from the friendships established as young musicians at residential courses, and have emerged around the country playing very significant roles.'[14]

---

[1] The Ireland Fund was established in Pittsburgh, Pennsylvania, in 1976 as a philanthropic organisation whose purpose was to channel donations from the USA towards deserving causes in Ireland, with a special emphasis on peaceful, charitable and cultural projects. Their grant to the Schools' Scheme in 1979 was actually $3,000.

[2] Richards' Report, page 54, section 14.19.

[3] Email of 29 November 2017, following interview with the author on 20 November 2017. The singer Anne Cant Fitzpatrick held various administrative posts at the NCH between 1981 and 2005. She was Hon. Sec of the MAI in the 1980s and served on the Executive Committee of the Feis Ceoil for many years.

[4] Eoin Garrett is a pianist, organist and former choirmaster. He has been an examiner for the RIAM Local Centre since 1990, and served as a Senior Examiner for eight years, four of those as chairman.

[5] In 1980, sponsorship was obtained from the cigarette company Carrolls, for five concerts at the National Gallery. Niamh Cusack (flute), Donal Bannister (trombone), Colette McGahon (mezzo-soprano), Eithne Tinney (piano) and Frank Schaeffer (cello) gave recitals. A number of other performers were included in a future series – Leonora Carney (piano), Geraldine Malone (oboe), Anna Caleb (soprano) and Brenda Hurley (piano).

[6] NLI – ACC 6000, box 18, beige folder 10.

[7] Ibid. box 10, red file.

[8] NLI Collection – IR7805 S13.

9 Quoted from Eilís MacGabhann's interview with Pat O'Kelly, 26 November 2002.

10 Lindsay Armstrong – Oboist with the RTÉSO from 1963 to 1979, Co-founder and Manager of NICO from 1970 to 1980, General Manager of the NCH - 1981, Director of the RIAM from 1982 to 1993, Manager and Artistic Director of the OSC from 1995 to 2014.

11 *The Irish Times*, 7 January 1982.

12 The final meeting of the Trustees was held on 27 May 2014.

13 Interviewed by the author, 9 January 2018.

14 Email to the author, 31 January 2018.

EPILOGUE

From early 1982 until mid 1985 my mother lived in complete enjoyment of her house and garden at Derrylahan in Connemara. She always had green fingers and cultivated an array of peat-loving flowering shrubs – hydrangeas, rhododendrons, azaleas and ragusa roses – which provided a riot of colour throughout the summer months. Even in her late seventies she had amazing physical energy and insisted upon mowing the steeply sloping grassy areas herself. Our daughters have given me some memories of Derrylahan. Deirdre (Dee) reminisced about the wonderful beaches that were within an easy walk, and helping my mother to bring seaweed up from the shore by the barrowful, as fertiliser for the plants. On summer visits there were always garden peas to be podded! Caitriona observed that my mother's hands were gnarled from gardening and often scratched with thorns. Also that Derrylahan had some idiosyncracies – water came from a well and was very drinkable, but when soap was added the water turned blue! The telephone was an antiquity – one turned a little handle on a small box and waited for the exchange in the local post-office to respond. The post-mistress would then try to connect to the requested number. My mother's number was Moyard 13 because this was the only line available when she moved there – none of the neighbours wanted number 13!

She liked to have old friends to visit – Pat McKnight, Lily Butler from Cork, Kenneth Armstrong and his wife Adrienne, Vincent and Anne Trotman, Mrs Mac and her husband Tommy (who did some work in the garden while he was there), Jimmy and Pauline Cavanagh, and her sister and brother-in-law from London. My mother had a powerful Peugeot car and thought nothing of the drive to Shannon airport to meet Kay and

David, taking a detour on the return journey to spend a couple of nights in the Burren, which they all loved. But she expressed distress to me at the gradual decline in her sister's health, due to the onset of Alzheimer's disease, and the prospect that Kay would soon not be able to visit anymore.

There were kindly neighbours – the Barry family and Garnet Irwin in particular – however my mother appeared to be contented and self-sufficient on her own, though there must have been lonely times on stormy winter evenings. However Mairtín McCullough made the interesting comment[1] that he did not consider my mother's move to Derrylahan to be wise, as she had been too involved with people all her life to more or less cut herself off. Indeed, I was aware that the moments of confusion and forgetfulness which I had noticed during the Greek cruise in 1981 were becoming more frequent, and was beginning to accept that the slow decline of Alzheimer's would be my mother's fate also. It was Pat McKnight who raised concerns, following a weekend visit in early 1985, noting that my mother had lost some confidence in driving and was finding it difficult to manage. It seems that my mother had also realised that there was a problem, as very soon afterwards she informed me that a neighbour was interested in buying Derrylahan, and that she would like me to find her an apartment to buy in Dublin. We were living in Rathgar at that time, and it was very fortunate that a block of new flats, just round the corner from us, was nearing completion. There was one available on the upper floor with a lovely view of the Dublin mountains and by early September the move was complete. It was an ideal situation, a return to the area she had known all her life, and close to our house so that she could see more of her grand-daughters and join us for her main meal on most days.

There was no escaping the steady deterioration of my mother's illness. Mrs Mac became one of her carers for a while, and then a new friend, Maura Walsh from Waterford who was also my home-help. Vincent and Anne Trotman were regular and devoted visitors, and the most wonderful support came from Pat McKnight whose friendship, of course, went right back to 1930. By the autumn of 1989 it was clear that the care of family and friends was not sufficient, and reluctantly it was decided that my mother should move into residential care. She died at Highfield Healthcare on the Swords Road on 12th September 1993, just two days short of her 61st wedding anniversary.

My mother and I had never discussed her wishes for her funeral, but I was very mindful of her long-standing aversion to formal religious services. As a family, we felt that something of the nature of a memorial, including some of the music she particularly loved, would be the most appropriate. A large attendance was anticipated, and as Revd Mary Hunter, Minister of Christ Church, Rathgar, was willing to conduct such a service, it seemed the right decision to return to that church, given its long association with both my father's and mother's families. Members of the National Chamber Choir, under their conductor Colin Mawby, sang Schubert's setting of 'The Lord's My Shepherd', a piece which my mother herself had often conducted in the days of the Olivian Singers. Brian O'Rourke and a string quartet of our orchestra colleagues, led by Mary Gallagher, played the slow movement of Mozart's Clarinet Quintet, and finally Bernadette Greevy sang 'Erbarme Dich' (Have mercy, Lord) from Bach's *St Matthew Passion* with Mary playing the wonderful violin solo. It was an extremely wet day, so only a small number of people made the journey out to the graveyard at St Patrick's Church in Enniskerry, where my mother was laid to rest in the same grave as my father.

---

[1] Interviewed by Pat O'Kelly, 3 February 2003.

APPENDIX 1

In memoriam Olive Smith

In the years that followed my mother's death, events have taken place at which she was remembered:-

15 October 1993: Appreciation in *The Irish Times*, page 15, written by Edgar Deale – 'I recall with pleasure Olive's enormous enthusiasm and devotion to duty. And her self-effacement – foremost in action, and the last to claim credit. She was gifted with remarkable capacity . . . Olive was a natural leader.'

1998: The programme booklet for the 50th Anniversary celebration of the MAI at the NCH on Saturday 10 October 1998 contained tributes to my mother from Bernadette Greevy, Gerard Gillen and Edgar Deale.

1999: The MAI organised the first of three **Olive Smith Commemorative Lectures** on 9th May 1999 at the Bank of Ireland Arts Centre, Foster Place, Dublin 2, at 8.00 p.m. This was given by Professor Donald Burrowes of the Open University, who spoke on 'The Last and First: Handel's Dublin Performances of *Imeneo* and *Messiah*.' The second in the series was on 11 November 2001 when Mícheál Ó Súilleabháin spoke about 'A River of Sound: the Changing Course of Irish Music'. The final lecture was given by Professor Gerard Gillen on the subject 'The Church and Musical Patronage' on 24 November 2002.

2003: The National Library of Ireland received the archive of the papers of the MAI on 5 November 2003. An official reception was held in the

Library on 19 February 2004 to mark the formal presentation by the then chairman, Rodney Senior. In 2007 an organisation called the Friends of Classical Music was founded by former MAI members.

2005: The 35th Anniversary of the NYOI was marked by a weekend reunion in Cork of former members, combining celebrations with rehearsals and an afternoon concert on Sunday 3 July. The printed programme featured a comprehensive history of the Orchestra over the 35 years, including warm tributes to Hugh Maguire and my mother. At the break in the Sunday morning rehearsal at the City Hall, Joanna Crooks asked me to go up onto the conductor's podium to say a few words to the assembled players. Almost as an aside, I mentioned that the 100th anniversary of my mother's birth would occur the following year. Joanna's acute hearing picked up my remark, and almost before I left the stage she was starting to plan how this event might be commemorated.

2006: The NYOI and Joanna Crooks could not have marked my mother's centenary more generously. A two-page account of her life and work, complete with photographs, occupied pride of place in the programme, and the leader's position in the under-18 orchestra (formerly the JIYO) was designated as the Olive Smith Chair 2006. I decided to invite a small group of her closest friends and relations to the concert on 29 July and to a meal beforehand. Her niece Helen and nephew Brian, together with their spouses Dan and Liz, came from England. Lindsay and I and our younger daughter Caitriona, as well as our eldest grandson Tycho, represented my mother's immediate descendents, and the Richardson-Smith Trustees were represented by Kenneth Armstrong and Brian Howlett. There was also a heart-warming attendance of old friends – Pat McKnight, Vincent and Anne Trotman, and Mrs Mac with her daughter June. Brian spoke a few words at the meal and we drank a toast in my mother's memory.

2007: Towards the end of 2006, the RTÉ producer Celia Donoghue, a former clarinettist with the NYOI, proposed the idea of a radio programme about my mother, to mark the 100th anniversary of her birth. Lasting about 30 minutes, it is a very well-conceived and fitting tribute, with extracts from archived spoken recordings by my mother and Hugh Maguire, and some musical contributions from the NYOI. My voice is there too, as a linking commentary. It was broadcast on Lyric FM on 7 January 2007 as part of the series *Sunday Sequence*.

2010: On 17 April, Teresa O'Donnell delivered a paper *A Woman's Touch: Olive Smith guiding the musical education of a generation* at the 'Women in Music in Ireland' conference at NUI Maynooth. Teresa had researched the MAI archives in preparation for her doctoral thesis (see below).

2010: The NYOI celebrated its 40th anniversary by once again bringing together former members to play in a special concert at the NCH on 28 November. A shortened version of the article on my mother, written for her 100th anniversary, with the title 'A Life in Music' was printed in the programme, which included a reprint of Ian Fox's *Counterpoint* account of the first course in 1970. There were also contributions from Hugh Maguire and Joanna Crooks. Gearóid Grant conducted the 40th Anniversary Orchestra in Dvořák's 'New World' Symphony and Evelyn Grant was the compère for the evening.

Evelyn also made a wonderful radio documentary about the NYOI in 2010, which celebrated the 40th anniversary through many of the voices and music of the preceding years. This was broadcast on Lyric FM. Plans are already underway to celebrate the 50th anniversary of the NYOI in the year 2020.

2012: Teresa O'Donnell completed her doctoral thesis on the work of the MAI – *The Music Association of Ireland: A Cultural and Social History* – and this is lodged in the Cregan Library of St Patrick's College, Drumcondra, now a constituent college of Dublin City University. To date this is the only other major study of the MAI and, unlike this present account, covers the entire period of the Association's existence, including the years of its decline. Having stated in section 1.2 that: 'Olive Smith's involvement in the MAI eclipses all others', Teresa goes on to devote the whole of Chapter 5 to 'The contribution of Olive Smith to the MAI.'

In her Conclusion (section 5.12) she writes: 'Olive Smith was a visionary whose dogged resilience and determination assured the realisation of her vision. She made no personal gain from her enterprises; her only wish was to assist young aspiring musicians and to make music accessible to all. Olive Smith, in her various volunteer roles in the MAI, made a considerable difference to music education in Ireland. Though not a pedagogue, composer or professional musician, her efforts, more than any other member of the MAI, helped realise its objectives, leaving a lasting impression on the cultural life of Ireland'.

APPENDIX TWO

Over the years, a number of organisations have come into existence as spin-offs from the pioneering work of the NYOI.

Dublin Youth Orchestras (DYO)

This organisation, planned originally in late 1981 by Joanna Crooks and three friends, Agnes O'Kane, Vanessa Sweeney and Charmian Arbuckle, was inaugurated in early 1982. Their concern was to provide orchestral training to children who had tuition with private teachers. The main music schools in Dublin (RIAM and College of Music) had orchestras, but it was a big step for young instrumentalists to get into the IYO without some previous orchestral experience. The DYO provided this stepping-stone and also, through its Junior and Intermediate Orchestras, an opportunity for orchestral playing from a very young age. There has been a strong emphasis in the DYO on playing in small chamber groups, and its summer chamber-music courses at Aravon School in Bray started in 1984. (www.dyo.ie)

Irish Youth Wind Ensemble (IYWE)

This was founded in 1985 by Professor James Cavanagh of the RIAM and Colonel Fred O'Callaghan, director of the Army School of Music. There was an awareness that, by its very nature, a Youth Orchestra accommodates many more strings than wind, brass and percussion, and it was hoped that the formation of a symphonic wind ensemble would go a long way towards filling this gap. The IYWE has some 70 members and meets each August for an annual residential course of about a week. It offers the young players an opportunity to study, perform and experience music specifically composed for wind ensemble, and to present music that would not otherwise be heard by Irish audiences. The present director is Ronan O'Reilly. (www.iywe.iayo.ie)

Irish Association of Youth Orchestras (IAYO)

Dating from 1994, the IAYO grew from the simple idea of compiling a list of the growing number of youth orchestras in various parts of Ireland, and possibly forming an Association for their mutual benefit. The impetus came from some of the people involved in the DYO chamber courses at Aravon, notably Joanna Crooks, Agnes O'Kane, Vanessa Sweeney and Carmel Ryan, with some very persistent encouragement from Sr Concepta who ran the Donegal Youth Orchestra. Agnes had recently moved to Cork with her family and agreed to act as organiser, funded by a small subvention of £200 from the DYO. An initial meeting was arranged in Ennis where Andrew Robinson, Vanessa's brother-in-law, was director of Maoin Cheoil an Chláir. This meeting was also attended by Conor Ó Ceallacháin, representing the Cork Youth Orchestra (the oldest youth orchestra in Ireland), as well as Adrian Petcu from the Cork School of Music and Kay O'Sullivan of the City Music College in Cork. Following this meeting, Agnes was delighted when Hugh Maguire accepted her invitation to become President of the new organisation.

The first AGM of the IAYO was held in Cork in September 1994, at which a chairman and committee were elected and a mission statement prepared, but there was surprise at the enthusiastic response from potential member orchestras. Agnes is quoted: 'This network was bigger than I had realised. We needed an event or a programme to channel interest and resources to our new organisation. How should we do this?' (from *Ten Years Making Music in Ireland*, published by the IAYO in 2004). It was Joanna who suggested a Festival at the NCH, and it was the wonderful sponsorship of Penneys in Cork which made it possible. The first Festival of Youth Orchestras took place in February 1995 and will celebrate its 25th year in 2020. About 500 young musicians in eight orchestras, a different selection each year, perform in this day-long annual concert.

Nowadays the IAYO represents over 5,000 musicians in 108 youth orchestras throughout Ireland. It runs an instrument bank, a music library, workshops for conductors, chamber music courses, and in general acts as an umbrella body for the development of orchestral playing. Membership is open to all youth orchestras in Ireland, whether linked to a school, a school of music, a college or university, or to an independent or community-based organisation. The IAYO is funded by the Arts Council and is a member of the European Youth Orchestras Federation. (www.iayo.ie)

ConCorda

Following his retirement as conductor of the NYOI, Hugh Maguire was still interested in working with young Irish string players and in 1994, together with his second wife, Tricia, set up the chamber music course which he called ConCorda. He involved Agnes O'Kane, as administrator of the IAYO, from the outset and also Adrian Petcu. The purpose of ConCorda is to provide players beween the ages of 14 and 26 with the opportunity to explore string quartet repertoire for a week each year, under the guidance of world-class coaches. A string orchestra is also formed by the participants during the week. This organisation is still flourishing with the support of the IAYO, the Irish Chamber Orchestra and the Arts Council. Its present directors are Katherine Hunka and Jonathan Roewer of the ICO. (www.concorda.iayo.ie)

Scoil Úna Naofa Violin and Orchestra Project

Originally named the St Agnes School Violin and Orchestra Project, this is the brainchild of Sister Bernadette Sweeney and Joanna Crooks, former Director of the NYOI. Founded in September 2006, it aims to bring the opportunity of playing a string instrument to every child in this primary school in the Dublin district of Crumlin. More than 400 children receive a free weekly music lesson, and the Project supports second-level pupils who want to continue with their instrumental tuition. A number of professional musicians, who were themselves formerly members of the NYOI, have been deeply involved with the Scoil Úna Naofa Project, notably Jimmy and Pauline Cavanagh, their daughter Ciara and son Shane, Seamus Doyle, Eimear O'Grady, Nicole Hudson, Naoise Dack and Richard Thomas. In 2010 the St Agnes' Parents String Orchestra was formed and the St Agnes Musical Society came into being in 2011, with its first production in 2012. The St Agnes Chamber Orchestra is for young players who have moved from primary to secondary school (www.stagnesmusiccrumlin.com). The St Agnes Community Centre for Music and the Arts opened in 2013 and offers music tuition to people of all ages in a wide range of instruments, classical and traditional, and also provides art and ballet classes (www.stagnesccma.ie).

APPENDIX THREE

Repertoire played by the Irish Youth Orchestra – July 1970 to January 1982

The following works were conducted by Hugh Maguire.

Arnold, Malcolm	Overture *Peterloo*
Bartók, Béla	Concerto for Orchestra, movements 1, 2 & 4
Bartók, Béla	*Romanian Dances*
Beethoven, Ludwig van	Symphony No. 5 in C minor
Beethoven, Ludwig van	Symphony No. 7 in A major
Beethoven, Ludwig van	Overture *Egmont*
Berlioz, Hector	Overture *Le Carnaval Romain*
Berlioz, Hector	*Hungarian March*
Bizet, Georges	Suite *L'Arlésienne* No.1
Brahms, Johannes	Symphony No. 4 in E minor
Britten, Benjamin	*Soirées Musicales*
Chabrier, Emmanuel	*España*

Dvořák, Antonín	Symphony No. 8 in G major
Dvořák, Antonín	Symphony No. 9 in E minor 'From the New World'
Gabrieli, Giovanni	*Canzonas* for Wind and Brass
Glinka, Mikhail	Overture *Ruslan and Ludmilla*
Handel arr. Harty	Suite *The Water Music*
Kelly, Thomas C.	*Fantasia on Two Irish Airs*
Kodály, Zoltán	*Dances of Galánta*
Larchet, John F.	*The Dirge of Ossian* & *MacAnanty's Reel*
Mendelssohn, Felix	Overture *The Hebrides*
Mozart, Wolfgang Amadeus	Symphony No. 39 in E flat major
Mozart, Wolfgang Amadeus	Concerto for Bassoon and Orchestra
Nielsen, Carl	Symphony No. 1 in G minor
Prokofiev, Sergey	*Peter and the Wolf*
Rakhmaninov, Sergey	Piano Concerto No. 2 in C minor
Rimsky-Korsakov, Nikolay	Symphonic Suite *Sheherazade*
Rossini, Gioachino	Overture *The Thieving Magpie*
Saint-Saëns, Camille	Concerto No. 1 for Cello and Orchestra
Schubert, Franz	Symphony No. 8 in B minor 'The Unfinished'
Schumann, Robert	Symphony No. 3 in E flat major
Shostakovich, Dmitry	Symphony No. 1 in F minor
Sibelius, Jean	Symphony No. 1 in E minor
Sibelius, Jean	Symphony No. 2 in D major
Sibelius, Jean	Tone Poem *Finlandia*

Sibelius, Jean	Suite *Karelia*
Smetana, Bedřich	Symphonic Poem *Vltava*
Strauss, Richard	Horn Concerto No. 1 in E flat major
Strauss, Richard	Tone Poem *Ein Heldenleben*
Tchaikovsky, Pyotr Il'yich	Symphony No. 4 in F minor
Tchaikovsky, Pyotr Il'yich	Symphony No. 5 in E minor
Tchaikovsky, Pyotr Il'yich	Fantasy Overture *Romeo and Juliet*
Tchaikovsky, Pyotr Il'yich	Suite *The Nutcracker*
Vivaldi, Antonio	Concerto for Four Violins
Vivaldi, Antonio	Concerto for Two Trumpets
Weber, Carl M. von	Overture *Oberon*
Weber, Carl M. von	Overture *Der Freischütz*

The Junior Irish Youth Orchestra played the following works in 1980/'81:
This repertoire was conducted by Gearóid Grant.

Beethoven, Ludwig van	Symphony No. 1 in C major
Bizet, Georges	Suite *L'Arlésienne* No. 2
Duff, Arthur	*Irish Suite for Strings*
Grieg, Edvard	Suite *Peer Gynt* No. 2
Haydn, Franz Joseph	Concerto for Trumpet and Orchestra
Rossini, Giaochino	Overture *The Italian Girl in Algiers*
Schubert, Franz	Symphony No. 8 in B minor 'The Unfinished'

APPENDIX 4

Music Association of Ireland Coming-Out Recitals 1957 – 1984

All recitals took place in the Royal Hibernian Hotel, Dawson St, Dublin, unless otherwise stated.

15/01/57: Mary O'Brien (violin) with Kitty O'Callaghan (piano).

30/04/57: Florence Ryan (piano).

14/10/57: Margaret Hayes (violin) with Kitty O'Callaghan (piano).

29/01/58: Julian Dawson (piano), Hazel Morris (alto) with Dorothy Stokes (piano).

28/04/58: Brendan O'Reilly (violin) with Kitty O'Callaghan (piano).

29/09/58: Valerie Walker (piano).

17/02/60: Mary Gallagher (violin) with Rhona Marshall (piano).

06/06/60: Bernadette Greevy (alto) with Jeannie Reddin (piano).

28/02/62: Brighid Mooney (cello) with Gerard Shanahan (piano).

10/10/62: Carmel O'Byrne (soprano), Patricia Dunkerley (flute) with Jeannie Reddin (piano).

25/10/62: Deirdre McNulty (piano).

20/02/63: Eily Markey (soprano) with Gerard Shanahan (piano).

23/04/64: Emily Wilson (piano).

08/10/64: Máire Ní Chuilleanáin (violin) with Veronica McSwiney (piano).

05/11/64: Gerard Gillen (organ) in Leeson Park Church.

04/02/65: Anne Cant (soprano) with Dorothy Stokes (piano).

03/11/65: Brian McNamara (violin) with Veronica McSwiney (piano).

09/03/66: Gillian Smith (piano).

17/11/66: Eileen Donlon (soprano) with Havelock Nelson (piano).

12/11/67: John O'Conor (piano).

24/01/68: Anne Woodworth (mezzo) with Dorothy Stokes (piano).

19/11/70: Lynda Byrne (piano).

12/03/71: Thérèse Timoney (violin) with John O'Conor (piano) in the Examination Hall, TCD.

23/11/71: Moninne Vaneček (violin) with Veronica McSwiney (piano) in the Examination Hall, TCD.

08/11/73: Peter Sweeney (organ) in the Pro-Cathedral, Marlborough Street.

03/02/74: Emer Buckley (harpsichord) in St Ann's Church, Dawson Street.

17/10/74: Áine Nic Gabhann (alto) with Darina Gibson (piano) in St Catherine's Church, Thomas Street.

30/09/76: Maureen Elliman (piano) in the Examination Hall, TCD.

28/06/79: Malcolm Proud (harpsichord) in the Examination Hall, TCD.

10/04/80: Una Hunt (piano) in the Law Society, Blackhall Place.

09/10/80: Denise Kelly (harp) in St Ann's Church.

During 1980/81 P. J. Carroll & Co. gave the MAI sponsorship for a series of Coming-Out recitals in the National Gallery. No record of dates or accompanists was found for the first five musicians making their debut: Niamh Cusack (flute), Donal Bannister (trombone), Colette McGahon (mezzo-soprano), Eithne Tinney (piano) and Frank Schaeffer (cello). Four more players were listed with dates:

02/06/81: Leonora Carney (piano).

20/10/81: Geraldine Malone (oboe) with Mary O'Sullivan (piano).

24/04/82: Anna Caleb (soprano), no accompanist listed.

17/05/82: Brenda Hurley (piano).

Finally – after a gap of two years:

15/05/84: Aisling Heneghan (piano and harpsichord) in the John
     Field Room, National Concert Hall.

BIBLIOGRAPHY

Archived papers of the Music Association of Ireland, including the papers of Concert and Assembly Hall Ltd – National Library of Ireland, ACC 6000 (53 boxes + 2 extra boxes).

Arts Council Report for 1975.

Beausang, Ita and de Barra, Séamus, *Ina Boyle: A Composer's Life*. (Cork: Cork University Press, 2018).

Bell, The – selected issues from 1941 to 1954: articles on music by Joseph O'Neill, Frederick May, Brian Boydell, John Beckett, Aloys Fleischmann, Michael Bowles and Michael McMullin.

Boydell, Brian (ed. Barra Boydell), *Rebellious Ferment: A Dublin Musical Memoir and Diary*. (Cork: Atrium, 2018).

Butler, Patricia and O'Kelly, Pat, *The National Concert Hall* (Dublin: Wolfhound Press, 2000).

Cox, Gareth, *Seóirse Bodley*. (Dublin: Field Day Publications, 2010).

Cox, Gareth, Klein, Axel and Taylor, Michael (eds.), *The Life and Music of Brian Boydell*. (Dublin: Irish Academic Press, 2004).

Composing the Island: programme notes to accompany the first week of concerts in the 1916 – 2016 'A Century of Music in Ireland' project.

Culwick Choral Society: celebrates one hundred years 1898 – 1998. Editorial committee: Jane Clare, Magdalen O'Connell and Ann Simmons.

Dervan, Michael (ed.), *The Invisible Art: A Century of Music in Ireland, 1916-2016*. (Dublin: New Island, 2016).

Bibliography

Dictionary of Irish Biography: entry under Smith, (Mabel) Olive (author: Simon Taylor) (Cambridge University Press, 2009).

Dungan, Michael, *Man of the Century*: conversation with Edgar Deale to mark his 95th birthday (*New Music News*, May 1997).

Finan, Gillian, *A Hundred Years A-Growing: A History of the Irish Girl Guides*. (Dublin: Liberties Press, 2010).

Fitzgerald, Mark, *The Life and Music of James Wilson*. (Cork: Cork University Press, 2015).

Fitzgerald, Mark and O'Flynn, John, *Music and Identity in Ireland and Beyond*. (UK & USA: Ashgate Publishing, 2014).

Fleischmann, Aloys (ed.), *Music in Ireland: A Symposium*. (Cork: Cork University Press, 1952).

Fleischmann, Ruth (ed.), *Aloys Fleischmann: A Life for Music in Ireland*. (Cork: Mercier Press, 2000).

Gannon, Charles, *John S. Beckett: The Man and the Music*. (Dublin: Lilliput Press, 2016).

Garret, Eoin, *The Music Association of Ireland: founded 70 years ago*. (Spring 2018 issue of *Sound Post*, the magazine of the Musicians' Union of Ireland).

Houston, Kerry and White, Harry (eds.), *A Musical Offering: Essays in Honour of Gerard Gillen*. (Dublin: Four Courts Press, 2018).

O'Donnell, Teresa, *The Music Association of Ireland: A Cultural and Social History*. (PhD Thesis, 2012 – available through the library of St Patrick's College, DCU, Dublin 9).

O'Donnell, Teresa, *The Music Association of Ireland: Fostering a Voice for Irish Composers and Compositions*. (*Journal of Music Research* online/a journal of MusicAustralia, 2016).

O'Donnell, Teresa, *Musical Legacies: The Contribution of the Music Association of Ireland to an Irish Musical Infrastructure*. (JSMI: *Journal of the Society forMusicology in Ireland*, 2014-15, issue 10, p.3).

O'Donovan, Donal, *God's Architect: A Life of Raymond McGrath*. (Bray, Co. Wicklow: Kilbride Books,1995).

O'Kelly, Pat, *The National Symphony Orchestra of Ireland, 1948-1998: A Selected History.* (Dublin: Radio Telefís Éireann,1998).

Parkes, Susan M. (ed.) *A Danger to the Men?: A History of Women in Trinity College Dublin, 1904 – 2004.* (Dublin: Lilliput Press, 2004).

Pine, Richard (ed.), *Music in Ireland 1848-1998: Thomas Davis Lectures (RTÉ).* (Cork and Dublin: Mercier Press,1998).

Quinn, Patricia, *Olive Smith: Woman of Action.* (Article in *SoundPost* Aug/Sept 1983, music periodical published bi-monthly by The Music Association of Ireland).

Richards, J. M., *Provision for the Arts.* (A report published by the Arts Council and the Gulbenkian Foundation, January 1976).

White, Harry and Boydell, Barra (eds.), *The Encyclopaedia of Music in Ireland.* (Dublin: UCD Press, 2013).

Wikipedia – entry under Olive Smith.

SOURCES OF THE ILLUSTRATIONS

Nos. 1 - 9:	Richardson family collection.
No. 10:	Photograph by Gillian Smith.
Nos. 11 - 16:	Collection of the late Pat McKnight.
Nos. 17 - 19:	Smith family collection.
Nos. 20 - 22:	Courtesy of the Culwick Choral Society.
Nos. 23 - 35:	Smith family collection.
Nos. 36 - 42:	Photos of Sri Lanka (Ceylon) by Olive Smith.
Nos. 43 - 60:	Smith family collection.
No. 61:	Courtesy of Mairtín McCullough.
Nos. 62 - 64:	Smith family collection.
Nos. 65 - 68:	These images are reproduced courtesy of the National Library of Ireland (ACC 6000 – Archive of the Music Association of Ireland).
Nos. 69 - 74:	Smith family collection.
No. 75:	Courtesy of Mairtín McCullough.
No. 76:	Reproduced courtesy of the National Library of Ireland (NLI).
Nos. 77 & 78:	Smith family collection.
Nos. 79 - 81:	Reproduced courtesy of the NLI.
No. 82:	Smith family collection.
Nos. 83 & 85:	Reproduced courtesy of the NLI.
No. 84:	Photograph by Gillian Smith.
No. 86:	Smith family collection.
No. 87:	Reproduced courtesy of the NLI.
No. 88:	Courtesy of David Laing.
No. 89:	Reproduced courtesy of the NLI.

No. 90:	Courtesy of Brian O'Rourke.
No. 91:	Reproduced courtesy of the NLI.
Nos. 92 & 93:	Smith family collection.
Nos. 94 - 96:	Courtesy of David Laing.
Nos. 97 - 99:	Reproduced courtesy of the NLI.
No. 100:	Courtesy of David Laing.
Nos. 101 & 102:	Reproduced courtesy of the NLI.
No. 103:	Smith family collection.
Nos. 104 – 108:	Reproduced courtesy of the NLI.
Nos. 109 – 118:	Smith family collection.
Nos. 119 – 123:	Reproduced courtesy of the NLI.
No. 124:	Courtesy of the National Youth Orchestra of Ireland (NYOI).
No. 125:	Smith family collection.
No. 126:	Reproduced with kind permission of Jim Harkin.
Nos. 127 & 128:	Courtesy of Gearóid Grant.
No. 129:	Courtesy of James Cavanagh.
No. 130:	Courtesy of the NYOI.
Nos. 131 – 136:	Smith family collection.

NOTE: all images from the MAI Archive are reproduced courtesy of the National Library of Ireland (ACC 6000).

INDEX